Dear Reader,

Sams Publishing is proud to introduce *TCP/IP Blueprints*. This is the first in a new series of *Blueprints* books. We are confident these books will be the resources you turn to when you need answers to your tough questions.

Books in the *Blueprints* series present their information with a high degree of technical detail, yet they are written in a style to make them accessible to everyone. Inside, you won't find information on how to click "Next" to get through a Wizard. Instead, you'll find detailed information showing you exactly how the technology works! Included with each book is a CD-ROM, which contains a searchable collection of the industry standards and whitepapers that define the technology covered in the book, along with useful utilities and applications.

The layout of the book has also been specially designed to make it easier for you to navigate through it. The use of academic numbering and indented headings lets you zero in on the information you need quickly and easily.

Thank you for choosing Sams Publishing as your source for the most up-to-date and technically accurate information available. As the publishing manager of the group that created this book, I welcome your comments. You can fax, e-mail, or write me directly to let me know what you did or didn't like about this book, as well as what we can do to make our books stronger.

Sincerely,

Dean Miller

Dean Miller
Sams Publishing
201 W. 103rd Street
Indianapolis, IN 46290
opsys_mgr@sams.mcp.com
Fax: (317) 581-4669

TCP/IP
Blueprints

Robin Burk
Martin J. Bligh
Thomas Lee
et al.

SAMS
PUBLISHING

201 West 103rd Street
Indianapolis, IN 46290

Publisher and President	Richard K. Swadley
Publishing Manager	Dean Miller
Director of Editorial Services	Cindy Morrow
Managing Editor	Kitty Wilson Jarrett
Director of Marketing	Kelli S. Spencer
Product Marketing Manager	Wendy Gilbride
Assistant Marketing Manager	Rachel Wolfe

Acquisitions Editor
Cari Skaggs

Development Editor
Jeffrey J. Koch

Software Development Specialist
Patricia J. Brooks

Production Editor
Colleen Williams

Copy Editor
Kimberly K. Hannel

Indexer
Craig Small

Technical Reviewer
Robert Bogue

Editorial Coordinator
Katie Wise

Technical Edit Coordinator
Lynette Quinn

Editorial Assistants
Carol Ackerman
Andi Richter
Rhonda Tinch-Mize

Cover Designers
Tim Amrhein
Karen Ruggles

Cover Production
Aren Howell

Book Designer
Gary Adair

Copy Writer
David Reichwein

Production Team Supervisors
Brad Chinn
Charlotte Clapp

Production
Rick Bond
Jeanne Clark
Mary Ellen Stephenson
Andrew Stone

Overview

Introduction xix

Part I Introduction

1   Introduction to TCP/IP 3

Part II Network Layer

2   A Close Look at IPv4 and IPv6 19

3   IP Addressing and Subnetting 57

4   Address Resolution Protocol (ARP) 79

5   IP Routing 93

6   Address Discovery Protocols 117

7   IP Over SLIP, PPP, and PPTP 137

Part III Transport Layer

8   Quality of Service 157

Part IV Application Layer

9   Introduction to the Application Layer 193

10   Support Services 211

11   Application Services 237

12   Naming Services 281

Part V Running with TCP/IP

13   Operating and Administering a TCP/IP Network 309

14   Troubleshooting Common TCP/IP Problems 335

Part VI Appendixes

A   RFCs and Standards/Further References 363

B   Service Port Numbers 387

C   Technical Glossary 439

Index 457

Contents

Part I   Introduction

1   Introduction to TCP/IP   3

    1.1. The History of TCP/IP 4

    1.2. The TCP/IP Protocol Stack 6

    1.3. The Internet Protocol 8

    1.4. Client/Server Relationships in TCP/IP Networks 10

        1.4.1. Open Systems 11

        1.4.2. Servers and Services in a TCP/IP Network 11

    1.5. Who's in Control Around Here? 12

    1.6. Summary 14

Part II   Network Layer

2   A Close Look at IPv4 and IPv6   19

    2.1. Relating TCP/IP to the ISO OSI Model 20

        2.1.1. ISO OSI Model 20

        2.1.2. TCP/IP Model 23

        2.1.3. Comparison of Layers 25

        2.1.4. Encapsulation and Demultiplexing 27

    2.2. How IPv4 Packets Are Put Together 29

        2.2.1. Basic IPv4 Packet Layout 29

        2.2.2. IPv4 Header Layout 30

        2.2.3. IP Fragmentation 36

        2.2.4. IP Address Types 38

    2.3. How IPv6 Packets Are Put Together 39

        2.3.1. IPv6 Basic Header Layout 39

        2.3.2. IPv6 Extension Headers 42

        2.3.3. IPv6 Address Types 49

    2.4. Comparing IPv4 and IPv6 49

        2.4.1. Addressing 50

        2.4.2. Headers and Header Processing 52

        2.4.3. Configuration 52

        2.4.4. Security and Encryption 53

        2.4.5. Routing 53

        2.4.6. Multicasting 54

        2.4.7. Address Resolution 54

        2.4.8. Performance 54

        2.4.9. Address Types 55

    2.5. Summary 55

3   IP Addressing and Subnetting 57

   3.1. IPv4 58

      3.1.1. IPv4 Network Classes 59

      3.1.2. IPv4 Multicasting 61

      3.1.3. Subnetting in IPv4 62

      3.1.4. Reserved Addresses 65

   3.2. Classless Inter-Domain Routing (CIDR) with IPv4 65

   3.3. IPv6: Next Generation Internet Addressing 68

      3.3.1. IPv6 Address Representation 68

      3.3.2. IPv6 Address Types 69

      3.3.3. Unicast Addresses 71

      3.3.4. Anycast Addresses 75

      3.3.5. Multicast Addresses 75

      3.3.6. Required Address Support 77

   3.4. Summary 78

4   Address Resolution Protocol (ARP) 79

   4.1. Overview of ARP 80

   4.2. What Happens When an ARP Packet Is Received? 81

   4.3. IP Address Conflicts 82

   4.4. Managing the ARP Cache Table 88

   4.5. ARP Packet Format 88

   4.6. The Use of a Static ARP Address 89

   4.7. Proxy ARP 90

   4.8. Summary 91

5   IP Routing 93

   5.1. Why Do We Need IP Addresses and IP Routing? 94

   5.2. How IP Routing Works 96

      5.2.1. The Address Resolution Protocol (ARP) 96

      5.2.2. The Reverse Address Resolution Protocol 97

   5.3. Internetworking: Options for Connecting Network Segments 98

      5.3.1. Repeaters 98

      5.3.2. Bridges 98

      5.3.3. Routers 99

   5.4. Router Protocols 103

   5.5. Routing Inside the LAN 103

      5.5.1. Routing Information Protocol 104

      5.5.2. The Hello Protocol 106

      5.5.3. Open Shortest Path First 107

        5.5.4. Intermediate Host to Intermediate Host 108
        5.5.5. Extended Interior Gateway Routing Protocol 108
    5.6. Routing Outside the LAN 109
        5.6.1. Bridging Considerations 109
        5.6.2. Routing Considerations 111
        5.6.3. Gateway to Gateway Protocol 112
        5.6.4. Exterior Gateway Protocol 112
        5.6.5. Border Gateway Protocol 113
        5.6.6. Inter-Domain Routing Protocol 113
    5.7. Moving to IP Version 6 (IPv6) 113
        5.7.1. Conversion Considerations 115
    5.8. Summary 116

6   Address Discovery Protocols 117
    6.1. Introduction 118
    6.2. Address Allocation Policies 119
        6.2.1. Manual 119
        6.2.2. Automatic 119
        6.2.3. Dynamic 119
        6.2.4. Which Allocation Policy to Use? 119
    6.3. Reverse Address Resolution Protocol 120
    6.4. BOOTP 121
    6.5. Dynamic Host Configuration Protocol 123
        6.5.1. DHCP Leases 123
        6.5.2. Initial Lease Allocation 123
        6.5.3. Lease Renewal 124
        6.5.4. Lease Deletion 125
    6.6. BOOTP Relay 126
    6.7. BOOTP Vendor Extensions and DHCP Options 127
        6.7.1. BOOTP Extension/DHCP Option Field Format 127
        6.7.2. Shared BOOTP Extensions and DHCP Options 127
        6.7.3. DHCP-Specific Options 134
    6.8. Summary 136

7   IP Over SLIP, PPP, and PPTP 137
    7.1. SLIP 138
        7.1.1. The SLIP Protocol 139
        7.1.2. Limitations of SLIP 140
    7.2. PPP 140
        7.2.1. Overview of PPP 140
        7.2.2. PPP Link Operation 143
    7.3. IPv6 and PPP 149
        7.3.1. PPP Operations with IPv6 149
        7.3.2. Network Control Protocol under IPv6 149

7.4. Tunneling and Virtual Private Networks 151
    7.4.1. Point-to-Point Tunneling Protocol—PPTP 152
    7.4.2. Layer 2 Forwarding—L2F 153
    7.4.3. Layer Two Tunneling Protocol—L2TP 153
7.5. Summary 154

Part III Transport Layer

8 Quality of Service 157

8.1. What Is Quality of Service 158
8.2. The Transmission Control Protocol (TCP) 159
    8.2.1. TCP Basic Concepts: Multiplexing, Reliability, and
          Flow Control 160
    8.2.2. TCP Datagram Format 162
    8.2.3. TCP Header Options and Maximum Segment Size 164
    8.2.4. TCP Multiplexing and Connection Management 165
    8.2.5. Flow Control—The TCP Window 169
    8.2.6. TCP Timers and the Reset Flag 172
    8.2.7. Terminating a TCP Connection 173
    8.2.8. T/TCP and Other TCP Extensions 173
8.3. The User Datagram Protocol (UDP) 174
    8.3.1. UDP Header Format 175
    8.3.2. UDP and the IP Pseudoheader 175
8.4. Interactive Audio and Video over the Internet—
    The Real Time Protocol (RTP) 176
    8.4.1. Fixed Fields in the RTP Header 178
    8.4.2. RTP Operating Concepts 179
    8.4.3. The Real Time Control Protocol (RTCP) 180
8.5. The Resource reSerVation Protocol (RSVP) 181
8.6. Multilink PPP 183
    8.6.1. Operational Concepts 184
    8.6.2. MPPP Encapsulation 185
    8.6.3. Link Control for MPPP 186
8.7. TCP/IP and Broadband Transmission Services 186
    8.7.1. Broadband Concepts 186
    8.7.2. Integrated Services Data Network (ISDN) 187
    8.7.3. Frame Relay 187
    8.7.4. Asynchronous Transfer Mode (ATM) 188
8.8. Summary 189

Part IV Application Layer

9 Introduction to the Application Layer 193

9.1. The TCP Application Interface Model 194
    9.1.1. TCP Connection States 195

9.1.2. Application Requests to TCP 198
9.1.3. TCP-to-Application Messages 201
9.2. TCP/IP Applications in the UNIX Environment 201
9.2.1. The Internet Daemon and Service Processes 202
9.2.2. Service Configuration in BSD UNIX 202
9.2.3. The BSD Socket Model 204
9.2.4. Service Configuration in System V UNIX 205
9.2.5. Security Considerations 205
9.3. TCP/IP Applications in the Microsoft Windows Environment 206
9.3.1. The WinSock API 206
9.3.2. The WinInet API 207
9.3.3. Server Facilities in Windows NT 208
9.4. Summary 208

10 Support Services 211
10.1. Timing Services: NTP and SNTP 213
10.1.1. NTP 213
10.1.2. SNTP 218
10.2. Management Services: SNMP 218
10.2.1. SNMP Operations 219
10.2.2. SNMP Management Information Base 221
10.2.3. SNMPv2 225
10.3. File Services: NFS 226
10.3.1. NFS Operations 227
10.3.2. NFS RPCs 228
10.3.3. WebNFS 229
10.4. NetBIOS Over TCP/IP 230
10.4.1. NetBIOS Operations 230
10.4.2. Supporting NetBIOS Over TCP/IP 232
10.4.3. Datagram Formats 233
10.4.4. IP Over NetBIOS 233
10.5. Summary 234

11 Application Services 237
11.1. Telnet 238
11.1.1. The NVT 240
11.1.2. Option Negotiation 241
11.1.3. Specifying Options 242
11.1.4. Control Functions 247
11.2. FTP 248
11.2.1. FTP Sessions 251
11.2.2. FTP Commands 253
11.2.3. FTP Response Messages 256
11.2.4. FTP Data Transfer 258
11.3. SMTP 259
11.3.1. SMTP Commands 261

11.3.2. SMTP Reply Codes 264

11.3.3. SMTP Mail Format 266

11.3.4. SMTP in the Enterprise 269

11.4. HTTP 269

11.4.1. HTTP Methods 272

11.4.2. HTTP Header Fields 273

11.4.3. URI Format 275

11.4.4. Response Codes 276

11.4.5. HTTP Futures—HTTP 1.1 and Beyond 277

11.5. Summary 279

12 Naming Services 281

12.1. Overview 282

12.2. DNS Concepts 283

12.2.1. The Domain Namespace 283

12.2.2. Reverse Lookups 285

12.2.3. Zones versus Domains 286

12.2.4. Primary and Secondary Servers 287

12.2.5. Iterative versus Recursive Queries 288

12.2.6. Forwarders and Slaves 288

12.2.7. Resolvers 288

12.3. DNS Data and Protocols 289

12.3.1. Resource Records 289

12.3.2. Glue Records 292

12.3.3. Queries in Detail 293

12.3.4. Zone Transfers 295

12.4. Debugging with `nslookup` 296

12.4.1. Invoking and Setting Options 296

12.4.2. Search Lists 296

12.4.3. Zone Transfers 296

12.4.4. Debugging 297

12.5. NetBIOS Name Service (WINS) 297

12.5.1. WINS versus DNS 297

12.5.2. NetBIOS Names 298

12.5.3. `LMHOSTS` 299

12.5.4. Node Types 300

12.5.5. NetBIOS Name Service in Action 301

12.5.6. Name Encoding 305

12.6. Summary 305

Part IV Running with TCP/IP

13 Operating and Administering a TCP/IP Network 309

13.1. Designing for Growth 310

13.2. Design Guidelines 311

13.3. The Departmental Network 312
    13.3.1. Configuring the Departmental Network 312
    13.3.2. Use of Virtual LANs 313
    13.3.3. Sizing the Network 314
13.4. The Company Backbone 314
    13.4.1. Fault Tolerance 315
    13.4.2. Switching versus Routing 316
13.5. The Internet Service Provider's Network 317
    13.5.1. An Example of an ISP's Network 317
13.6. Network Security 319
    13.6.1. Security Policy 319
    13.6.2. Passwords 319
    13.6.3. Router Security 320
    13.6.4. Firewalls 321
    13.6.5. Packet Filtering 321
    13.6.6. Building a Firewall 322
    13.6.7. Configuring Your Firewall 323
    13.6.8. Restricting Traffic by Service Type 323
    13.6.9. Bastion Hosts 324
    13.6.10. Proxy Hosts 325
    13.6.11. TCP Wrappers 326
    13.6.12. Intranets 327
    13.6.13. Mail Server Security 328
13.7. Network Management 329
    13.7.1. Capacity Planning 329
    13.7.2. New IP Allocations 330
    13.7.3. Remote or Satellite Sites 331
    13.7.4. Software Licensing 331
    13.7.5. Client/Server Backup—Tuning IP Accordingly 331
13.8. Summary 334

14 **Troubleshooting Common TCP/IP Problems 335**
14.1. Analyzers and Sniffers 337
14.2. Software Tools to Help You Solve Problems 338
    14.2.1. `ping` 338
    14.2.2. `traceroute` 339
    14.2.3. `tcpdump` 340
14.3. Windows NT Network Monitor 341
14.4. Common Problems 343
    14.4.1. Unable to Connect to a Remote Host 343
    14.4.2. Slow Performance 346
    14.4.3. Printing to a Remote Host via LPD Doesn't Work 346
    14.4.4. Name Resolution Problems 347
    14.4.5. DNS Problems 347
    14.4.6. MAC Level Broadcast Storms 348

14.5 Analyzing Packet Dumps and Examples of Common Sequences 349
    14.5.1. An ICMP Echo Request 349
    14.5.2. An ICMP Echo Reply 350
    14.5.3. Initiating a TCP Connection (Stage 1) TCP: SYN 351
    14.5.4. Initiating a TCP Connection (Stage 2) TCP: SYN, ACK 353
    14.5.5. Initiating a TCP Connection (Stage 3) TCP: ACK 354
    14.5.6. Sending Data via TCP (an EOF Character) TCP:
        PSH, ACK 355
    14.5.7. Terminating a TCP Connection (Stage 1) TCP: FIN, ACK ... 357
    14.5.8. Terminating a TCP Connection (Stage 2) TCP: FIN, ACK ... 358
14.6. Summary 359

Part VI Appendixes

A RFCs and Standards/Further References 363

A.1. Internet Standards—An Overview 364
    A.1.1. RFCs—What Are They? 364
    A.1.2. Do I Need an RFC? 365
    A.1.3. Getting RFCs 365
    A.1.4. Internet Drafts 367
    A.1.5. FYIs 367
A.2. RFCs by Subject 367
    A.2.1. Address Resolution Protocol/Reverse ARP
        (ARP/RARP) 368
    A.2.2. April Fools Spoof RFCs 368
    A.2.3. Assigned Numbers 369
    A.2.4. Asynchronous Transfer Method 369
    A.2.5. Bootstrap Protocol (BOOTP) 369
    A.2.6. Border Gateway Protocol 369
    A.2.7. Classless Inter-Domain Routing... 370
    A.2.8. Dynamic Host Control Protocol 370
    A.2.9. Domain Name Service 371
    A.2.10. Exterior Gateway Protocol 371
    A.2.11. File Transfer Protocol 371
    A.2.12. Finger 372
    A.2.13. Gopher 372
    A.2.14. Hypertext Markup Language 372
    A.2.15. Hypertext Transfer Protocol 372
    A.2.16. Internet Control Message Protocol 373
    A.2.17. Internet Group Multicasting Protocol 373
    A.2.18. IPv4—Internet Protocol 373
    A.2.19. IPv6—Internet Protocol 374
    A.2.20. IPv6—Security 374
    A.2.21. Internet Relay Chat 375
    A.2.22. Multipurpose Internet Mail Extension 375
    A.2.23. NetBIOS 375

A.2.24. Network File System 376

A.2.25. Network News Transfer Protocol 376

A.2.26. Open Shortest Path First 376

A.2.27. POP3—Post Office Protocol 376

A.2.28. Point-to-Point Protocol 377

A.2.29. Routing Information Protocol 378

A.2.30. Simple Mail Transfer Protocol 378

A.2.31. Simple Network Management Protocol 378

A.2.32. SNMP—Management Information Bases 380

A.2.33. Systems Network Architecture 382

A.2.34. Transmission Control Protocol 382

A.2.35. Telnet 382

A.2.36. Trivial File Transfer Protocol 384

A.2.37. User Datagram Protocol 384

A.3. Other References 384

A.3.1. Ethernet 384

A.3.2. Frequently Asked Questions 385

A.3.3. Microsoft White Papers 385

B   Service Port Numbers 387

C   Technical Glossary 439

Index 457

Acknowledgments

Special thanks to Roger for support and grocery shopping. Also to the Laurelwood English Cockers, who intuitively understand how to negotiate a communications session (beg), allocate resources (if it's on the counter, it's ours!), and travel in encapsulated cells (show crates) over broadband highway networks. Thanks, also, to Stephen P. Kowalchuk, who provided an IS manager and practicing network administrator's point of view.

—*Robin Burk*

First, I'd like to say thanks to the team at Sams Publishing who have prodded, pushed, cajoled, and obtained my output in good time and have managed to make it presentable to you, the reader. Also, I'd like to say a very big thank-you to my wife, who has tolerated the long days and longer nights and has supported and organized me.

—*Thomas Lee*

About the Authors

Robin Burk

Robin Burk has over 25 years of experience in advanced software and communications technologies, having contributed to the development of packet-switched network software, multiple operating systems, and multimedia applications. After serving as a successful executive in entrepreneurial companies, she now consults on the software development and business use of the Internet.

Robin's other passion is breeding and training show dogs. She moderates an e-mail list for English Cocker Spaniel fanciers, and she can be reached at `robink@wizard.net`.

Robin holds an undergraduate degree in Physics/Math and an MBA in finance and operations.

Martin J. Bligh

Martin J. Bligh is a communications specialist, working for Sequent Computer Systems in the United Kingdom. He has experience in planning, designing, and implementing networks, specializing in UNIX and Windows NT communications and LAN/WAN technologies. He holds a degree in Mathematics and Computing from Oxford University, England, and his interests include distributed operating systems, the application of neural networks, and playing the game of Go. He can be contacted via e-mail at `mbligh@sequent.com`.

Thomas Lee

Thomas Lee is a computer consultant and educator living in the United Kingdom. He has been working with Windows NT since 1993. Educated at Carnegie Mellon University in the United States, he worked on two successful operating systems projects (Comshare's Commander II and ICL's VME) before joining Andersen Consulting in 1981. Thomas founded PS Partnership, a Microsoft Solutions Provider, in 1987, and today is a partner. He is a Fellow of the British Computer Society as well as an MCSE, MCT, and MVP. You can contact Thomas at `tfl@psp.co.uk`.

Richard J. Maring

Richard J. Maring is a Senior Programmer/Analyst for the National Association of Securities Dealers (NASD). He is currently tasked with the design and development of an enterprise-scale, Web-based OLAP solution for the internal Executive Information System. He is also a freelance Microsoft Certified Trainer, specializing in all 32-bit Microsoft operating systems. His extensive background includes LAN/MAN/WAN construction, capacity planning, performance tuning, database design, and system development/integration, as well as extensive experience in project management/budgeting. Richard has recently been acquired by Microsoft to serve in their elite Internet Infrastructure and Architecture division as the Site Architect and QA Manager for all `microsoft.com` Web sites throughout the world. He can be reached via e-mail at `maringr@hotmail.com`.

Christopher Fisher

Christopher Fisher has a B.S. in Anthropology and Computer Science from Trent University and an MBA specialized in MIS from McMaster University. He currently works as a Technology Specialist for a major Canadian bank.

Mark Vevers

Mark Vevers is a consultant for Research Machines PLc in the United Kingdom, which designs and delivers high-performance networks to the education sector, specializing in IP network design and LAN/WAN connectivity. Mark was educated at Oxford University, England, and holds a Masters degree in Engineering and Computing Science. His background includes UNIX/Windows NT cross-network backup and mass data storage technologies. His other interests include robotics and fast motorcycles. Mark can be reached via e-mail at `mvevers@rmplc.net`.

Tell Us What You Think!

As a reader, you are the most important critic and commentator of our books. We value your opinion and want to know what we're doing right, what we could do better, what areas you'd like to see us publish in, and any other words of wisdom you're willing to pass our way. You can help us make strong books that meet your needs and give you the computer guidance you require.

> **NOTE** If you have a technical question about this book, call the technical support line at (317) 581-3833.

Do you have access to CompuServe or the World Wide Web? Then check out our CompuServe forum by typing `GO SAMS` at any prompt. If you prefer the World Wide Web, check out our site at `http://www.mcp.com`.

As the publishing manager of the group that created this book, I welcome your comments. You can fax, e-mail, or write me directly to let me know what you did or didn't like about this book—as well as what we can do to make our books stronger. Here's the information:

Fax: (317) 581-4669
E-mail: `opsys_mgr@sams.mcp.com`
Mail:

Dean Miller
Sams Publishing
201 W. 103rd Street
Indianapolis, IN 46290

Introduction

Once known only to researchers and true hackers, the TCP/IP stack of communications protocols has risen to prominence along with the explosion of the Internet and the World Wide Web. It seems every PC these days comes with dial-up protocol software for Net access, and every LAN and WAN has a gateway into the TCP/IP Internet world. Many companies and individuals are setting up Web servers on desktop computers using shareware or the latest commercial server software packages.

The proliferation of computers accessing the public Internet is itself sufficient reason for network and information systems professionals to want to master the ins and outs of TCP/IP. An even more pressing reason, however, is the increasing use of private and public TCP/IP networks to link corporate networks into enterprise-wide, distributed computing and information systems. Mission-critical corporate applications require new levels of security, throughput, and reliability. As you'll see throughout this book, the TCP/IP protocol suite has been evolving to meet those challenges.

There are new opportunities to exploit as well—technologies such as interactive multimedia conferencing and object- and component-based Java and ActiveX applications. These, too, place new demands on the network infrastructure.

Inside this book, you'll find answers to many of the questions you might have about the TCP/IP stack. If you are new to packet-switched approaches, this book will help you master the concepts and architecture of a leading technology. If you've been working with TCP/IP-based networks, you will find useful information on recent extensions that support new forms of multimedia, multicasting, and multiple protocol/interoperable networks, along with enhanced addressing and security features. You'll also find out where to get more information and how to stay abreast of rapidly changing communications standards.

Who This Book Is For

This book is primarily aimed at readers who have advanced familiarity with networking, protocols, and administration. The advanced and expert user will find this a useful reference and an excellent introduction to the newest members of the TCP/IP protocol family. Less experienced readers will find that care has been taken to explain the usefulness and relevance of this material as an aid to mastering the rich layers of the TCP/IP protocol stack.

It's an exciting time because networking technologies evolve rapidly. The authors of this book invite you to explore the *TCP/IP Blueprints* on which so much of today's newest advances are based.

Conventions in This Book

This book uses the following conventions:

TIP Tips indicate the author's simple and direct advice on how to do specific tasks better and easier.

NOTE Notes contain pertinent information that will help expand on the information in the text.

WARNING Warnings let you know something you should watch out for. The information presented in these warnings could help save you from disaster.

Program names are indicated in all uppercase.

Screen messages and commands are shown in a monospaced type style like the command below:

```
ROUTE PRINT
```

Discussions of commands sometimes include variables that are shown in *italicized monospace*. You should substitute your command or statement where an italicized command or statement is shown.

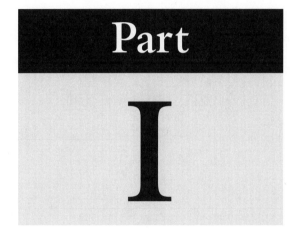

Introduction

1.1. The History of TCP/IP

1.2. The TCP/IP Protocol Stack

1.3. The Internet Protocol

1.4. Client/Server Relationships in TCP/IP Networks

1.5. Who's in Control Around Here?

1.6. Summary

Chapter

1

Introduction to TCP/IP

by Robin Burk

The Transmission Control Protocol and the Internet Protocol are the key data communication mechanisms that underlie the Internet and, in a quiet way, have enabled its rapid growth.

In actuality, TCP/IP means more than just these two protocols. As you'll see throughout the book, the TCP/IP protocol suite is a rich, open, and flexible facility that continues to evolve by adapting to new hardware, software, and application environments. It is this adaptability, along with the accessibility of the World Wide Web, which has led to increasing use of the Internet and TCP/IP–based intranets and extranets, by incorporating MIS groups previously wed to stable, vendor-proprietary networks.

Inside these chapters you'll find answers to many of the questions you might have about the TCP/IP stack. If you are new to packet-switched approaches, this book will help you master the concepts and architecture of a leading technology. If you've been working with TCP/IP–based networks, you'll find useful information on recent extensions that support new forms of multimedia, multicasting, and interoperable communications. You'll also find out where to get more information and how to stay abreast of rapidly changing communications standards.

1.1. The History of TCP/IP

By now, many computer professionals are familiar with at least some of the history behind the development of the TCP/IP protocol stack. In the mid-1960s, the dominant computing technology consisted of transistor-based mainframes with proprietary operating systems. The Department of Defense (DOD), noting that the development of Integrated Circuit chips (ICs) was in turn enabling the development of powerful minicomputers, foresaw the potential for a distributed military communications and control system using switched telephone lines. Through its Defense Advanced Research Projects Agency (DARPA), DOD funded research for advanced computing and communications technologies that resulted in a prototype packet-switched network called the ARPANET. (DARPA's role in advancing data communications and computing was not limited to the ARPANET project; other areas of funding included extensive research into robotics, artificial intelligence, high-density chip design/manufacture, massively parallel computer architectures, and Reduced Instruction Set (RISC) CPUs, among other topics. Most of the resulting technology has found its way into leading commercial products.)

The goal of the ARPANET project was to create a robust, reliable, and self-healing network architecture that could withstand substantial loss of equipment and still function with the remaining configuration of computers and communications circuits. Because DOD already operated a wide variety of computers and because the pace of breakthroughs in computing was accelerating, such a network would be based on the idea of an open system—that is, one which was not restricted to a given vendor's proprietary equipment or software. In order to provide the greatest flexibility in adding or losing equipment and circuits, and to respond to network congestion, the desired network would be based on the transfer of small packets of information that could be independently switched from node to node until delivered to the destination, where they would be reassembled into the original message. Finally, in order to encourage advances in software techniques and protocol design over time, and to accommodate changing interface hardware, the various data communication steps would be segmented into separate protocols, each implemented as a separate software program, which interact with one another through well-defined interfaces.

The idea of layered or stacked protocols was not unique to DARPA's vision. IBM was working toward its own SNA family of communications protocols, and the International Standards Organization (ISO) later defined an eight-layer model as well. What distinguished the DARPA model was its balance between openness and specificity. Whereas SNA was a proprietary model embodied in one vendor's product line, the protocols that were developed for the ARPANET were independent of any vendor, or even of any operating system or hardware architecture. And on the other hand, whereas the OSI model was generic and abstract in many ways, DOD had specific performance and use criteria that guided the development of its prototype network.

Perhaps inevitably, the original nodes of the prototype ARPANET consisted of academic computers. Many of them were the new Digital Equipment Corporation's VAX minicomputers that proliferated rapidly throughout engineering and scientific departments across the country. Over time, many of these VAXes came to host the UNIX operating system, and DOD sponsored a model implementation of the ARPANET protocols, including TCP and IP, on the Berkeley version of UNIX. The marriage of UNIX to TCP/IP proved particularly successful because both were open systems favored by many researchers.

The ARPANET led to the Internet, which eventually opened for use beyond the research community to the wider public. Today we are seeing enormous interest in the commercial application of TCP, IP, and related protocols for private intranets and extranets, along with commercial uses for the public Internet itself. As you will see throughout this book, the success of the Internet and of TCP/IP can be attributed to the success of its designers in achieving the goals originally laid out by DOD and DARPA: robustness, reliability, and flexibility in an open, multivendor environment.

The TCP/IP suite of protocols was not the only candidate for this leading role. Commercial packet-switched communication services based on the X.25 protocol and the OSI model were offered during the 1970s, but failed to find a sufficiently large base of customers outside the proprietary mainframe environment.

The design and architecture of the TCP/IP protocol stack was ahead of its time. Since the development of the ARPANET, the computing world has seen the marriage of TCP/IP with UNIX, the rise of the personal computer/workstation, digitally switched high-speed telephone lines and object-oriented GUIs. As a result of the widespread adoption of these technologies, the early promise of TCP/IP is finally coming to fruition.

If the success of the Internet is based in great part on the open system approach of both UNIX and the TCP/IP protocol stack, it is also due to the organizational home in which the Internet settled as it migrated from DOD to the academic community and into general public and commercial use. As we will see later in this chapter, the Internet and its associated protocols and standards are continuously evolving by means of a process that is itself analogous to the open system model—a process in which all interested and competent parties can participate.

1.2. The TCP/IP Protocol Stack

A stack architecture divides out the functionality of a data communications capability into discrete layers. Rather than tightly coupling the hardware interface with addressing, for instance, the stack model deliberately identifies a separate interface through which these functions shall cooperate, thereby incurring some inefficiency in order to isolate not only implementation details, but the whole design of one layer from that of another.

Figure 1.1 shows the comprehensive OSI architecture model. The higher layers are less well defined than those at the bottom of the OSI stack, which is not surprising given the breadth of applications to which they must apply. In comparison, the complexity involved in the lower levels of the stack consists of independent protocols to support specific hardware interfaces, transport mechanisms, and so forth.

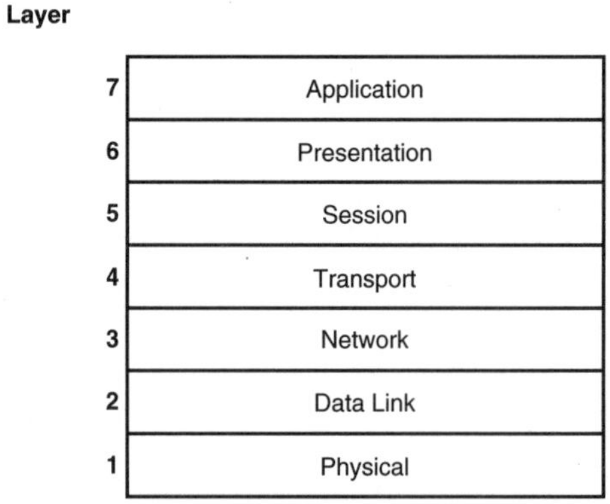

Figure 1.1.

The OSI architecture model.

Layer

#	
7	Application
6	Presentation
5	Session
4	Transport
3	Network
2	Data Link
1	Physical

Figure 1.2 shows the TCP/IP model. It is less ambitious in scope than the OSI model with regard to application and user interfaces; however, it's richer in available protocols that currently populate the various lower layers.

Figure 1.2.

The TCP/IP architecture model compared to the OSI model.

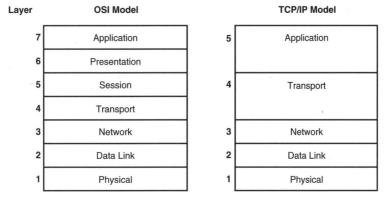

The TCP/IP stack layers serve the following functions:

- Media Access (Physical) Protocols—They specify the mechanisms for client and server nodes on a network to interface to the transmission media, generally through network interface cards (NICs).

- Data-Link Protocols—They specify the control characters and lowest level mechanisms for transmitting packets of data in successive small segments (called *frames*) between nodes. The data link layer does not know the sender or receiver of this information, nor the applications that are exchanging information in this way; this layer is solely concerned with getting the packet as a whole from node A to node B, where it will be reassembled and potentially forwarded again and again until it reaches the destination node.

- Network Protocols—These are the means by which packets of data are routed through the network from sender to receiver. The network layer is concerned with the path that a packet takes through the network, but is not concerned with information content or reliable reassembly of complete application messages at the destination node.

- Transport Protocols—They assume responsibility for delivering a potentially large message from the sending application on one network node to the receiving application on a destination node. Different transport protocols offer trade-offs between quality of service and efficiency.

- Application Protocols—They form the working toolset for network users and the applications that are written to support them. Service applications in effect extend the operating system and network functionality for user applications by providing timing, administration, and file management capabilities across the network.

In the original TCP/IP stack, the network layer consisted of the Internet Protocol (IP), and the transport layer consisted of the Transport Control Protocol (TCP) for reliable delivery of application messages and the User Datagram Protocol (UDP) for efficient exchange of small packets—primarily for control and administrative purposes.

As you will see, the TCP/IP suite has evolved significantly since its inception. The challenges of integrating dial-up communications and proprietary LANs and WANs with packet-switched networks are being met by utilizing IP and TCP to carry these foreign protocols across the public Internet and private TCP/IP networks to corporate gateways leading to other LANs and WANs using the same proprietary technologies. As a result, TCP/IP networks are increasingly able to interoperate with enterprise networks for critical applications.

In addition, the promise of interactive multimedia, including over-the-net teleconferencing, has led to the development of new protocols allowing resources to be allocated on demand, specific quality of service to be offered (and ultimately, to be paid for), and the demands of real-time applications to be met over networks that originally were not optimized for time efficiency of delivery, but rather for robustness and reliability.

The adoption of protocols such as Multilink PPP, the RealTime Protocol, and the ReSource reserVation Protocol (RSVP) somewhat blur the definition of stack layers, but nonetheless validate the stack architecture model. It is precisely because the original layers of the TCP/IP stack were isolated behind well–thought-out interfaces that this new functionality can be added successfully to the complex, rapidly changing Internet.

1.3. The Internet Protocol

As the name implies, IP is designed to route traffic between networks—that is, across a network of networks. Applications running on a client machine or a LAN generate messages to be sent to a machine residing on another network. IP receives these messages from the transport layer software residing on a server that provides the gateway from the LAN or WAN onto the Internet (or other TCP/IP network).

The addressing function embedded in IP embodies the topology of the Internet as a whole. IP addresses consist of a network identifier and a host (server) identifier, with the capability to designate subnetworks as necessary. Thus, at least one combination of network and host identifier is associated with each node on an IP-based network such as the Internet.

Not all nodes on the network are end-user machines or gateways to LANs and WANs. Some nodes are devoted to routing packets along the various potential pathways from the sending node to the receiving node. This approach differs from other network architectures in several ways.

Many LANs are based on a broadcast/collision model. Ethernet-based networks, for instance, simply tell everything to everyone; each machine on the LAN listens for the traffic that is relevant to itself and ignores the rest. Computers on a Token Ring LAN take turns listening and broadcasting.

Mainframe computers for many years also did not make use of message routing when communicating with other computers or with remote terminals. Instead, they required a physical and logical connection to be established directly between the two pieces of equipment over a leased or dial-up line.

By separating the logical destination of a packet from the route by which it arrives at that destination, packet-switched protocols such as IP allow network equipment to automatically respond to the addition or loss of nodes, or to momentary or persistent traffic jams on portions of the network. In fact, in an IP network *no* nodes (even on the backbone circuits) know the entire topology of the network at any given time. Instead, the routing computers know about the nodes in their immediate vicinity and can update their information by exchanging it with other adjacent nodes. In addition to the identity of adjacent nodes, routers also keep track of the relative distance to farther nodes along alternate pathways. When combined with information regarding current transmission times across those pathways, this information allows routers to decide how to forward a given packet at a given time so that it moves through the network expeditiously.

The explosive growth in the Internet, plus the creation of private intranets and extranets, has led to extensions of the original IP addressing mechanism. IP version 6 increases the address size and hence the potential address space of the Internet. In addition, new protocols, such as L2TP, have been proposed to allow non-TCP/IP network traffic to tunnel, or pass transparently, over the Internet and continue on its way through a remote network or dial-up line. This approach bypasses the need to accommodate differing network architectures through a common interface or redesign; instead, it allows the routing of essentially non-switched communications through the switched network.

IP pathways are inherently one packet wide. A multipacket message may be transmitted across diverse paths before the packets are reassembled at the destination node. However, it is sometimes useful to construct a virtual pipeline through a TCP/IP network in order to pass through higher volume data. Multilink Point-to-Point Protocol (MPPP) is one protocol advanced for this purpose. MPPP also utilizes the power and flexibility of routed IP to convey non-TCP/IP information to a remote gateway computer and ultimately to the destination user machine.

Finally, the emergence of digital telephony services such as Asynchronous Transfer Mode support IP by expanding the options available for establishing connections between network nodes. Here, too, new protocol extensions are being developed to allow open system interoperability between these service layers.

1.4. Client/Server Relationships in TCP/IP Networks

The TCP/IP protocol stack is built around the idea of client machines that receive service from other machines on the network. For instance, a PC that accesses the Internet through a LAN gateway relies on that gateway server to "speak TCP/IP" across the Internet on its behalf. Similarly, the home PC that dials into an Internet service provider's network server to access the Web communicates with that server via a non-TCP/IP protocol. The server then provides translation and transmission services on behalf of each of its clients.

More directly, each successively higher layer within the TCP/IP stack software on a given machine is a client to the layer beneath it (see Figure 1.3). IP is a client of the data link layer software, using that software's services to accomplish its physical transmission of packets. TCP and UDP are clients of IP, using the IP routing mechanisms to move messages across the switched network, and application layer programs are clients of the transport layer, relying on TCP, UDP, or other transport protocols to package their information correctly and to see that it is delivered reliably and in a timely fashion across the network to the receiving application on a remote machine.

Figure 1.3.
Client/server relationships in TCP/IP.

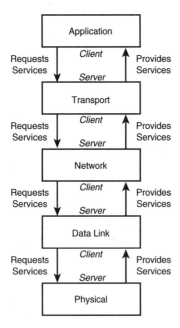

1.4.1. Open Systems

A client/server architecture does not automatically mean that the resulting system is open in the sense of allowing transparent interoperation of diverse hardware and software. By segregating functionality into discrete layers, however, the client/server relationships built into the TCP/IP stack remind protocol designers and implementers that it is desirable to keep vendor or other specific characteristics out of the definition of protocol interfaces wherever possible.

With the exception of protocols specifically designed to provide service to proprietary network protocols and services, the TCP/IP stack elements do meet the definition of an open system. Neither the implementation of a given protocol server process in software nor the hardware environment within which it executes is reflected in the packet headers, control message formats, or other details of the protocols that make up the stack. This is appropriate—given the goal of the original ARPANET and of its successors today—that diverse existing computers and networks be interconnected in a reliable, robust, and extensible way. A computer communicating over the Internet or another TCP/IP network neither knows nor cares about the software or hardware to which it is talking. In addition, an application neither knows nor cares what network protocol or media are used by TCP to transfer a file or a transaction across the Net.

The advantage of an open systems approach is that network technology can evolve seamlessly and flexibly over time without disrupting existing capabilities. Thus corporate mainframes, UNIX-based workstations, and family PCs can all communicate with one another by means of the simple addition of a TCP/IP stack implementation and a suitable access to a transmission medium, in the form of a modem and dial-up line, a LAN gateway, or direct network connection. Similarly, various router technologies can be deployed over time, without impact on existing router or end-user equipment.

Roughly speaking, the effort to centrally manage a network increases geometrically with an increase in the complexity of the network topology. By distributing this management task across an open system network architecture, the TCP/IP protocols bypass this difficulty and allow the Internet and related networks to expand, contract, and change with the least burden on the system as a whole.

1.4.2. Servers and Services in a TCP/IP Network

We've talked about the client/server model that obtains both servers and services within the protocol modules on a given machine and among machines in the network. The examples given so far are generally invisible to the end user or even to system and network administrators.

Additional servers exist at the application layer and are directly visible to humans. These may be grouped into applications that serve network administrators and those that serve the end user.

There is a sense in which *network administrator* is a contradiction in terms when applied to TCP/IP networks. To a fair degree, IP-based networks administer themselves in that new routing information is propagated automatically. However, routers must be programmed with initial information regarding their neighbors. Protocol modules must be configured with parameter settings appropriate to the capacity of the local hardware and software environment, and cross-protocol support must be explicitly evoked, where desired, in LAN and WAN gateways. In addition, ISPs and others need information regarding the health and performance of network nodes and pathways. Simple Network Management Protocol (SNMP) provides a non-intrusive, non-directive means of gathering such information.

Similarly, the various nodes in a network must be synchronized as to time because many of the decisions executed automatically by TCP/IP protocol modules and routers are time-dependent. The Network Time Protocol (NTP) allows network administrators to identify primary, external sources of reliable time information, which can then be propagated throughout the wider network.

Finally, the Domain Name System (DNS) gives network administrators and users a convenient, easy-to-memorize means of assigning mnemonic names to IP numeric addresses and other network resources.

End user application services vary in scope and power. The Network File System (NFS), devised by Sun Microcomputers and made available for wider adoption, allows users to access remote files and directories as though they were local resources. The File Transfer Protocol (FTP) allows files to be exchanged among machines and users. SNMP supports the ubiquitous e-mail we've all come to depend upon, and the Hypertext Transfer Protocol (HTTP) underlies the popular graphical WWW.

Each of these applications depend on the lower layers of the TCP/IP protocol stack for essential services to carry out their own operations. Thus, the TCP/IP stack is a rich, complex set of capabilities that has evolved over time in response to the opportunities and challenges posed by new user requirements and new technical opportunities.

1.5. Who's in Control Around Here?

The Department of Defense has long since given up its role in guiding the evolution of TCP/IP–based networks. So how do new protocols get approved, the Internet backbone circuits get configured, and corporate enterprise needs get met over the public Internet? Who's in control around here, anyway?

The community of organizations and people involved in the evolution of the Internet and of the TCP/IP protocol suite is as rich, diverse, and evolving as the Net itself. Key groups include

- Internet Society (ISOC)
- Internet Architecture Board (IAB)
- Internet Engineering Steering Group (IESG)
- Internet Engineering Task Force (IETF)
- Internet Assigned Numbers Authority (IANA)
- InterNIC

The IETF is an open community of network designers, equipment manufacturers, service providers, and researchers. IETF is organized into working groups for various technology areas. Area directors join together in IESG, under the overall guidance of IAB, to resolve technical conflicts and confirm new standards. IANA is the central coordinator for the assignment of unique parameter values for Internet protocols.

IANA and IESG are chartered by the Internet Society, which has overall responsibility for the operation and evolution of the Internet and associated protocols.

The InterNIC is a cooperative effort by the National Science Foundation, Network Solutions, Inc., and AT&T. InterNIC accepts registrations of domain names for DNS and manages an archive of Internet-related documents.

TIP Newcomers to the IETF and its activities are directed to RFC 1718, "The Tao of IETF," for a light-hearted (but serious) introduction to the culture and norms of the Task Force in action. A running account of the standards adopted officially for Internet use is maintained in successive RFCs as Standard 1; the version current when this chapter was being written can be found in RFC 1920. The InterNIC site's RFC index identifies those RFCs that have been rendered obsolete, along with their replacements. You can search these links to identify the version of the Internet protocols currently in effect at any given time.

The IETF is a truly open, international, and dynamically changing group. Most work is done in the working groups by means of e-mail, and the atmosphere is collegial.

The central mechanisms for proposing new protocols or new versions of established protocols and for recommending implementation approaches are the IETF draft and the Request for Comments (RFC). Individuals and organizations are free to submit draft memos and protocol standards for IETF discussion. These drafts have a six-month lifetime, after which they must advance to RFC status or expire.

RFCs are proposed for information or as potential standards. Once adopted as a standard, an RFC governs the manner of support for various Internet capabilities, including protocols in the stack. Informational RFCs are used, among other purposes, to make corporate standards such as the Network File System (NFS) available for general adoption. Such protocols often become *de facto* standards for Internet usage, but are not adopted officially because the originating organization retains control of the evolution of that protocol. The text of published drafts and RFCs is available over the Web and by FTP from numerous repositories. The most complete repository can be accessed from the InterNIC's home page on the Web at `http://ds.internic.net`.

This site contains IETF drafts, RFCs and conference documents, ISOC papers, and other detailed information regarding the operation and evolution of the Net and related protocols. A search engine is provided to support content-related browsing.

 Additionally, an electronic copy of some of the RFCs is included on the CD-ROM that comes with this book.

1.6. Summary

TCP and IP are the central protocols underlying the public Internet and increasing numbers of private intranets and extranets.

The TCP/IP protocol stack is designed around a layered architecture model in which higher layers are clients for the services provided by the lower layers. At the top of the stack are application programs; at the bottom are the physical transmission media forming the network connections.

One reason for the explosive growth of the Internet and the widespread adoption of the TCP/IP protocol suite is its resolute adoption of an open systems approach. The capability of diverse computers to interoperate transparently, combined with protocol extensions and additions, has resulted in the adoption of TCP/IP protocols and networks by large corporate enterprises as well as by individual users of the Internet.

The community of those who guide the development, evolution, and operation of the Internet and its protocols is as open and diverse as the technologies they manage. Central to this process is the Internet Engineering Task Force that, through its RFC process, responds to new user requirements and proposed protocol enhancements. Under the guidance of the Internet Architecture Board, the IETF and its working groups continue to adopt and extend the original TCP/IP protocols to support interactive multimedia, resource and service management, and the interconnection of TCP/IP networks with existing enterprise environments.

The evolution of the TCP/IP suite is not limited to hardware interfaces or low-level protocols. It also includes applications that serve both end users and network administrators, including naming services, access to remote file resources, and the mechanisms that underlie open system e-mail and the Web. These capabilities help to make the Internet and related networks a mature environment that the general public and corporate information systems, as well as the academic community, can utilize effectively. That this maturity does not come at the price of static standards or a rigid exclusion of new approaches is a measure of the care and ingenuity that went into both the original ARPANET and the evolving community into whose hands the care of the current Internet has come.

Introduction to TCP/IP

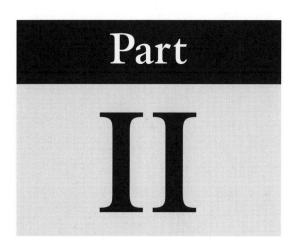

Part

II

Network Layer

2. A Close Look at IPv4 and IPv6

3. IP Addressing and Subnetting

4. Address Resolution Protocol (ARP)

5. IP Routing

6. Address Discovery Protocols

7. IP Over SLIP, PPP, and PPTP

2.1. Relating TCP/IP to
the ISO OSI Model

2.2. How IPv4 Packets Are
Put Together

2.3. How IPv6 Packets Are
Put Together

2.4. Comparing IPv4 and
IPv6

2.5. Summary

Chapter

2

A Close
Look at IPv4
and IPv6

by Thomas Lee

The Internet Protocol (IP), the workhorse of the TCP/IP protocol suite, deals with key functions such as the addressing and the routing of packets through an internetwork. The version of IP deployed in the Internet and virtually all private intranets is IP version 4 (IPv4), which was defined in RFC 791. This version of IP was designed when internetworking, as we know it today, was in its infancy and when most environments were smaller and simpler. Although IPv4 has many strengths, it also has some weaknesses that have only become apparent, and a problem with the explosive growth of the Internet. These are addressed in the updated version of IP, IPv6, which is defined in RFC 1883.

This chapter examines both versions of IP: IPv4 and IPv6. We'll start with a discussion of the International Standards Organization Open Systems Interconnect (ISO OSI) model and look at how the architecture of TCP/IP relates to this model. This is followed by a more detailed look at how IPv4 and IPv6 packets are put together. Finally the chapter reviews the key differences between the IPv4 and IPv6 protocols. The important issues surrounding IP addressing are discussed in Chapter 3, "IP Addressing and Subnetting."

2.1. Relating TCP/IP to the ISO OSI Model

Computer networks and the protocols they employ are complex. To help us understand this complexity, it is useful to have some sort of reference model. The ISO OSI model is appropriate for this purpose.

2.1.1. ISO OSI Model

The International Standards Organization (ISO) began the development of a detailed data communications model in 1977. Known as the Open Systems Interconnect Reference Model, it is often referred to as the OSI model, the ISO model, or just the seven-layer model. The original intention was that this model would eventually lead to software that would allow communications between heterogeneous systems.

The OSI model defines communications between two systems in terms of seven distinct layers. A diagram of the OSI model is shown in Figure 2.1.

Each layer in the OSI model represents a discrete set of functions and services available to a higher layer. Each layer performs those functions by calling functions in a lower level and offering up functions to a higher layer. These layers assist protocol designers to manage the inherent complexity of modern computer networks.

Figure 2.1.
The OSI Model.

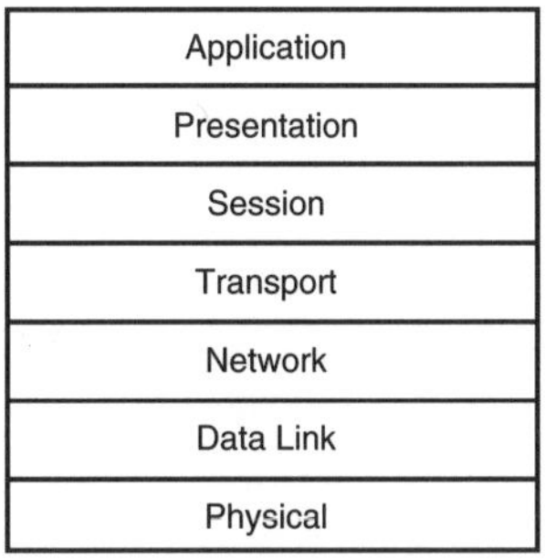

| Application |
| Presentation |
| Session |
| Transport |
| Network |
| Data Link |
| Physical |

TIP

For those who need to remember the layers and their relationship, use a simple memory trick—a saying in which the first letter of each word corresponds to the name of each layer. One such saying is "All People Seem To Need Data Processing"—a top-down approach. More cynical anti-NT advocates suggest a bottom-up version is more appropriate: "Please Deliver NT Some Plausible Answers." In the UK, some folks use another bottom-up saying: "Princess Diana Never Tried Snagging Prince Andrew." There are loads more, but I hope these will act as memory aids.

The seven–layer model does not define any specific protocol or protocols but rather the functions that will be carried out by each layer. It is assumed that these functions are implemented as one or more formalized data communication protocols, such as the IEE 802.2, TCP, IP, or FTP. Before looking at the specifics of these protocols, it is useful to have a good framework model.

You also will note that the layers, as shown in Figure 2.1, resemble a set of child's building blocks, one on top of the other. For this reason the set of implemented protocols is often referred to as a *protocol stack*.

The functions of the seven layers in the ISO OSI model are shown in Table 2.1.

Table 2.1. The functions of each of the OSI layers.

Layer	Function
Physical	This layer defines the specific characteristics of the hardware over which any actual data communications will take place. The key functions of the physical layer are to define some sort of communication channel, often referred to as the *wire*, to put binary numbers onto that wire, and then to transmit those bits to other systems also connected to the wire. The specific bits that are to be put on the wire are the function of the higher layers.
Link	The data link layer defines how to transmit reliably a packet, or frame, of information between two stations on the same physical network (that is, the physical network provided by the physical layer).

continues

Table 2.1. Continued.

Layer	Function
Network	The network layer defines how a single packet is transmitted between two stations on different physical networks, also known as an internetwork. The network layer also isolates the higher layers from the details of the physical network. IP is a network layer protocol.
Transport	The transport layer uses the functions of the network layer to provide reliable end-to-end communications between two hosts. TCP is a transport layer protocol.
Session	This layer sessions between two systems. Sessions between two systems consist of a number of datagrams passed between two systems. Sessions are useful because they allow the sender and receiver to remember details about each other. There is no specific session layer protocol in the TCP/IP suite; although, NetBIOS, as used on Microsoft networks, is broadly a session layer protocol.
Presentation	The presentation layer provides translation between different data representations. There are no protocols to speak of at this layer of the model. Most presentation layer functions are carried out by the actual network application.
Application	The application layer comprises all the functions which the user applications directly access, such as FTP or SMTP.

NOTE I've always thought there was one layer missing from the OSI model—the user interface. Most of the application layer protocols are, by themselves, somewhat inaccessible by the end user; they need some sort of user interface. This might include an FTP program for the FTP protocol or a rich Internet client, acting as a UI to multiple protocols (SMTP, NNTP, and so on). Rather, the OSI model leaves this layer as an exercise for the reader or the software vendor. Some formalization of the client interface might have been useful, albeit contentious.

The OSI seven-layer model provides a good basis for understanding the functions and features that need to be provided in the protocols that implement the model. It provides a less useful basis for the direct implementation of a "pure" OSI stack, and there are not many implementations. This is partly for implementation considerations. With seven layers, a pure OSI stack could be inefficient, with a lot of parameter passing between each layer. It would be more efficient to have fewer layers, the approach taken by the designers of TCP/IP.

The process of creating an ISO standard is complex, not to mention that the labyrinthine politics have not helped either. The OSI standards documents are available only for purchase and are quite expensive. The specifications of TCP/IP, the Request for Comments (RFC) documents, are by comparison freely available from a large number of sites (see Appendix A, "RFCs and Standards/Further References," for more details on obtaining RFCs and other related documents). The openness of both the specifications and the process leading to their adoption has certainly made TCP/IP more attractive to developers, vendors, and users.

2.1.2. TCP/IP Model

The development that led to the TCP/IP protocols was originally funded by the U.S. Department of Defense's Advanced Research and Projects Authority (ARPA, later known as DARPA) and was begun as a research project in 1969. The original network that was developed, ARPANET, was built to study the techniques involved in reliable packet-switching networks, as well as to allow ARPA contractors to share their very expensive computing resources. The first version of the network linked a mere four organizations: the University of California at Los Angeles (UCLA), the University of California at Santa Barbara (UCSB), the University of Utah, and SRI International.

The original ARPANET succeeded beyond the wildest dreams of the first implementers. By the 1980s, the ARPANET connected hundreds of organizations, many of them commercial, and provided the basis for today's Internet. The original ARPANET protocols were, in effect, replaced with TCP/IP in 1984. With the incorporation of TCP/IP source code as a part of BSD 4.2, the success of TCP/IP was ensured.

The protocol model for TCP/IP is conceptually simpler than the OSI model. It consists of just four layers, as shown in Figure 2.2.

A Close Look at IPv4 and IPv6

Figure 2.2.

The TCP/IP architecture model.

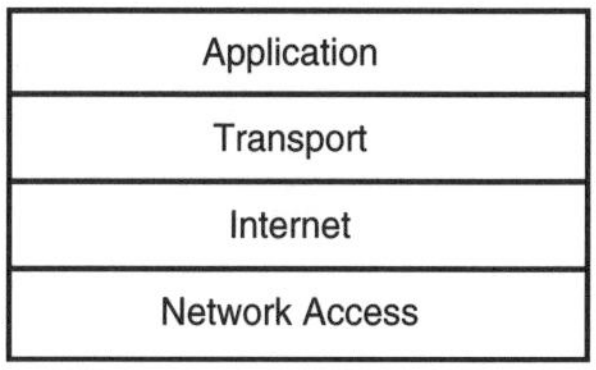

Application
Transport
Internet
Network Access

The functions of the four layers in the TCP/IP model are shown in Table 2.2.

Table 2.2. The functions of the TCP/IP model layers.

Layer	Function
Network Access	This corresponds to the physical and data link layers in the OSI model. There are no TCP/IP protocols at this layer as such. Rather, the higher layers are defined to work over existing physical networks, such as Ethernet, Token Ring, FDDI, ATM, and so on.
Internet	This corresponds to the network layer on the OSI model. The protocols at this level include Internet Protocol (IP), Internet Control Message Protocol (ICMP), and Internet Group Management Protocol (IGMP). Address Resolution Protocol (ARP) straddles these two layers.
Transport	This layer corresponds to the transport layer in the OSI model and includes the Transmission Control Protocol (TCP) and User Datagram Protocol (UDP).
Application	This broadly corresponds to the presentation and application layers in the OSI model. There are a large number of protocols at this layer, including File Transfer Protocol (FTP), Hypertext transfer Protocol (HTTP), Simple Mail Transfer Protocol (SMTP), Network News Transport Protocol (NNTP), and so on.

Figure 2.3 is a more complete picture that shows the key TCP/IP protocols implemented in IPv4. A similar picture can be drawn for IPv6, although in IPv6, the functions of ARP and RARP are contained within a revised ICMP.

Figure 2.3.
TCP/IP protocol architecture.

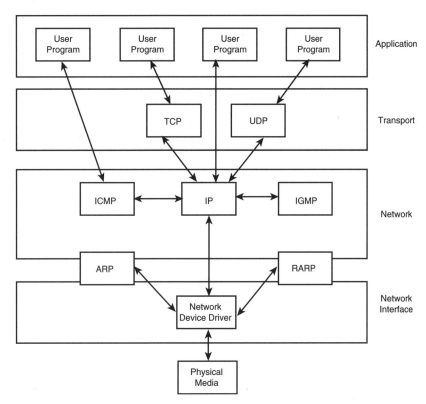

2.1.3. Comparison of Layers

Figure 2.4 shows a comparison of the layers in the ISO OSI and TCP models.

Figure 2.4.
Comparing the ISO OSI model with TCP/IP.

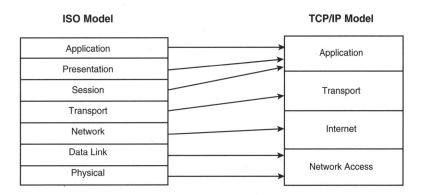

As can be seen in Figure 2.3, the TCP/IP model incorporates both the ISO physical and data link layers into a single layer, the network access layer. To a large degree, this is because IP can be implemented on top of virtually any sensible method of connecting two computers. This is true for both IPv4 and IPv6.

A large number of RFCs describe how this is achieved for both IPv4 and IPv6. These include the following:

- RFC 2023—IP version 6 over PPP
- RFC 2019—Transmission of IPv6 packets over FDDI
- RFC 1972—A method for the transmission of IPv6 packets over Ethernet networks
- RFC 1932—IP over ATM: A framework document
- RFC 1577—Classical IP and ARP over ATM
- RFC 1390—Transmission of IP and ARP over FDDI networks
- RFC 1331—The Point-to-Point Protocol (PPP) for the transmission of multiprotocol datagrams over point-to-point links
- RFC 1201—Transmitting IP traffic over ARCnet networks
- RFC 1149—A standard for the transmission of IP datagrams on Avian carriers
- RFC 1051—A standard for the transmission of IP datagrams and ARP packets over ARCnet networks
- RFC 1042—A standard for the transmission of IP datagrams over IEEE 802 networks
- RFC 894—A standard for the transmission of IP datagrams over Ethernet networks

Although RFC 1149 was intended as a spoof, it, along with the other RFCs, describes how higher IP datagrams can be carried by a number of different physical network types.

The functions of the ISO network layer are broadly implemented in the TCP/IP Internet layer. The main protocols defined for IPv4 at this layer are Internet Protocol (IP), defined in RFC 791, and Internet Control Message Protocol (ICMP), defined in RFC 792. For IPv6, the Internet Protocol is defined in a number of RFCs—the main one being RFC 1883. In IPv6, the functions of the ARP and RARP protocol have been subsumed within a revised ICMP.

The functions of both the ISO and TCP/IP transport layers are broadly similar—that is, they both provide reliable end-to-end communication across different networks. In the TCP/IP architecture, the designers added User Datagram Protocol (UDP). UDP offers an unreliable datagram delivery protocol that was not something originally envisaged by the ISO model because the ISO transport layer concerns itself with reliable transport. TCP is defined in RFC 793 while UDP is defined in RFC 768.

The top three layers in the ISO model (session, presentation, and application) are combined into the TCP/IP application layer. This approach makes the TCP/IP application layer rather large. A wide variety of protocols are defined at this layer, including key protocols used regularly by most Internet users. Examples include File Transfer Protocol (FTP), defined in RFC 959; Simple Mail Transfer Protocol (SMTP), defined in RFC 821; and Network News Transfer Protocol (NNTP), defined in RFC 977.

In summary, TCP/IP is a popular and widely deployed implementation of the ISO model. The functions described in the ISO model have largely been implemented in TCP/IP and are now widely deployed both in private corporate intranetworks as well as on the Internet itself.

While considerable work has been done to improve the performance, usability, and scalability of TCP/IP since the TCP/IP specifications were first published, much remains to be done. A major undertaking is the upgrading of IP from version 4 to version 6. Given the number of hosts utilizing IPv4, this upgrading will take a long while, and in the interim, many sites will be running a mixture of both versions.

Before moving on into the details of IPv4 and IPv6, let's first look at an important concept in layered communication protocol stacks—encapsulation and demultiplexing.

2.1.4. Encapsulation and Demultiplexing

A key characteristic of a layered network stack is the way each layer communicates with peer layers in different machines. This is achieved through the use of the protocols provided in a lower layer. Each layer in the model will transmit data to its peer layer in a receiver by using a protocol at a lower layer. This lower layer will encapsulate the data passed by the higher layer and will continue to pass it down the stack and eventually onto the wire. When the data is received at the destination host, these encapsulations are stripped away as the data is passed up the stack. Encapsulation is illustrated in Figure 2.5.

A Close Look at IPv4 and IPv6

Figure 2.5.

Communication protocol encapsulation.

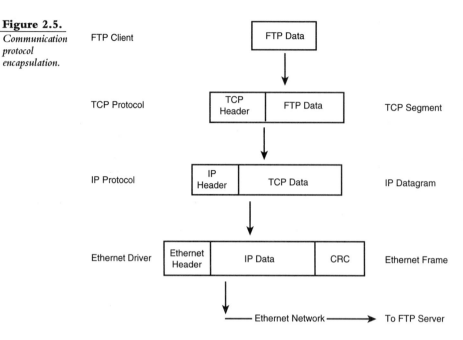

Figure 2.5 gives a simple example of an FTP client sending data to an FTP server. In this example, the protocols in the sender would carry out a number of distinct steps:

1. The FTP client asks TCP to transmit some data to an FTP server, having previously established a TCP session with the FTP server.

2. The TCP protocol takes this FTP data and adds a TCP header to create one or possibly more TCP segments. TCP then asks IP to send these segments to the FTP server.

3. IP packages this data, along with an IP header, into one (or possibly more) IP datagrams and asks Ethernet to transmit these.

4. Finally, Ethernet constructs an Ethernet frame containing the IP data along with a header and trailing Cyclical Redundancy Check (CRC), and has the network adapter transmit this onto the Ethernet LAN.

When the Ethernet Frame reaches the destination system (that is, the one hosting the FTP server), the reverse process known as demultiplexing occurs, and eventually the FTP data reaches the FTP server.

This example excludes the complexities of IP routing and packet fragmentation (fragmentation is discussed later in this chapter in the "IP Fragmentation" section). Additionally, the communication between FTP client and FTP server would normally involve a number of data exchanges, with each side sending encapsulated data across the physical network to be demultiplexed at the receiving end.

NOTE Not all implementations use pure encapsulation. Services on some servers bypass this in search of performance. One NFS developer, in a posting in the Internet `comp.procools.tcp-ip` newsgroup, stated, "Our server intercepts NFS packets early in UDP input process before the IP checksum is done and [they] are passed to NFS server threads. These [server threads] do the checksums, thereby loading the message into the cache of the CPU that will process the request. On output, we bypass the UDP and IP code completely and pass each reply fragment to the MAC level code for Ether/FDDI processing." In some instances, therefore, the normal encapsulation can be and is being bypassed. However, this is not the norm and is possible only when highly skilled programmers are involved. This is *not* something to try at home.

At each level in this model, the protocol has no knowledge of the higher-level data; it's just data to be transmitted. At first sight, this approach seems quite wasteful. Why not have the applications (in this example, the FTP client and server) just talk directly to the Ethernet LAN?

If such an approach were to be taken, each application would need full knowledge of all the functions of all the layers; it would be huge and complex. And unless the developers were extremely competent, most applications (both client and server sides) would most likely be inefficient. While there is overhead involved with encapsulation and demultiplexing, it is ultimately an efficient and leveraged way to implement data communication protocols.

The next two sections look at how the IP layers, IPv4 and IPv6, construct the IP datagrams. In later chapters, the details of how the higher-level protocols work will be presented.

2.2. How IPv4 Packets Are Put Together

IP is the workhorse of the TCP/IP suite. It handles the key functions of addressing and routing as well as packet fragmentation and reassembly. Each IP datagram consists of an IP datagram header and data.

2.2.1. Basic IPv4 Packet Layout

Figure 2.6 shows the basic format of an IPv4 datagram.

Figure 2.6.
IPv4 datagram layout.

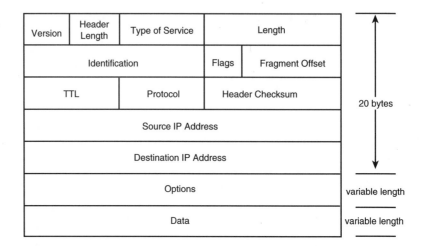

> **NOTE** Although IP datagrams are typically transmitted on a reliable physical link (for example, Ethernet, Token Ring, and so on) provided by the network interface layer, IP itself is an unreliable datagram protocol. It accepts data from the higher-level protocols, such as TCP and UDP, and offers a best-effort attempt to transmit this data to target a host utilizing some physical network. IP treats every datagram independently, and thus it has no concept of application data.

An IPv4 datagram consists of three primary components:

- Header—This is 20 bytes long and contains a number of fields. These fields are described in the next section.

- Options—This is a variable length set of fields which may or may not be present. These options also are discussed in the next section.

- Data—This is the encapsulated data from the higher level, usually a whole TCP segment or UDP datagram. Fragments of a TCP segment of a UDP datagram may also be carried, as described in the next section.

2.2.2. IPv4 Header Layout

The IP header is used by the IP software in a host or a router to determine what to do with the datagram (for example, route it to another host, pass it up the stack, demultiplex it, and so on). The IP header consists of the following fields:

- Version—The version number of IP (4 bits).

- Internet Header Length (IHL)—The total length of the IPv4 header, in 32-bit words (4 bits).

- Type of Service (TOS)—This is used to indicate the service level this IP datagram should be given (8 bits).

- Total Length—The total length of the IP datagram in octets (16 bits).

- Identification—A value assigned by the IP sender of an IP as an aid to reassembling fragmented packets (16 bits).

- Flags—Used to control fragmentation (3 bits).

- Fragment Offset—An offset into a nonfragmented datagram, used to reassemble a datagram that has become fragmented (13 bits).

- Time-To-Live (TTL)—The maximum time the datagram is allowed to exist within the networks it travels through (8 bits).

- Protocol—Identifies what higher-level protocol the data portion of the datagram belongs to (8 bits).

- Header Checksum—A checksum on the header (16 bits).

- Source IP address—The IP address of the sender of the IP datagram (32 bits).

- Destination IP address—The IP address of the host to which this datagram is to be sent (32 bits).

- Options—A set of fields, which may or may not be present in any given datagram, describing specific processing that must take place on this packet (variable length).

- Padding—Although not shown in Figure 2.6, some additional padding may be necessary to ensure that the header takes up a complete set of 32-bit words (variable).

The Version number is the version number of the IP datagram. The following version numbers, shown in Table 2.3, have been assigned by RFC 1700.

Table 2.3. IP version numbers.

Version number (Decimal Value)	Keyword	Version
0	Reserved	
1–3	Unassigned	
4	IP	Internet Protocol (that is, IPv4)
5	ST	ST datagram mode
6	SIP	Simple Internet Protocol (that is, IPv6)
7	TP/IX	TP/IX: The Next Internet

A Close Look at IPv4 and IPv6

continues

Table 2.3. Continued.

Version number (Decimal Value)	Keyword	Version
8	PIP	The P Internet Protocol
9	TUBA	TUBA
10–14	Unassigned	
15	Reserved	

Although several different version numbers have been assigned, only one is commonly used today (4, indicating IPv4). The SIP value (6) is used to indicate IPv6, which will become more common once working implementations of IPv6 begin to be deployed.

The Internet Header Length (IHL) is the total length of the header, including any Option fields, in 32-bit words. The minimum value for the IHL field is 5 (five 32-bit words or the 20 bytes of the IPv4 header). However, such a packet would not be particularly useful because it would have no payload.

The TOS field is used to indicate the level of service the IP datagram should be given while it is being transmitted through an internetwork. This field, an 8-bit value, is formatted as shown in Table 2.4.

Table 2.4. The format of the TOS field.

Bit	Parameter	Values
0–2	Precedence	111 = Network Control
		110 = Internetwork Control
		101 = CRITIC/ECP
		100 = Flash Override
		011 = Flash
		001 = Immediate
		001 = Priority
		000 = Routine
3	Delay	0 = Long Delay
		1 = Low Delay
4	Throughput	0 = Normal Throughput
		1 = High Throughput
5	Reliability	0 = Normal Reliability
		1 = High Reliability
6–7	Reserved for future use	

RFC 1349 gives further guidance on the use of the TOS field. This is augmented by recommendations contained in RFC 1700 for the default type-of-service values for the most important Internet protocols.

Although networks and IP stacks can offer the capability to utilize the TOS fields to discriminate between the different options, others do not, and the TOS field tends to be ignored. The Microsoft implementation of TCP/IP on NT 4.0, for example, will usually set the entire TOS field to zeros, indicating normal precedence, delay, throughput, and reliability. Microsoft's `PING.EXE` program, supplied on Windows NT, offers the capability to set a value for the TOS field for both the Echo Request and the Echo Reply. This can be useful when used on networks where these options are used.

The Total Length field specifies the length of the entire IP datagram, including the header and any payload. Unlike the Header Length field, the Total Length field is measured in octets and because this field is 16 bits wide, the maximum permitted length of an IP datagram is 65,535 octets. However, such large packets would not be practical, particularly on the Internet where they would be heavily fragmented. RFC 791 mandates that all hosts must accept IP datagrams up to 576 octets; however, it goes on to suggest that sending larger packets should be done only if the sender can be assured that the destination host is prepared to accept larger datagrams. This would be unlikely on the Internet, for example. A typical upper limit is 8,176 octets, although most datagrams are usually much smaller than this.

The Identification field is used to assist a destination host to reassemble a fragmented packet. It is set by the sender and uniquely identifies a specific IP datagram sent by a host. RFC 791 suggests that the Identification number is set by the higher-layer protocol, but in practice this tends to be set by IP.

The Flags and Fragmentation Offset fields govern fragmentation and are used to reassemble a fragmented packet at a destination host, as discussed in the "IP Fragmentation" section.

The Flags field is 3 bits long:

- Bit 0—Reserved

- Bit 1—May Fragment/Don't Fragment (the DF flag)

- Bit 2—Last Fragment/More Fragments (MF flag)

The Fragmentation Offset field is 13 bits long and indicates where in the reassembled datagram the data carried by a fragmented datagram should go.

The Time-To-Live (TTL) field indicates how long an IP datagram may live on the wire. This field, measured in seconds, is modified each time an IP datagram passes through an IP router. Each router that forwards the datagram will decrement

A Close Look at IPv4 and IPv6

the TTL by 1 prior to forwarding the packet. If the TTL reaches 0, it will be discarded and a suitable ICMP message will be sent back to the source host.

In the days when data communications were, relatively speaking, very slow, measuring TTL in seconds was sensible. Today, however, the TTL mainly uses a maximum hop count, rather than an actual time to live, and this is reflected in the proposals for IPv6. RFC 1700 recommends a default TTL of 64, although many stacks set a different value. The Windows NT 3.51 and the Windows 95 TCP/IP stacks, for example, both use a default TTL of 32, while the IP stack in Windows NT 4.0 uses a default TTL of 128. Naturally these values are easily changed.

The Protocol field indicates what higher-level protocol the data portion on the datagram relates to. RFC 1700 defines the values to be used in this field, but some of the more common protocols and their related values are shown in Table 2.5.

Table 2.5. Values of the Protocol field, as defined by RFC 1700.

Value	Name	Protocol
1	ICMP	Internet Control
2	IGMP	Internet Group Management
4	IP	IP in IP
6	TCP	Transmission Control (TCP)
17	UDP	User Datagram (UDP)
29	ISO-TP4	ISO Transport Protocol Class 4
45	IDRP	Inter-Domain Routing Protocol
46	RSVP	Reservation Protocol
80	ISO-IP	ISO Internet Protocol
83	VINES	VINES
88	IGRP	IGRP (Cisco)

The Header Checksum field contains a checksum for the header fields only. This checksum is calculated as a 16-bit one's complement of the one's complement of all the 16-bit words in the header. The value of the Checksum field, for the purposes of calculating the actual IP Header Checksum, is set to zero. Because the header, and therefore the checksum, contains the TTL field, the Header Checksum must be recalculated by every router or IP module that decrements the TTL. Although this is extra work, the header checksum is relatively quick to calculate.

As described in Chapter 1, "Introduction to TCP/IP," each host—whether on a single Ethernet LAN, a corporate intranet, or the Internet—must have a unique 32-bit IP address. The Source IP address and the Destination IP Address fields in the IP header hold the IP address for the sender and the ultimate destination of the IP datagram. If an IP datagram is to be routed, the source and destination addresses are not modified during the routing process.

The IPv4 header offers the capability to specify a number of options. There may be zero or more of these options present in the IP header. Although the carrying of one or more options is optional, the processing of these options must be implemented in any IPv4 stack.

The IP Header Option is a variable length field, consisting of zero, one, or more individual options. An option can consist of either a single octet or multiple octets. The more common options include the following:

- Security—See RFC 1108 for more details. Note that the security options tend not to be used in most commercial networks.

- Record route—This option has each router record its IP address in the Options field, which can be useful for tracing routing problems.

- Timestamp—This option requests each router to record both the router address and the time. Like the record route option, this can be useful for debugging router problems; although, the use of a trace-route program is preferred.

- Strict/loose source routing—This enables a host to define the routers the packet is to be transmitted through.

RFC 791 defines a number of option fields with additional options defined in RFC 1700. Although there are a large number of options defined, they tend not to be used and represent a significant overhead, especially for IP routers, a weakness addressed in IPv6. The record route, timestamp, and source routing options are discussed in more detail in Chapter 5, "IP Routing."

Because the IP Option fields are variable length, it might be necessary to add additional octets to the header to make it a whole number of 32-bit words (that is, the length defined in the Header Length field). If required, additional padding bytes are added to the end of any specified options to pad out the header. All padding octets have the value of zero.

As you can see, the IPv4 header is complex and contains a number of fields that, although not in common use today, still need to be catered for in any implementation of IP that can impose performance penalties on IP routers. This complexity has been taken into consideration in the design of IPv6.

A Close Look at IPv4 and IPv6

2.2.3. IP Fragmentation

As noted in the last section, it is possible for an IP datagram to be fragmented during transmission across an internetwork. Fragmentation can occur in two places:

- At the source host—When IP gets a request to transmit a datagram (for example, containing a TCP segment or a UDP datagram) to a destination host, it will check the local interface over which the datagram is to be transmitted for the Maximum Transmission Unit (MTU). The MTU is the maximum size of a physical packet on the network. If the amount of data to be transmitted (which must include the length of the IP Header, or 20 octets) is greater than the MTU, then the datagram is fragmented into several, smaller datagrams.

- In a router—If the router is connected to networks supporting different packet sizes, such as Token Ring and Ethernet, fragmentation can be created. If the router received a large IP datagram for routing onto a network, which doesn't support such large datagrams, the router must divide the packet into a number of discrete IP datagrams for transmission.

Once fragmented, these fragment datagrams will not be reassembled until they reach the destination host. Because fragmentation creates extra datagrams that require extra processing, it can result in a degradation in performance. Further, because IP is an unreliable protocol, if any of the fragmented datagrams are lost, then all the fragments (that is, the entire original datagram) will have to be retransmitted. It is the responsibility of the higher layers, such as TCP or a UDP application, to detect this problem and take corrective action.

In general, the sender of a datagram wants to keep the size of any transmitted IP datagram to the maximum size that can be transmitted, without causing fragmentation. This value is referred to as the Path MTU. Some stacks will automatically calculate this, while other stacks leave this as an exercise for the user. Path MTU is defined in RFC 1191.

Fragmentation utilizes several fields from the IP header:

- Identification—The Identification field has a unique value for each datagram transmitted. Each of the fragmented datagrams will have the same Identification field value, which enables IP to reassemble fragmented datagrams correctly.

- Flags—If the MF flag (bit 2 of the Flags field) is set, this indicates that this datagram is a fragment to be reassembled, but not the last. The last fragment datagram will have the MF flag set to 0.

- Fragmentation offset—This is used by IP when it is reassembling the fragment datagrams into a whole datagram. The offset tells where the data in a fragmented datagram should be placed into the datagram being reassembled.

IP datagram fragmentation is illustrated in Figure 2.7.

Figure 2.7.
IP datagram fragmentation.

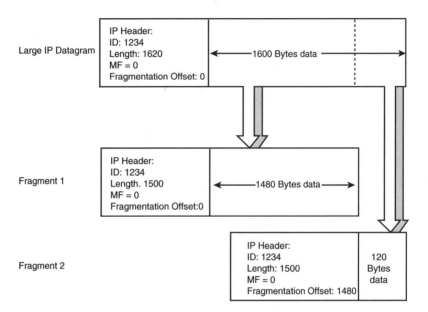

In this example, a single, large IP datagram is fragmented into two smaller frames. The large IP datagram has an Identification field value of 1234, a Total Length of 1620 octets, and the More Fragments flag is set to 0. In the first fragment datagram, IP will set the MF flag to 1, indicating more fragments to come, and the Fragmentation Offset to 0, indicating that the data in this fragment is the start of the larger unfragmented datagram. The second fragment datagram will have the remaining data, 120 octets, and will have the MF flag set to 0 and the Total Length set to 140 (20 octets of header and 120 of IP data). In this second fragment, IP will set the Fragmentation Offset to 1480, indicating that the 120 bytes of data are to be reassembled into offset 1480 of the reassembled, larger datagram.

In carrying out the fragmentation, IP will have to copy across any Options fields, if any, from the larger Datagram into the header of each fragment, as well as recalculate any change in IP header length. IP will also calculate new checksums for both fragments.

A Close Look at IPv4 and IPv6

It might be desirable for a sending host to indicate it does not wish any datagram to be fragmented. It can do this by setting the DF flag in the Flags field (bit 2). If a datagram reaches a router that needs to fragment the packet for onwards transmission and discovers the DF flag is set, it will send an ICMP Destination Unreachable error back to the originating host with a code of 4, indicating "Fragmentation Needed and Don't Fragment was Set," as described in RFC 792.

One possible approach to minimizing fragmentation is for the application sending data, which would also include TCP and UDP, to determine the Path MTU—that is, the size of the largest single datagram that could be transmitted without fragmentation occurring and not sending datagrams larger than this. This means more work initially to determine path MTU, but can result in much better throughput, especially for TCP. In IPv6, the sender must know the MTU.

2.2.4. IP Address Types

IPv4 uses three types of addresses in the Source and Destination fields:

- Unicast—This represents a single interface to a single system. IP datagrams sent to a unicast address will be sent to a single interface on a single IP host.

- Multicast—This represents one or more interfaces, but typically not all. IP datagrams sent to a multicast address will be sent to all hosts participating in this multicast group.

- Broadcast—This represents all interfaces on all hosts. Usually, this is restricted to all hosts on the local subnet.

Most hosts that implement IP will have a single net card or modem, and this interface will have a single IP address—a unicast address. When communicating between hosts, most IP traffic will have unicast addresses in both the Source and Destination addresses.

Multicast addresses are used to allow a host to join a multicast group and to receive all IP datagrams destined for that multicast group. Multicasting is not heavily used in most installations, although its use is growing. Multicast addresses are generally specified only in a Destination address.

The IP Broadcast address is 255.255.255.255 (all binary 1s) and represents all IP hosts on the subnet (discussed in the next chapter). Broadcasts are used for a variety of purposes, usually to find a station or stations (for example, find the system whose system name is \\SERVER21). Some older IP stacks used the address 0.0.0.0 for broadcast, and most IP stacks have a method of enabling this older form if required. As broadcasts are sent to all stations, most IP routers will filter broadcasts; thus, these are never usually routed. It is possible to have the router relay these broadcasts, but this is not recommended. A datagram sent to the IP broadcast address will result in all stations (typically on the subnet) receiving the packet. Note that this will usually generate a CPU interrupt on *all* hosts on that subnet, even those that are not running TCP/IP.

2.3. How IPv6 Packets Are Put Together

IP version 6 (IPv6) is the new version of the Internet Protocol, designed to be a full replacement for IPv4. RFC 1883 defines the new IPv6 protocol, with other RFCs providing additional details.

IPv6 differs from IPv4 in a number of significant ways, including the following:

- Increased address size—The IP address length in IPv6 is increased from 32 to 128 bits, which allows for significantly larger numbers of IP addresses.

- Simplified setup and configuration—IPv6 can automatically configure local addresses and locate IP routers, thus reducing configuration and setup problems. It can also work with DHCP, as required.

- Simplified header format—The IPv6 header format has been simplified, and some header fields have been dropped or made optional. This new header format should improve router performance and make it easier to add new header types as necessary.

- Improved support for options and extensions—The way header options are specified has been improved, which should improve the performance of option performance, as well as make it easier to add new option types.

- Support for authentication and data encryption—Support for authentication, data integrity, and data confidentiality are part of the IPv6 architecture, rather than being add-ons.

- Flow labeling—A new concept of flows has been added to IPv6 to enable the sender to request special handling of datagrams. This will assist the use of IP for handling application data such as video and audio.

The differences between IPv4 and IPv6 are discussed in the "Comparing IPv4 and IPv6" section later in this chapter.

2.3.1. IPv6 Basic Header Layout

The generic IPv6 packet format, defined in RFC 1883, is shown in Figure 2.8. It consists of a basic header, optional extension headers, and data. In IPv6, the data portion of the datagram is called the payload. Figure 2.8 shows the format of a datagram with no extension headers.

A Close Look at IPv4 and IPv6

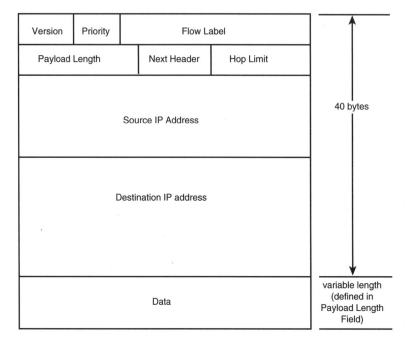

Figure 2.8.
*The IPv6
datagram layout.*

The Version field in the IPv6 header serves the same purpose as in the IPv4 header—identifying version 6 packets. IPv6 datagrams have this 4-bit field set to a value of 6.

The Priority field is a 4-bit value that enables the sender of IPv6 datagrams to indicate the priority of datagrams, with respect to other packets originating from the same sender. The Priority field contains two value ranges: values between 0 and 7 are used when the sender is able to provide congestion control (for example, for TCP type traffic) and the values between 8 and 15 are used to specify the priority for datagrams where the sender is not providing flow control (for example, for UDP or datagrams transmitted at a constant rate such as video or audio). There is no relationship between these two classes.

For congestion-controlled traffic, RFC 1883 suggests the following Priority values shown in Table 2.6.

Table 2.6. Priority values suggested by RFC 1883.

Priority value	Type of traffic
0	Uncharacterized traffic
1	"Filler" traffic (for example, NNTP news has a fairly low priority)

Priority value	Type of traffic
2	Unattended data transfer (for example, e-mail)
3	Reserved
4	Attended bulk transfer (for example, FTP and NFS)
5	Reserved
6	Interactive traffic (for example, Telnet and X)
7	Internet control traffic, such as routing protocols or SNMP

For non-congestion controlled traffic, RFC 1883 suggests that the lower the value (in the range 8–15) the more willing the sender is to have the datagrams discarded should congestion occur. For both classes of Priority values, the higher the Priority value, in general, the less willing the sender is to see the datagram discarded.

RFC 1883 defines a *flow* as a sequence of packets sent from one host to a particular unicast or multicast destination where the sender wants some special handling by any intervening routers (for example, non-default quality of service or "real-time" service, and so on). The details of the special handling desired will be defined either by a control protocol, such as a resource reservation protocol, or by information within the flow's packets themselves, such as might be contained in a Hop-by-Hop Option Extension Header (discussed later in this section). The 24-bit Flow Label field is used by a source to label those packets for which it requests such handling. This aspect of IPv6 is currently considered experimental and subject to change.

The Payload Length field is used to define the size of the data carried in the packet—the Data portion shown in Figure 2.8. As this field is 16 bytes long, standard payloads can be as large as 65,535 bytes long. If the sender needs to send a datagram with a larger payload, IPv6 offers a "jumbo payload" feature. This is indicated by setting the Payload Length field to zero and indicating the true length in the Jumbo Hop-by-Hop Extension Header.

IPv6 datagrams may have multiple Extension headers, each with a defined architecture and format. The Next Header field is used to tell whether another header is present and to identify the header. RFC 1883 defines the number of header types that are described in the "IPv6 Extension Headers" section.

A Close Look at IPv4 and IPv6

> **NOTE** How many IP addresses do you really need?
>
> IPv6 uses address lengths of 128 bits, which will enable a large number of potential addresses. Assuming that there were no inefficiencies in the assignment and usage of IP addresses, 128 bits provide in the region of 665,570,793,348,866,943,898,599 addresses per square meter of the earth's surface. The creation of IP address hierarchies, however, will reduce the efficiency of address assignment and this theoretical number of hosts. Christian Huitema presents in RFC 1715 an analysis in which he concludes that the 128-bit IPv6 addresses could accommodate between 8×10^{17} to 2×10^{33} nodes per square meter of the earth's surface. Even his most pessimistic estimate suggests that the new address size would create 1,564 addresses per square meter of the earth's surface. Huitema concludes that this is sufficient to last for at least another 30 years to come! No doubt this will come back to haunt him if this estimate is proved wrong!

The Hop Limit field is an 8-bit field that broadly serves the same purpose as IPv4's TTL field—to limit the length of time a packet can live on the wire. In IPv6, however, this is strictly a hop count limit. Each node that forwards an IPv6 datagram will decrement the Hop Limit field by 1. If the value drops to 0, the datagram is discarded. If the packet is discarded, the IPv6 node that discarded it will send an ICMP Time Exceeded-Hop Limit Exceeded in Transit message back to the source host, identified by the source IP address in the IPv6 Basic Header.

Like IPv4, the IPv6 header contains a Source Address and a Destination Address, although in the IPv6 header, these fields hold 128-bit IPv6 IP addresses. Unlike IPv4, the IPv6 Destination Address may not hold the IP address of the datagram's final destination. When source routing is being used, the Destination Address may indicate an intermediate host, via which this datagram will be routed with the final destination host IP address being contained in a routing header. In such cases, the ultimate destination IP address is contained in the routing extension header. The IPv6 Routing Extension Header is discussed in the "IPv6 Address Types" section and in Chapter 5.

2.3.2. IPv6 Extension Headers

IPv6 greatly simplifies the handling of options, in comparison to IPv4, by creating separate extension headers for each option. These extension headers are aligned on word or byte boundaries within the datagram to minimize the cost of processing each option. None of these headers is examined or processed, except by the destination host specified in the header, with the exception of the Hop-by-Hop extension header.

All IPv6 datagrams contain the basic header, as previously described, but a given IPv6 datagram may carry zero, one, or more of these extension headers. These extension headers are pointed to by the Next Header field in the datagram header.

Each extension header is assigned a separate 4-bit Next Header value. Currently assigned Next Header values are shown in Table 2.7.

Table 2.7. Extension header types and their assigned values.

Header type	Next header value
Hop-by-Hop Options	0
Routing Header	43
Fragment Header	44
Encapsulating Security Payload	50
Authentication Header	51
Destination Options Header	60
No Next Header	59

In general, if any of these headers are present, they should be presented in the order shown in the table. If there are options to be processed during source routing, there may be more than one Destination Options Header. This would be placed before the routing header.

Hop-by-Hop Option Header

Hop-by-Hop options are special options that require hop-by-hop processing. The Hop-by-Hop extension header can contain multiple options to be processed. Each option is contained in variable length using a type-length-value (TLV) format. The Option Type is an 8-bit field, and Option Length is represented by an 8-bit unsigned integer field.

The Hop-by-Hop Option Types have values coded so that the two high-order bits can be used to determine what IP should do if it cannot recognize the option type. These two bits are coded as follows:

Bit Value	Action to be taken
00	Skip over this option and continue processing the Hop-by-Hop header.
01	Discard the datagram.
10	Discard the datagram and send the Source Host an ICMP Parameter Problem message (Unrecognized Option Type).
11	Discard the packet. If the Destination host is *not* a multicast address, send the source host an ICMP Parameter Problem message (unrecognized Option Type).

The third bit in the Hop-by-Hop Option Type is coded to indicate whether the value of this option can change during transmission:

A Close Look at IPv4 and IPv6

Bit Value	Action to be taken
0	Option does not change en route.
1	Option may change en route.

There are three Hop-by-Hop Option Types defined thus far:

- Pad1—This is a one-byte padding option. This is a special case Option Type and has the value 0, contained in 8-bits.

- PadN—This pads the header by *n* bytes. This has an Option Type of 1.

- Jumbo-payload—This enables payloads greater than 65,525 octets long. This has an Option Type of 194.

Some option headers, such as the Jumbo-payload option, need to be aligned so that when some values (for example, the Jumbo Payload Length, or JPL) fall on convenient boundaries (on a 32-bit word boundary for the JPL field), padding of the Pad1 or PadN is used. These paddings have no purpose other than to pad out the header to enable the next component to begin on an appropriate word/byte boundary. In the case of the Jumbo-payload option, note that this is already properly aligned, assuming it is the only Hop-by-Hop Option Type specified.

The Hop-by-Hop Option Header layout and the layout of these three Option Types are shown in Figure 2.9.

Figure 2.9.
The Hop-by-Hop extension option header layout.

Hop-by-Hop Option Header Layout

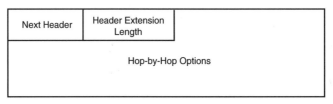

Hop-by-Hop Pad1 Option Type Layout

Hop-by-Hop PadN Option Type Layout

Hop-by-Hop Jumbo Payload Option Layout

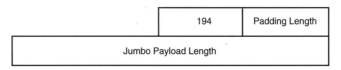

Routing Extension Header

In most cases, a source host will send datagrams to a destination host, allowing the underlying network to use its best efforts to route those datagrams. In some cases, it might be desirable or even necessary for a source host to guide the packets to the host by a specific route or via certain hosts. This guidance, or source routing, can be either strict or loose. With *strict source routing*, the source will list the exact path the datagram must take, whereas for *loose source routing*, the source host will list certain way points the datagram must travel.

The Routing Header layout is shown in Figure 2.10.

Figure 2.10.
The Routing Header layout.

Next Header	Header Extension Length	Routing Type	Segments Left
Routing-Type Specific Data (variable length)			

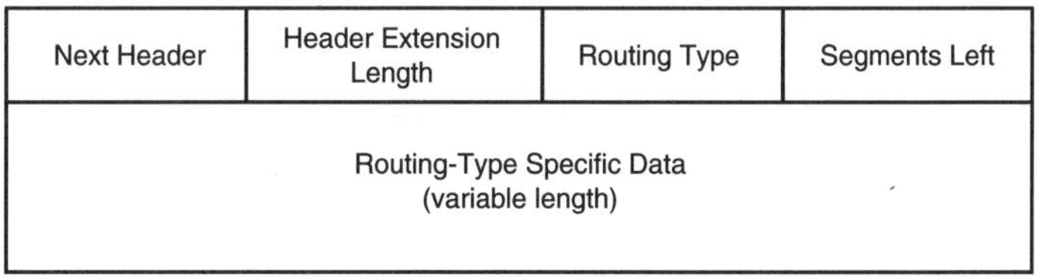

There is currently only one routing header defined, a Type routing header. The layout of the Type 0 routing header is shown in Figure 2.11. The use of this header is detailed in Chapter 5.

Figure 2.11.
The Type 0 routing header.

Next Header	Header Extension Length	Routing Type (0)	Segments Left
Reserved	Strict/Loose Bit Map		
Address [1]			
Address [2]			
• • •			
Address [n]			

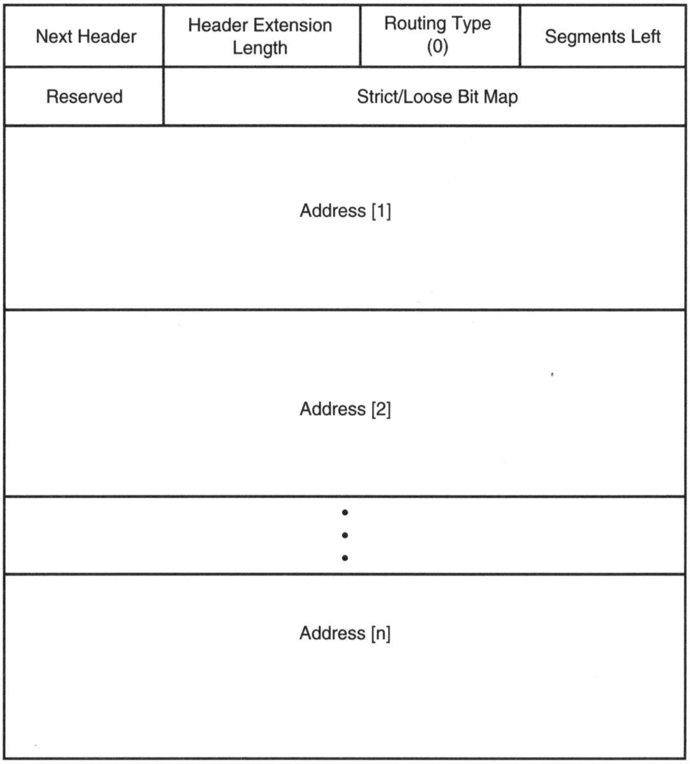

The Fragmentation Header

Unlike IPv4, IPv6 datagrams are generally not fragmented. If fragmentation is required, it will be carried out not by routers, but by the source of the datagram. If a sender decides to fragment a datagram, it can use the fragmentation and reassembly extension header to indicate this. The Fragmentation Header layout is shown in Figure 2.12.

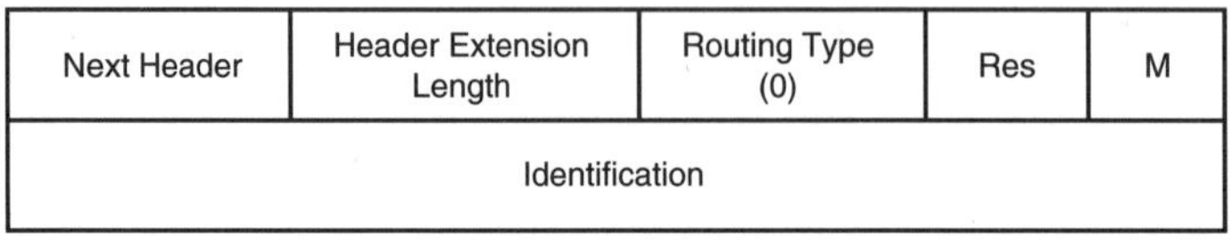

Figure 2.12.

*The Fragmenta-
tion Header
layout.*

Next Header	Header Extension Length	Routing Type (0)	Res	M
Identification				

In order to transmit a datagram greater than the Path MTU, the source host will divide the packet into individual fragments. These will be reassembled by the final destination host.

For each datagram that will be fragmented, the source host will generate a unique identification value, which must be different from that used in any other datagram sent *recently* to the final destination host. Recently means, according to RFC 1883, "with the maximum likely lifetime of a packet including transit time from source to destination and time spent awaiting reassembly." This does not mean that the IP must know the maximum lifetime of a packet. RFC 1883 assumes that this can be met by maintaining a simple wraparound counter that is incremented for each datagram that must be fragmented before transmission.

The Authentication Header

The Authentication Header (AH), described in RFC 1826, has been designed to provide authentication and prove the integrity of IP datagrams. The AH provides the receiver of an IPv6 datagram with confidence that the datagram was sent by the sender indicated in the header and that the packet was not altered in any way during transmission. Depending on the specific algorithm used to create this header, it may also allow for nonrepudiation—that is, for a receiver to know that a datagram came from a particular source even if that source subsequently wished to deny that it ever sent the datagram. The AH does not provide confidentiality. The Authentication Header layout is shown in Figure 2.13.

Figure 2.13.
*The Authentica-
tion Header
layout.*

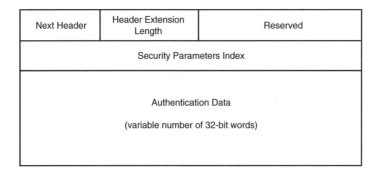

Next Header	Header Extension Length	Reserved
Security Parameters Index		
Authentication Data (variable number of 32-bit words)		

The basic concept of the Authentication Header is to generate a unique signature, or cryptographic checksum, of some part of the datagram. This checksum is based on an algorithm and a key or keys on which both the sender and receiver have previously agreed. This checksum is generated by the sender and transmitted to the receiver in the Authentication Header. The receiver then can use this checksum to confirm that the datagram's payload was not altered during transmission and, potentially, to confirm who sent it.

In order for the authentication process to work, the sender and receiver must have previously agreed on the encryption algorithm to be used, the key or keys to be used by that algorithm, as well as other data, such as the lifetime of the key, and so on. This set of parameters constitutes a security association between the sender and receiver. When a datagram is received, the receiver will only be able to provide datagram authentication if it can link the datagram back to that security association.

The Security Parameters Index (SPI) is used to indicate to the receiver how the AH was generated and the type and nature of the key or keys used in the generation process; it is the security association noted in the preceding paragraph. Typically this will be negotiated prior to the commencement of datagram transmission. The authentication data in the Authentication Header is the cryptographic checksum.

The calculation of the authentication data can have a significant impact on the overall performance of datagram transmission because the sender has to calculate the Authentication Data for each datagram, and the receiver has to verify that the datagram was not tampered with. The trade-off between speed and authentication is an issue that each site will have to evaluate.

Encapsulating Security Payload

The Encapsulating Security Payload (ESP) header, defined in RFC 1827, is used to provide confidentiality of payload data, rendering it unreadable by all but the destination host. This is different than the authentication provided by the Authentication Header, although the keys and algorithms used can be the same or similar.

Depending on the algorithm used to encrypt the encapsulated payload, the ESP header may also provide a measure of authentication and integrity, although this is not its prime purpose.

There are two modes of ESP. The first, the tunnel mode, involves encapsulating and encrypting an entire IP datagram (complete with header). This can provide secure transmission of confidential datagrams over a less secure network (for example, the Internet). The second mode, the transit mode, just encapsulates and encrypts data from a higher level protocol, such as an UDP datagram or a TCP segment.

When the ESP is used, only part of the data is encrypted—namely anything that follows the ESP header (plus a portion of the ESP header itself). The ESP header is shown in Figure 2.14.

Figure 2.14.
The ESP header layout.

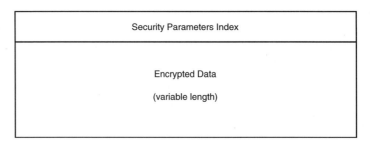

The Security Parameter Index (SPI) in the ESP header is used to define the security association for this datagram. Like the Authentication Header, the ESP header relies on a strong encryption algorithm and its correct implementation by sender and receiver; the strength and security of the key or keys used in the encryption process; and the correct implementation of the processing of both headers by the IP modules within the sender, receiver, and any intermediate security hosts (for example, a security gateway). The management of keys is also an area of potential vulnerability. Manual key distribution, while potentially secure, does not scale well. Before widespread adoption of the ESP header can take place, some automated form of key registration and distribution must be developed, such as extensions to DNS.

Destination Options

The final header in the IPv6 chain is the Destination Options header. At present, there are no real destination options specified, except for the two padding options defined previously in the Hop-by-Hop header. It's doubtless that this header will become used for a variety of things, such as server- or organization-specific data.

2.3.3. IPv6 Address Types

IPv6 has three different types of addresses that can be used in the Source and Destination fields of the IPv6 header:

- Unicast—This represents a single interface to a single system. IP datagrams sent to a unicast address will be delivered to a single interface on a single host.

- Multicast—This represents one or more interfaces, but typically not all. IP datagrams sent to a multicast address will be sent to all interfaces/hosts.

- Anycast—This represents some, but not all, interfaces. IP datagrams sent to an anycast address will be sent to one of possibly many interfaces/hosts.

Unicast addresses in IPv6 are similar to IPv4, although they use the longer 128-bit address format. It is also expected that many interfaces can have multiple IP addresses obtained from different ISPs.

Multicast addresses in IPv6 are also very similar to IPv4, although IPv6 makes much more use of multicasting. For example, in IPv6, all IP hosts on a particular subnet will not be reached via a broadcast address (as in IPv4), but rather by the hosts on this link multicast address, `FF00::2`.

The broadcast address used in IPv4 is not used in IPv6. Broadcasts, as used in IPv4, have been replaced by multicast addresses. This is likely to provide great benefit for those organizations that are not totally TCP/IP based because it will allow the network card to filter out packets sent to a multicast address that are not relevant to a particular host.

The anycast address represents one of possibly many interfaces/hosts. This feature, not present in IPv4, allows a host to send a datagram to one of many servers. The datagram will be delivered to only one interface/host, typically the nearest. Anycast addresses are still experimental.

2.4. Comparing IPv4 and IPv6

This section looks at some of the key differences between IPv4 and IPv6. Because there is little working IPv6 code available, the impact of these differences is as yet theoretical; large scale deployment of IPv6 will be needed before some of the differences can be truly quantified.

A Close Look at IPv4 and IPv6

2.4.1. Addressing

Perhaps the most obvious difference between IPv4 and IPv6 is the larger, 128-bit IP address supported in IPv6. As noted in the "How IPv4 Packets Are Put Together" section, this larger address space gives rise to a large number of potential hosts—more than enough for the foreseeable future.

The larger address space provided by IPv6 is urgently needed for the Internet, which is rapidly running out of usable addresses. Techniques such as Classless Inter-Domain Routing (CIDR), discussed in Chapter 5, have reduced the pressure, but the popularity of the Internet with both business and private individuals means that a solution, such as that provided by IPv6, will be needed within the next few years.

The IPv6 space is not, as in IPv4, just divided up into a few simple address classes to be handed out on a first come-first served basis. The address space in IPv6 is much more highly structured and has been designed to cater to a number of different uses.

This structure, like the IPv4 class approach, is based on the first high-order bits of the IPv6 IP address. RFC 1884 defines the initial address space allocation, as shown in Table 2.8.

Table 2.8. The IPv6 address space allocation.

Allocation	Prefix	Fraction of space
Reserved	`0000 0000`	1/256
Unassigned	`0000 0001`	1/256
Reserved for NSAP Allocation	`0000 001`	1/128
Reserved for IPX Allocation	`0000 010`	1/128
Unassigned	`0000 011`	1/128
Unassigned	`0000 1`	1/32
Unassigned	`0001`	1/16
Unassigned	`001`	1/8
Provider-based unicast address	`010`	1/8
Unassigned	`011`	1/8

Allocation	Prefix	Fraction of space
Reserved for geographic-based unicast addresses	100	1/8
Unassigned	101	1/8
Unassigned	110	1/8
Unassigned	1110	1/16
Unassigned	1111 0	1/32
Unassigned	1111 10	1/64
Unassigned	1111 110	1/128
Unassigned	1111 1110 0	1/512
Link local use addresses	1111 1110 10	1/1024
Site local use addresses	1111 1110 11	1/1024
Multicast addresses	1111 1111	1/256

A Close Look at IPv4 and IPv6

This allocation scheme provides several highly desirable features:

- It provides for the allocation of addresses by an ISP. This will greatly simplify the provision of address blocks and routing within the global Internet.

- It provides for Site- and Link-Local addresses. These IPv6 addresses are based on the network card address and are for use when a host does not wish to utilize a network either outside its link or outside its site. This greatly simplifies the assignment of IP addresses to a host.

- It provides larger address ranges for multicasting. A large block of multicast addresses is defined. These addresses are used for a variety of things, such as host autoconfiguration, routing, and so on.

- It provides for substantial future growth. The majority of the address space has been left unallocated, which allows for better future growth and expansion as well as for new classes of applications or hosts.

One downside to this new address size is that addresses are no longer memorable. Addresses such as `193.195.190.200` or `193.195.190.25` (the IPv4 addresses of the machines on which this chapter was developed) are memorable. On the other hand, a fictional IPv6 provider-based address such as `4890:0AF:1212:0:0:0:3434:11F3` is harder to remember.

While the user interface issues appear not to have been considered part of the development of the IPv6 RFCs, the size of the address presents challenges to organizations developing IPv6 products. The IPv6 suppliers will need to work hard to reduce the inherent difficulty people will have with such large addresses.

Another aspect this larger address space and configuration will allow is provider choice. IPv6 is designed to handle multiple IP addresses per interface, which will allow organizations, in effect, to ask for bids for transit services. Greater choice of provider, possibly on a connection-by-connection basis, becomes much easier with IPv6.

2.4.2. Headers and Header Processing

Header processing in IPv4 is complex. Many implementations did not implement some features, such as security. Indeed, many of the fields in the header, such as the Type Of Service, are simply not used or are ignored if encountered. The RFCs that define IPv6 give much more guidance on the nature and handling of header fields, which will increase interoperability.

Another important aspect of the design of IPv6 headers has been the efficiency of processing. By ensuring that key values are on natural byte or word boundaries, modern computers can process IPv6 headers more efficiently. This will have a great impact on the performance of routers and large servers, such as those found at major WWW or FTP sites.

This increased processing efficiency and larger IPv6 address, however, comes at the price of larger IP datagrams. This will put pressure on many organizations to upgrade or replace existing infrastructures. The transition arrangements for the implementation of IPv6, however, will enable most organizations to carry out these improvements in a planned and phased manner, thus reducing the negative impact.

2.4.3. Configuration

Configuration of IPv4 hosts, especially in large organizations and for private Internet users, can be a minefield. While skilled IP practitioners can configure a host easily and with little effort, the efficient configuration of larger, dynamic organizations can be a substantial support burden.

IPv6 handles this by providing what is known as stateless autoconfiguration. For small networks, the IPv6 address of any host is a concatenation of the site or link local header with a host's IP card MAC address. This makes host configuration virtually automatic.

This autoconfiguration also allows for automatic detection of routers. Each router is automatically a member of the All Routers Multicast group. Thus, as part of a host's configuration process, it can send a multicast ICMP message to a multicast group consisting of all routers on the local link, which will allow the host to determine its local gateway.

Wherever an organization wishes to require hosts to have more structured IPv6 addresses or wherever specific parameters must be used (rather than being discovered), an IPv6 version of DHCP may be utilized.

2.4.4. Security and Encryption

The requirements of most organizations or individuals in the area of authentication, integrity, and confidentially can be met using existing protocols and techniques. However, none of them are automatic nor are they especially easy for end users to implement. The AH and ESP extension headers allow these requirements to be met easily.

However, this extra security comes at a price. Initial calculations suggest that the AH header might increase the time to process an individual datagram by 10–15%. The ESP might add 50%, which would have a noticeable effect on throughput. Given the relentless increase in processing power, the costs are probably acceptable.

2.4.5. Routing

With the growth of the Internet has come a growth in the size and complexity of routing tables and router processing. If a router in the Internet, as it presently exists, needs to determine the best path to take for a distant host, it would need to maintain a routing table entry for every host. With the size of the Internet today, this simply is not practical. With 128-bit addresses, better approaches are required.

One way around this difficulty has been route aggregation—encapsulated in CIDR. With CIDR, all addresses in Europe could, in theory, share the same high-order prefix to allow fewer routing table entries to be held for addresses in routers outside Europe. This approach has certainly helped control the relentless growth of routing table sizes, but it is not the long-term answer.

With IPv6 comes a new variant of routing protocol. Today, the exterior-routing protocol in use on the Internet is the Border Gateway Protocol. BGP4 supports the route aggregation necessary for CIDR, but the designers feel that it is so optimized for IPv4 that upgrading it to handle IPv6 is impractical.

For this reason, with the deployment of IPv6 will come new routing protocols based on the Interdomain Routing Protocol (IDRP). IDRP was originally designed to be a part of the OSI family of protocols. Chapter 5 discusses IDRP in more detail.

2.4.6. Multicasting

While multicasting—sending an IP datagram to multiple hosts—has long been supported, most users and products tend to not make much use of it. In Microsoft Windows 95 and Windows NT stacks, there is no real use made of multicasting—except for the WINS Server, which uses it to discover replication partners.

IP V6 makes heavy use of multicasting, and this may assist in improving performance in some mixed environments. When, for example, an IPv6 node performs autoconfiguration, it will attempt neighbor and router discovery. These multicasts will be sent to multicast groups, thus not interrupting non-IPv6 hosts.

2.4.7. Address Resolution

In IPv4, the ARP protocol is used to resolve an IP address into a physical address that can be used by the network interface layer. In most cases, this is done by a link layer broadcast, which causes CPU interrupts in every system that receives the packet.

2.4.8. Performance

The performance of a suite of protocols is a key issue in their acceptance. TCP/IP does not perform as well in very small networks in comparison to, say, NetBEUI, but it comes into its own in the larger organizations and the Internet. Because IP is the workhorse of the TCP/IP protocol suite, the designers of IPv6 needed to ensure that the additional features added would not affect overall throughput.

The increase in packet size directly affects the communications latency time—the time it takes to transmit a datagram from sender to receiver. Initial estimates suggest that this might amount to a 10-15% degradation, although that does leave out any improvements in processing performance as a result of better header field alignment and simplified routing.

The AH and ESP headers will add additional overhead, but only for those organizations and individuals who utilize them. From experience with SNMPv2, which uses basically the same techniques, the costs of AH may increase per datagram processing time in the region of 5–10%. The ESP might add another 50%. These additional costs have to be seen in light of the benefits they provide.

2.4.9. Address Types

As noted in the "IPv6 Address Types" section, there are differences in the types of addresses used in IPv4 and IPv6. Both versions support both unicast and multicast addresses.

IPv4 makes heavy use of broadcasting (for example, with ARP and DHCP). In IPv6, multicast addresses will be used in place of the IPv4 Broadcast addresses. This will allow much more filtering to be done by the network card. This should result in performance improvements across the network because it eliminates the CPU interrupts associated with broadcasts.

2.5. Summary

This chapter looks at the design of IPv4 and IPv6 and broadly compares them to the ISO OSI model. You also looked at how IPv6 works and the key differences between IPv4 and IPv6.

IP, as the workhorse of the overall TCP/IP protocol suite, is an important component, but there are other protocols that also affect performance, reliability, robustness, and ease of use.

Chapter 5 examines the issue of IP routing, with the higher-level protocols in the following chapters.

A Close Look at IPv4 and IPv6

3.1. IPv4

3.2. Classless Inter-Domain Routing (CIDR) with IPv4

3.3. IPv6: Next Generation Internet Addressing

3.4. Summary

Chapter

3

IP Addressing and Subnetting

by Robin Burk

The purpose of the Internet Protocol (IP) is to support the routing and delivery of packets. To accomplish this, IP is based on a digital addressing scheme suited to the nature of the Internet as an internetwork—that is, a network whose elements are networks themselves.

This chapter examines how IP addressing works and how it flexibly adapts to network topologies. Chapter 5, "IP Routing," discusses how these addresses are used to route packets through the network.

3.1. IPv4

Version 4 of the Internet Protocol has been in use since 1981 and is implemented in most parts of the public Internet, along with many private TCP/IP–based networks. In keeping with the "network of networks" concept, IPv4 addresses are hierarchical. That is, they consist of subfields that successively divide the overall address space into smaller portions until the total address uniquely identifies a single network interface on a network node.

The relative age of this addressing scheme is reflected in the simplicity of the original hierarchy and the somewhat contorted extensions made to it as the public Internet, in particular, grew in complexity.

At their most basic, IPv4 addresses consist of two subfields: a *network identifier* and a *host* (or local) *identifier*. Figure 3.1 shows this hierarchical addressing approach.

Figure 3.1.
IPv4 hierarchical address approach.

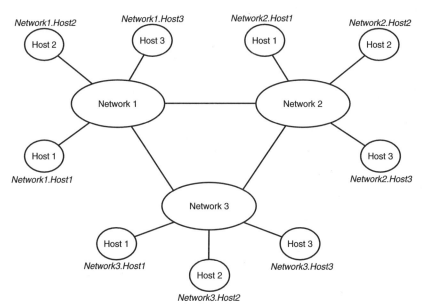

NOTE When the IPv4 addressing
scheme was being developed,
most computers had only a single network
interface that connected it to its local network.
Therefore, the practice arose of referring to the
local portion of the address as the *host*. RFC 791
alternates between carefully referring to this as
the *rest* of the address (after the network subfield)
and using the term *multihomed host* for those
computers with more than one physical interface
to the network.

Today, many of the computers present on the
public Internet (and in private intranets and
extranets) are routers or servers with multiple
network interfaces, so that the distinction
between host computer and interface becomes
more important to maintain. In keeping with
traditional practice, let's continue to call this local
address the host identifier, but keep in mind that
a given computer may have several such addresses
that refer to it.

The IPv4 network identifier uniquely specifies a
LAN, WAN, or complex grouping of linked
computers. Historically, there may have been
only a single gateway from such a network into
the Internet, defined by the entire address space.
Today, of course, there are often many more
such gateways. Nevertheless, the network
remains the fundamental grouping for IPv4
addresses because network identifiers must be
unique across the public Internet and as a result
are assigned by the InterNIC.

The host address uniquely identifies a given
physical interface (usually a network interface
card) between a specific computer and the
network to which it is linked locally. Unlike
network identifiers, host identifiers are assigned
by the network administrator, Internet service
provider (ISP), or other owner of a network.

3.1.1. IPv4 Network Classes

NOTE Some server software extends the
IP address-to-host mapping a
further step by supporting more domain names
than there are interfaces on a given server
computer. This is typically accomplished by
assigning virtual port numbers to user processes
while they are active.

The architects of the IPv4 standard were faced
with a dilemma: How to accommodate the
wide range of network complexities that might
arise within the Internet address space, while
keeping the IP address size (and hence overhead
burden on communications circuits, routers, and
server computers) as low as possible?

The approach they chose was to identify different classes of networks. A minority
of networks, such as the enterprise-wide nets of a major corporation, might
require a large number of local addresses. A larger number of networks would be
of medium size. And still more networks might contain relatively few local
computers. These constitute Groups A, B, and C, respectively.

The IPv4 architects defined a fixed address length of 32 bits for all IP addresses.
The 32 bits of address are allocated differently, however, based on the class to
which the network identifier belongs. It is customary to write IPv4 addresses as a
series of four decimal numbers, one per byte pair, separated by periods; this is
referred to as *dotted decimal* or *dot notation*.

IP Addressing and Subnetting

Figure 3.2 shows the respective bit allocations for Class A, B, and C addresses.

Figure 3.2.
*IPv4 address bit/
byte allocations.*

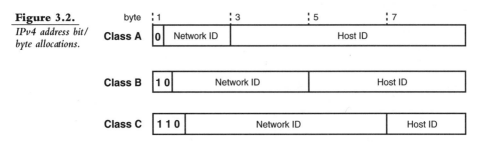

Figure 3.3 gives some IP address examples in binary/hexadecimal format and their corresponding dot notation forms.

Figure 3.3.
*Sample IPv4
addresses.*

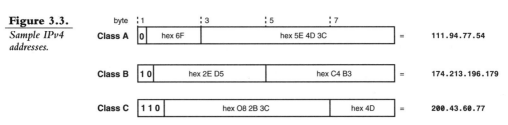

Note that the use of leading bits as class prefixes means that the class of a computer's network can be determined by the numerical value of its address. Table 3.1 shows the range of values for each network class. (Class D is used for multicast addresses; see the "IPv4 Multicasting" section. Class E is reserved for experimental protocol use.)

Table 3.1. Network class address ranges.

Class	Address Range
A	000.000.000.000–127.255.255.255
B	128.000.000.000–191.255.255.255
C	192.000.000.000–223.255.255.255
D	224.000.000.000–239.255.255.255
E	240.000.000.000–255.255.255.255

3.1.2. IPv4 Multicasting

TIP Note the difference between the network identifier assigned by the InterNIC and the first bytes of the IP address. In the Class B example from Figure 3.3, the network identifier is hexadecimal 2E D5. When combined with the Class B prefix, however, the first four bytes of the address yield AE D5, and the first two decimal numbers in the dot notation are 174 and 213.

If you are new to IP addressing, take time to work out the bit and byte placements to verify these values—it's an excellent way to familiarize yourself with the intricacies of IP address formats.

IPv4 addresses that begin with a byte value of hexadecimal 7 or lower belong to Class A networks. Those that begin with a value of 8 through B belong to Class B networks; those whose first byte value is C through D belong to Class C networks.

IPv4 addresses that begin with a byte value of E or F belong to network class D and E, respectively.

Most IPv4 addresses fall into one of the previously mentioned three classes. A fourth class, Class D, is used for multicasting.

The term *multicasting* refers to transmission of a packet to several networks at once. Unlike subnetting, which is a conceptual mechanism for adding a layer of addressing hierarchy within a network, multicast groups allow a sender to reach all the hosts on multiple networks with a single IPv4 address.

Host group addresses may be permanently or transiently assigned. A permanent group address is the one assigned by the Internet Assigned Numbers Authority (IANA).

Routers on the public Internet must be configured to support multicasting and to map host group addresses (multicasting addresses) to one or more network interfaces. The routers do *not* need to be aware of the specific hosts that are present on each network. Instead, the gateway computers for each network treat a multicast packet as a broadcast to all the network hosts. This reduces the administrative effort for router configuration to a more manageable level of complexity.

Figure 3.4 shows the format of a multicast address.

Figure 3.4.
The IPv4 multicast address format.

byte 1   3   5   7
Class D | 1 1 1 0 | Host group address

WARNING Take the time to work through the examples in Figure 3.3. The dot notation is not intuitively obvious, nor do the decimal subfields automatically correspond to meaningful subfields in the IP address types.

Although the multicast address format suggests that the Class D addresses may extend from 224.0.0.0 to 239.255.255.255, address 224.0.0.0 is never used and 224.0.0.1 is assigned to the permanent group of all IP hosts, including gateways. A packet addressed to 224.0.0.1 will reach all multicast hosts on the directly connected network.

IP Addressing and Subnetting

IPv4 multicasting is defined in RFC 1112. As might be expected, this document primarily discusses the changes required in routing computers to map a given Class D IP address to the networks that form the group in question. Although client software must know about this addressing format in order to make use of IP multicasting, the bulk of the programming changes occur in routers because their central job is to interpret IP addresses and to forward packets.

3.1.3. Subnetting in IPv4

From the beginning, the two-layer hierarchy established in IPv4 addresses (`network.host`) has lacked the flexibility and information richness needed for any sophisticated size or topology of network.

To begin with, it provided administrators few ways to manage large, heterogeneous networks. A Class A network can contain 16,777,216 host identifiers! This is far too many identifiers to configure and manage as a flat address space. Many of those hosts are likely to reside on various locally administered LANs, with different media and data-link protocols, different access needs, and in all likelihood, different geographical locations. The IPv4 addressing scheme has no way to reflect these subdivisions within a large enterprise WAN.

In addition, Class A, B, and C network identifiers are a limited and scarce resource, whose use under the class addressing scheme was often inefficient. For example, many mid-sized enterprises found Class C network identifiers too small (each Class C network can contain fewer than 256 hosts). Instead, they often requested Class B identifiers despite having far fewer than the 65,536 network interfaces a Class B address supports. As a result, many of the network/host combinations were allocated but unused, being superfluous to the network owner and unusable by other organizations.

Subnetting provides the answer to both of these problems, which result from the rapid expansion of the public Internet beyond academic use, and from the adoption of TCP/IP for corporate use. The term *subnetting* refers to a discipline of assigning and interpreting IP addresses in such a way as to increase the depth of the address hierarchy on large networks.

NOTE   All three of these subnet approaches can and do co-exist across TCP/IP internetworks. CIDR does not replace the class-based IPv4 subnet approach so much as it generalizes and extends it, while preserving the 32-bit IPv4 address format. IPv6 does change the address format itself, but has provisions for interacting with IPv4 networks.

Subnet addressing has evolved through three phases:

- Class-based IPv4 subnetting

- Classless Inter-Domain Routing (CIDR)

- Distributed subnetting—IPv6

We'll examine the first, and least flexible, form of subnetting in this section. CIDR, a more general solution that was designed as a stopgap while IPv6 was under development, is described in the "Classless Inter-Domain Routing (CIDR) with IPv4" section. Finally, with the introduction of IPv6 (see the "IPv6: Next Generation Internet Addressing" section), the IPv4 addressing scheme is abandoned entirely in favor of an inherently distributed allocation of the IP address space.

Class-Based IPv4 Subnetting

Figure 3.5 shows how subnetting adds an intermediate layer to the address hierarchy. In this figure, hosts are grouped by their geographical location into subnetworks. Such groups might correspond, for instance, to different department LANs within a large office building, which are linked to a common backbone (Network 1).

Figure 3.5.

Subnetting in an IPv4 address space.

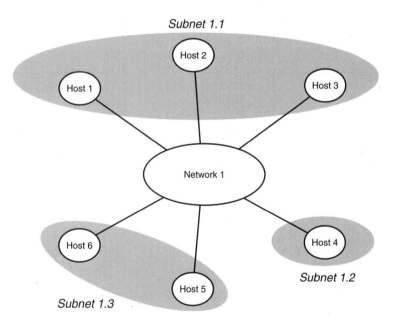

As Figure 3.5 also shows, IPv4 subnetting is accomplished by dividing the host identifiers into groups. The easiest way to do this is by allocating the first several bits of the host identifier—no matter which class the network identifiers belongs to—to the subnet number.

For instance, if you have a Class C network, the first 6 bytes (24 bits) comprise the network ID, leaving 8 bits for host IDs. Because identifier fields consisting of all 0s or 1s are by convention not allocated to hosts, this leaves a possible network size of 254 nodes, with host IDs ranging from hexadecimal 01 to hexadecimal FE.

Figure 3.6 illustrates how a Class C network might be subnetted by allocating the high-order bits in the host identifier to the subnet number. The most obvious approach would be to allocate 2 bits to the subnet ID because that is adequate to differentiate four different bit patterns (00, 01, 10, 11). However, one of the ground rules for subnetting is that the subnet ID itself cannot take a value of all 1s. Therefore, if you truly need four subnets, you would have to assign 3 bits to the subnet identifier, as shown in Figure 3.6.

Figure 3.6.

An example of an IPv4 Class C address subnet.

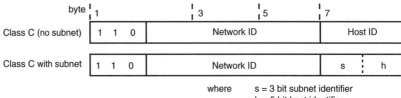

In this example, each subnet can assign 5-bit host identifiers to the nodes on that subnetwork. Leaving out all the 0 and 1 identifiers, that leaves 30 hosts per subnet, for up to six subnets in all. As this example illustrates, the use of class-based subnets means that the total pool of *subnet.host* identifiers is smaller than it would be with no subnetting in effect. The advantages to this approach, however, are that it imposes no changes at the InterNIC for address allocation and does not disrupt the IPv4 class-based address scheme.

Subnet Masks

The purpose of IP addresses is to guide the routing of packets through a network. Special computers dedicated to this purpose, called routers, use the network portion of the address to determine the destination node or network gateway on the internetwork. The routers then move the packet from node to node until it reaches that gateway.

Class-based IPv4 subnetting continues this practice, but extends the information in routing tables to include a binary mask used to isolate the network and subnetwork portions of the address.

For example, in Figure 3.6, a total of 27 bits in the address are dedicated to the network and subnet identifiers. The mask for this case would consist of 27 1s, followed by five 0s. When this mask is ORed to an incoming IP address, the resulting 32 bits can be compared to the network and subnet combinations in the router's tables. Where they match, this router knows the physical location of the intended host node and can deliver the packet to that node directly.

By isolating the subnet identifier as well as the network identifier, routers are able to distinguish the physical (or geographical) region in which the intended host resides. If hosts were assigned randomly to subnets, no routing or management efficiency would be gained. However, if subnets are assigned to correspond to different Internet gateways, for example, or to different campus backbones, detailed information regarding the location of specific hosts needs to be maintained only in the router closest to that group of computers. This significantly reduces the cost of the routing infrastructure as the complexity of the Internet (or of private TCP/IP networks) grows, improving throughput and response time.

3.1.4. Reserved Addresses

WARNING	Because the InterNIC is not involved in allocating addresses in

the private range, it is quite likely that multiple organizations are using duplicate addresses in their private networks. This works fine as long as all such networks remain private, but poses problems and a potential administrative headache when one or more of these networks connect to the public Internet.

Good practice is to acquire addresses from the InterNIC for any network that may in the future exchange packets with other organizations or make use of the Internet backbone for internetwork communications. These addresses can be kept private merely by configuring the network so that they are not advertised to the wider Internet system.

An alternative approach to segregating private networks from the wider Internet world is to filter them through a firewall or to access the Internet through a proxy server. The former approach inflexibly keeps out all packets except those originating from approved IP addresses. A proxy server, alone or combined with an address-translating firewall, masks the originating computer behind a shared IP address.

A number of IPv4 addresses are reserved or given specific meaning. The address `0.0.0.0` is reserved and left unused, as is `224.0.0.0`. Addresses in the range `10.0.0.0` through `10.255.255.255` are available for use in private intranets.

Address `224.0.0.1` is used to address all multicast groups that are defined at a given time.

Addresses in the range `240.0.0.0` through `255.255.255.254` are Class E addresses and are reserved for experimental use when new protocols and protocol extensions are under development.

Address `255.255.255.255` is the broadcast address, used to reach all systems on a local link. In addition, a host ID of `255` specifies all systems within a given subnet, and a subnet ID of `255` specifies all subnets within a network.

IP Addressing and Subnetting

3.2. Classless Inter-Domain Routing (CIDR) with IPv4

The original IPv4 address hierarchy model built on network classes was a useful mechanism for allocating identifiers when the primary members of the public Internet were academic and research organizations. This model proved insufficiently flexible and inefficient as the Internet grew rapidly to include gateways into corporate enterprises with complex networks.

We've seen how the use of multicast groups enables a packet to be forwarded efficiently to hosts on several network identifiers at once. This mechanism, along with the use of class-based subnetting, provided an interim solution that extended the original IPv4 model without requiring major rewrites of client IP software modules or substantial reprogramming of routers.

Neither multicasting nor subnetting address the needs of an organization whose network complexity falls between that of Class B and Class C, however, nor do they make up for the relative scarcity of Class C network identifiers.

Solving the addressing challenges that have arisen as a result of the rapid adoption of IP and of the public Internet requires a redesign of the IP addressing model from the bottom up. This has, in fact, been accomplished in the definition of IP version 6. By September 1993, however, it was clear that the exponential growth in Internet users would require an interim solution while the details of IPv6 were being hammered out.

The resulting proposal was submitted as RFC 1519 by the Network Working Group of the IETF. This Request for Comment is titled "Classless Inter-Domain Routing (CIDR): an Address Assignment and Aggregation Strategy." As the title suggests, CIDR is

- *Classless*, representing a continued move away from the original IPv4 network class model

- Primarily concerned with *interdomain routing* (rather than host identification)

- A *strategy* for the allocation and use of IPv4 addresses, rather than a new protocol

The strategy proposed in RFC 1519 addresses the need to conserve address space within the routing equipment already in place in the Internet (and private IP-based networks).

The exponential growth in Internet users created a corresponding growth in the size and complexity of data structures required by routing computers, which forward IP packets through the Internet. In addition to posing a substantial administrative headache, incomplete routing tables impose a serious overhead burden on network traffic as routers query their neighbors to identify local network topologies. Most ISPs, at both the retail and wholesale levels, and the backbone circuits themselves were expanding infrastructure as fast as they could to keep up with demand. Upgrading routing equipment already in place was far too costly to do unless no other alternatives could possibly be adopted.

Therefore, a strategy for allocating and aggregating IPv4 addresses to conserve IP address space and slow the growth of router tables would allow service providers to expand capacity and support growing network use in the most cost-efficient way.

CIDR accomplishes this by aggregating IP addresses that refer to topologically (physically and logically) adjacent networks and hosts into transit-routing domains. Efficient use of these domains includes two elements:

- Variable-length subnetting

- Supernetting

Variable length subnetting allows IPv4 address space to be allocated in address quantities based on any power of 2, rather than in subnets of 2^8 hosts each. Routers and gateways are updated to accept subnet masks with variable-length fields as well. The combination of network and subnet masks then can be used to route even noncontiguous space with reasonable efficiency and frees otherwise unused address space for allocation to other organizations.

Supernetting is a strategy for overcoming the early exhaustion of Class B network identifier space and the scarcity of Class A network IDs. Under this scheme, organizations with complex networks can acquire contiguous blocks of Class C identifiers and advertise a single route for reaching all of them. (*Advertising* refers to the mechanism by which routers and gateways inform neighboring Internet nodes of their location in the physical Internet topology, and hence of the best way to route packets so as to reach them. See Chapter 5.)

Taken together, the variable-length subnetting and supernetting schemes solve an additional problem caused by the rapid expansion of the Internet—namely the resulting administrative demands placed by a single address allocation body, the InterNIC.

By shifting responsibility for the definition of subnets and the aggregation of network identifiers into supernets, the CIDR approach essentially delegates address allocation authority to service providers, enterprise network administrators, and other middlemen. As a result, the CIDR approach also supports the recent expansion in number and scope of ISPs.

The key to the success of CIDR in operation is the fact that it has no impact at the client machine. Client PCs *may* allow subnet masks to be defined when the TCP/IP stack is being configured—the Microsoft Windows clients are configured in this manner, for example—but this is a matter of design choice and network administration convenience. It is equally acceptable, if more cumbersome, for server software to maintain tables that allocate specific client machines to various subnets, as well as to define supernetting relationships.

Because the client software can remain unaware of subnetting and supernetting strategies, ISPs and corporate network administrators have found it relatively easy to create prepackaged software bundles and installation instructions for new user machines. By supporting the growth in Internet use in this way, CIDR also has directly contributed to the shape of the ISP industry at present. As you'll see in

IP Addressing and Subnetting

the following section, this approach has been enhanced and extended in the design of IPv6. Rather than being merely a stop gap measure, CIDR is a prototype of the wider solution to IP addressing.

3.3. IPv6: Next Generation Internet Addressing

By December 1995, the Network Working Group of the IETF was ready to propose a longer-term solution to specifying and allocating IP addresses. The address space model associated with the resulting version 6 of IP is described in RFC 1884.

As seen in the previous sections of this chapter, IPv4 addressing has several shortcomings that became obvious once the Internet grew substantially in size and complexity. These shortcomings include the following:

- Limited size of the address space imposed by the 32-bit address size

- Awkwardness of the original network class model

- Inflexibility imposed by limiting the address space hierarchy to only two layers: network and host

- Concentration of responsibility for address allocation in a single organization

IPv6 improves upon IPv4 in each of these areas. IPv6 allocates 128 bits for addresses. Analyses of potential IP use suggest that this address space will suffice for the remaining life of the protocol.

The new address model officially endorses the practical migration away from the IPv4 class model. The IPv6 address space is allocated in variable-sized segments for subsequent suballocation by service providers, enterprise administrators, and other middlemen. As a result, administration of the IPv6 address space is distributed in much the same way as network development and packet-routing decisions.

3.3.1. IPv6 Address Representation

Like IPv4 addresses, IPv6 addresses are represented as strings of digits divided by separators. However, IPv6 address representations differ from those of IPv4 in several important ways:

- The basic representation takes the form *nn:nn:nn:nn:nn:nn:nn:nn* where each *nn* represents the hexadecimal form of 16 bits of address.

- Because some styles of IPv6 address will predictably contain sequences of zero bits, the convention has arisen of using a double colon (::) to indicate an arbitrarily long sequence. Only one such abbreviation is permitted in a given address, so the full address expansion is always unambiguous. Thus, the following two address representations are equivalent:

```
1234:5678:9ABC:DEF0:0000:0000:0000:1234
1234:5678:9ABC:DEF0::1234
```

The double colon may be used at the beginning or end of the address representation, if appropriate.

- IPv6 has facilities for operating in a mixed IPv4/IPv6 environment. IPv4 addresses are right-aligned within the 128-bit IPv6 format, with the leftmost bit smeared for an additional 16 bits. This ensures that the one's complement arithmetic used for checksums operates correctly with both the 32-bit and 128-bit versions of the address. In such cases, hybrid addresses may be represented in a hybrid fashion, as in the following:

```
0:0:0:0:0:0:15.34.52.7        (or ::15.34.52.7)
0:0:0:0:0:FFFF:129.132.67.43  (or ::FFFF:129.132.67.43)
```

3.3.2. IPv6 Address Types

From its inception, IPv6 has identified three types of addresses, based on their use rather than on network size. These three types are

- Unicast—Associated with a specific physical interface to a network

- Multicast—Associated with a set of physical interfaces, generally on multiple hosts (network nodes)

- Anycast—Associated with a set of physical interfaces, generally on different nodes

These address types are distinguished by the scope of packet delivery they specify. Packets sent to a *unicast* address are delivered to the interface uniquely specified by the address. Packets sent to a *multicast* address will be delivered to all the interfaces to which the address refers. And packets sent to an *anycast* address will be delivered to at least one interface specified by the address (usually the one that is "nearest" in routing protocol terms).

IP Addressing and Subnetting

Figure 3.7 illustrates these address differences.

Figure 3.7.
IPv6 address types.

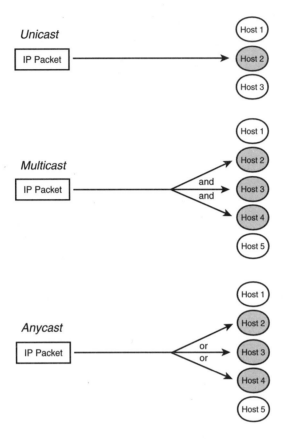

IPv6 does not assign fixed-length address subfields across all types. Instead, each IPv6 address begins with a variable-length Format Prefix, which specifies the type and subtype of the address.

Table 3.2 shows the Format Prefixes defined by the IPv6 standard.

Table 3.2. IPv6 Format Prefixes.

Prefix (binary)	Allocated to
0000 0000	Reserved
0000 0001	Unassigned
0000 001	Reserved for NSAP
0000 010	Reserved for IPX allocation
0000 011	Unassigned

Prefix (binary)	Allocated to
0000 1	Unassigned
0001	Unassigned
001	Unassigned
010	Provider-based unicast addresses
011	Unassigned
100	Reserved for geographic-based unicast addresses
101	Unassigned
110	Unassigned
1110	Unassigned
1111 0	Unassigned
1111 10	Unassigned
1111 110	Unassigned
1111 1110 0	Unassigned
1111 1111 10	Link-Local use addresses
1111 1110 11	Site-Local use addresses
1111 1111	Multicast addresses

As the table shows, multicast addresses (including the special purpose multicasts that specify Link-Local and Site-Local scopes) are distinguished by an initial octet of hexadecimal value FF.

All other addresses are presumed to be unicast. Anycast addresses are taken from the unicast address space and are handled differently due to routing table setups.

3.3.3. Unicast Addresses

IPv6 unicast addresses encompass variable-length subfields, beginning with the Format Prefix.

The developers of IPv6 anticipated the need for various organizations to introduce varying degrees of hierarchy in address allocation and interpretation. Subnet identifiers of varying lengths can be incorporated into addresses, as can other layers of hierarchy that reflect physical topology or logical relationships within complex networks such as enterprise WANs.

> **NOTE** NSAP refers to OSI Network Service Access Provider Allocation. IPX is a part of the Novell network protocol suite. Formats for IPv6 addresses in these ranges were undefined at the time of this writing.
>
> RFC 1884 reserves portions of the unicast addressing space specifically for future use in mapping non-IP addresses onto IP networks. This is in keeping with the long-term intent of the Internet Architecture Board—the TCP/IP protocol family will interoperate across many protocol architectures and eventually converge with other standards, such as the OSI suite.
>
> More pragmatically, this development reflects the increasing business use of the Internet and the desire to achieve interoperability between LANs and WANs, on the one hand, and IP-based networks such as the public Internet, on the other hand.

One salient feature of IPv6 is the way in which the Format Prefix assignments explicitly anticipate that many addresses will be allocated by service providers rather than by the InterNIC. As we saw with regard to CIDR, the explosive growth of the Internet and of private IP-based networks makes address allocation and administration a major bottleneck. IPv6 reflects the growth of the ISP industry, but also recognizes that the Internet is now an international entity for which multiple address registries might be appropriate.

One common address scenario in IPv6 assumes multiple registries, each of which allocates address space to various service providers, who in turn allocate subdivisions of their space to subscribers. Subscribers such as corporate enterprises or large university campuses may organize their networks into subnets of hosts (interfaces).

A typical allocation of address bits in this scenario might be:

- 3 bits—`010` indicating this is a provider-based address

- 5 bits—Registry identifier

- 16 bits—Provider identifier

- 16 bits—Subscriber type

- 8 bits—Subscriber identifier

- 32 bits—Subnetwork identifier

In this example, 80 bits have been allocated to the address hierarchies above the individual network interface. In fact, four (or possibly five, depending on the use of the subscriber type subfield) layers of such hierarchy can be distinguished.

The choice of 80 bits for noninterface information in the preceding example is more than casual; it reflects the fact that most LAN media access level addresses, for instance, require 48 bits. The authors of RFC 1884 specifically anticipated the use of LAN workstation addresses and other link-layer addresses for the interface-specific portions of IPv6 addresses where applicable. Such a convention facilitates semiautomatic or automatic translation of local addresses into IPv6 format for interoperable, multiprotocol enterprises.

Embedded IPv4 Addresses

As previously mentioned, the IPv6 addressing model anticipates the need for IPv6 networks to exchange packets with IPv4-based networks. To facilitate this exchange, the IPv6 address model allows IPv4 addresses to be embedded using the following bit allocations:

80 bits	Must be zero
16 bits	Hex `0000` = IPv4-compatible IPv6 address
	Hex `FFFF` = IPv4-mapped IPv6 address
32 bits	IPv4 address

An IPv4-compatible IPv6 address denotes an IPv6-capable node that must exchange packets with an IPv4 network. To facilitate this exchange, the IPv6 node's significant address information is restricted to 32 bits in IPv4 format.

An IPv4-mapped IPv6 address is an IPv6 representation of the address for an IPv4-only node. This extension of the IPv4 address facilitates the tunneling of IPv4 packets over IPv6 links.

Global Provider-Based Unicast Addresses

Service providers adopt their own address hierarchy and bit allocation for the IPv6 address space assigned to them. The designers of IPv6 anticipate that service providers will use at least the following layers of hierarchy in their addressing schemes:

3 bits—010 = service provider-based unicast addressing

n bits—Registry identifier

m bits—Provider identifier

s bits—Subscriber identifier

125-n-m-s bits—For subscriber use

NOTE   It may seem to some that this global unicast address "format" is so generic as to be of no use. Its inclusion in RFC 1844 and the IPv6 definition, however, is neither a wasted effort nor a mistake. The protocol's developers are clearly signaling a major shift in design philosophy from IPv4 by underscoring the fact the IPv6 offers a variable, distributed capability to define useful address hierarchies when and as they make sense. In this way, the designers are ensuring the capability of this protocol to adapt to new technical, business, and regulatory initiatives as the use of the public Internet and the TCP/IP suite continues to grow.

Note that this generic, global unicast address type is more fully instantiated in the example in the "Unicast Addresses" section.

Local Use Unicast Addresses

The designers of IPv6 did include two specific Format Prefixes identifying specific scopes of address hierarchy. These are the Link-Local and Site-Local address types.

Link-Local addresses are defined in order to support configuration, management, or pseudorouting activities on a local network link. They are, by definition, not intended for interpretation by foreign nodes, including routers on the wider Internet.

The format of a Link-Local unicast address is

10 bits	Binary 1111111010 (Format Prefix)
n bits	Zero
118-n bits	Interface identifier

The Link-Local unicast address consists of the local identifier, generally from the media access layer or data link layer of the local protocol suite and an IPv6 Format Prefix.

Site-Local unicast addresses are intended to help organizations prepare for eventual connection to the public Internet. The format of the Site-Local address is

10 bits	Binary 1111111011 (Format Prefix)
n bits	Zero
m bits	Subnet identifier
118-n-m bits	Interface identifier

When the organization connects to the public Internet, it can migrate addresses by substituting the appropriate registry, provider, and subscriber information for the prefix and zero fields.

Special Purpose Unicast Addresses

The address 0::0 is called the *unspecified address* and must never be assigned to a specific interface. It indicates the absence of a known address in situations such as an IPv6 sender who does not yet know its own address during initialization. Therefore, this address must never be used as a destination for IPv6 packets.

The address 0::1 is called the *loopback address*. It is used by a node to send a packet back to itself, and may neither be assigned to a specific interface nor used as the destination for an IPv6 packet intended for another node.

3.3.4. Anycast Addresses

IPv6 anycast addresses are allocated out of the unicast address space and otherwise look like unicast addresses. Unlike unicast addresses, however, anycast addresses are mapped into multiple interfaces onto one or more networks. The nodes to which these interfaces belong must advertise the mapping with knowledge that the address in question refers to multiple interfaces and potentially multiple nodes.

One purpose for the anycast address is to update routing information in one of a group of routers, which would then propagate that information throughout its vicinity. A related purpose might be the propagation of control or status information throughout a given logical or physical topology.

An anycast address may encompass any set of relationships between the interfaces to which it refers, with the following exceptions:

- Anycast addresses may not be used as source addresses in an IPv6 packet.

- An anycast address may, for the present, refer only to routers, not to end nodes (host computers).

3.3.5. Multicast Addresses

An IPv6 multicast address identifies a group of nodes. A given network computer, whether host or router, may belong to multiple multicast groups at once. The format for an IPv6 multicast address is

8 bits	11111111 (Format Prefix)
4 bits	Flags, consisting of `000T`
	T = 0 indicates this is a well-known address
	T = 1 indicates this is a transient address
4 bits	Scope
	`0` = Reserved
	`1` = Node-Local scope
	`2` = Link-Local scope
	`3–4` = (Unassigned)
	`5` = Site-Local scope
	`6–7` = (Unassigned)
	`8` = Organization-Local scope
	`9–D` = (Unassigned)
	`E` = Global scope
	`F` = Reserved
112 bits	Group identifier

Multicast addresses may not be used as the source address for any IPv6 packet.

Well-Known Multicast Addresses

Multicast addresses may be permanently assigned as a result of permanent group definitions. For any given group with identifier GG, the following addresses are automatically well known:

FF01::GG	All group members on the same node as the sender
FF02::GG	All group members on the same link as the sender
FF05::GG	All group members on the same site as the sender
FF08::GG	All group members belonging to the same organization as the sender
FF0E::GG	All group members in the Internet

Transient Multicast Addresses

Groups that are not assigned permanent, well-known group identifiers have validity only within the scope and during the lifetime of their definition. For instance, two different sites might define groups with the same identifier and each site's nodes could legitimately send multicast messages to the members of the Site-Local group. Neither would know of, nor be able to address, the nodes that belong to the other site's group with the same identifier.

Predefined and Reserved Multicast Addresses

Some addresses in the multicast format are reserved or otherwise predefined. These include the following:

- Group 0—Addresses of the format FF0x::, where $0 < - x - < F$ (reserved; do not use)

- Group 1—All nodes' addresses, which identify every IPv6 node in a given scope:

FF01::1	All Node-Local nodes
FF02::1	All Link-Local nodes

- Group 2—All routers' addresses

FF01::2	All Node-Local routers
FF02::2	All Link-Local routers

- Group C—DHCP server/relay agents:

FF02::C	All Link-Local DHCP servers and relay agents

■ Solicited-node addresses of the form `FF02::1:xxxx:xxxx`, where `xxxx:xxxx` is the low-order 32 bits of the node's unicast or multicast address; eliminates the need for redundant group membership (and hence redundant multicast traffic) for a given node

3.3.6. Required Address Support

The IPv6 protocol is quite flexible in formats and address space hierarchies, but does impose some requirements regarding the minimum set of addresses that must be supported by any IPv6 implementation.

Subnet–Router Anycast Address

This address format consists of an anycast address for which the interface identifier subfield contains zeroes. Packets sent to this anycast address will be delivered to at least one router in the subnet specified by the higher position, nonzero bits of the address. This address format is intended to support applications such as mobile computing access to IP networks.

Required Host Address Support

A host must recognize the following addresses as identifying (referring to) itself:

■ The Link-Local address for each interface

■ All assigned unicast addresses associated with interfaces

■ The Loopback address

■ The All-Nodes multicast addresses (Node-Local and Link-Local)

■ Solicited-Node multicast addresses for all unicast and anycast addresses assigned to it

■ Multicast addresses for each group to which it is assigned

Required Router Address Support

A router must recognize the following addresses as identifying itself:

■ The Link-Local address for each interface

■ All assigned unicast addresses associated with interfaces

■ The Subnet-Router anycast addresses for all links to which it has interfaces

IP Addressing and Subnetting

- All other anycast addresses with which it has been configured

- The All-Nodes multicast addresses

- The All-RouterNodes multicast address

- Solicited-Node multicast addresses for all unicast and anycast addresses assigned to it

- Multicast addresses for each group to which it is assigned

3.4. Summary

The Internet Protocol constitutes the core capability that makes the public Internet possible. Its capability to route packets through the Internet is based on a digital addressing scheme. Router nodes on the Internet decipher portions of IP addresses when determining where to forward a given packet next.

IP version 4 was defined when the Internet was small and consisted of networks of limited size and complexity. It offered two layers of address hierarchy—network identifier and host identifier—with three address formats to accommodate varying network sizes.

Both the limited address model and the 32-bit address size in IPv4 proved to be inadequate in the face of rapid adoption of TCP/IP–based networks and the public Internet. Address allocation and aggregation techniques such as subnetting, supernetting, and CIDR extend the usefulness of IPv4 addressing and preserve an extensive investment in IPv4-based equipment and operating procedures.

A more permanent solution is offered by IPv6. This protocol revision incorporates flexible hierarchies and distributes the responsibility for allocation and management of the IP address space. The power and scope of the IPv6 address model reflects a mature architecture informed by extensive use of TCP/IP–based networks in significant, complex topologies. Along with support for IPv4 interoperability, IPv6 incorporates support for accessing the public Internet and private IP-based internetworks from existing enterprise LANs and WANs.

Chapter

4

4.1. Overview of ARP

4.2. What Happens When an ARP Packet Is Received?

4.3. IP Address Conflicts

4.4. Managing the ARP Cache Table

4.5. ARP Packet Format

4.6. The Use of a Static ARP Address

4.7. Proxy ARP

4.8. Summary

Address Resolution Protocol (ARP)

by Martin Bligh

IP addresses are an abstract mapping defined by the network administrator—IP doesn't have to worry whether its datagrams are transmitted over Ethernet, Token Ring, or FDDI. However, for the network cards to be able to communicate with each other, they must have their own addressing scheme, dependent on the network type. These *MAC addresses* are derived from the IP address by the Address Resolution Protocol (ARP). ARP is capable of resolving addresses for other protocols, too, but let's only consider IP here.

An ARP request is not necessary for every datagram sent. The responses are cached in the local ARP table, which keeps a list of `<IP address, MAC address>` pairs. This keeps the number of ARP packets on the network very low. ARP is generally a low maintenance protocol that raises few problems; it is normally seen only when there is a conflicting IP address on the network. A knowledge of ARP will make understanding IP routing much easier.

4.1. Overview of ARP

In Figure 4.1, interface A wants to send a datagram to interface B, where both interfaces are on the same physical network. Interface A only has the IP address for B (*B-IP*, which is `9.8.7.2`); it must first find the MAC address for B (*B-MAC*). Interface A sends an ARP broadcast specifying the desired IP address (`9.8.7.2`) and requesting *B-MAC*. Interface B receives the broadcast and replies with a unicast to A, giving the MAC address corresponding to `9.8.7.2` (*B-MAC*).

Figure 4.1.
An ARP exchange between machines on the same network.

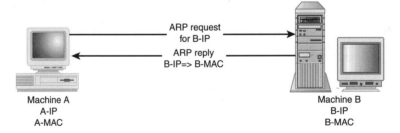

Machine A
A-IP
A-MAC

ARP request
for B-IP
ARP reply
B-IP=> B-MAC

Machine B
B-IP
B-MAC

Note that only interface B responds to the request, although other interfaces on the network may have the relevant information. This ensures that responses are correct and do not provide out-of-date information.

In Figure 4.2, the more complex case is shown, where interface A and B are not on the same network. It is important to understand that ARP requests are only sent out for the next-hop gateway, not always for the destination IP address. Thus, if interface A wants to send a datagram to interface B, but its routing table tells it that traffic must pass through router C, it will send out an ARP request for router C, not for interface B.

Figure 4.2.
ARP exchanges when traffic passes through a router.

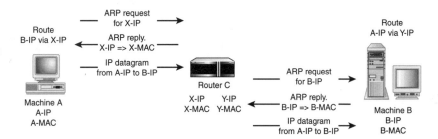

The sequence of events involved in sending a datagram from A to B is shown in Figure 4.2. The first event is shown at the top of the diagram, and subsequent events follow underneath. Router C has two interfaces, X (on the same network as interface A) and Y (on the same network as interface B).

4.2. What Happens When an ARP Packet Is Received?

The flowchart in Figure 4.3 details the process followed when an ARP packet is received. Note that the `<IP address, MAC address>` pair of the sender is inserted in the local ARP table, and a reply is sent. If A wishes to talk to B, it is likely that B also will need to talk to A.

Address Resolution Protocol (ARP)

Figure 4.3.

A receipt of an ARP packet (constructed from information in RFC 826).

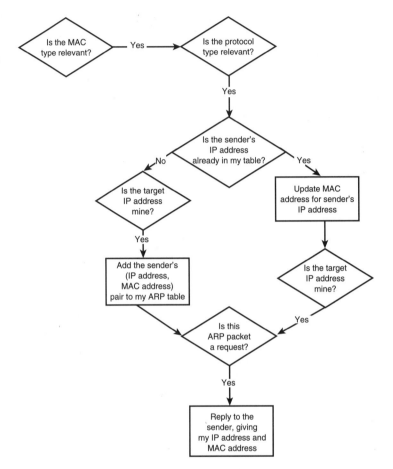

4.3.   IP Address Conflicts

The most common error that the user sees produced by ARP is an IP address conflict, where two different stations claim to own the same IP address. IP addresses *must* be unique on any connected set of networks.

IP address conflicts are apparent when two replies answer an ARP request—each specifying a different MAC address. This is a serious error with no easy solution. Which MAC address do you send the datagrams to?

To avoid IP address conflicts, when interface A first initializes it will send out an ARP request *for its own IP address.* If no response is sent back, it is assumed that the IP address is not in use. However, suppose that interface A wishes to use IP address `6.6.6.1`, but interface B is already using this address. Interface B will send an ARP reply, stating that IP address `6.6.6.1` maps to MAC address *B-MAC*. Interface A now knows that the IP address is already in use; it must not use the address and will flag an error.

There is still a problem, however. Suppose that before interface A sent out an ARP request for `6.6.6.1`, host C had a correct ARP table entry mapping `6.6.6.1` to *B-MAC*. On receipt of the ARP broadcast from interface A, host C will update its ARP table to map `6.6.6.1` to *A-MAC*. If C now sends a datagram to B, it will be sent to *A-MAC* and B will never receive it. To correct such errors, interface B (the "defending" system) will now send out an ARP request broadcast for `6.6.6.1` again. Host C will now update its ARP entry for `6.6.6.1` to *B-MAC* again, and the network state is now back as before. Any IP datagrams that C may have sent to B while its ARP tables were temporarily incorrect will have gone to *A-MAC* and effectively will have been lost. This is unfortunate, but because IP does not guarantee delivery, it should not cause major problems.

Table 4.1 gives the manufacturer of the interface card from the first half of the MAC address (this information is taken from RFC 1700; the ownership of some addresses is unclear, hence the question marks against some entries).

When trying to resolve IP address conflicts, you may have difficulty tracking down the offender, because you only have a MAC address to work from. Unless a list of MAC addresses is kept, you'll often need to check the configurations of many systems in order to find the misconfigured system.

On a multivendor network, knowing the manufacturer of the Ethernet card often helps greatly. Suppose that I have a network with 20 NCD X-terminals, 30 Sun workstations, and 30 PCs with 3Com Ethernet cards. If I know that the offending host's MAC address begins with `080020`, looking at Table 4.1, I can see that it is a Sun system. I now have to search just 30 machines, instead of 80.

Table 4.1. Ethernet vendors indexed by MAC address.

First half of the MAC address	Manufacturer
00000C	Cisco
00000E	Fujitsu
00000F	NeXT
000010	Sytek
00001D	Cabletron
000020	DIAB (Data Industrier AB)
000022	Visual Technology
00002A	TRW

continues

Address Resolution Protocol (ARP)

Table 4.1. Continued.

First half of the MAC address	Manufacturer
000032	GPT Limited (reassigned from GEC Computers, Ltd.)
00005A	S & Koch
00005E	IANA
000065	Network General
00006B	MIPS
000077	MIPS
00007A	Ardent
000089	Cayman Systems (Gatorbox)
000093	Proteon
00009F	Ameristar Technology
0000A2	Wellfleet
0000A3	Network Application Technology
0000A6	Network General (internal assignment, not for products)
0000A7	NCD (X-terminals)
0000A9	Network Systems
0000AA	Xerox (Xerox machines)
0000B3	CIMLinc
0000B7	Dove (Fastnet)
0000BC	Allen-Bradley
0000C0	Western Digital
0000C5	Farallon phone net card
0000C6	HP Intelligent Networks Operation (formerly Eon Systems)
0000C8	Altos
0000C9	Emulex (Terminal Servers)
0000D7	Dartmouth College (NED Router)

First half of the MAC address	Manufacturer
0000D8	3Com? Novell? PS/2
0000DD	Gould
0000DE	Unigraph
0000E2	Acer Counterpoint
0000EF	Alantec
0000FD	High Level Hardvare (Orion, UK)
000102	BBN (BBN internal usage [not registered])
0020AF	3COM ???
001700	Kabel
008064	Wyse Technology / Link Technologies
00802B	IMAC ???
00802D	Xylogics, Inc. (Annex terminal servers)
00808C	Frontier Software Development
0080C2	IEEE 802.1 Committee
0080D3	Shiva
00AA00	Intel
00DD00	Ungermann-Bass
00DD01	Ungermann-Bass
020701	Racal InterLan
020406	BBN (BBN internal usage [not registered])
026086	Satelcom MegaPac (UK)
02608C	3Com (IBM PC; Imagen; Valid; Cisco)
02CF1F	CMC (Masscomp; Silicon Graphics; Prime EXL)
080002	3Com (Formerly Bridge)
080003	ACC (Advanced Computer Communications)

Address Resolution Protocol (ARP)

continues

Table 4.1. Continued.

First half of the MAC address	Manufacturer
080005	Symbolics (Symbolics LISP machines)
080008	BBN
080009	Hewlett-Packard
08000A	Nestar Systems
08000B	Unisys
080011	Tektronix, Inc.
080014	Excelan (BBN Butterfly, Masscomp, Silicon Graphics)
080017	NSC
08001A	Data General
08001B	Data General
08001E	Apollo
080020	Sun (Sun machines)
080022	NBI
080025	CDC
080026	Norsk Data (Nord)
080027	PCS Computer Systems GmbH
080028	TI (Explorer)
08002B	DEC
08002E	Metaphor
08002F	Prime Computer (Prime 50-Series LHC300)
080036	Intergraph (CAE stations)
080037	Fujitsu–Xerox
080038	Bull
080039	Spider Systems
080041	DCA Digital Comm. Assoc.
080045	???? (maybe Xylogics, but they claim not to know this number)

First half of the MAC address	Manufacturer
080046	Sony
080047	Sequent
080049	Univation
08004C	Encore
08004E	BICC
080056	Stanford University
080058	??? (DECsystem-20)
08005A	IBM
080067	Comdesign
080068	Ridge
080069	Silicon Graphics
08006E	Concurrent (Masscomp)
080075	DDE (Danish Data Elektronik A/S)
08007C	Vitalink (TransLAN III)
080080	XIOS
080086	Imagen/QMS
080087	Xyplex (terminal servers)
080089	Kinetics (AppleTalk–Ethernet interface)
08008B	Pyramid
08008D	XyVision (XyVision machines)
080090	Retix, Inc. (Bridges)
484453	HDS ???
800010	AT&T
AA0000	DEC (obsolete)
AA0001	DEC (obsolete)
AA0002	DEC (obsolete)

continues

Address Resolution Protocol (ARP)

Table 4.1. Continued.

First half of the MAC address	Manufacturer
AA0003	DEC (Global physical address for some DEC machines)
AA0004	DEC (Local logical address for systems running)

4.4. Managing the ARP Cache Table

The ARP cache table is a list of `<IP address, MAC address>` pairs, indexed by IP address. The table can often be managed via the `arp` command. Common commands include the following:

- `arp -s <IP address> <MAC address>`—Add a static entry to the cache table

- `arp -d <IP address>`—Delete an entry from the cache table

- `arp -a`—Display all entries in the cache table

Dynamic entries in the ARP cache table (that is, those that have not been manually added with `arp -s`) are normally deleted after a period of time. This period is determined by the specific TCP/IP implementation, but an entry would commonly be destroyed if unused for a fixed time period (for example, five minutes).

4.5. ARP Packet Format

An ARP packet is *not* encapsulated within an IP datagram, but travels over the link layer (for example, an Ethernet frame). Table 4.2 describes the fields that make up an ARP packet, which should allow you to debug any ARP problems from the output of a link layer trace.

Table 4.2. Construction of an ARP packet.

Size (bytes)	Description
2	MAC address type (for example, 10Mbps Ethernet = 1)
2	Protocol type (for example, IP = 0800)

Size (bytes)	Description
1	Byte length of MAC address (h-len)
1	Byte length of protocol address (p-len)
2	Opcode (specifying a `REQUEST = 1` or a `REPLY = 2`)
h-len	MAC address of sender
p-len	Protocol address of sender
h-len	MAC address of target (if known)
p-len	Protocol address of target

4.6. The Use of a Static ARP Address

A typical use of a static ARP entry is to set up a standalone printer server. These units can usually be configured via Telnet, but first they will need an IP address. The obvious way to feed them this initial information is to use the built-in serial port, but it is often inconvenient to find an appropriate terminal and serial cable, set up baud rates, parity settings, and so on. Using a static ARP entry provides a neat way to circumvent this problem, but this may not work with some print servers that insist on using RARP or BOOTP.

Suppose you want to set up a print server P with an IP address of P-IP, and you know the print server's MAC address is P-MAC. A static ARP entry is created on workstation A to map P-IP to P-MAC. Any IP traffic from workstation A to P-IP will now be sent to P-MAC, although the print server does not yet know its IP address. You can now telnet to P-IP, which will connect to the print server and configure its IP address. Tidy up by deleting the static ARP entry.

Figure 4.4.
Using a static ARP address to set up a print server.

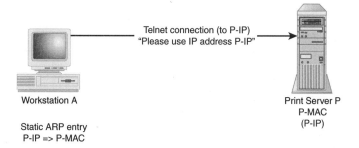

Telnet connection (to P-IP)
"Please use IP address P-IP"

Workstation A

Static ARP entry
P-IP => P-MAC

Print Server P
P-MAC
(P-IP)

It is often useful to use the print server on one subnet, but configure it on another. This is easy to achieve by a process similar to the preceding one, providing you know the MAC address of the print server (*P-MAC*). Suppose that the print server will be used on subnet `6.6.6` with IP address `6.6.6.36`, but it will be configured on subnet `6.6.10`, using a temporary IP address `6.6.10.99`:

1. Connect the print server to subnet `6.6.10`.

2. On a workstation (A) connected to subnet `6.6.10`, create the static ARP entry mapping `6.6.10.99` onto *P-MAC*.

3. Create a telnet session from workstation A to the print server using address `6.6.10.99`.

4. Configure the print server to use IP address `6.6.6.36`.

5. Move the print server to subnet `6.6.10`.

6. On workstation A, delete the static ARP entry for the temporary IP address `6.6.10.99`.

Figure 4.5.
Setting up a print server using a temporary IP address.

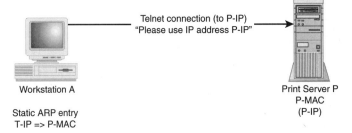

Telnet connection (to P-IP)
"Please use IP address P-IP"

Workstation A

Static ARP entry
T-IP => P-MAC

Print Server P
P-MAC
(P-IP)

4.7. Proxy ARP

It is possible to avoid configuring the routing tables on every host by using *proxy ARP*. This is particularly useful where subnetting is being used, but not all hosts are capable of understanding subnetting.

The basic idea is that a workstation will send out ARP requests even for machines that are not on their own subnet. The ARP proxy server (often the gateway) will respond with the MAC address of the gateway. See Figure 4.6, where proxy ARP is used, and compare it to Figure 4.2, where routing tables are used. The figures are very similar, but note that neither A nor B has routing tables in Figure 4.6, and that although the initial ARP request is for *B-IP* (instead of *X-IP*), the MAC address *X-MAC* of the gateway is still returned.

Figure 4.6.
A workstation using proxy ARP.

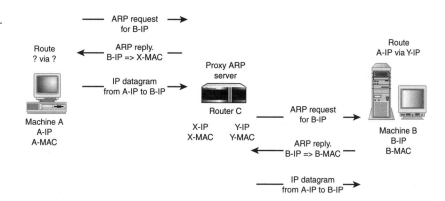

Proxy ARP makes the management of hosts' configurations much simpler. However, it increases network traffic (although not significantly) and potentially requires a much larger ARP cache. An entry for each IP address off the local subnet is created, all mapping to the gateway's MAC address.

In the eyes of a workstation using proxy ARP, the world is just one large physical network with no routers in sight!

4.8. Summary

ARP maps the abstract IP address to the physical MAC address. It is used to contact machines on the same network; traffic to remote networks is sent via routers. Hosts hold a cache of known MAC addresses, commonly called the *ARP table*, and this can be manipulated via the `arp` command.

ARP allows machines to send traffic over the local network; IP routing allows you to send traffic to remote networks.

Chapter

5

IP Routing

by Robin Burk &
Richard Maring

5.1. Why Do We Need IP Addresses and IP Routing?

5.2. How IP Routing Works

5.3. Internetworking: Options for Connecting Network Segments

5.4. Router Protocols

5.5. Routing Inside the LAN

5.6. Routing Outside the LAN

5.7. Moving to IP Version 6 (IPv6)

5.8. Summary

TCP and IP together are often referred to as *packet-switched* protocols. The term calls our attention to the fact that packets given to IP by TCP (or other protocols that are higher in the stack) are switched, or routed, from node to node through the network as they make their way to their destination.

The fact that packets must be routed through an IP network becomes clear when we remember that IP is above all the protocol for internetwork communications. You would expect that data traffic within a LAN will find its way to the destination host quickly and efficiently. By definition, a single network must have some standard means of identifying all of the hosts on the network. In most LANs, such as those based on the IEEE 802.3 (Ethernet) standard, the sender specifies the actual Media Access Control identifier for the destination network interface card. All the stations on an Ethernet LAN must have such a card, and therefore, all of the stations can be addressed in the same direct fashion by using their physical identifiers.

With the introduction of internetworks, beginning with the ARPANET and continuing through today's public Internet and private intranets, physical addressing alone cannot support message delivery. Internet users reside on a wide variety of networks based on diverse media and MAC protocols. For this reason alone, the Internet Protocol requires a logical addressing scheme in which hosts are identified both by the network on which they reside and by a logical host ID. During the time that a packet is being switched through the internetwork, its immediate destination is the network (or subnetwork) itself. Only when it reaches that (sub)network is the host ID of interest. At that point, the logical host identifier contained within the IP address must be translated into the specific MAC address necessary to find the destination host on the local network.

This chapter describes the means by which IP packets are routed through an internetwork and reach their intended destination nodes. Let's begin by looking at LAN addressing as it contrasts with IP addressing, then take a close look at the equipment and configuration issues involved in the adoption of IP. Finally, I'll describe the behavior of the various routing algorithms and routing management protocols that support IP packet switching.

5.1. Why Do We Need IP Addresses and IP Routing?

Chapter 3, "IP Addressing and Subnetting," described the IP addressing scheme. Before you see how IP addresses are used to route messages, it's useful to understand why IP uses its own address scheme and why routing is necessary in an IP-based network.

The movement of messages through a network can be managed at any of several layers in the OSI protocol stack model. These layers include the physical layer, governed by the Media Access Control, or MAC, address; the data link layer, including the Logical Link Control (LLC); and the network layer, where most routing takes place.

IEEE 802.3 (Ethernet) networks manage message delivery at the MAC level. Ethernet addresses, called *node addresses,* are created from the combination of the network adapter card serial number and a special manufacturer number.

Because each Ethernet network interface card (NIC)—and therefore the host in which it resides—has an address guaranteed to be unique among all possible Ethernet NICs, no two workstations will ever bear the same Ethernet address. Also, because the Ethernet address is used at the Media Access Control (physical) level, no address translation is required to deliver an Ethernet packet within an Ethernet LAN.

If the Ethernet address of a workstation uniquely identifies it, why does IP require a second, logical identifier in order to deliver packets to the same workstation? In particular, why does IP use a logical addressing scheme, which ultimately requires some way to translate that IP address into a physical address on a given wire or other network medium?

The answer to these questions lies in the purpose for the TCP/IP protocol stack. Remember that IP originally was designed to support a network of networks, not a network of workstations. In order to deliver a packet to the right workstation or other host, IP must first locate the network on which the host resides. Then, IP can pass the packet to the destination network for delivery to the (now local) recipient.

Because an internetwork might contain LANs based on a variety of protocols, it is most efficient to have IP use a neutral addressing scheme. For example, if Ethernet-style addresses were used for all IP routing, such addresses would need to be assigned to every host that might use an internetwork, whether or not that host contained an Ethernet NIC. Managing the assignment of Ethernet addresses, which is now a distributed task, would require massive and cumbersome administration.

Nor would it be helpful (even if it were possible) to mandate that all internetworks adopt a physical (as opposed to logical) addressing discipline. Ethernet and Token Ring, for example, require all messages to pass through the entire network. While this is manageable in LANs, it rapidly becomes impractical in larger networks, even in the perfect world where no messages are lost or corrupted while traveling through switched phone lines and a variety of transmission media.

IP Routing

> **TIP** Understanding the rationale behind the IP addressing scheme can help you make sense of the sometimes bewildering details of subnetting, supernetting, and the other steps you might take as a network administrator when introducing TCP/IP communications into your corporate computing environment.

Rather than attempt to scale LAN technologies beyond their useful scope, IP layers a logical addressing scheme above the local, physical address. Much of the power of the TCP/IP protocol suite results from the fact that IP does not require every node to know about every other node, nor every network to use the same local technology. Instead, IP moves messages one step at a time, deciding the next step based on information available in the intermediate node computers. These computers, which are usually dedicated to moving IP-encapsulated packets through the internetwork, are called *routers*.

5.2. How IP Routing Works

The aim in the delivery of packets in an IP network is always to move the packet to the network that is local to its destination node—that is, to the network on which the destination node resides. Once the packet reaches a routing computer that is connected to the destination network, the node's MAC address must be identified and used to deliver the packet locally.

As you will recall from Chapters 2, "A Close Look at IPv4 and IPv6," and 3, "IP Addressing and Subnetting," a packet that is encapsulated for IP routing includes a header specifying the IP address of the sender and the destination host. The TCP/IP suite includes protocols that enable a network node to identify its own IP address (if it is not otherwise identified to the TCP/IP software stack on the node) and the IP and physical addresses of neighboring nodes. The suite also includes means by which routing computers can update and share information regarding the topology of the internetwork, the IP addresses associated with user-accessible hostnames, and similar information.

5.2.1. The Address Resolution Protocol (ARP)

The Address Resolution Protocol (ARP) is used to identify the MAC address associated with an IP node that resides on the same network as the sender.

When a node wants to transmit an IP packet, it first checks to see if the destination node's network identifier is the same as its own. If it is, the sender transmits an ARP packet encapsulated inside an Ethernet (or other LAN protocol) broadcast message. This ARP query asks the owner of the destination IP address to reply with its MAC address. Because this is a broadcast message, every node on the local network will read the message, and those that support IP will compare the desired IP address to their own addresses. The node with the desired IP address will reply with an ARP response packet, again encapsulated as a LAN message but specifically addressed to the inquiring host. Once it receives the destination MAC address, this host encapsulates the IP packet within a properly addressed MAC packet and puts it onto the LAN for delivery.

In order to minimize ARP broadcast traffic, all host IP software processes maintain an *ARP cache*. This cache contains the local MAC address equivalents of destination IP addresses, updated each time a new address is discovered by means of an ARP query. The software is configured (typically by the software developer rather than by a network administrator) with a parameter specifying the maximum time a cache entry will be considered valid. When that time has expired, the entry is deleted and subsequent IP transmissions to that address will require a fresh ARP query, thereby providing a means to automatically keep up with changes in hardware and network configuration.

If the destination IP address is not on the local network, ARP cannot help the source deliver the IP message. Therefore, the source mails the IP packet to the local router instead. Again, this is accomplished by encapsulating the IP packet within a LAN packet addressed to the MAC address of the local router. TCP/IP hosts must be configured with the address of at least one local router, referred to as the *default gateway*. The default gateway receives all IP traffic that is destined for a remote network and for which the host has no other routing information.

5.2.2. The Reverse Address Resolution Protocol

The Reverse Address Resolution Protocol (RARP) is used by a workstation to learn its own IP address, which it needs in order to initiate any IP transmissions. RARP is required by diskless workstations and, in some cases, by other hosts whose TCP/IP stacks have not been configured with this information.

In order to identify itself, the host must broadcast an RARP packet requesting response from any RARP server on the network. Because the host does not know its own IP address assignment, the RARP packet lacks IP information and is therefore restricted to the physical segment (local network) only.

If there is more than one RARP server on the physical segment, the first available RARP server will send a response packet to the querying workstation. This response will be addressed properly at the MAC level, but will also contain the workstation's logical IP address, which the server finds by doing a reverse lookup in the routing table.

IP Routing

5.3. Internetworking: Options for Connecting Network Segments

IP routing is only one of several possible ways to interconnect network segments. In this section we'll examine several alternative technologies in order to understand what benefits IP routing brings and the cost in complexity that these benefits entail.

5.3.1. Repeaters

Repeaters are the simplest way to interconnect two physical network segments. A repeater operates at the level of the electrical signals traveling through the network medium. Because all transmission media offer some resistance to electrical currents (or wireless transmissions), signals inevitably attenuate, or fade, as they traverse a network segment.

A *repeater* is a device that reconditions an incoming signal and passes it along to the next segment. This reconditioning restores signal strength and clarity, but does not in any way interpret the signal as containing useful information. Therefore, repeaters can only connect two segments, which adopt exactly the same MAC-level protocols. For instance, repeaters are often used in Ethernet networks, especially when these are implemented as ring buses.

Although they do no protocol interpretation or translation, repeaters can join segments using different media, such as optical fiber to copper wire. As you might expect, repeaters do not identify or correct any transmission or addressing errors.

Repeaters can be useful in building LANs of modest size and are cost-effective for this purpose. Their limited functionality makes them unsuitable for larger or more complex internetworking situations.

5.3.2. Bridges

A *bridge* is a hardware device used to manage networks of medium complexity. Bridges operate at the Media Access Control level of the protocol stack and are *store and forward* devices. That is, a bridge accepts a packet and examines the hardware address before deciding whether to forward that packet to another network segment.

Most LAN-oriented protocols, such as Ethernet and Token Ring, were developed to allow local networks to be implemented and managed with a minimum of expertise and administrative burden. To achieve this goal, Ethernet and Token

Ring networks broadcast all messages to all network nodes. Each node must read the message header to determine if that node is the intended message destination. As a result, these networks require little software or other configuration as nodes are added or removed from the network.

As LANs grow in size, however, the broadcast approach becomes increasingly inefficient. Bridges allow medium and large LANs to be segregated into smaller local segments, while still ensuring that any workstation on the LAN can reach another LAN workstation with a message when necessary.

The most common type of bridge, called a *transparent* or *spanning tree bridge*, accomplishes this by examining the hardware address of each packet that comes to it and determining whether the destination node is on the originating segment of the network. If it is, the packet does not need to be forwarded to the nodes on the other LAN segments. If it is not, the packet is forwarded on to the adjacent segment, where it resumes standard LAN processing.

Other types of bridges include

- *Source routing bridges*, typically used in Token Ring networks, which are specific to a given LAN protocol and make forwarding and filtering decisions based on network topology and the destination address.

- *Source route transparent bridges*, which perform source routing if the packet is understood, but transparent routing otherwise.

- *Translational bridges*, which are able to pass traffic between two specific LAN types, most commonly Ethernet and Token Ring, by translating the packet headers accordingly.

Because a bridge intrinsically functions as a repeater (because it regenerates the signal each time it forwards a packet), it can be used to expand the overall length of a LAN. However, a good rule of thumb is never to use more than seven bridges to concatenate segments within the same network.

5.3.3. Routers

Repeaters function at the physical wire and signal level of the protocol stack and make no decisions regarding a packet's contents or destination.

Bridges function at the Media Access Control (and sometimes the Logical Link Control) level. They make limited decisions regarding the checksum integrity of a packet and the physical location of the packet's destination node. Some bridges also provide a limited degree of interoperability between LANs that use different MAC-level protocols.

Routers function at the network level of the OSI model and are significantly more sophisticated and complex than either repeaters or bridges. A router not only makes complex decisions regarding packet transmission, it also actively exchanges information regarding the overall internetwork topology and adjusts those decisions in response to network traffic and even outages within the telecommunications infrastructure.

Whereas repeaters and bridges are primarily intended to work within a local network or to extend LAN capabilities across multiple local networks, routers are primarily intended to support networks of networks, such as the public Internet or complex corporate intranets. Routers increasingly are also used within complex LANs and WANs, but their functionality—especially in the context of TCP/IP—is shaped by the goals for the TCP/IP suite as a whole. Namely, to allow transparent data communications between computers that reside on separate and perhaps very diverse networks.

Routing Concepts

Because IP uses logical addresses, Table 5.1 shows a very simple routing table taken from a Windows NT 4.0 workstation residing on an Ethernet LAN.

Table 5.1. A minimal routing table.

Network Address	Net mask	Gateway Address	Interface	Metric
		Active Routes		
0.0.0.0	0.0.0.0	131.107.5.1	131.107.5.12	1
127.0.0.0	255.0.0.0	127.0.0.1	127.0.0.1	1
131.105.0	255.255.255.0	131.107.5.12	131.107.5.12	1
131.107.255.255	255.255.255.255	131.107.5.12	131.107.5.12	1
131.107.5.12	255.255.255.255	131.107.5.12	131.107.5.12	1
224.0.0.0	224.0.0.0	131.107.5.12	131.107.5.12	1
255.255.255.255	255.255.255.255	131.107.5.12	131.107.5.12	1

In this example, the enterprise IP network received a Class B IP address of 131.107.x.x. The workstation resides on subnet (LAN) number 5 and has been assigned a host ID of 12. Its own IP address, therefore, is 131.107.5.12 and its subnet mask is 255.255.255.0.

The workstation's routing table associates a subnet mask and gateway address with each IP destination address in the table. Because hosts running Windows NT can serve as routers for small networks—and can contain more than one NIC, each with its own IP address—the table also specifies the particular interface to be used in IP transmissions to the specified destination.

The final column in this table is a metric that expresses the relative distance of the destination from the workstation itself. In routers and intermediate nodes, the distance metric is used to choose the best next step in routing a message. Our NT workstation will use RIP to route messages, so this metric is a *hop count*, or a count of the number of nodes required for reaching the destination. End nodes such as this workstation are limited to broadcasting messages, sending them to local nodes via the MAC protocol or sending them to a specific gateway machine for further routing. In these cases, therefore, the hop count is always 1. We'll examine hop counts and other distance metrics in greater detail in the "Router Protocols" section later in this chapter.

In Table 5.1, all the entries are labeled active routes because they were created during protocol handshakes and TCP/IP stack initialization. This is referred to as *dynamic acquisition* of router table entries. Within intermediate nodes and dedicated router machines, the number of active routes in the table will grow over time as the router exchanges information with neighboring nodes and issues queries to the wider network.

Table 5.1 contains little new information, because its entries consist of the network, a subnet, the loopback address, broadcast scopes, and a multicast group, most of which can be deduced from the workstation's address and its associated subnet mask. Even an end node like this workstation might need more information in its routing table, however.

Consider the situation in which a specific workstation needs to know which of multiple gateways on its LAN should be used to route messages to one or more hosts on a different subnet. Perhaps the sending machine is assigned to a network administrator or to an employee who has temporarily been assigned to a project in another department. In this case, it is useful to be able to specify routing information that will always be present when the workstation and its TCP/IP stack boot up, but which could not be deduced by the workstation's own address. This is done by creating *static* route entries, labeled *persistent* routes in the preceding NT example.

NOTE NT's use of the label *persistent* to refer to static entries calls our attention to the fact that routing table information that has been acquired dynamically will eventually age and be discarded. This ensures that the routing information used by a node is current and reflects any recent changes in network topology. Static entries are neither discarded nor automatically updated using any of the relevant protocols, however. For this reason, their use should be limited to network installation, troubleshooting, and well-considered network administration situations.

The most common (and platform-independent) way to create static route entries is with the `route` utility. This program, originally developed in the UNIX environment, is a flexible network administration and debugging tool that has been ported to several other operating systems. To add a routing table entry on the NT workstation, go to the command-line prompt and issue the following command:

```
>route add 131.107.7.0 mask 225.225.225.0 131.107.5.2
➥131.107.5.12
```

TIP   The route utility is only one of several tools available for troubleshooting and administering TCP/IP networks. The ipconfig utility tells you what configuration settings are active on a workstation. The ping utility tests your ability to reach a given node from this workstation. You will probably use nslookup to verify that the workstation can reference destinations as DNS or NetBIOS names and with IP addresses. Don't forget to investigate the network monitor software available for your platform, which allows you to see exactly what packets are being sent and received at a node.

This command adds an entry stating that any host on subnet 7 of the corporate network can be reached by going through a second gateway, host 2, on our local LAN. To add a specific destination node only, modify this command as follows:

```
>route add 131.107.7.23 mask
➥225.225.225.255 131.107.5.
➥2 131.107.5.12
```

Once the entry is added, you could generate a new listing of the routing table, again with the route command, as follows, and generate Table 5.2:

```
>route -p print
```

Table 5.2. Routing table with static entry.

Network Address	Net mask	Gateway Address	Interface	Metric
Active Routes				
0.0.0.0	0.0.0.0	131.107.5.1	131.107.5.12	1
127.0.0.0	255.0.0.0	127.0.0.1	127.0.0.1	1
131.105.0	255.255.255.0	131.107.5.12	131.107.5.12	1
131.107.255.255	255.255.255.255	131.107.5.12	131.107.5.12	1
131.107.5.12	255.255.255.255	131.107.5.12	131.107.5.12	1
224.0.0.0	224.0.0.0	131.107.5.12	131.107.5.12	1
255.255.255.255	255.255.255.255	131.107.5.12	131.107.5.12	1
Persistent Routes				
131.107.7.23	255.255.255.255	131.107.5.2	131.107.5.12	1

5.4. **Router Protocols**

So far, we've discussed in a general way what a router does and the basics of a routing table. In order to fully understand how a TCP/IP network functions—and in particular, to become knowledgeable about selecting and administering equipment for such a network—it's necessary to understand the various protocols in the stack that specifically support the IP routing process.

Router protocols serve three functions:

- Learning routes—Creation of a routing table by learning the parts of a network and where they are (dynamic acquisition of information).

- Selecting routes—Router will determine if there are multiple routes to get to a destination segment and will choose the best one.

- Maintaining routes—Each router will listen for changes in the network and will update their routing tables as necessary. The time it takes for all the routers to update their routing tables is called *convergence*.

In order to accomplish these tasks, a routing protocol must embody a set of rules, or algorithms, that will govern the means by which information is acquired and way in which that information will govern routing choices. Existing router protocols generally rely on one of two such algorithms, called *distance vector* and *link state*, respectively. The distance vector approach is older, simpler, and far more traffic-intensive, but is cost-effective for small networks adopting TCP/IP for the first time. The link state approach is more software-intensive, responds more dynamically to network performance, and generally requires more expensive routing equipment.

This section examines the various router protocols with an eye to those that are best suited for certain situations.

5.5. **Routing Inside the LAN**

Routing and bridging are best broken down by what is inside and outside the LAN. Because each solution is implemented differently, it is better to work from the inside out of your network, allowing for growth as well as identifying the potential problems that might occur within your personalized network setup.

Routers use protocols or sets of rules to determine how data packets will be directed through the network. For internal LANs, there are five alternatives from which to choose:

- Routing Information Protocol (RIP)

- Hello protocol

- Open Shortest Path First (OSPF)

- Intermediate Hosts to Intermediate Host (IS-IS)

- Extended Interior Gateway Routing Protocol (EIGRP)

These protocols are all referred to as *Interior Gateway Protocols* (IGPs). Their general purpose is to define routes through the local LAN and then advertise to the *Exterior Gateway Protocols* (EGPs), which connect remote LANs together.

5.5.1. Routing Information Protocol

The Routing Information Protocol (RIP) is probably the most widely used IGP on the market today. It was originally designed and implemented at the University of California in Berkeley to provide consistency to routing information in local LANs. It was first implemented in Berkeley's BSD UNIX host and was later adopted as the standard from there.

RIP uses network broadcasts to dynamically update routing tables and make changes quickly using the standard distance vector–routing algorithm to learn, select, and update routes.

RIP breaks all routers into two categories: active and passive. Active routers advertise their routing information to other routers, whereas passive routers update their information based on these active broadcasts but never broadcast themselves. These broadcasts occur every 30 seconds and are based on the most current information taken from the active router's routing table. Regardless of whether the router is active or passive, all routing information that is broadcasted will be captured and used to update the routing tables.

The distance is measured in what is known as a *hop count metric*. In an RIP format, every time the packet crosses a router, it is considered one hop. For example, if the hop count metric is three, the network crossed three routers to get to the network destination. If two paths are found that have the same hop count, RIP will give priority to existing routes and use those until a route with a smaller hop count is discovered. Based on this fact alone, RIP does not provide *load balancing,* or the distribution of data across multiple paths to increase performance. Once a route path is selected, it will be used until the route stops functioning. The only time that this value might be inaccurate is if, for example, a connection that has three hops is significantly faster due to the network topology than a path with only two hops. To compensate for the lack of speed considerations on the RIP algorithm, some routers will artificially "inflate" the hop counts for known slow links.

RIP as a small internal solution works very well. If RIP is used in a larger LAN/ WAN environment, certain precautions must be made to keep all the routing information consistent. Being based on the 30-second count to allow all routers to update and validate their information can be problematic on hosts that either have slow links or multiple routers to cross. Consider two different buildings within a LAN campus that are connected with a 56Kbps leased line. If the information does not travel a round trip in 30 seconds, areas of the network potentially would cease to exist and hosts on the other end of the leased line would not be aware of it. The second part of the figure goes to the other extreme. If the environment has a lot of routers, the time for each router to process and the number of routers crossed can hinder throughput as well. Also be aware in the second example that RIP has a maximum limit of 16 routers it may cross. Any number higher than this is considered an unreachable route, and the route is discarded. These problems of slow performance and limited router hops are known as the *slow convergence* or more commonly *count to infinity* problems. If one of the end routers were to fail, it is conceivable that the routers based on the time delay could fall out of sync and a router towards the middle could be potentially faced with a problem. If one router on one end registers a failure and returns all packets addressed through it while a router at the other working end that has not been updated continues to retransmit the failed transmit attempts, the data could be bounced back and forth until each data packet's hop count goes above 16 and the packet is discarded. In order to combat this problem, three solutions have been implemented:

- Split Horizon Update

- Hold Down

- Poison Reverse

Split horizon update basically uses a forward motion–only implementation of RIP. For example, if router 1 goes down, router 2 is notified immediately. Router 2 stops broadcasting back to router 1 and marks the path as unreachable. Routers 3 and 4 will also eventually be updated, each router being updated as the routers broadcast. Eventually, all paths will be updated. None of the notified routers will allow the packets to pass through them until they are notified by the originator (in this case router 2) of the downed connection. Be aware that this implementation can be slow because the whole network must be updated before traffic is routed, regardless of whether the connection comes back up or not.

Hold down takes a more time-based approach, similar to the basic RIP protocol. If a router using hold down receives a message indicating that a route is downed, it will *hold* packets destined for that path for a period of 60 seconds. The basic principle is to give the network an additional amount of time to notify all routes within the LAN. The major negative to this solution is that to be effective all routers must be synched to the same hold down time schedules. If routers are out of sync, they could loop bad information to each other every 60-plus seconds, causing the propagation of bad route paths as well as the effective blocking of functional ones.

Poison reverse uses a method whereby, upon a connection being broken, the router that identified the break will retain the route and label it as unreachable. It will then broadcast to the rest of the network, immediately notifying all routers, causing them to reassess the best path to the desired subnetwork and update their routing tables.

RIP is discussed in RFCs 1388 and 1508.

5.5.2. The Hello Protocol

The Hello protocol predates even the RIP protocol; it was used in the original NSFnet (National Science Foundation network) as a standard for packet passing. Whereas RIP uses a cost-based hop metric, Hello is based on time synchronization. It functions in two steps:

- All clocks between the routers are synchronized to provide a base time.

- Each machine then calculates the shortest path to the desired destination based on the shortest time discovered.

In order to do these two functions, each Hello packet bears a timestamp along with routing information so that when a packet passes through a router, the router's table will be updated with the time value from the packet allowing the computation of delay. The concept of how many routers were crossed is not an issue; all that is important is how long it takes to send and receive the packet. In order to handle the possibility of packet delay, each router will also periodically contact its nearest routing neighbors to get time updates to verify their tables. If its neighbor's routing information has a entry that has a shorter time delay then its own, it will update the routing tables with the new information and route the packets through a new pathway.

The main disadvantage of this packet is the time delay factor. This protocol cannot handle rapidly changing routing environments effectively. Here's how Hello works: Packets sent by computer 1 go to router 1 that, based on its previous time calculation, chooses router 2 as its preferred path to router 3 and the destination at computer 2.

Router 1 continues to pass packets to router 2 until the line becomes congested or until it receives an update telling it that the path from router 1 to 3 to 5 is much faster. In such a case, router 1 would divert the flow of data to that path, causing the new route to eventually become saturated. This flip-flop effect is a common problem within redundant path environments, and the only real solution is to embed a weighing factor into its calculation cycle for judging if the delay is substantial enough to move all the data to a new path.

5.5.3. Open Shortest Path First

The OSPF protocol is a relatively new standard developed by the Internet Engineering Task Force (IETF) as a way to handle the limited connectivity of RIP and the time delays of Hello. OSPF includes the following new features, making it a popular choice among large network installations:

- The capability to identify multiple routing paths through a network and to give each a designation, such as paths for better performance or optimized for packet bursts.

- The capability to balance the data from one location to another using multiple paths.

OSPF also has additional features that make it suitable for dealing with multitopology networks or LANs that have been segmented together. The concept of *network areas*, similar in concept to Apple Computer's *zones*, allows each segment's topology to be tracked and maintained independently. This allows for the flexibility of both newer and legacy hosts. As long as both hosts speak OSPF, the architecture is ignored. To handle these differences, OSPF has the capability to verify its own topology strengths and weaknesses. Therefore, each segment certifies itself as a valid path through the connecting routers, and OSPF assumes that each network is trusted and valid to receive/forward packets. Once the networks are all trusted, IS managers can track the network on a more logical versus physical level, allowing for more focus on performance tuning to be performed.

Interior Gateway Protocols are realistically simple to understand, based on the relative complexities of the rest of your network. If your network is small and relatively point to point, the Hello protocol may be a good implementation. The time it takes to get from one point to another is relatively static in the case of a failure; the routers are immediately notified. If the network needs another path, all that is necessary is to remove the faulty router and replace it. The routers essentially reconfigure themselves, by identifying the new connection, and the packets are forwarded to that path. If your network has fewer than 16 segments and your media allows for the propagation of packets around your network in under 30 seconds, RIP is an excellent choice in both ease of installation and documentation. RIP is most effective if your network has the same equipment and relative connection speeds throughout, allowing the protocol to optimize itself based on the physical layout of your environment. When the needs of the network involve the move to connect multiple sites with existing mixed topologies or legacy hosts with newer high-speed burst segments, OSPF with its user configurable options allows for a better balancing and monitoring of the internal segment environment. The downside to OSPF is that the user needs a much higher degree of understanding as to the setup of each specific router and an overall understanding of his network. If one router is incorrectly configured, it can degrade the performance of the rest of the network, causing bottlenecks in unlikely places.

For more detailed information regarding OSPF, see RFCs 1131, 1247, and 1583.

5.5.4. Intermediate Host to Intermediate Host

This protocol and the one that follows (EIGRP) are relatively new in architecture terms. IS-IS is similar in design to OSPF but has modifications based on its initial design restraints. To discover its neighbor nodes, it utilizes the same Hello packets that OSPF does as well as use *flooding* or *pyramid* packets to send out its link information to the neighbor nodes. However, because OSPF uses an *exchange* protocol to allow routing information to be updated dynamically, IS-IS relies on the flood packets to stream data in one direction, allowing effective updating. IS-IS was originally developed for use exclusively for OSI networks and because of this, it follows the strict constraints of the OSI breakdown in the connectivity of subnets. Due to this constraint, IS-IS has two major flaws:

- IS-IS uses a small metric number (6 bits) in its message sequence number. Due to this factor, packets are restricted to a smaller division number than in OSPF, causing larger packets not to be effectively sent or possibly discarded due to packet size restrictions.

- IS-IS is restricted to an 8-bit link state value. This restriction limits the number of packets that one router can effectively broadcast to another router to 256. Any destinations over this number will be ignored until the older packet paths are discarded or packets are refreshed and reordered.

5.5.5. Extended Interior Gateway Routing Protocol

EIGRP is unique in that it is not a uniform open standard. It was developed by Cisco hosts before OSPF had been formalized by the IETF as a way to combat the limitations faced within the then standard RIP. The original protocol, IGRP, was a distance vector protocol similar to RIP, but it did not incur RIP's problems or limitations. Whereas RIP broadcasted every 30 seconds, IGRP broadcasted every 90 and supported some of the more complex features found in the now standardized OSPF, such as composite metrics, loop protection, and multipath routing. Instead of limiting itself to distance (hops) or time (ticks), its preferred routing destinations were determined by the following components:

- Delay (equivalent to a tick time)

- Bandwidth (how large is the segment's transmission bandwidth)

- Reliability (based on count of lost or dropped packets on that particular route)

- Load (how busy is the route)

These values, which can also be manipulated by the network administrator, allow for the designation of a preferred path to each destination subnet. In the case of two paths that essentially provide the same preferred path, the source host will split the packets down both paths to allow for better performance. OSPF supports a similar multipath concept but will drop all but the first best preferred path found. EIGRP uses the same IGRP mechanics, but has an improved distance vector algorithm that all but eliminates routing loops. Due to these new modifications, however, one problem with EIGRP is that it is not compatible with IGRP; thus older hosts must upgrade to take advantage of the reliability options.

5.6. Routing Outside the LAN

Information can easily be routed within a LAN using protocols that employ broadcast techniques because LANs generally are optimized for broadcasting in any case.

Outside the LAN, however, the focus changes. Networks like the Internet can't have protocols like RIP broadcasting every 30 seconds to every other network; the network would become bogged down. The purpose of external hosts is to simply identify which network holds the desired destination and if the destination is reachable.

5.6.1. Bridging Considerations

When bridging is implemented, it is usually talked about using one of two terms: remote or local. A local bridge simply connects two segments of a local LAN. Remote bridges connect two networks via a WAN-type link. Remote bridges are usually connected to things like public-switched telephone networks (PSTN), private T-1 data links, or X.25 remote point-to-point or multipoint gateways. With the addition of faster technologies, such as FDDI and ATM, the X.75 standard is also being added using packet-switched network gateways.

The difficulty with remote bridging lies in the speed factors between LAN- and WAN-based connectivity. LANs usually are connected via physical media and, due to their close proximity, they allow data to be transferred much faster than the slower gateway-type WAN connectivity. Remote bridges can compensate for this performance discrepancy by implementing sufficient buffering capability, allowing the bridge at the end of the WAN link to reassemble the packet before it forwards it to the faster LAN link. This also has the benefit of working on the other direction to allow larger, faster packets to be broken down and fed slowly to the WAN link. This eliminates the possibility of the WAN link being oversaturated with packets and potentially causing packet collisions or packets to be dropped due to the bandwidth being used up.

In addition to the oversaturation factor, the inconsistencies of different media must also be addressed. Because transparent bridges are found mainly in Ethernet networks and source route bridges are mainly found in Token Ring networks, it is logical to wonder what mechanism is necessary to get these two devices to talk to each other.

The technology is known as *translational bridging*. It was first developed in the mid-1980s, and in 1990 was implemented by IBM in its source route transparent bridging architecture. In order for this protocol to be an effective translator, it had to deal with the oddities of each protocol and be able to convert it. Common issues addressed were as follows:

- Incompatible Bit Ordering:

    Token Ring—First bit is High Order Bit

    Ethernet—First bit is Low Order Bit

- Maximum Transfer Unit (Packet) Size:

    Token Ring—4,202 bytes

    Ethernet—1,500 bytes

- Frame Status Bit:

    Token Ring—Three possible settings: Bit A—Frame Seen; Bit C—Frame Copied; Bit E—Errors in Frame

    Ethernet—No such technology

- Explorer Frames:

    Token Ring—No such technology

    Ethernet—Used by transparent bridges to identify the network topology

- Routing Information Field (RIF):

    Token Ring—Uses the RIF field to hold routing information sent in each packet

    Ethernet—No such technology

Due to the fact of vast differences between the overall packet structures, the following rules were implemented to allow a consistent conversion process to occur. These rules, while not enforced standards, aid the manufacturer in addressing potential "holes" in the translation schemes:

- Source and destination bits are reordered on both frame types. Embedded MAC addresses are separated from the packet as it enters the bridge and, using a software translation host, the bridge chooses which port to send the packet through.

- The RIF field is broken down into a subfield that indicates the largest frame size. The bridge records this information, and any packets sent to this destination port will be scaled down or have multiple packets joined together to fit into the network's topology model.

- Token Ring's error trapping and frame status bits are dropped in favor of having the transport layer functions of the network verify the frame's validity.

The translation bridge creates artificial environments on each of its ends to trick the topologies into thinking they are only connected to one of their own. On the Token Ring networks, the bridge has a ring number and bridge number, causing it to look like a standard source-route bridging host. On the Ethernet networks, the source-route bridging is stripped away and replaced with RIF information cached from other incoming Ethernet packets. If the destination has not been cached, the bridge will implement the Spanning Tree Algorithm and will explore the network for the destination.

5.6.2. Routing Considerations

The purpose of the IGPs is to locate and identify destination information and pass it on to the EGPs. The purpose of the EGPs is to notify their network neighbors that the routes are valid and located on their perspective networks.

This section looks at four EGPs:

- Gateway to Gateway Protocol (GGP)

- Exterior Gateway Protocol (EGP)

- Border Gateway Protocol (BGP)

- Inter-Domain Routing Protocol (IDRP)

The exterior gateway protocols all have different implementations; however, they all follow the same basic needs of what information is placed in their routing tables and how do they get it. Different environments handle their problems differently. Some routers will start and sync with a secondary host, while others will start with a totally empty table and execute external commands to generate the route tables. Others may simply contact their neighbors at startup to ask them for their routing information and then alter that information to reflect their own locations on the network.

5.6.3. Gateway to Gateway Protocol

This protocol was one of the first exterior gateway protocols, and while it is no longer used as a standard in the community, it gives a very basic theoretical understanding of the structure needed.

GGP was created to travel inside or *tunnel* in the standard TCP and UDP data packets.

Every packet carried with it a standard format header that identified what type of information it carried. Once the type of information was identified, the packet was read and processed. When a new router was created on the network, all that was necessary was to identify its neighbor or a reference router. As the neighbor had already been communicating with the rest of the network, all that was necessary for the new router to do was to tap into the working router's information and copy it. The new router then identified what routes it contained by communicating with the IGPs inside its host. It, in turn, contacted and propagated its information to all the other routers in the external community. Any failures that occurred internally to each host would be handled by the IGPs and fed out to all the EGPs. Any gateway failures would be identified by each gateway as they tried to forward packets and found the remote host unreachable.

5.6.4. Exterior Gateway Protocol

EGP follows the GGP standards in a more formalized manner. EGP implements a neighbor acquisition method, whereby each exterior router agrees that it can and should communicate reachability information with the other. Once this link is established, each router sees the other as a *trusted peer*. The routers will subsequently verify that their peers are operational and will transmit routing information to each other as necessary in the form of routing update messages. The problem with EGP lies in that it does not understand the concept of distance in its algorithm. If there are two paths to the destination in its own network, it does not advertise which is better or worse, only that the destination is on its network and is operational. At this point, the concept of a default route path comes into play as the possibility of packet loops or unnecessary delays caused by incorrect choices becomes obvious. If the preferred pathway through the EGP goes down for any reason, the paths to its destination are totally unreachable. IS managers must manually configure an alternative path as well as make manual decisions as to which path should be loaded to deliver the best performance.

For the basic EGP definition and documentation, see RFCs 827 and 904.

5.6.5. Border Gateway Protocol

BGP expands on the EGP. Not only does it deliver the requested routing information, but it embeds within its packets path attributes that provide more information about each route as well as provide alternate paths that allow data to be streamed across different internal pathways, thus eliminating the possibility of packet loops as found in the EGP example.

The path attributes also notify the external router that the packet was generated from internal routing information, external routing information, or from another source. When external trusted peers are identified and validated, they are issued a path number that ties to the routing information that goes to that specific router. Due to the design of BGP, each peer is directly connected to its subnet in order to eliminate potential distance delays or inconsistencies found in the EGP protocol. Each packet then has the path number in its header, which eliminates the possibility of misdirected packets. The packets are captured by the neighbors who embed their own unique numbers to the source information of the packet they have just received in their corresponding routing tables. In this way, every destination is identified and the specific paths are predefined. Any packets received without this unique number are considered to be generated within the router's own internal network and are labeled as internal.

You can review the details of BGP by reading RFCs 1105, 1163, and 1267.

5.6.6. Inter-Domain Routing Protocol

This protocol was designed by the OSI as a companion protocol to IS-IS. It was developed by the same design team that created BGP, and while it follows the same basic form, it has several differences, including the following:

- Whereas BGP packets are exchanged within the TCP protocol, IDRP uses the raw datagram, allowing better and faster transfer of information and more compatibility with older host architectures.

- BGP identifies all the autonomous hosts that are included in a path to transfer data from source to destination. IDRP uses the concept of Routing Domain Confederations, which identifies "virtual" pathways between domains. This allows for improved reliability in the case of a potential path failure.

5.7. Moving to IP Version 6 (IPv6)

With the increased activity centering around getting connected to the Internet, more resources and time are being diverted into finding a solution that handles the exchange of both large numbers of packets and routers as well as doing so in an expedient manner. However, the routing protocols are just part of the problem. The current IP addressing scheme (version 4) will not handle the increase in the size of the routing table caused by the immense numbers of active workstations and servers. The current scheme was developed in the 1970s when a 32-bit address was considered enough to handle any configuration of hosts. IP version 6 reworks this methodology by increasing the address size to 128 bits. These 128 bits are further broken down into 8 16–bit integer clusters separated by colons like this:

```
[2A:FFFA:0::15:1075:111:1B]
```

This address format drops all leading zeros (**002A** becomes **2A**); null values are represented by double colons (**::**); and a standard address cannot hold more than one pair of double colons.

Whereas IPv4 was divided into three general classes (A, B, and C), IPv6 reads the raw 128-bit packet and uses variable-length prefixes (from 1 to 128 bits). The routers then store this prefix and base their routing decisions upon this factor. Within the prefixes, there are several special addresses that have reserved functions, including the following:

- Unspecified addresses (denoted by 16 null bytes)

- Loopback addresses (**::1**)

- Local addresses (identified by the binary number **1111 1110 11**)

- Legacy IPv4 addresses (96 zero bits prepended by the 32-bit IPv4 address)

- Multicast addresses (identified by the binary number **1111 1111**)

Along with the capability to multicast information to a select group at once, the IPv6 also implements anycast, allowing transfer of information to the nearest certain group of targets. Anycast follows the same syntax as unicast. With the capability to define a select group of targets, a hierarchy can be created to specify which targets get the updated routing information and handle potential transmission errors. This select group is otherwise known as a *provider list*.

The providers allow for a subsectioning of the packets into a virtual region instead of being limited to physical- or domain-oriented constraints currently implemented in IPv4. The current constraints are not valid because a domain can span several physical locations, making it difficult to route correctly. The only problem with the IPv6 scenario is when a host moves from one provider to another. Because the provider determines routing selection, moving the host would mislead the network regarding the location of the host, and any traffic that was addressed to the host's physical address would have difficulty either locating the correct routing information or seeing two possible routes to the same machine, one being no longer existent. The following are two possible options to handle the move and to deal with the virtual duplication problem:

- The host moves to the new provider and forces the new provider to advertise to the entire network of the host's new location. While this would be transparent to the host, the amount of broadcast traffic that would be incurred and the amount of misdirected data packet traffic that would need to be retransmitted once the new route was obtained would cause several potential routing and performance problems, especially if this happened regularly or involved whole domains moving at once.

- The host changes its workstation within its network to use the new IP addresses. This would involve lots of work for the workstation users in reconfiguration, depending on the number or workstations moved, but to the network, it would simply accept the change and route correctly with very few packet errors.

The second option is probably the more realistic choice because it will have the least impact on the overall performance of the network. IPv6 has put in place autoconfiguration procedures that easily remap a domain, a group, or workstations to its new location. Depending on the load constraints of the network paths involved, both providers could be used to map to the same IP address and physical address. This allows data to be streamed through two routing pathways.

5.7.1. Conversion Considerations

While the preceding section deals with implementing IPv6 as a standard and the problems inherent to its model, the biggest concern with Internet developers is the migration process from IPv4 to IPv6. All existing IPv4 hosts have to be given new IP addresses. Because this cannot be done all at once, IPv6 allows IPv4 packets to be right-justified inside a 128-bit IPv6 address field (prefixed with 96 zero bits), and thereby routed using the IPv6 scheme. However, because the IPv4 routing algorithms are based on location and the IPv6 are based on hierarchical routing, a router must be able to separate the two packet types and route them differently. Even if a router could handle the decision-making involved in the process, the final result would be small, growing IPv6 areas separated by the rest of the Internet, which is IPv4. The routers would need some mechanism to seek out other IPv6-compatible routers in order to deliver the IPv6 packets effectively. If none exist for a particular pathway, some mechanism must be able to break down and encapsulate the IPv6 packets into an IPv4 format.

While IPv4 does support this type of fragmentation scheme, it would waste the bandwidth and not take advantage of the IPv6 architecture enhancements. Also, if the IPv6 packet was fragmented, the destination router would need to receive and reassemble all of the fragments in order to deliver the packet to an IPv6 host. If any of the fragments were lost or dropped, the remaining fragments would be held in the destination buffer until the Time-To-Live on the packet had expired.

The Time-To-Live on a IPv4 packet fragmentation must be altered anyway to compensate for a packet that is four times the size of a standard packet it is used to carrying.

5.8. Summary

Judging which tools will best suit your environment is an important decision.

As a general guide in decision making, keep these factors in mind:

- Bridges are good for smaller networks with fewer slow WAN links.

- Bridges must be used in certain situations where the protocols cannot be encapsulated or tunneled.

- Bridges usually are more cost-effective. In a cost-to-speed ratio, a low-end router is more expensive than a low-end bridge.

- Routers require human intervention; they need to be set up, whereas bridges are plug and play.

- Routers handle larger networks with different speed links better.

- Routers are better at filtering things such as broadcasts and bandwidth utilization.

- Routers are more intelligent and can make decisions based on upper-OSI layer sections of the packet.

Chapter

6

Address Discovery Protocols

by Martin Bligh

6.1. Introduction

6.2. Address Allocation Policies

6.3. Reverse Address Resolution Protocol

6.4. BOOTP

6.5. Dynamic Host Configuration Protocol

6.6. BOOTP Relay

6.7. BOOTP Vendor Extensions and DHCP Options

6.8. Summary

6.1. **Introduction**

Every host wishing to use TCP/IP needs a unique IP address and other configuration information. This is normally stored on the hard disk of each system, but there are advantages to storing the information centrally:

- It makes the workstation easier to configure. This is particularly useful if users are expected to configure their own workstations.

- One of the few parameters that is unique to each workstation is the IP address. If address allocation can be automated, it is possible to set up a workstation by dumping one centrally held image onto its hard disk. This saves a huge amount of time if you are performing a mass rollout of workstations.

- If IP addresses are controlled centrally, it is much easier to avoid IP address conflicts. The information can also be fed into network management systems.

- Machines without local storage can get the information they need to use IP. This applies more to diskless PCs than X terminals (which will often have non-volatile RAM in which to store IP settings).

- If a workstation obtains its IP address automatically from a local network server, this makes it much easier to move machines between subnets. Instead of having to reconfigure the machine, it will automatically work out its own position and appropriate configuration parameters. This is very useful for the increasing number of portables using IP.

Some of these advantages are obtained only with specific address allocation polices. See the section "Address Allocation Policies."

Apart from the IP address, other information that hosts using IP might need include

- Subnet mask

- Static routing information (for example, default gateway)

- Address of boot file servers

- Name of boot file to boot from

- Addresses of name servers

- Addresses of other servers (time, print, and so on)

- Detailed IP and TCP configuration settings

6.2. Address Allocation Policies

There are three main address allocation policies: manual, automatic, and dynamic.

6.2.1. Manual

In manual address allocation, the administrator must create a database of `MAC address -> IP address` mappings, with an entry for every host on the subnet. Both mapping insertions and deletions must be done manually.

6.2.2. Automatic

In automatic address allocation, the server creates the `MAC address -> IP address` mappings as they are needed. IP addresses are taken from a pool given to the server. Once allocated, they stay in the database until manually removed. Mapping insertions are automatic, but deletions must be done manually.

6.2.3. Dynamic

> **NOTE** Manual and automatic policies are collectively called *static address allocation*.

In dynamic address allocation, the server creates the `MAC address -> IP address` mappings as they are needed. IP addresses are taken from a pool given to the server, but they are only allocated for a fixed period of time. If the client does not renew its claim to the address before that time is expired, the mapping will be removed by the server. Mapping insertions and deletions are both automatic.

6.2.4. Which Allocation Policy to Use?

There is no best allocation policy. Which allocation policy you should use is dependent on your own network. Some advantages and disadvantages are listed in the following sections.

Disadvantage of Manual Allocation

Typing an Ethernet address by hand is extremely tedious and error-prone. Automatic and dynamic address allocations require little information to set up—just a range of IP addresses to allocate. Static address allocation requires an IP address and MAC address for each interface on the network.

Address Discovery Protocols

Disadvantage of Dynamic Allocation

With dynamic allocation, name servers may need updating every time a machine boots. DNS (the prevalent name service) is not designed to cope with these regular changes. Static address allocation makes using name services much easier. Name servers only need to be updated when a machine is put onto or removed from the network.

Advantages of Dynamic Allocation

Dynamic address allocation is particularly useful for notebook computers. They can be plugged into any subnet with an appropriate server and can obtain a correct IP address for that subnet without information being manually fed to the server.

Dynamic address allocation saves IP addresses. One address is needed for each interface currently connected to the network, whereas static allocation requires one address for each interface that could possibly connect to the network. This is particularly useful for Internet service providers, who will normally have only a small proportion of their customers connected at any one time.

Workstations versus Servers

Most of the advantages of dynamic address allocation apply to workstations, not servers. Servers generally have a static address to make it easier for other hosts to find them. As servers are rarely reconfigured, they often do not use any of these address allocation policies, but store their configuration information on their hard disks.

However, it is an excellent idea to keep static entries in your address allocation database for all servers. Even if they are not used by the servers themselves, it means that your information database will be complete and therefore much more useful.

6.3. Reverse Address Resolution Protocol

Reverse Address Resolution Protocol (RARP) operates at the data link layer (over Ethernet frames) and provides a static address allocation policy. If the network stack does not already provide an open interface to send and receive data link layer frames, low-level modifications will be necessary to implement RARP (as a server or a client).

An RARP client will send out a data link layer broadcast. Any RARP servers seeing the broadcast and knowing the correct IP address for the client will send a response. The client may get no response, in which case it should retry after a set timeout period and eventually give up. The client may receive multiple RARP replies from different servers.

RARP has a different Ethernet frame type from ARP, but uses the same data format, shown in Table 6.1.

Table 6.1. Construction of an RARP packet.

Size (bytes)	Description
2	MAC address type (for example, 10Mbps Ethernet = 1)
2	Protocol type (for example, IP = 0800)
1	Byte length of MAC address (h-len)
1	Byte length of protocol address (p-len)
2	Opcode (specifying a REQUEST REVERSE = 3 or a REPLY REVERSE = 4)
h-len	MAC address of sender
p-len	Protocol address of sender
h-len	MAC address of target (if known)
p-len	Protocol address of target

Address Discovery Protocols

6.4. BOOTP

BOOTP (boot protocol) is a more complex protocol than RARP, providing a facility for bootfile selection and custom vendor extensions. BOOTP runs over UDP, and hence is much easier to implement than RARP (which runs at the data link layer). BOOTP uses a static address allocation policy.

The BOOTP client broadcasts a *bootrequest* message to ask for its IP address and other configuration information. The IP source address is set to 0 if the client does not already know its own IP address. The BOOTP server then sends a *bootreply* message, containing the correct IP address for the client, in addition to any other configuration information it is able to provide.

How is the bootreply sent? The reply must be sent over IP, but the client does not yet know its IP address. There are two possibilities:

- The reply is broadcast back. This is not really desirable because hosts that do not need to see the reply will receive it. However, BOOTP requests are sent only on bootup, so the traffic levels involved are low. It is also an easy solution to implement.

- The reply is sent via unicast. This requires special handling to avoid the normal ARP process. The client's MAC address must be directly inserted into the packet. One easy way of doing this is to put a static entry into the ARP table.

BOOTP uses two UDP ports—BOOTP clients use 68; servers use 67. Using two separate ports means that BOOTP clients listening for a BOOTP reply don't have to process all the broadcast BOOTP requests to servers.

The packet format for BOOTP is given in Table 6.2.

Table 6.2. Construction of a BOOTP packet.

Size (bytes)	Description
1	Opcode (bootrequest = 1 or bootreply = 2)
1	MAC address type (for example, 10Mbps Ethernet = 1)
1	Byte length of MAC address (h–len)
1	Number of hops (client sets to 0)
4	Transaction ID; a randomly generated key for each request
2	Seconds elapsed since client started trying to boot
2	Unused
4	Client's knowledge of its own IP address (set to 0 if unknown)
4	Server's knowledge of client's IP address
4	Server IP address
4	Gateway IP address (optional)
16	Client MAC address
64	Server hostname (optionally set by client)
128	Boot filename (generic name can be set in bootrequest)
64	Vendor extensions area

6.5. Dynamic Host Configuration Protocol

Dynamic Host Configuration Protocol (DHCP) is a much more complex protocol than RARP or BOOTP. It provides a dynamic address allocation policy, while still providing the capability to allocate certain addresses manually (called a *reservation*). This is particularly useful for servers.

6.5.1. DHCP Leases

DHCP allocates an IP address to an interface for a fixed period of time. This temporary allocation is called a *lease*. If a interface still needs the IP address, it must renegotiate the lease before it expires. The automatic address allocation policy can be implemented by using dynamic allocation, but setting the lease time to be infinite.

6.5.2. Initial Lease Allocation

Figure 6.1 illustrates the sequence of DHCP messages that are exchanged in order to negotiate the lease. Note that all messages from the client are broadcast because the client doesn't yet have an IP address.

Figure 6.1.
DHCP lease allocation.

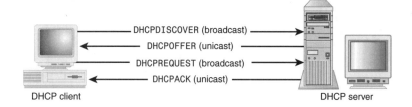

Each type of DHCP messages is explained in the following:

DHCPDISCOVER   This message is broadcast from a DHCP client in order to locate DHCP servers.

DHCPOFFER   This message is an offer of an IP address sent from a DHCP server to a DHCP client in response to a DHCPDISCOVER. A DHCP client may receive offers from multiple DHCP servers. It is free to accept any of these, although it will usually take the first received. An offer is not a cast-iron guarantee that the address will be allocated to the client (that is done by DHCPACK); however, in the interest of efficiency, servers will normally reserve the address until the client has had a chance to send a DHCPREQUEST.

Address Discovery Protocols

DHCPREQUEST	This message is a formal request for an IP address that has already been offered to the client by a DHCPOFFER message. The request is broadcast so that all DHCP servers may see it; servers whose offers have not been accepted may reclaim the IP address.

Instead of the DHCPREQUEST, the client could send a DHCPDECLINE:

DHCPDECLINE	This message is sent from the DHCP client to the DHCP server to indicate that the configuration parameters sent in a DHCPOFFER are invalid. This is an error condition, indicating that something is misconfigured somewhere along the line.
DHCPACK	This is an acknowledgment to confirm that the IP address requested in a DHCPREQUEST has been allocated to the client.

Instead of the DHCPACK, the server could send back a DHCPNAK:

DHCPNAK	This is a denial, meaning that the IP address requested in a DHCPREQUEST has not been allocated to the client. These normally should not be sent and should indicate either an error or that the client has been so slow in responding to a DHCPOFFER that the server has reallocated the address.

6.5.3. Lease Renewal

A DHCP client will attempt to renew its lease before it expires. This ensures continuous service (attempting to change an IP address while booted is most impractical). It will also renew the lease when it reboots, to check that no other host has taken the address.

The sequence of messages for an attempted lease renewal is similar to the second half of the initial lease allocation and is shown in Figure 6.2.

Figure 6.2.
DHCP lease renewal.

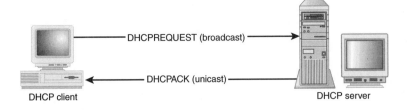

DHCP client — DHCPREQUEST (broadcast) → DHCP server

DHCP client ← DHCPACK (unicast) — DHCP server

If the lease is successfully renewed, a `DHCPACK` message will be sent back to the DHCP client from the DHCP server. If the renewal is unsuccessful, a `DHCPACK` message will be sent back. A `DHCPACK` message is much more likely during lease renewal than in the initial lease allocation. The lease may have expired while the machine has been turned off, and another interface may have taken the address.

The client maintains two times, T1 and T2, which are offsets in seconds, relative to the client's clock. After T1 seconds, the client will start attempting to renew its lease. After T2, the client attempts to rebind its lease to any available server. Both T1 and T2 are configurable by the server by using options, although they default to 1/2 and 7/8 of the lease time, respectively.

6.5.4. Lease Deletion

DHCP provides a mechanism for a client to release a lease. The DHCP client sends a `DHCPRELEASE` message containing the lease identification transaction ID to the DHCP server. Note that addresses are not normally released when a client is shut down, only when the client knows that it is being moved to another subnet. In practice, `DHCPRELEASE` messages are hardly ever sent; the lease is just left to expire.

DHCP messages use a similar format to BOOTP messages. The fields of a DHCP packet are described in Table 6.3.

Table 6.3. Construction of a DHCP packet.

Size (bytes)	Description
1	Opcode (`client->server` = 1 or `server->client` = 2)
1	MAC address type (for example, 10Mbps Ethernet = 1)
1	Byte length of MAC address (h–len)
1	Number of hops (client sets to 0)
4	Transaction ID; a randomly generated key for each request
2	Seconds elapsed since client started trying to boot
2	Flags field (this is unused in BOOTP)
4	Client's knowledge of its own IP address (0 if unknown)
4	Server's knowledge of client's IP address
4	Server IP address (for next step in boot process)

continues

Table 6.3. Continued.

Size (bytes)	Description
4	Gateway IP address (optional)
16	Client MAC address
64	Server hostname (optionally set by client)
128	Boot filename (generic name can be set in bootrequest)
312 (min)	DHCP Options (this is a 64-byte "vendor extensions area" in BOOTP)

DHCP messages from client to server set the Opcode field to 1 (BOOTP bootrequest). DHCP messages from server to client set the Opcode field to 2 (BOOTP bootreply).

The main changes include the introduction of the Flags field (unused in BOOTP) and the extension of the Options field, which is now a variable length, with a minimum of 312.

DHCP message types (for example, `DHCPDISCOVER`) are defined in an Options field of type 53.

6.6. BOOTP Relay

BOOTP and DHCP clients send out broadcast messages to UDP port 67 (the server port) in order to find their BOOTP or DHCP server. If the server is not on the same subnet as the client, it will never see the request. To avoid the necessity of having a boot server on every subnet, BOOTP relay agents have been invented to forward client requests to a remote server. They do not simply relay the packet, but have to change fields to indicate where the request came from. BOOTP relay agents work both for BOOTP and DHCP.

When forwarding a packet, the relay agent will examine the gateway IP address field. If this field is zero, it will be filled with the IP address of the receiving interface on the relay agent. If it is not zero, it will be left unchanged. The information in this field is used by the BOOTP/DHCP server to select an appropriate IP address for the client (see Figure 6.3).

Client-to-server messages will be forwarded to a configured IP address (for example, a DHCP server). Server-to-client messages are more complex, because the client does not yet know its own IP address. The message is sent back to the relay agent and is broadcast back on the interface that the relay agent originally received the message on (stored in the gateway IP address field).

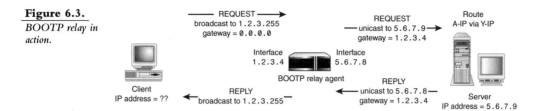

Figure 6.3.
BOOTP relay in action.

6.7. BOOTP Vendor Extensions and DHCP Options

There is a huge variety of BOOTP vendor extensions and DHCP options available. This section gives you an idea of the configuration power of BOOTP and DHCP. The available extension types are defined in RFC 1533 (from where the following information is taken), and only about a third of the possible options are listed here. For a complete reference, see the RFC, but most of the options in common usage are given here, ordered by option code. The options defined here may be used by both BOOTP and DHCP, except for those in the DHCP extensions section, which are specific to DHCP.

6.7.1. BOOTP Extension/DHCP Option Field Format

BOOTP vendor extensions and *DHCP options* have the same format. All options begin with a tag byte, which uniquely identifies the option. There are two fixed length options (0 and 255) that consist of only their tag bytes. All other options are variable-length, with a length byte following the tag (the length does not include the two bytes specifying the tag and length). The length is followed by the specified number of bytes of data. In the case of some variable-length options, the length field is a constant but must still be specified. All multibyte quantities are in network byte-order.

The first four bytes of the Options field start with the magic cookie sequence `99,130,83,99`. Option codes `128` to `254` (decimal) are reserved for site-specific options.

6.7.2. Shared BOOTP Extensions and DHCP Options

The options in this section can be used by both BOOTP and DHCP.

Pad Option

The pad option can be used to cause subsequent fields to align on word boundaries. The code for the pad option is 0, and its length is 1 octet:

Code   0

End Option

The end option marks the end of valid information in the vendor field. Subsequent octets should be filled with pad options. The code for the end option is 255, and its length is 1 octet:

Code   255

Subnet Mask Option

The subnet mask option specifies the client's subnet mask per RFC 950. If both the subnet mask and the router option are specified in a DHCP reply, the subnet mask option *must* be first.

The code for the subnet mask option is 1, and its length is 4 octets:

Code   1
Len   4
Subnet Mask   *subnet mask* (4 bytes)

Router Option

The router option specifies a list of IP addresses for routers on the client's subnet. Routers *should* be listed in order of preference. The code for the router option is 3.

The minimum length for the router option is 4 octets, and the length *must* always be a multiple of 4:

Code   3
Len   *n*
Address 1   *IP address* (4 byte)
Address 2   *IP address* (4 byte)
  ...   ...

Domain Name Server Option

The domain name server option specifies a list of Domain Name System (STD 13, RFC 1035 [8]) name servers available to the client. Servers *should* be listed in order of preference.

The code for the domain name server option is 6. The minimum length for this option is 4 octets, and the length *must* always be a multiple of 4:

Code	6
Len	*n*
Address 1	*IP address* (4 byte)
Address 2	*IP address* (4 byte)

Cookie Server Option

The cookie server option specifies a list of RFC 865 cookie servers available to the client. Servers *should* be listed in order of preference.

The code for the log server option is 8. The minimum length for this option is 4 octets, and the length *must* always be a multiple of 4:

Code	8
Len	*n*
Address 1	IP address (4 byte)
Address 2	IP address (4 byte)
...	...

Host Name Option

The host name option specifies the name of the client. The name may or may not be qualified with the local domain name (see the section "Domain Name" for the preferred way to retrieve the domain name).

The code for this option is 12, and its minimum length is 1:

Code	12
Len	*n*
Host Name	*domain name*

Boot File Size Option

The boot file size option specifies the length in 512-octet blocks of the default boot image for the client. The file length is specified as an unsigned 16-bit integer.

The code for this option is 13, and its length is 2:

Code	13
Len	2
Boot file size	*integer* (2 bytes)

Domain Name Option

This option specifies the domain name that client should use when resolving hostnames via the Domain Name System.

The code for this option is 15. Its minimum length is 1:

Code	15
Len	*n*
Domain name	*domain name*

Swap Server Option

The swap server specifies the IP address of the client's swap server.

The code for this option is 16, and its length is 4:

Code	16
Len	4
Address 1	*IP address* (4 byte)

Root Path Option

The root path option specifies the pathname that contains the client's root disk. The path is formatted as a character string consisting of characters from the NVT ASCII character set.

The code for this option is 17. Its minimum length is 1:

Code	17
Len	*n*
Root path	*string* (n bytes)

Broadcast Address Option

The broadcast address option specifies the broadcast address in use on the client's subnet.

The code for this option is 28, and its length is 4:

Code	28
Len	4
Broadcast address	*IP address* (4 byte)

Perform Mask Discovery Option

This option specifies whether the client should perform subnet mask discovery using ICMP. A value of 0 indicates that the client should not perform mask discovery. A value of 1 means that the client should perform mask discovery.

The code for this option is 29, and its length is 1:

Code	29
Len	1
Perform mask discovery flag	0 or 1

Static Route Option

The static route option specifies a list of static routes that the client should install in its routing cache. If multiple routes to the same destination are specified, they are listed in descending order of priority.

The routes consist of a list of IP address pairs. The first address is the destination address, and the second address is the router for the destination.

The default route (0.0.0.0) is an illegal destination for a static route. See the next section for information about the router option.

Router Option

The code for this option is 33. The minimum length of this option is 8, and the length *must* be a multiple of 8:

Code	33
Len	*n*
Destination 1	*IP address* (4 bytes)
Router 1	*IP address* (4 bytes)
Destination 2	*IP address* (4 bytes)
Router 2	*IP address* (4 bytes)
...	...

Network Information Service Domain Option

The network information service domain option specifies the name of the client's NIS domain. The domain is formatted as a character string consisting of characters from the NVT ASCII character set.

The code for this option is 40. Its minimum length is 1:

Code	40
Len	*n*
NIS domain name	*string*

Network Information Servers Option

The network information servers option specifies a list of IP addresses indicating NIS servers available to the client. Servers *should* be listed in order of preference.

The code for this option is 41. Its minimum length is 4, and the length *must* be a multiple of 4:

Code	41
Len	*n*
Address 1	*IP address* (4 bytes)
Address 2	*IP address* (4 bytes)
...	...

Vendor-Specific Information

This option is used by clients and servers to exchange vendor-specific information. The information is an opaque object of *n* octets, presumably interpreted by vendor-specific code on the clients and servers. The definition of this information is vendor specific. The vendor is indicated in the class-identifier option. Servers not equipped to interpret the vendor-specific information sent by a client *must* ignore it (although it may be reported). Clients that do not receive desired vendor-specific information *should* make an attempt to operate without it, although they may do so (and announce they are doing so) in a degraded mode.

If a vendor potentially encodes more than one item of information in this option, the vendor should encode the option using *encapsulated vendor-specific options*, as described here.

The encapsulated vendor-specific options field *should* be encoded as a sequence of code/length/value fields of identical syntax to the DHCP Options field with the following exceptions:

- There *should not* be a magic cookie field in the encapsulated vendor-specific extensions field.

- Codes other than 0 or 255 *may* be redefined by the vendor within the encapsulated vendor-specific extensions field, but *should* conform to the tag-length-value syntax defined in the section "BOOTP Extension/ DHCP Option Field Format."

- Code 255 (END), if present, signifies the end of the encapsulated vendor extensions, not the end of the vendor extensions field. If no code 255 is present, the end of the enclosing vendor-specific information field is taken as the end of the encapsulated vendor-specific extensions field.

The code for this option is 43 and its minimum length is 1:

Code	43
Len	*n*
Vendor-specific information	variable

When encapsulated vendor-specific extensions are used, the information bytes 1-n have the following format:

Code	*T1*
Len	*n*
Data item	variable
...	...
Code	*T2*
Len	*n*
Data item	variable
...	...

NetBIOS over TCP/IP Name Server Option

The NetBIOS name server (NBNS) option specifies a list of RFC 1001/1002 [19] [20] NBNS name servers listed in order of preference. The most common implementation of a NetBIOS name server is Microsoft's WINS.

The code for this option is 44. The minimum length of the option is 4 octets, and the length *must* always be a multiple of 4:

Code	44
Len	*n*
Address 1	*IP address* (4 bytes)
Address 2	*IP address* (4 bytes)
...	...

NetBIOS over TCP/IP Node Type Option

The NetBIOS node-type option allows NetBIOS over TCP/IP clients that are configurable to be configured as described in RFC 1001/1002. The value is specified as a single octet that identifies the client type as follows:

Value	Node Type
0x1	B-node
0x2	P-node
0x4	M-node
0x8	H-node

In the preceding chart, the notation 0x indicates a number in base-16 (hexadecimal).

The code for this option is 46. The length of this option is always 1:

Code	46
Len	1
Node type	option from above table

Address Discovery Protocols

6.7.3. DHCP-Specific Options

This section details the options that are specific to DHCP and are not usable by BOOTP. These options relate mostly to the dynamic nature of DHCP and its extended command syntax.

Requested IP Address

This option is used in a client request (`DHCPDISCOVER`) to allow the client to request that a particular IP address be assigned.

The code for this option is 50, and its length is 4:

Code	**50**
Len	**4**
Address 1	*IP address* (4 bytes)

IP Address Lease Time

This option is used in a client request (`DHCPDISCOVER` or `DHCPREQUEST`) to allow the client to request a lease time for the IP address. In a server reply (`DHCPOFFER`), a DHCP server uses this option to specify the lease time it is willing to offer.

The time is in units of seconds, and is specified as a 32-bit unsigned integer.

The code for this option is 51, and its length is 4:

Code	**51**
Len	**4**
Lease time	*integer* (4 bytes)

DHCP Message Type

The DHCP message type option is used to convey the type of the DHCP message. The code for this option is 53, and its length is 1. Legal values for this option are the following:

Value	*Message Type*
1	DHCPDISCOVER
2	DHCPOFFER
3	DHCPREQUEST
4	DHCPDECLINE
5	DHCPACK
6	DHCPNAK
7	DHCPRELEASE

The code is 53, and the length is 1:

```
Code        53
Len         1
Value       1–7
```

Server Identifier

This option is used in DHCPOFFER and DHCPREQUEST messages, and may optionally be included in the DHCPACK and DHCPNAK messages. DHCP servers include this option in the DHCPOFFER in order to allow the client to distinguish between lease offers. DHCP clients indicate which of several lease offers is being accepted by including this option in a DHCPREQUEST message.

The identifier is the IP address of the selected server.

The code for this option is 54, and its length is 4:

```
Code        54
Len         4
Address     IP address (4 bytes)
```

Renewal (T1) Time Value

This option specifies the time interval from address assignment until the client transitions to the RENEWING state.

The value is in units of seconds and is specified as a 32-bit unsigned integer.

The code for this option is 58, and its length is 4:

```
Code          58
Len           4
T1 interval   integer (4 byte)
```

Rebinding (T2) Time Value

This option specifies the time interval from address assignment until the client transitions to the REBINDING state.

The value is in units of seconds and is specified as a 32-bit unsigned integer.

The code for this option is 59, and its length is 4:

```
Code          59
Len           4
T2 interval   integer (4 byte)
```

Address Discovery Protocols

6.8. Summary

RARP covers only the basic need—obtaining an IP address. A RARP server holds a database containing MAC address–to–IP address mappings. RARP uses a static address allocation policy.

BOOTP is more useful for machines without local storage. A host needs more information than an IP address to boot. For instance, BOOTP provides the name of a server and a filename from which you obtain its boot program (typically via TFTP). BOOTP can also provide much more information, via *vendor extensions*. BOOTP uses a static address allocation policy.

DHCP is based upon BOOTP, but is much more flexible—proving manual, automatic, and dynamic address allocation policies (instead of just manual). DHCP uses the BOOTP message format, and the two protocols can interoperate. DHCP is the prevalent address discovery protocol for Microsoft operating systems.

The features of RARP, BOOTP, and DHCP are compared in the following table to show which is the most appropriate protocol for a given situation.

Table 6.4. Feature comparison of RARP, BOOTP, and DHCP.

Protocol	Manual	Automatic	Dynamic	IP	Bootfile address	Other info info
RARP	X			X		
BOOTP	X			X	X	via extensions
DHCP	X	X	X	X	X	via options

7.1. SLIP

7.2. PPP

7.3. IPv6 and PPP

7.4. Tunneling and Virtual Private Networks

7.5. Summary

Chapter

7

IP Over SLIP, PPP, and PPTP

by Robin Burk

Although TCP and IP together address several layers of the OSI protocol stack model, they do not operate alone. IP manages the transfer of datagrams, but depends upon lower-level data-link protocols and physical links for actual transfer of the information it has encapsulated.

The Internet Engineering Task Force (IETF) has adopted standards addressing the interaction of IP with some of the more common data-link protocols. These include NetBIOS, Ethernet LANs (IEEE 802.3), Token Ring LANs (IEEE 802.5), and HDLC (the data link under X.25). When IP runs in these environments, both the physical (layer 1) and data (layer 2) layers contain extensive and sophisticated error checking and transmission control, typically over a dedicated medium such as coax cable or fiber. Network Interface Cards (NICs) link the client computer to this backbone, and the transmission is handled as a digital stream from end to end.

However, many Internet and intranet users connect to a TCP/IP server using only a modem and a dial-up telephone line. Standard telephone lines operate on an analog basis only. This means that each dial-up computer communication session is treated as an end-to-end voice conversation, and the entire link must be switched as the data travels through the telephone system. Routed protocol stacks such as TCP/IP assume fixed connections between network nodes and switch individual data packets, not entire connections. As a result, there is a significant design conflict to overcome when using connection-oriented dial-up services to access a TCP/IP network.

This chapter describes the most common protocols used for dial-up access to TCP/IP servers, the Serial Line Interface Protocol (SLIP), and its successor, the Point-to-Point Protocol (PPP). Unlike SLIP, which was defined to provide a low-overhead, easily implemented terminal connection for low-volume transfers, PPP is an IETF standard that addresses such issues as error correction, diagnostics, and peer-to-peer negotiation.

We'll also take a look at the implications of running IPv6 over PPP. Finally, we'll look at how the TCP/IP protocol stack is being extended to provide secure remote access to non-TCP/IP corporate networks across the Internet.

7.1. SLIP

The Serial Line Interface Protocol was first developed in the early 1980s to provide a non-proprietary way for remote users to access open systems. Prior to the definition of SLIP, serial line protocols tended to be vendor specific. The 3Com UNET TCP/IP included the first implementation of SLIP. Shortly after, around 1984, Rick Adams implemented SLIP for Sun Microsystems workstations and version 4.2 Berkeley UNIX to support remote software development and systems administration, and then released the code for public use. Thereafter, SLIP was included in the reference standard version 4.3BSD release of UNIX and hence passed into wide use.

Unlike most protocols developed today, SLIP does not address error correction, compression, or Quality of Service. Instead, SLIP is limited to a simple packet-framing protocol. As a result, the two systems communicating via SLIP must know what higher protocols are being used. In addition, the system that initiates the call must know exactly how to reach the destination computer (that is, by telephone number for dial-up), because SLIP does not include any facility for logical or physical addressing as part of the protocol.

These limitations of SLIP were outweighed for years by the ease of implementing SLIP framing and by the low demands it places on system resources. As a result, SLIP quickly became available on early PCs and hence accelerated the adoption of TCP/IP and the growth of the Internet for personal use.

However, SLIP has never been adopted as an IETF standard. With the advent of inexpensive high-speed modems and increasing desire to transfer large blocks of information, such as graphics and multimedia files, SLIP has been overshadowed by standard protocols such as PPP. It is still supported by many Internet service providers, however. SLIP is described by RFC 1055.

7.1.1. The SLIP Protocol

SLIP defines two protocol-specific characters: END (octal 300, decimal 192) and ESC (octal 333, decimal 219).

> **NOTE** The SLIP ESC character is *not* the same as the ASCII Escape character. Don't confuse them! Throughout this section, ESC means the SLIP framing character.

Encapsulation of any datagram, including those passed to SLIP by IP, is a simple process:

1. Transmit an ESC character.

2. Transmit the datagram, character by character. Replace any byte that contains the same code as the ESC character with a 2-byte sequence of ESC and octal 335 (decimal 221). Replace any byte that contains the same code as the END character with a 2-byte sequence of ESC and octal 334 (decimal 220).

3. Transmit an END character.

The receiving system reverses this process, stripping off all ESC and END characters and restoring the original byte values inside the datagram.

IP Over SLIP, PPP, and PPTP

7.1.2. Limitations of SLIP

> **NOTE** As a serial line protocol, SLIP does not "think" in terms of packets or frames, only in terms of a sequence of individual characters. This approach dates back to the days when a terminal might not even display the character as a user typed it, but only when it was echoed back by the receiving computer and hence acknowledged.
>
> For this reason, and because SLIP was never formalized as a standard, there is no defined maximum packet size for SLIP. Most implementations conform to the Berkeley UNIX drivers, which stipulate a maximum of 1,006 characters, including the IP and transport protocol headers but excluding the SLIP framing characters.

Although it offers an easily implemented, low-overhead way to transfer information over a dial-up line, SLIP has several distinct shortcomings as a data-link protocol underneath IP and TCP. These include

- Addressing—Because SLIP does not transmit either the sender or the recipient's network address, this must be established at higher levels in the protocol stack. In practice, the sender dials into a server, which must perform an address translation and, usually, repackage the datagram for routing using another data-link protocol.

- *Type identification*—Because SLIP does not provide a header with protocol type information, a serial line must be dedicated to the SLIP session and cannot support other protocols or virtual sessions simultaneously. Significant potential bandwidth goes unused.

- *Compression*—The original SLIP protocol had no provision for compressing the datastream. Although RFC 1144 describes a Compressed SLIP, the resulting protocol still is inadequate for most current applications that make use of TCP/IP stacks for network communications.

7.2. PPP

Like SLIP, the Point-to-Point Protocol is intended for use over serial lines, including dial-up telephone connections. Unlike SLIP, however, PPP was designed from the ground up by the Network Working Group of the Internet Engineering Task Force, with an eye to supporting a wide variety of other protocols. The result is RFC 1548, adopted as Standard 51, and several supporting RFCs that address the use of PPP in specific environments.

7.2.1. Overview of PPP

PPP is designed to transport datagrams from multiple protocols over point-to-point links in a dynamically changing network. As a result, the design of PPP addresses three areas of functionality:

- Encapsulation—How PPP nests within the stack of protocols that make up the entire communications environment in a network

- Link Control Protocol—How PPP establishes, configures, and monitors the data-link connection

- Network Control Protocols—How PPP interacts with a variety of network-layer protocols, including IP

A key element in PPP is its dependence on configuration parameters and peer-to-peer negotiation to establish the specific ground rules under which a given PPP connection will be managed. Characteristics such as the maximum size of datagram that a given peer will accept, the authentication protocol (if any) that should be applied to datagrams originating from that sender, and compression schemes are all open to negotiation between the two systems being linked via PPP. This negotiation takes the form of a series of packet exchanges until both systems have agreed to the parameters under which the link will operate. (See Figures 7.1 and 7.2.)

PPP is intended for use in simple links that transport datagrams between two peers. PPP supports full-duplex lines with simultaneous bi-directional traffic. Unlike some link-level protocols, however, PPP assumes that datagrams arrive in the order they were sent. Within this limitation, PPP offers an easy connection protocol between hosts, bridges, routers, and client computers. It has become the protocol of choice for dial-up access of PCs and workstations with Internet servers and other TCP/IP hosts. In particular, the link-testing features of PPP enable more robust transfer of graphics, binary files, and World Wide Web pages to and from PCs and the public Internet or private intranets.

PPP Encapsulation

PPP allows the peers on a given link to establish the encapsulation to be used for datagrams. The default PPP encapsulation resembles HDLC framing in OSI-compliant X.25 networks. Frames transmitted via PPP have three fields, as shown in Figure 7.1.

Figure 7.1.
PPP frame format.

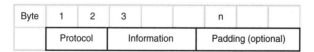

IP Over SLIP, PPP, and PPTP

The fields in the PPP frame are used as follows:

- Protocol field—Establishes the network protocol that sent the datagram and with regard to which it should be interpreted

- Information field—The packet received from the network-level protocol to be transmitted over the physical medium under the control of the PPP data-link software

- Padding—Optional bytes added to extend the length of the overall frame to any length needed by the receiving protocol stack

The Protocol Field

The Protocol field defaults to two bytes in length, but may optionally be shortened to one byte if both peers agree. It is transmitted in big-endian fashion—that is, most significant byte first.

In accordance with the ISO requirements for address fields, all protocol codes must be odd, and the least significant bit of the least significant byte must equal 0.

Protocol field values are defined in RFC 1700, "Assigned Numbers." The following values (given in hexadecimal) are of special interest when PPP is used along with TCP and IP:

0021	Internet Protocol
002d	Van Jacobson Compressed TCP/IP
002f	Van Jacobson Uncompressed TCP/IP
8021	Internet Protocol Control Protocol
c021	Link Control Protocol
c023	Password Authentication Protocol
c025	Link Quality Report
c223	Challenge Handshake Authentication Protocol

Other protocol codes that might be seen in a mixed network include

0029	AppleTalk
002b	Novell IPX
0035	Banyan VINES
003f	NetBIOS Framing
0041	Cisco Systems
004f	IP6 Header Compression
8029	AppleTalk Control Protocol
802b	Novell IPX Control Protocol
8031	Bridging NCP
8035	Banyan VINES Control Protocol
803f	NetBIOS Framing Control Protocol
8041	Cisco Systems Control Protocol
804f	IP6 Header Compression Control Protocol

Codes in the `0000–02ff` range identify network-layer protocols. Codes in the `8000–bfff` range identify packets belonging to Network Control Protocols. Codes in the `c000–ffff` range identify link-layer control protocols such as PPP's Link Control Protocol (LCP).

The Information Field

The Information field contains the packet sent down by the network level. As is usual in stacked protocols, PPP encapsulates the packet without in any way interpreting it. Unless otherwise established by peer-to-peer negotiation, the default Maximum Receive Unit length for the Information field is 1500 bytes, including any padding but excluding the Protocol field.

The Padding Field

The Padding field supports protocols and equipment that prefer (or require) that the overall packet length be extended to a 32-bit boundary or be otherwise fixed. Its use is not mandatory except as implied by configuration options negotiated between the peers in the link.

7.2.2. PPP Link Operation

> **WARNING** It's tempting to use the terms *message*, *datagram*, *packet*, and *frame* interchangeably. Properly speaking, however, each of these terms is used at a different level in the OSI protocol stack. Messages are exchanged between applications. The transport layer breaks large messages into datagrams before sending them to the network layer. The network layer may divide datagrams into multiple packets, if necessary, before passing them on to the data link layer.
>
> Some data link–layer protocols, such as HDLC, also divide packets into multiple frames, which then become the smallest unit of information that is routed and switched through a network. PPP does *not* do so, however, and the terms *datagram* and *packet* are often used to describe the unit of information transmitted by PPP. When establishing a multiprotocol network, be careful to ensure that the Maximum Receivable Unit (MRU) sizes for all peers are compatible, because PPP will simply pass on what was given to it by the upper protocol layers.

Before user information can be sent across a point-to-point link, each of the two endpoint systems comprising the desired link must test the link and negotiate an agreement regarding the parameters under which the link will operate.

These functions are performed using the Link Control Protocol. The PPP software on each peer (endpoint) system creates packets for this purpose, framed with the standard PPP protocol field. Once the link has been established, each peer authenticates the other if so requested. Finally, PPP must send Network Control Protocol packets to negotiate the network-layer protocol(s) that will be supported in this link.

Once the link has been established and both peers have agreed to support a given network-layer protocol on this link, datagrams from that network-layer protocol may be sent over the link.

The link will remain available for communications until it is explicitly closed. This can happen at the LCP or NCP level, either by administrator intervention or through a time-out interrupt. Specific network-layer protocols can be enabled and disabled on the link at any time, without affecting the capability of the PPP link to support other network-layer protocol transmissions.

Link Control Protocol

All Link Control Protocol packets are encapsulated within a PPP frame, with a Protocol field value of c021. Each LCP packet is contained in the Information field of a separate PPP datagram. However, some LCP packet types, such as the configuration packets, may themselves contain a variable number of data subfields.

The format of a Link Control Protocol packet within the Information field is shown in Figure 7.2.

Figure 7.2.

The Link Control Protocol packet format.

Byte	1	2	3	4	5			
	Code	Identi-fier	Length		Data			

LCP packet fields are used as follows:

- Code—One byte; identifies the type of packet

- Identifier—One byte; used to match replies and responses

- Length—Two bytes; specifies the length of the LCP packet (must not exceed the MRU of the link)

- Data—Zero or more bytes; contains code-specific information

The basic code types for LCP packets include the following:

01	Configure-Request
02	Configure-Ack
03	Configure-Nak
04	Configure-Reject
05	Terminate-Request
06	Terminate-Ack
07	Code-Reject
08	Protocol-Reject
09	Echo-Request
0a	Echo-Reply
0b	Discard-Request

LCP Packets—Negotiating Configuration

The Link Control Protocol software on each system must initiate Configure-Request packets stating the system's desired values for PPP operating parameters. Each endpoint system also responds to the configuration packets sent by the other, either accepting the proposed values or proposing alternate values for given parameters. When this exchange ends in mutual Configure-Ack packets, the link has been established.

Figure 7.3 shows half of a simple negotiation. Peer 1 notifies Peer 2 of the parameters under which it would prefer to communicate. Peer 2 responds by accepting those parameters.

Figure 7.3.

A simple PPP configuration negotiation.

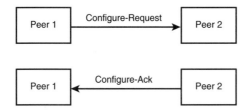

Figure 7.4 shows half of a more complex negotiation. Here Peer 1 again proposes the parameters under which it would like to communicate, but Peer 2 cannot support one or more of them. Therefore, Peer 2 responds with alternative values for one or more parameters and Peer 1 adopts these in a modified request, which is accepted by Peer 2.

Figure 7.4.

A more complex PPP configuration negotiation.

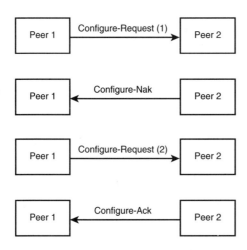

IP Over SLIP, PPP, and PPTP

Note that Figures 7.3 and 7.4 show only half of the negotiation process—namely, establishing the characteristics of communications initiated by Peer 1. A parallel negotiation process occurs from Peer 2 to Peer 1. Peer 2 does *not* need to communicate using the parameters established for Peer 1—it simply must get Peer 1's agreement to its own set of communications options.

To lower the overhead of this negotiation process, default values have been established in the PPP standard for all configuration options. A system that is willing to accept the default value for a given option need not propose that value. In the simplest case, both endpoint systems agree to all the defaults in their initial Configure-Request packets, and the negotiation completes with their mutual Configure-Ack packets.

The Data field for configuration packets contains option subfields. A Configure-Request packet contains a unique identifier chosen by the sender. The corresponding Configure-Ack or Configure-Nak repeats this identifier value during the negotiation.

If the recipient agrees to all the configuration option values proposed by the sender, the software process responds with a Configure-Ack message that repeats back all of the specified options and values. If the recipient cannot support one or more proposed option values, he responds with a Configure-Nak message whose data field contains ONLY the unacceptable options and their values.

Options that have no value subfields are Nak-ed using a Configure-Reject packet instead.

Most configuration options are *half-duplex*. That is, the sender is requesting the recipient to support this value in traffic initiated by the sender, but is not requiring the other party to send using the same parameters.

When the Data field of the LCP packet contains options, each option is given as a subfield of the Data field and itself contains three sub-subfields, as follows:

- Option Type—One byte

- Option Length—One byte; indicates the length of this option (including type, length, and data sub-subfields)

- Option Data—Zero or more bytes; type-dependent

A current list of defined option codes is given in RFC 1700. Among those most commonly seen when PPP supports TCP/IP are the following:

01	Maximum Receive Unit
03	Authentication Protocol
04	Quality Protocol
05	Magic Number
07	Protocol Field Compression
08	Address and Control Field Compression

RFC 1548 (Standard 51) gives detailed formats for the parameter data associated with each option code in a Configure-Request LCP packet, or in the corresponding Configure-Ack, Configure-Nak, or Configure-Reject response packets. Once the initiating peer has established a list of options under negotiation for its half-duplex side of the link operation, the responding peer must retain that order of options in responding Configure-Ack and Configure-Nak packets.

LCP Packets—Termination

TIP The Identifier field is used to provide a unique identity to a given exchange of packets during the course of a PPP connection's life, not to the peer who initiated the exchange. For instance, a PC negotiating a PPP link with an Internet server will establish an identifier in its initial Configure-Request packet. If the server agrees to support the PPP parameters that the PC is requesting, it will return a Configure-Ack packet *with the same identifier*. If the server does not agree, it will return a Configure-Nak packet, again with the same identifier. The PC must then initiate another Configure-Request packet, *continuing to use the original identifier*, that offers different values for the Nak-ed options. This negotiation process continues until the server has Ack-ed all options proposed by the PC.

While this is happening, the server has also sent out a Configure-Request packet with its own identifier and the option values that the server would prefer to see govern the transmissions it will make over the PPP connection. This negotiation is a different exchange and carries its own identifier.

Subsequent LCP exchanges, such as Terminate-Request and Terminate-Ack pairs, are assigned a new identifier, distinct from either identifier used to establish and configure the connection.

A separate parameter, the Magic Number, may be negotiated by a peer when the data link is established. The intent of the Magic Number is to uniquely identify this peer among all others who may be communicating with the other system. It is generally created using random or pseudo-random seeds so as to maximize the chance that it is truly unique during the connection's lifetime.

The Terminate-Request packet code is used when one of the two peers on a PPP link wants to shut down the data-link connection. The peer who receives a Terminate-Request packet must respond with a Terminate-Ack packet containing the same identifier.

When a peer receives a Terminate-Request packet, it means that the sender cannot continue operations over the link as things currently stand. The sender may be shutting down, the user may have ended the applications above the data link and requested that it be disconnected, or some other event may require that connection parameters be renegotiated.

The Data subfield of the LCP packet may be used to report status codes or other termination-related information. PPP does not interpret this field in Terminate-Request and Terminate-Ack packets.

LCP Packets—Code Reject

The PPP frame format and LCP packet formats do not provide a way to distinguish future versions of the protocol from the current standard. However, LCP does provide a way for one peer on a PPP connection to inform the other that the software process has received an LCP packet with an unknown code.

The Code-Reject packet must be sent whenever a peer on a PPP connection receives an

LCP packet with an unknown code. The Data field of the packet contains a copy of the full LCP packet being rejected, beginning with the Information field (that is, without any data link–layer headers, including the PPP frame) and truncated to comply with the recipient's established Maximum Receivable Unit length.

LCP Packets—Protocol Reject

If one peer on a PPP connection receives a PPP frame with an unknown protocol value, the frame must be rejected using an LCP Protocol-Reject packet. The Data field of the packet contains the Protocol and Information fields of the rejected frame, truncated to comply with the recipient's established Maximum Receivable Unit length. As with rejected LCP packets, data link–layer headers and framing characters are stripped from the rejected frame before it is inserted into the Protocol-Reject packet.

LCP Packets—Loopback Checking

PPP's Link Control Protocol includes a facility for looping back data link–layer traffic. Loopback checking is useful for checking link quality and performance, and as part of network checkout.

Either peer on a PPP connection may initiate Echo-Request packets. When an Echo-Request packet is received and the PPP connection is otherwise opened (that is, configuration negotiation has completed), the Echo-Reply must be transmitted in response.

The Echo-Request packet's Data field begins with a 4-byte Magic Number subfield. If the sender has not negotiated a successful Magic-Number configuration option, this subfield must contain zeros. If the option has been successfully negotiated, this subfield contains the unique Magic Number established for the sender at configuration time.

The Echo-Reply packet is sent in response to an Echo-Request, with a Data field including the Magic Number subfield and any subsequent data from the Echo-Response packet, truncated to comply with the MRU of the Echo-Request's sender. The Identifier field of the Echo-Reply matches that of the Echo-Response packet.

LCP Packets—Discard-Request

PPP includes a Discard-Request code in the Link Control Protocol. This allows a one-way exercise of the link, typically from the local PC to a remote server, in order to test the link. As with the Echo-Request, the Discard-Request packet includes a Magic Number subfield. The recipient must silently discard any packets received with the Discard-Request code, but may log receipt of the packet, along with any other information in the Data field, for use in network analysis.

7.3. IPv6 and PPP

The introduction of version 6 of the IP protocol was also the occasion for suggested revisions in the PPP protocol. In particular, there is an overlap of control functionality between parts of the Link Control Protocol specified in RFC 1548 (Standard 51) and the new features added to IP in IPv6.

As a result, RFC 2023 was submitted to the IETF standards track in October 1996. This RFC describes a new Network Control Protocol to be supported by PPP and some restrictions on standard PPP Link Control Protocol functions when supporting IPv6 as a network layer protocol.

7.3.1. PPP Operations with IPv6

Under IPv6, PPP retains its three areas of functionality: encapsulation, a Link Control Protocol, and support for Network Control Protocols.

PPP encapsulation does not change under IPv6. Hex code **0057** has been added to the list of protocol codes to indicate that the datagram originated from Internet Protocol version 6.

As with the original PPP, a Link Control Protocol is used to establish communications over a point-to-point connection, configure and test the data link, and negotiate optional link parameters. Once the link has been established, PPP then uses Network Control Protocol packets to establish the network layer protocols that will be supported over the link. Once a given NCP has been established, datagrams originating from that protocol can be exchanged. The link remains active until explicit LCP or NCP packets terminate the link (or use a given NCP across the link), or until external administrative or other events occur to interrupt link use.

7.3.2. Network Control Protocol under IPv6

The original PPP standard defines the Link Control Protocol (hex code **8021**) as the network control protocol associated with links that will carry IP (hex code **0021**) datagrams.

Similarly, RFC 2023 proposes a new Network Control Protocol called the IPv6 Control Protocol, or IPv6CP, to support the use of IPv6 over PPP links. Because IPv6 has been assigned the PPP Protocol field code of **0057**, IPv6CP is assigned the Protocol field code of **8057**.

IPv6CP parallels the original Link Control Protocol used with version 4 of IP, with a few exceptions.

IP Over SLIP, PPP, and PPTP

IPv6CP Packet Codes

The following are the only legal codes for IPv6CP packets:

01	Configure-Request
02	Configure-Ack
03	Configure-Nak
04	Configure-Reject
05	Terminate-Request
06	Terminate-Ack
07	Code-Reject

All others should be explicitly rejected using the Code-Reject packet response.

Note that the codes for loopback testing in standard PPP have been removed for PPP running under IPv6. As you will see in the following section, IPv6CP no longer uses the Magic Number concept, but instead provides a configuration option allowing negotiation of a unique interface token. This new option supports the autoconfiguration capabilities added to IPv6.

Configuration Options in IPv6CP

IPv6CP uses the same configuration option format defined in RFC 1548 for the Link Control Protocol, but specifies a separate set of options that may be negotiated. As with LCP, options that are not specifically requested to take given values are assumed to be requested to take the default value, and are not included in the option list presented in the Configure-Request packet.

The options initially defined for IPv6CP in RFC 2023 are assigned values as follows:

1	Interface-Token
2	IPv6-Compression-Protocol

The IPv6CP Interface-Token Option

IPv6CP supports the negotiation of a 32-bit interface token to be used in forming IPv6 addresses at the local end of the PPP link. This token *must* be unique within the link; in practice, this means that the two communicating systems must negotiate different tokens.

As with Magic Numbers in the standard PPP Link Control Protocol, each of the two peer systems negotiating a PPP link must begin by choosing a tentative Interface-Token, using as random a seed (or seeds) as possible so as to maximize the likelihood that the other system will choose a different Token value.

When a Configure-Request packet is received by a peer that supports this option, the peer will either Ack this Token value or suggest an alternative non-zero value in the responding Nak packet. If this option is requested of a peer that does not support it, Configure-Reject must be sent.

The Interface Token option type code is 1. It is followed in the Option subfield by the usual 1-byte Length field and the 4-byte Interface Token.

The IPv6CP Compression-Protocol Option

The Compression-Protocol option is used to signal that the requester can accept packets compressed in one of the IPv6 packet-compression protocols. The default is uncompressed packets. Note that enabling IPv6 compression for traffic originating in one direction on the link does not require that traffic originating in the other direction be compressed as well. For full-duplex compression, both peers must negotiate this option.

Also, note that this option enables IPv6 compression only. The Compression Control Protocol may be used to force compression on all datagrams passing over a PPP link, without regard to the network protocol through which the datagram was sent to the data link–layer software.

The IPv6 Compression-Protocol option type code is 2. It is followed in the Option subfield by the usual 1-byte Length field, a 2-byte Compression Protocol field, and optional additional data as required by the protocol specified.

At present, the only IPv6 compression protocol supported for this option is IPv6 Header Compression, specified by hexadecimal code 004f.

7.4. Tunneling and Virtual Private Networks

On the one hand, there are private data networks. For those who access them in the form of a corporate LAN or WAN, they provide secure, high-speed access to critical information. But these advantages disappear when key personnel must access information from a hotel or customer site while traveling.

On the other hand is the public TCP/IP–based Internet. It is easy to access from anywhere using SLIP or PPP dial-up. It is built on robust protocols. But it offers little or no security, and generally has no gateway into corporate networks.

And then there is the corporate intranet—an Internet developed for private use, complying with Internet standards for address allocation but either not registering allocated addresses or exploiting the IP address space set aside for multiple use. It is secure and flexible, but expensive and isolated from the larger Internet world.

IP Over SLIP, PPP, and PPTP

Surely there must be a way to have it all—to access corporate networks and data using the routed TCP/IP protocols and the backbone of the public Internet while maintaining security and the flexibility to establish connections from anywhere, anytime.

7.4.1.   Point-to-Point Tunneling Protocol—PPTP

In March 1996, a group of companies led by Microsoft Corporation announced their proposal for a new, Point-to-Point Tunneling Protocol (PPTP). The term *tunneling protocol* refers to a mechanism for passing PPP and other data link–layer communications across TCP/IP networks (such as the Internet) with the PPP packets preserved intact. Such tunnels allow PPP to carry other protocols, such as LAN/WAN standards like IPX and NetBEUI, across the Internet, thereby providing access to private corporate networks by simply dialing up through the Internet.

The approach originally proposed by the Microsoft-led consortium focused primarily on dialing into Windows NT–based servers across the Internet. The Point-to-Point Tunneling protocol envisions corporate users who dial into an ISP server using a PPP connection that might carry other protocols, including NetBEUI. The ISP server would then encapsulate the PPP packets using a modified version of the Generic Routing Encapsulation Protocol (GRE). These packets would be routed across the Internet to the appropriate domain server, which would strip off the GRE encapsulation and transfer the PPP packets to the corporate NT-based server designated as a gateway into the company's LAN/WAN.

PPTP offers several attractive features to corporate Information Systems professionals; it extends the life and usefulness of existing corporate network equipment, software, and training. The primary burden for upgrades to support PPTP would rest on Internet service providers, who would need both to implement PPTP on their servers and to administer the database of hard bindings between the ISP server and one or more corporate gateways.

However, PPTP does not include the robust capability of establishing a secure Virtual Private Network across the Internet, nor does it include support for ISDN connections to ISP servers. Finally, because it requires hard binding between the ISP server and the corporate gateway, it does not scale up easily for generalized or rapidly growing use.

As a result, the Internet Draft proposing PPTP did not advance to RFC status and expired in 1996.

7.4.2. Layer 2 Forwarding—L2F

In April of 1996, Cisco Systems proposed a different way to mesh private and public networks in the form of a new Layer 2 Forwarding protocol. L2F also describes a way to tunnel data link–layer protocols such as PPP across a TCP/IP network. However, as the leading supplier of Internet routers, Cisco took a significantly different approach than the PPTP proposal. Instead of focusing on the corporate network itself, Cisco proposed an extension of the data link layer and IP addressing schemes to provide dynamic ways to address corporate networks using standard Internet mechanisms.

L2F provides a means for logically separating the location of the server accessed by a dial-up user on the one hand and the location at which the protocol connection is terminated and gateway access is provided on the other hand. The result is a means by which IP addresses can be assigned to the corporate gateway server, in essence extending the IP addressing to these PPP dial-up links. L2F allows multiple ways for addresses to be assigned, and supports authentication and encryption to be applied at several levels in the TCP/IP stack.

Because it primarily approaches tunneling as a routing problem, L2F supports GRE, Frame Relay, and UDP as encapsulations, unlike PPTP. It imposes low-overhead requirements, especially as a packet travels across the public Internet, and allows (but does not require) authentication both at the network access server (ISP) and at the corporate or home gateway. More fundamentally, L2F is inherently bi-directional in its design philosophy, whereas PPTP primarily addresses remote access into corporate networks rather than access out from the corporate LAN/WAN to the public Internet.

7.4.3. Layer Two Tunneling Protocol—L2TP

Although the Microsoft consortium and Cisco each forwarded their proposals in the form of Internet Drafts, neither adequately addressed all the requirements for general protocol tunneling or for the creation of Virtual Private Networks across the public Internet. However, these commercial initiatives did result in a meeting among representatives from each of the companies and across the IETF in the context of the PPP Working Group.

The result was the December 1996 Internet Draft titled "Layer Two Tunneling Protocol, L2TP."

L2TP allows a multiprotocol PPP tunnel to be established across the Internet, thereby giving corporate users Virtual Private Network access to their LAN/WAN gateway servers. Encryption and authentication can be specified as desired at the Network Access Server, the corporate gateway server, or both.

IP Over SLIP, PPP, and PPTP

L2TP supports Internet access both to LANs/WANs in their native protocols and unregistered IP addresses. Although IPv6 significantly expands the universe of legal IP addresses, obtaining and administering suitable addresses for corporate networks is cumbersome and expensive. By merging the protocol-tunneling richness of PPTP with the addressing flexibility and lower overhead of L2F, L2TP promises to preserve current investments in corporate networks while greatly expanding corporate use of the TCP/IP–based public Internet. It is likely that adoption of some form of L2TP will also accelerate the deployment of private networks based on TCP/IP, because the protocol will most likely be supported in protocol stacks appropriate for deployment on private servers as well by ISPs.

The December 1996 draft proposal for L2TP describes the following features:

- Connection-oriented sessions initiated by PPP dial-up of L2TP-enabled NAS

- Quality of Service control resulting in a unique L2TP tunnel for users who require the QOS of a given medium

- Switched Virtual Circuits

- Support for multiple authentication regimes

- Facilities for resource-use accounting at both the ISP and the corporate gateway servers

Given the extensive industry participation in the December 1996 draft, the maturity of existing TCP/IP services, and the desire of large corporations to access private networks using the facilities and standards of the public Internet, it is reasonable to assume that some form of L2TP will see rapid adoption.

7.5. Summary

The advantages of a layered approach to communications protocols become especially apparent when routed, packet-oriented TCP/IP networks can make use of dial-up, connection-oriented, data link–layer protocols such as SLIP and PPP. PPP, in particular, is well designed to carry multiple protocols across dial-up lines and hand them off to routed internetworks. This flexibility is rapidly leading to the use of the public TCP/IP Internet to provide remote, secure access to private corporate LANs and WANs, thereby providing a technology integration and migration pathway that will accelerate distributed computing applications and the continued growth of multiprotocol networks.

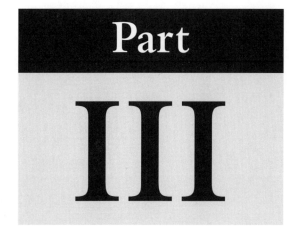

Part

III

Transport
Layer

Chapter

8

Quality of
Service

by Robin Burk

8.1. What Is Quality of
      Service?

8.2. The Transmisson
      Control Protocol (TCP)

8.3. The User Datagram
      Protocol (UDP)

8.4. Interactive Audio and
      Video over the
      Internet—The Real
      Time Protocol (RTP)

8.5. The Resource
      reSerVation Protocol
      (RSVP)

8.6. Multilink PPP

8.7. TCP/IP and Broadband
      Transmission Services

8.8. Summary

So far in this book we've been looking at the Internet Protocol (IP), its addressing/routing capabilities, and how it interacts with data link–layer protocols such as SLIP and PPP for dial-up access to TCP/IP server machines.

IP provides a flexible and powerful way to address and route user information across a network of networks, or an internetwork—the most famous being the public Internet. The capability of IP to accommodate varying complexities of network, as supported by the A, B, and C classes of network IDs, plus the translation services provided by the Domain Name System makes the Internet possible. The capability to layer IP above dial-up data-link protocols such as PPP extends the Internet down to the client desktop PC. Through commercial initiatives such as the Point-to-Point Tunneling Protocol (PPTP) and emerging IETF standards such as the Layer 2 Tunneling Protocol (L2TP), dial-in links can also use the IP and Internet for remote access to private LANs/WANs and even to hidden corporate intranets.

However, IP does not provide all the services and features that applications need for reliable, timely communications. Nor is IP well-suited to support data-intense, time-critical transmission of multimedia streams, especially for interactive response.

This chapter looks at the protocols that supplement IP in order to ensure the Quality of Service that is provided by the lower protocol layers to user applications. In addition, we'll dive below the data link–layer to consider new media capabilities and how TCP/IP stacks interact with Asynchronous Transfer Mode (ATM), Frame Relay, and Integrated Services Data Network (ISDN).

8.1. What Is Quality of Service

From the point of view of an application, all the protocol stack below the application interface, plus the physical data-link media, exist to provide a service—namely, to transmit and deliver information to another application executing on another computer.

Different protocol stacks and media will provide better or worse service to their clients. And different aspects of the data communications service will be of greater or lesser importance to any given application.

For instance, a character-based application such as Telnet wants communications to be moderately fast and reasonably reliable. Because Telnet transmits one character at a time, an effective network transmission rate much greater than human typing speed is not greatly important. If a character is lost in transmission, the user will be able to diagnose that fact and retype the command.

Digitized audio data absorbs much greater bandwidth, so effective transmission speed is important to audio applications. Although most digitizing and compression techniques allow modest bit loss without seriously degrading the information being transmitted, the size of audio data transmissions alone makes reliability a second concern. In addition, audio files logically take the form of long streams of sequenced data rather than the discrete, independent exchanges generated during a Telnet session. As a result, an audio application would prefer to have the logical equivalent of a dedicated circuit during data transmission.

Transactions such as credit card charges generate small amounts of data, but require strong security, high data integrity, and good-to-excellent delivery speed. In general, individual transactions are independent of one another and do not require the continuing presence of a virtual circuit for effective communications.

The quality of service provided by a communications pathway can be measured in terms of several different characteristics, including the following:

- Average throughput

- Response to congestion (flow control)

- Reliability of delivery

- Security

As you'll see, the original transport protocols—Transmission Control Protocol (TCP) and User Datagram Protocol (UDP)—give different emphases to each of these factors. Neither, however, is particularly well-suited to transport audio, video, or even large static graphics files. As a result, additional protocols have been proposed at both the transport, data link, and media access layers to meet the growing demand for rapid transmission of large multimedia data streams. This chapter covers several of these emerging technologies and how they interact with one another.

8.2. The Transmission Control Protocol (TCP)

TCP is the original transport layer protocol associated with IP. Developed as part of the Department of Defense Advanced Research Projects Agency's (DARPA's) ARPANET, TCP was revised and refined over a number of years before the final protocol definition was submitted as RFC 793 and adopted as Std 7 by the IETF.

From its earliest beginnings, TCP was designed to ensure robust delivery of information despite potential unreliability (or even partial unavailability) of particular communications paths or bandwidths.

Quality of Service

The original ARPANET was implemented to connect researchers from across the country, without regard to the proprietary operating systems and data communications protocols more commonly in use at the time. As a result, TCP was designed to facilitate open systems interconnect, adapting dynamically to differing host transmission capabilities and to data congestion in the network.

However, DARPA had a second reason for sponsoring the development of the ARPANET: to prototype a network that could allow military command, control, and tactical computers to communicate in the event that nuclear war, natural disasters, or other catastrophes disrupted normal telephone service and destroyed major sections of the telephone infrastructure.

This requirement is met in various levels of the protocol stack. IP and the routers that support it respond dynamically to changes in the physical topology of the public internetwork, dynamically exchanging information regarding network topology and optimal route segments. The transport layer, specifically TCP, was given the job of managing data flow rates in response to data congestion on the network or at the recipient host, although it is not directly concerned with actual throughput or network speed. In addition, TCP is responsible for ensuring the reliability of information delivery. As a connection-oriented protocol, TCP ensures that segments of information arrive in the proper order; however, it is not an optimal method for delivering large streams of information, nor does it provide more than minimal security or priority control mechanisms.

> **TIP**   RFC 793, which defines the TCP protocol, is supplemented by several other Requests for Comment. In particular, RFC 1700 (Assigned Numbers) and RFC 1122 (Host Requirements) specify additional field values for connection options, dynamic flow control algorithms, and window management constraints.

This chapter looks at TCP specifically from the vantage point of its approach to ensuring Quality of Service to the applications whose information it agrees to transport.

8.2.1. TCP Basic Concepts: Multiplexing, Reliability, and Flow Control

As a transport layer protocol, TCP accepts message information from application programs, divides it into multiple segments if necessary, and encapsulates each segment into a datagram. Each datagram is passed to the network layer protocol (usually IP) for transmission and routing. The receiver's TCP handler acknowledges each datagram as it is successfully received; datagrams that are not acknowledged are retransmitted. The receiver's TCP reassembles the message information and passes it to the appropriate application program when it has been received in its entirety.

Before datagrams are sent to a target machine, sender and receiver must negotiate to establish a temporary logical connection. This connection will typically stay open during an extended session corresponding to the period during which a user interacts with the application software.

The sender TCP process receives an entire information message from the application and will break it into datagrams at its leisure, encapsulate them, and hand them off to the network layer (IP) and lower-level protocols for delivery. As a result, the sender TCP process has little or no need to be concerned regarding the rate at which information is transmitted. The receiver, however, must ensure adequate buffer space for incoming datagrams and for reassembling the application message. Therefore, TCP provides the receiver with a mechanism for flow control over the connection. Flow control is accomplished dynamically by means of a window parameter, returned with each acknowledgment of a received datagram. The window parameter specifies the number of bytes that the sender may transmit before receiving additional permission. The sender TCP process compares this parameter to the number of bytes sent after the datagram being acknowledged and determines how much additional information, if any, can be sent at this moment. If the receiver's window size has been absorbed by datagrams in transit, the sender must wait until the receiver advertises a non-zero window size before sending more datagrams.

TCP does not assume that underlying protocols guarantee datagram delivery. Explicit acknowledgments must be received for outstanding datagrams. If transmitted datagrams are not acknowledged in a timely manner, the sending TCP process retransmits the datagrams and waits for a new acknowledgment to arrive.

To reduce network traffic, especially with regard to routing headers and other overhead data, TCP embeds control information such as datagram acknowledgment and window parameter values with the actual headers for datagram delivery. Figure 8.1 shows a conceptual model for the way in which TCP combines application datagrams with transport-level control information for efficient use of transmission resources.

Figure 8.1.
TCP nests transport control information within user datagram headers for efficient use of transmission resources.

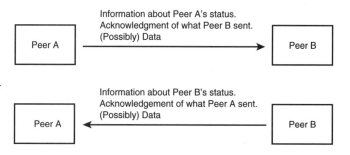

Quality of Service

8.2.2. TCP Datagram Format

TCP does not interact directly with computer users. That is the role of application-layer programs in the protocol stack.

Applications can generate message information in a wide variety of formats and sizes in order to serve a variety of purposes. A Web browser, for instance, will generate a request for the hypertext page associated with a given Universal Resource Locator (URL). The HTTP script might include pointers to graphics files, Java applets, or ActiveX controls or video clips, in which case the browser will also send requests to retrieve those files as well. At the other end of the connection, the computer that hosts the domain within which the Web page resides will respond by sending back the HTTP script and the various files as they are requested.

The TCP software on each of these machines must be capable of accommodating this wide variety of message content as efficiently as possible. One step in this process is to divide large messages into multiple segments of manageable size, then encapsulate each segment with a header. This allows the receiver to reconstruct the original message out of a series of segment datagrams.

Figure 8.2 shows the format of the TCP datagram header.

Figure 8.2.
The TCP datagram header.

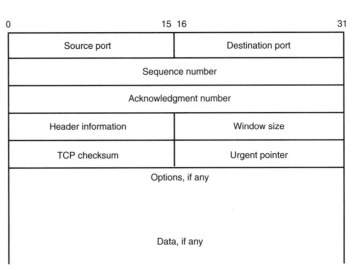

The header fields contain the following information:

- Source—A 2-byte port number assigned on the sending computer to the application program that passed this message to TCP for transmission.

- Destination—A 2-byte port number assigned on the receiving computer to the destination application for this message.

- Sequence—A 4-byte number identifying the starting byte number of this segment within the application message; if the SYN flag is set, this field contains the initial sequence number being forced and the contents of the Data field start with message byte Sequence+1.

- Acknowledgment—A 4-byte field specifying the next sequence number the sender expects to receive; valid only if the ACK flag is set.

- Header information—A 2-byte field containing the following subfields:

  > bits 0-3 = offset, the length of the TCP header in 32-bit words
  > bits 4-9 = reserved
  > bit 10 = URG flag
  > bit 11 = ACK flag
  > bit 12 = PSH flag
  > bit 13 = RST flag
  > bit 14 = SYN flag
  > bit 15 = FIN flag

- Window—A 2-byte field specifying the number of segment bytes the sender is willing to receive subsequent to the datagram being acknowledged.

- Checksum—A 2-byte TCP-type checksum (16-bit half-words, one's complement, summed).

- Urgent—A 2-byte pointer to the last byte within the segment which is urgent and should be expedited in delivery; valid only if the URG flag is set.

- Options—An optional, variable-length field containing other TCP parameters; most commonly used in negotiating a connection.

- Padding—An optional, variable-length field that is used to force the segment data onto a 32-bit word boundary.

- Data—The data segment being transmitted; begins at the 32-bit word offset specified in the Offset field.

The control flags convey the following information shown in Table 8.1.

Table 8.1. TCP header control flags.

Flag	Meaning If Set
URG	Contents of the Urgent field are valid
ACK	Contents of the Acknowledgment field are valid

Quality of Service

continues

Table 8.1. Continued.

Flag	Meaning If Set
PSH	Push function; this data must be pushed through to the receiving application immediately
RST	Reset the connection
SYN	Synchronize sequence numbers
FIN	Final data from the sender

Most of the flag meanings are self-evident. The PSH flag is used to force accumulated segments to be concatenated and delivered to the receiving application. It effectively signals the end of a given information message. The SYN, RST, and FIN flags are used in negotiating connections and managing connection integrity. See the "TCP Multiplexing and Connection Management" section for further discussion.

8.2.3. TCP Header Options and Maximum Segment Size

In addition to the fixed fields, the TCP header can convey optional information in the Option field. The most common use of options is during connection negotiation.

The major TCP header option that is specified when the connection is established is the *maximum segment size* (MSS). MSS is the maximum number of data bytes that the sending TCP process can ever receive in a given datagram. Senders may transmit datagrams with segments that are smaller than the receiver's MSS, but they may not exceed it.

A TCP header may include bytes between the Urgent Pointer field and the Data field. These may, but need not, contain a list of one or more option parameters. (Bytes in this area might simply be padding required to force the Data field onto a 32-bit boundary. Padding will also follow an options list, if necessary.) The receiving TCP process examines the first byte within a potential Option field and interprets it as follows:

- Value = 0 implies end of option list

- Value = 1 implies no operation

- Value = 2 implies that the next four bytes contain the sender's MSS

- Value > 2 implies some other TCP option, as documented in RFC 1700

The default MSS value is 536 bytes, and all TCP processes must be able to accept a segment at least this large. For efficient network operation, MSS should be as large as possible without causing IP fragmentation. Typically, the MSS is set to the Maximum Transmission Unit (MTU) size of the pathway, minus 40 bytes or so to account for lower-level encapsulation. Where the MTU is not known, a path MTU discovery mechanism should be used before a value other than the default MSS is specified.

8.2.4. TCP Multiplexing and Connection Management

> **NOTE**
>
> A socket can support multiple connections at once. For instance, an FTP process on a server might be sending files across multiple connections. Where the receiving computer on the Internet is a gateway providing dial-up access from PCs, the sending FTP process could participate in several different connections with that server at the same time, corresponding to several dial-up users. More commonly, the FTP process would be transmitting files over connections to a variety of Internet hosts.

IP assigns a network/host address to a given computer as a whole. It is not uncommon, however, for multiple applications on a given computer to simultaneously desire TCP/IP transmission or reception services, particularly if the computer is a server accessed by multiple dial-up connections or if it serves as the Internet gateway for a LAN or WAN.

To support multiple simultaneous communications sessions, TCP further qualifies IP addresses with port numbers. For most purposes, a port signifies a given application process on that computer. The combination of an IP address and port constitute a socket. A pair of sockets defines a given TCP connection.

Initiating the Connection

Before two application processes can communicate across a network using TCP/IP, they must each indicate to the TCP process on their own host that they are ready to send and/or receive information. A process that wants to initiate or accept connections must provide the TCP process with a port number that is unique, at that time, on that machine. Certain network-oriented applications have been assigned specific Well Known Port Numbers. Other applications must first request a port assignment from the TCP process.

An application process that is ready to initiate a connection must also provide the TCP process with a socket identifier for the receiver. If the receiving application does *not* have a permanently assigned port, the initial connection will be made to a process on the receiver machine, which will identify and return the desired port.

Quality of Service

Well Known Port Numbers

The Internet Assigned Numbers Authority (IANA) has the responsibility for assigning fixed values for various parameters in Internet-related protocols, including TCP. These parameter values are documented in RFC 1700 (Std 2) and include port numbers that are reserved for the use of key applications and other processes on host machines.

Port numbers ranging from 0 to 1023 (decimal) are managed by IANA as Well Known Port Numbers. These are port assignments that may be assumed by TCP processes and applications anywhere on the Internet, as they are incorporated in an IETF standard.

> **TIP** Many standard UNIX processes have also been assigned Well Known Port Numbers. If you are operating in an UNIX environment or managing a network that accesses a UNIX-based server, you will find that RFC 1700 is a useful aid for interpreting TCP dumps and traces.
>
> Similarly, Well Known Port Numbers have been assigned to many of the most common proprietary LAN/WAN protocols, widely-used mainframe middleware, and other applications that might be active in your computing environment. A quick scan of both the Well Known Ports and the reserved numbers can give you a valuable insight into the mechanisms that make your corporate intranet or your network's use of the public Internet possible.

Ports 1024–65535 are not officially assigned to application processes. Many port numbers in this range, however, are unofficially reserved for use by proprietary network management packages and other specific uses. RFC 1700 also documents these reserved numbers, which do not carry the force of an IETF standard.

Table 8.2 shows some of the most commonly used Well Known Port Numbers. Where a given application process can be contacted using more than one transport layer protocol (for instance, TCP and UDP), the same port number is used by either protocol for that purpose.

By convention, ports are specified as decimal numbers.

Table 8.2. Some Well Known Port Numbers.

Keyword	Port	Assigned To
tcpmux	1	TCP Port Service Multiplexer
echo	7	Echo
discard	9	Discard
ftp-data	20	File Transfer [Default Data]
ftp	21	File Transfer [Control]
telnet	23	Telnet
rlp	39	Resource Location Protocol
nameserver	42	Host Name Server
nicname	43	Who Is

Keyword	Port	Assigned To
domain	53	Domain Name Server
sql*net	66	Oracle SQL*NET
gopher	70	Gopher
finger	79	Finger
www-http	80	World Wide Web HTTP
hostname	101	NIC Host Name Server
snagas	108	SNA Gateway Access Server
pop3	110	Post Office Protocol, version 3
sunrpc	111	SUN Remote Procedure Call
auth	113	Authentication Service
sqlserv	118	SQL
cisco-fna	130	Cisco FNATIVE
cisco-tna	131	Cisco TNATIVE
cisco-sys	132	Cisco SYSMAINT
netbios-ns	137	NetBIOS Name Service
netbios-dgm	138	NetBIOS Datagram Service
netbios-ssn	139	NetBIOS Session Service
sql-net	150	SQL-NET
snmp	161	SNMP
snmptrap	162	SNMPTRAP
irc	194	Internet Relay Chat Protocol
dls	197	Directory Location Service
dls-mon	198	Directory Location Service Monitor
at-rtmp	201	AppleTalk Routing Maintenance
at-nbp	202	AppleTalk Name Binding
at-zis	206	AppleTalk Zone Information
ipx	213	IPX
ipcserver	600	Sun IPC server
doom	666	doom Id Software

Quality of Service

Negotiating the TCP Connection

Once an application process has asked TCP to establish a connection to a specific remote socket, the TCP process attempts to negotiate the connection. The negotiation process takes the form of an exchange of datagrams, often called the *three-way handshake*. Typically, one host TCP initiates a negotiation and the receiver responds; however, the protocol also supports a case where both hosts simultaneously attempt to start the negotiation process.

The SYN flag in a datagram header is used to signal to the receiver that a new connection is being negotiated. In effect, the presence of this flag indicates a new information message or user session at the application layer. As you'll see in the "TCP Timers and the Reset Flag" section, connections stay open unless specifically closed by the application, by lower-layer protocols, or by timing out. Good application design, however, suggests that connections be closed whenever there is likely to be an indeterminate time until additional messages need to be sent or when it is likely that the socket or socket-related resources within the TCP process (local or remote) would be in demand by other applications.

Figure 8.3 shows a simple three-way handshake.

Figure 8.3.

Three-way handshake negotiating a new TCP connection.

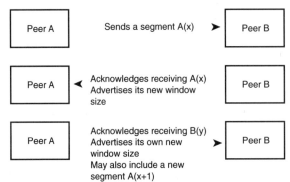

Negotiating a new TCP connection requires a minimum of three datagrams. Here Peer A wants to establish a connection with an application process on Peer B. Setting the SYN flag unambiguously tells the TCP process on Peer B that this is a new connection and that the sequence field indicates the "zero" counter of bytes in a new message—that is, the first data byte will be considered to be byte number Sequence+1.

When Peer B receives a SYN header, it also discards any remaining datagrams it has stored in buffers (or which might arrive after the SYN header) when those datagrams continue the sequence number otherwise expected over a previous connection to the same socket. Otherwise, there might be confusion regarding which application process is the intended recipient of the datagrams.

By choosing the initial sequence offset carefully to ensure no overlap with datagrams that might still be floating around the network, the sending TCP software ensures that only valid segments are concatenated by the receiving TCP process and passed on to the appropriate application. This is a central TCP mechanism that ensures reliability and integrity of message delivery. RFC 793 specifies that the initial sequence number offered during connection negotiation should be based on a 4-microsecond clock tick to ensure uniqueness from one connection to another between the same sockets.

NOTE	An acknowledgment value of n means that all bytes up to, but not including, the nth byte of the information message have been received. Therefore, the receiver is expecting a segment beginning with the nth byte next. However, if a segment with a sequence number greater than n is received, it will be stored in a buffer awaiting the prior segment *if it falls within the current window range for the receiver.*

Assuming the prior segment is delivered in time, both segments can be acknowledged with a single TCP header and thus unnecessary retransmittals can be avoided. It is possible that the timing will work out in such a way that both of these segments are retransmitted, in which case TCP works fine—there is merely a local inefficiency in using transmission resources. This occasional inefficiency is counterbalanced by the greater inefficiencies that would be introduced if each segment were required to be transmitted and acknowledged before a second were sent.

When Peer B receives a datagram with a SYN header, it acknowledges the SYN by setting the ACK flag and placing the sequence number of the next expected byte into the acknowledgment field. If the SYN header was sent with no segment data, this will be Peer A's segment value, incremented by 1. However, it is quite legal for Peer A to have included the first segment of data for this new connection along with the SYN header. In this case, the acknowledgment field will contain the value segment+n+1, where n equals the length of the first segment included along with the SYN header sent by Peer A.

In addition to acknowledging the new segment sequence initiated by Peer A, Peer B must also specify his own starting sequence number. As with Peer A, Peer B must ensure that the value he specifies allows Peer A to discard invalid datagrams that might arrive later or that might be lingering in buffers. However, there is no need for Peer B's segment value to be related to that of Peer A.

8.2.5. Flow Control—The TCP Window

Each peer on a TCP connection has the ability to control the flow of data into its receiving buffers. The mechanism for accomplishing flow control is a TCP header parameter called the *window*.

The window is used in conjunction with the acknowledgment parameter to provide ongoing feedback from the receiver to the sender. The acknowledgment field identifies the next segment that the receiver expects to receive; by implication, all previous segments have been successfully received and concatenated by the receiving TCP process. The window field identifies the maximum additional bytes the receiving TCP process is able to accept at the time of acknowledgment.

Quality of Service

The sender is not obligated to wait for acknowledgment of one segment before transmitting one or more additional segments. If it transmits too much data, however, there is a risk that some segments will be passively rejected by the receiving process. The only way the sender can tell whether this has happened is by the fact that it never receives an acknowledgment for that segment.

TCP processes set a timer for each segment they encapsulate into a datagram and transmit. If the timer expires before an acknowledgment is received for that segment, the process will assume that that segment must be retransmitted. It is likely that any additional unacknowledged segments will need to be retransmitted as well. If, however, segments were received out of order, retransmitting a single segment may result in the acknowledgment of multiple segments at once.

Congestion Management

> **TIP**   Remember that TCP is a full-duplex transport protocol. This means that each peer on a TCP connection can be both receiver and sender at the same time.
>
> Therefore, at any given moment there are *two* current window values, one for each direction of transmission.

Although a receiver has advertised its capability to receive a given amount of data, TCP processes do not send the full window count of segment data bytes. Instead, TCP takes into account the likelihood that there is congestion on the network.

An efficient TCP process will follow several practices to adjust transmission volume and timing in response to network traffic. The TCP sender constrains the actual number of transmitted, unacknowledged bytes to less than the receiver's current advertised window. This proportion is increased incrementally each time a segment is acknowledged until a segment times out. At this point, a potential state of congestion is diagnosed and the TCP process slows segment transmission. When segments are once again regularly acknowledged without timeout, the internal congestion window is slowly increased again.

Throttling transmission when congestion is suspected is the most globally efficient practice that can be adopted. Congestion typically takes the form of queues on multiple nodes at the IP or data-link level. All these intermediate queues must clear before retransmissions at multiple protocol layers can die down. Therefore, the higher in the protocol stack we go, the more conservative the approach to congestion management.

This is especially important at the transport layer, with a protocol like TCP. Unlike the lower-layer protocols, TCP deals with logical connections that extend over substantial time and potentially substantial transmission volume (from the perspective of equipment capabilities). Therefore, TCP implementations should take a wide view of optimality, maximizing overall throughput of the network layers beneath it as well as of its own simplicity of logic.

> **TIP** Understanding the way TCP responds dynamically to perceived network congestion will help you to make sense of the varying segment sizes and transmission rates you might see in a TCP dump.

Although RFC 793 spells out a detailed state-transition description of TCP processing, some parameters were left open to implementation choice. As TCP/IP stacks were ported to a variety of operating and hardware environments, and use of TCP/IP internetworks spread beyond the original academic ARPANET community, the IETF found it useful to provide more definitive guidance regarding implementation parameters within both the IP and TCP layers of software.

The resulting RFC 1222 specifies implementation details for TCP processes, including the rate and mechanisms by which a TCP sender shall dynamically adjust transmission in response to network congestion.

Silly Window Syndrome and Nagle's Algorithm

Window-based flow control schemes can suffer from silly window syndrome. This occurs when sender and receiver interact in such a way as to generate more and more datagrams with smaller and smaller amounts of segment data in them.

Either sender or receiver can trigger a silly window syndrome on one half-duplex side of a TCP link. A receiver who acknowledges each datagram as it is received may find itself advertising small window sizes when buffers are nearly full. A sender might also transmit small data segments rather than wait for additional message information from the application process. For instance, a TCP process serving a Telnet application might transmit each character as it is received from the Telnet software, rather than buffer them until a carriage return or other control character is identified or until the Telnet process requests that all data be pushed to the receiver.

In either case, the result is likely to be an exchange in which the overhead of protocol encapsulation far outweighs the actual application information being transmitted. Once a peer advertises a small window value, subsequent transmissions will be limited to that segment size until the connection ends or some other anomaly occurs.

If the sending application ever stops generating information to be transmitted, the receiver will eventually catch up, empty its buffers, and advertise large window space again. However, in large file transfers, the volume of data to be transmitted means that silly window syndrome, if allowed to occur and persist, might absorb as much as 80% or more of the connection's bandwidth into overhead.

Most TCP/IP stacks prevent silly window syndrome by implementing Nagle's algorithm, which prescribes the following behavior:

- Only one tinygram (segment consisting of one or a few characters) can be outstanding on a connection at any given time

- The receiver must not acknowledge the tinygram until it can advertise a window at least as large as the smaller of a half of its total buffer space *or* its full MSS

- The sender must not transmit until it can send a full-sized (MSS) segment, it can send a half or more of the largest window ever advertised by the recipient, or no acknowledgments are outstanding

The net effect of these constraints is to restore efficiently large segment sizes to the connection, while minimizing the need to retransmit segments.

RFC 1122 requires that all TCP implementations apply Nagle's algorithm in controlling data flow. However, all TCP implementations must also provide a way to disable the application of these rules under certain circumstances.

If silly window syndrome has the potential to seriously degrade network performance, why not apply the Nagle algorithm at all times? The answer lies in the fact that TCP does not originate the data segments it transports, but serves higher-layer applications. Applied strictly, the algorithm overrides an application's capability to push information through the connection at appropriate points, such as the completion of a file transfer or the submission of a small user command that must be processed before any other action may be taken by the application. Abnormal conditions, such as connection timeout, are also not addressed by the algorithm.

8.2.6. TCP Timers and the Reset Flag

TCP processes use timing mechanisms for several important functions.

It's already been mentioned that each transmission of a datagram sets a timer. If the timer expires before acknowledgment for the datagram is received, that datagram must be retransmitted.

In addition, each TCP/IP implementation has a maximum segment lifetime (MSL) value, typically ranging from 30 seconds to 2 minutes. The MSL value is used to discard datagrams that may remain within the network after a connection has been closed. This prevents old datagrams from being delivered when a new incarnation of the connection is established.

When a receiver's buffers fill up, it advertises a window size of 0 bytes. Once buffers free up, it advertises the availability of window space again. If, however, this advertisement were to be lost, the TCP connection would be deadlocked because nondata segments are not themselves acknowledged. To avoid such deadlock, the sender sets a *persist timer*, which causes the sender to periodically query the receiver for its window size.

TCP connections remain established until explicitly terminated by any of several means. As a result, a TCP connection can go idle, but will continue to remain in force. Some server-based applications such as Telnet want to monitor the state of the other peer on the connection so that server resources are not tied up waiting for a client process that has, in fact, crashed or otherwise become inactive. Many implementations of TCP include a *keepalive timer*, which causes the server to periodically probe the client to ensure that the connection should in fact continue to remain established. If the client does not respond to the probe, the server can wind down the connection cleanly. If the client receives the probe after a reboot, it sends an RST (reset) datagram to the server.

A reset will also be sent in response to any of the following conditions:

- When a connection request is made to a port on which no process is listening (invalid socket)

- When a connection is aborted without orderly release

- When one direction of the connection has closed without informing the other peer (half-open connection)

8.2.7. Terminating a TCP Connection

The normal way to terminate a connection is through an orderly release, signaled by sending a datagram with the `FIN` flag set.

The proper response on the part of the receiver is to wrap up processing and respond with a `FIN` in the other direction.

However, a peer can abort a connection by sending an RST instead. This is called an *abortive release*, and is used to inform the receiver that queued data may be invalid. The receiving application may then assume that the sending application crashed or otherwise terminated in an unorderly fashion, and take whatever steps may be appropriate in response.

8.2.8. T/TCP and Other TCP Extensions

TCP was designed to transport data streams over IP networks. It establishes connections that persist over some time. In order to administer these connections and ensure reliable delivery, TCP encapsulates message segments in information-rich headers and requires three-way handshakes.

UDP is connectionless and unreliable. It is particularly well-suited to the transport of short, occasional messages.

Neither TCP nor UDP is well-suited to transport a class of messages that is central to many corporate information systems, namely *transactions*. A transaction-oriented application sends relatively short messages, often of fixed or semifixed length, but requires high levels of reliability. If the standard TCP protocol were to be used to transport database transactions, the relatively long wait between transactions would require a connection to be established, the transaction content sent, and the connection terminated for each transaction—a minimum of 10 datagrams. In addition to imposing expensive overhead, this approach would be constrained by a requirement that TCP processes limit the number of connections that may be established to a maximum of 268 per second, far fewer than the number of transactions than would be required, for instance, by a mainframe computer supporting hundreds of automatic teller machines owned by a major bank.

As a result, RFC 1379 was adopted. It defines a minimized version of TCP to streamline transaction processing over TCP/IP networks. T/TCP has not yet achieved widespread use, however, perhaps because corporations require more data security than has been available over the public Internet. With the rise of private intranets and growing availability of authentication and encryption mechanisms, T/TCP may extend the useful life of existing mainframe database applications without requiring a re-engineering into client/server application architectures.

TCP has also been extended through the definition of additional options, including compression mechanisms, timestamping to extend sequence numbers, and support for vendor-specific application requirements. RFC 1700 documents the options that have been defined for standard use, along with the specific RFC that provides comprehensive information for each optional capability.

8.3. The User Datagram Protocol (UDP)

TCP provides a reliable, connection-oriented datastream transport capability over IP or other network layer protocols. In order to ensure this service, the TCP protocol encapsulates message segments in an information-rich header and requires extensive handshaking between sender and receiver.

There is a need, however, for some applications to exchange small amounts of information regularly. The Internet Name Server, the Trivial File Transfer, and similar application processes require efficient transfer of short messages on a transaction (datagram) basis at irregular intervals. These applications operate most efficiently if the overhead associated with a given transfer is minimized. In exchange, they can tolerate the possibility of unreliable transport or of duplicate copies of a message being delivered.

This need is met by UDP, which minimizes the protocol mechanism required for message delivery by tightly coupling its operations with IP (only) and by foregoing any acknowledgment activity.

8.3.1. UDP Header Format

UDP encapsulates the application message with a header. The format for a UDP header is shown in Figure 8.4.

Figure 8.4.
The UDP header format.

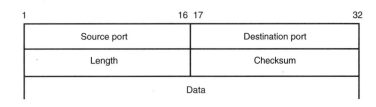

The header fields contain the following information:

- Source—An optional 2-byte port number assigned on the sending computer to the application program that passed this message to UDP for transmission; if unused, it contains zeros.

- Destination—An optional 2-byte port number assigned on the receiving computer to the destination application for this message; if unused, it contains zeros.

- Length—A 2-byte field specifying the number of bytes in this datagram, including the UDP header itself; minimum value = 8.

- Checksum—A 2-byte TCP-type checksum (16-bit half-words, one's complement, summed); value = 0 implies no checksum was generated.

- Data—The data segment being transmitted; word or half-word boundaries are not forced with padding.

8.3.2. UDP and the IP Pseudoheader

UDP prefixes its encapsulated message with a short IP header. This prefixed datagram is then passed to IP, which computes a checksum and transmits it.

The format of the pseudoheader is given in Figure 8.5.

Figure 8.5.
The UDP pseudoheader format.

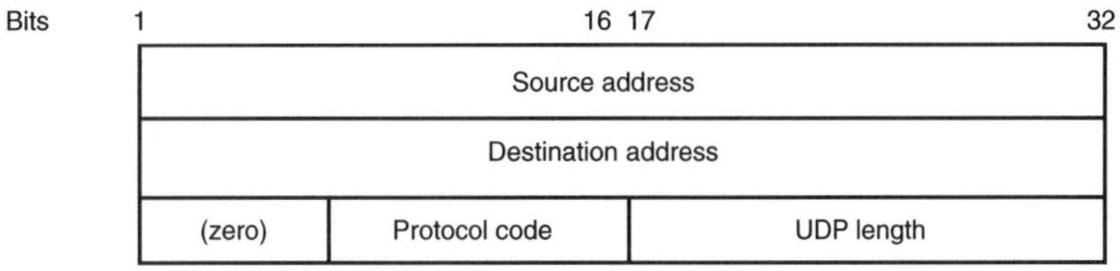

Bits 1	16 17	32
Source address		
Destination address		
(zero)	Protocol code	UDP length

Quality of Service

The header fields contain the following information:

- Source—A 32-bit standard IP address for the sender

- Destination—A 32-bit standard IP address for the receiver

- Protocol—The standard IP code designating the datagram as having originated from UPD; value = 17 (decimal)

- UPD length—A count of the bytes of the UDP datagram, including header

The IP process calculates an Internet header checksum, then transmits the datagram as addressed by UDP. In most cases, the destination IP address must be provided to UDP by the sending application.

8.4. Interactive Audio and Video over the Internet—The Real Time Protocol (RTP)

In May 1996, the Fifth International World Wide Web Conference was held in Paris, France. Many of the participants never left their homes or offices to attend, however, because they were able to participate in conference sessions via the Internet.

The conference sessions were multicast over an experimental virtual network called Mbone. Mbone sits on top of the public Internet and provides multicast delivery of real-time information. The network layer protocol used was IP multicasting, described in a series of RFCs beginning with RFC 966. (Multicast IP is now supported by many UNIX-based workstation vendors, including Sun, Silicon Graphics, Digital Equipment Corporation, and Hewlett-Packard.) Applications that supported the conference included interactive audio, video, and whiteboard capabilities.

Conference audio was multicast using the Real Time Protocol (RTP). RTP is one of a series of protocols intended for use with high-bandwidth, multimedia network applications. As you'll see, RTP proposes not only a new protocol, but a new approach to specifying protocols intended to accommodate rapid changes in application needs, network carrying capacity, and transmission media technologies.

TCP and UDP were designed to carry relatively low volumes of data in a few well-defined formats, primarily text and pre-formatted binary files such as executables. As a result, these protocols could be thoroughly and definitively specified in a single, unchanging definition document.

Multimedia information, however, is generated in large volumes, does not have the relatively well-defined and predictable format of an executable file, and is captured and interpreted by hardware and software that are themselves rapidly evolving. The IETF's Network Working Group and Audio-Video Transport Working Group, which drafted RFC 1889 defining RTP, deliberately designed RTP to be extensible over time. Unlike TCP or PPP, which can accommodate new field values alone, RTP separates the specification of much of its protocol format into separate files for each type of payload (media-encoding format) that will be transported using the protocol. The payload types currently supported by an implementation of RTP are defined in a profile specification document, which maps payload formats to their payload specification documents.

A second difference between protocols such as TCP and RTP is that RTP protocol handlers are likely to be integrated into specific applications rather than standing alone as a separate layer in a protocol stack. This approach, sometimes called integrated layer processing, is taken to meet the challenges inherent in providing adequate real-time response and data-integrity management for interactive multimedia transmissions.

RTP is typically layered over UDP in order to make use of its services for port assignment (multiplexing), checksums, and tight integration with IP.

In order to provide end-to-end transport functions for real-time data, RTP as a data transport protocol is augmented with a corresponding Real Time Control Protocol (RTCP). RTCP monitors data delivery over even large multicast networks and provides minimal control and identification services. Both RTP and RTCP are designed to be independent of the underlying transport and network layers, despite the typical use of UDP and IP for these services. RTP is dependent on these lower-layer protocols to provide a port mechanism or similar way to distinguish among specific users who share an IP address.

RTP accommodates technology differences in a third way as well. One hurdle to real-time conferencing and other multicast transmissions of multimedia data is the variety of equipment and capabilities available to participants.

Rather than force all participants to the lowest common denominator in terms of speed, encoding, and other media characteristics, RTP supports the use of mixers and translators. *Mixers* are RTP-level relays that reconstruct audio or other media streams into lower-bandwidth, lower-quality versions. Mixers allow participants to receive degraded versions of multimedia multicasts rather than be excluded from participation by reason of equipment limitations. They are made possible because RTP distinguishes between synchronization packets and content packets in the datastream. *Translators* funnel multicast streams through firewalls and other constriction points in the network, then separate them out again for delivery to the intended clients.

Quality of Service

The rest of this section describes the RTP and RTCP packet formats that are common across payload types. A brief description of RTP concepts is also provided.

8.4.1. Fixed Fields in the RTP Header

All RTP headers begin with the same fixed fields, then diverge according to the payload format being supported for a given datastream. Figure 8.6 gives the overall RTP header format.

 Figure 8.6.
The RTP header format.

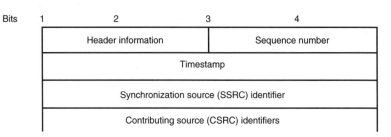

The header fields contain the following information:

- Header information—A 2-byte field containing the following subfields:

bits 0–1	version (V)—Current value = 2.
bit 2	padding (P)—If set, it indicates the presence of padding bytes at the end of the payload data; the final byte of the padding contains the count of padding bytes.
bit 3	extension (X)—If set, the fixed header is followed by exactly one header extension.
bits 4–7	CSRC count (CC)—Count of the CSRCs, if any, added by mixers to this payload.
bit 8	marker (M)—Profile-specific flag.
bits 9–15	payload type—Format of the payload, used to identify the profile to be used in interpreting the payload data; all packets emitted by a sender in a given stream are of the same payload type.

- Sequence number—A 4-byte number, incremented for successive packets in a datastream; the initial segment value is a random number chosen to make attacks on encryption more difficult. Successive sequence numbers increase monotonically.

- Timestamp—A 4-byte field specifying the sampling instant of the first byte in the RTP data packet; derived from a clock that increments monotonically and linearly in time to allow synchronization and jitter calculations. Initial value of the timestamp in a datastream is random, and multiple packets may carry the same timestamp if they resulted from the same example (for example, packets from the same video frame). Successive timestamps need not be monotonic because digitizing regimens such as MPEG interpolation do not transmit information in the order in which it was sampled.

- SSRC—A 4-byte field identifying the synchronization source; the SSRC is chosen randomly so that no two SSRCs within the same RTP session will be identical; if a source changes its source transport address, the SSRC must change as well.

- CSRC list—A list containing 0 to 15 items, each 4 bytes long, inserted by mixers to convey the SSRC identifiers of contributing sources.

RFC 1889 also defines an *extension header*. Extensions are intended to allow RTP implementations to experiment with additional services and functions that apply across multiple payload profiles while preserving interoperability with standard implementations.

8.4.2. RTP Operating Concepts

RTP was designed primarily in order to transport datastreams, such as multimedia content, in application contexts where timely delivery is a required service. Among these application contexts is interactive audio/video conferencing across TCP/IP networks such as corporate intranets or the public Internet.

Interactive conferencing requires a network layer protocol such as multicast IP, which is capable of establishing a group of addresses and exchanging packets among them all, without restricting specific addresses to send or receive mode alone.

In a typical operating scenario using RTP to support interactive conferencing, the conference coordinator would acquire a multicast IP address and two ports at that address: one for RTP data and the other for RTCP control packets. This information must be disseminated to participants before the conference begins. Encryption disciplines may also be defined and encryption keys distributed, as appropriate.

As the conference proceeds, audio data would be captured in manageable chunks and encapsulated in an RTP header within a UDP datagram. The RTP header would identify the media-encoding method, which would be used by mixers along the multicast pipeline to degrade the audio stream for users who required lower bandwidth usage.

Timing and sequence information in the RTP header would be used by the receiving RTP process to concatenate the audio chunks and play them at appropriate speeds in a continuous, if delayed, audio stream to the client computer's user.

Quality of Service

Each RTP process also periodically multicasts a report giving its name and such payload-specific information as the quality of audio reception for this participant, thereby supporting adaptive encode/decode algorithms to enhance analog audio output at the client computer.

RTCP signals the end of the user's participation in the session when requested to do so by the conferencing application software.

If simultaneous video and audio transmissions are desired, these are supported as separate pairs of RTP ports and separate datastreams. This flexibility allows participants to limit their reception to one or the other medium. The sequencing and timestamp information in the packet headers provides the information needed to synchronize audio and video output to the participant.

8.4.3. The Real Time Control Protocol (RTCP)

RTCP packets travel on a separate RTP port and allow participating processes to provide feedback regarding quality of datastream delivery. RTCP packets are multicast in the same way as the RTP data packets and allow the senders to diagnose distribution errors as well as media characteristics relating to digitization and playback of analog source information.

For maximum efficiency, multiple RTCP packets can be encapsulated and transmitted together. RTCP information transmittal rates are scaled to avoid network overload as additional participants join a multicast.

A key service provided by RTCP is to establish a persistent transport-layer identifier for an RTP source. This canonical name persists even if the SSRC identifier must be modified due to non-uniqueness across the multicast. The canonical name allows the synchronization and association of audio and video transmissions, for example, from a given participant in an interactive conference.

RFC 1889 defines several RTCP packet types, including the following:

- Sender Report (SR)—Transmission and reception statistics from participants who are active senders

- Receiver Report (RR)—Reception statistics from participants who are not active senders

- Source Description (SDES)—Items such as canonical name

- BYE—To indicate end of participation

- APPlication-specific functions

The RTCP overview in RFC 1889 also identifies processing guidelines for the concatenation and priority of RTCP packets that are encapsulated in a single UDP datagram.

8.5. The Resource reSerVation Protocol (RSVP)

TCP assumes fixed datagram formats. The nature of the data that TCP typically transports is not sensitive to the order and timing with which packets arrive. The receiver TCP process sorts the packets out, reconstructs the information message, and delivers it to the appropriate application. This elasticity of text and other traditional data formats allows TCP to provide reliable, robust transport.

> **TIP**
>
> If you are implementing RTP and want to be able to interpret a network trace, you will need appropriate documentation. In addition to your vendor's information, you may want to identify the RFCs that define the profile for the media formats that will be supported at your site.
>
> For quick reference, and as a useful way to master the complexities of RTP, consider extracting the relevant formats, along with digitizing standards such as Pulse Code Modulation for audio or MPEG for video, into an administrator's notebook.
>
> This can prove invaluable when you are trying to debug a pilot project such as corporate video-conferencing across a private intranet. A common failing of prototype projects is that they tend to be overwhelmed by the complexities of setup, the need for staff to understand new technologies, and the lack of familiar and user-friendly reference sources. An administrator's notebook addresses all three of these potential pitfalls early in the project, thereby allowing attention to turn to the wider issues of usability and cost-benefit trade-offs.

RTP introduces a new kind of malleability to transport protocols, allowing the adoption of varying payload formats as needed by the media applications that generate payload data. RTP also supports the open-ended topologies of multicast IP through RTCP.

The Resource reSerVation Protocol (RSVP) introduces yet another type of protocol that addresses Quality of Service issues on TCP/IP networks. Like RTP, RSVP appeared in response to the demands placed on networks by multimedia-based applications.

Multimedia applications require an extent and variety of services from the network that go far beyond those needed for more traditional information messages. One characteristic of multimedia traffic is that it is inelastic with regard to throughput and timing. If the majority of the bits do not arrive in sequence and on time, the information content of the multimedia datastream will be lost. However, neither IP (nor the data link layer– and media access control– protocols that support the public Internet and private internets) is designed with deterministic or optimal delivery speed in mind. Instead, TCP, IP, and the current Internet infrastructure are built, like the original ARPANET, to provide robustness and reliability in the face of varying traffic loads and a potentially dynamic network topology.

Given the existing investment in backbone, routing equipment, and applications that utilize these traditional protocols, it is unlikely that the requirements imposed by multimedia applications will be met by native, low-level redesign of the internetwork structure. Nor should they be, given the rapid evolution of multimedia capabilities and the investment in "legacy" applications such as static HTTP pages.

Quality of Service

There is a need, therefore, to find ways to provide adequate quality of services to multimedia applications within the framework of the existing packet-switched network. RSVP, defined in an IETF draft submitted in November 1996, addresses that need.

> **WARNING** The following discussion is based on the November 1996 draft document. Because drafts evolve over time, be sure to verify the current RFC status of draft proposals if you are planning an RSVP implementation and want to confirm the adoption and details of the protocol beyond your current equipment suppliers.
>
> This is particularly important because RSVP relies on implementation changes to the software in routers as well as in client computers and gateways. Unless your implementation is restricted to a corporate intranet, you will be dependent on the public Internet—and hence on equipment that is not under your control—to support RSVP sessions.

RSVP is not a protocol for transporting application data, although it resides roughly at the transport layer in the protocol stack. Instead, it provides a means by which adequate network resources can be reserved to ensure delivery of datastreams. In this sense it is a control protocol similar to ICMP and IGMP. RSVP requests are passed to all nodes in the path(s) to be taken by the datastream, requesting specific levels of service. In the typical case, the result will be that resources are reserved in appropriate nodes for this datastream.

Whereas TCP and other traditional protocols perform reliability control from the sender side, RSVP requests are made by the sender. As you might expect, this is because RSVP is intended to work together with unicast and especially multicast protocols. Just as RTP and RTCP address the varying capabilities of participants in a multicast, so too RSVP recognizes the usefulness of having each participant specify the quality of service it desires and can support. RSVP depends on other protocols such as IGMP to establish packet routing appropriately. In addition, RSVP has been designed to interoperate with both IPv4 and IPv6.

Like RTP, RSVP takes an integrated approach to protocols. It is anticipated that RSVP services will be embedded within various application software.

A key concept in the RSVP proposal is the packet classifier. This is a new process, hosted in routers, which evaluates the handling required for a given packet and forwards it in such a way as to ensure that the reserved quality of service is achieved. An admission control module decides whether there are sufficient resources to support the packet at the required level of service. A policy control module then decides if the receiver has administrative authority to reserve resources. If both are true, the packet classifier receives the information necessary for it to process the datastream packets as they arrive at that node and the requester is notified that resources have been reserved at this node. These three modules are jointly termed traffic control.

Because multicasts, especially, change size dynamically and must be able to scale efficiently, routers do not assume that participant membership and the topology of a multicast remain stable. Instead, routers regularly exchange information regarding the sessions and resources being managed by their traffic control functions. This is termed *soft state management*.

RSVP resource reservation requests are called flow descriptors and consist of a flowspec and a filterspec. The flowspec describes the specific Quality of Service desired for a given session. The filterspec, along with a session specification, identifies the data flow or set of data packets to receive this Quality of Service.

The flowspec is used by routers to establish parameters in the scheduler function on each node. The filterspec, on the other hand, is used by the packet classifier.

Packets that arrive at a router, but do not correspond to an accepted flow descriptor, are handled on a best-effort basis.

> **NOTE** Under some circumstances, merging multiple requests as they move upstream towards potential sending nodes may lead to confirmations to some recipients before the full pathway of the merged request arrives at the most distant sender.

Reservation requests are processed and propagated back from the receiver towards potential senders. Reservations for a given sender from multiple recipients are merged, with the maximum reservation always being passed upstream towards the sender node. Once the reservation request has been approved and processed back through the network to the sender, the sender responds with a confirmation message. Confirmation means that it is highly likely, but not absolutely certain, that the requested quality of service will be provided.

RSVP, as proposed, provides a scalable, robust, and flexible mechanism for ensuring quality of service for high-volume multimedia traffic and dynamic multicast topologies. Because it interoperates with existing network and data link–layer protocols, it extends the capabilities of existing TCP/IP networks, such as the Internet, while preserving the current investment in infrastructure, applications, and data.

8.6. Multilink PPP

RSVP is not the only proposal that addresses the need to transport large amounts of information to a given receiver using existing protocols and infrastructure.

RFC 1717 defines the PPP Multilink Protocol (MPPP). Multilink PPP exploits characteristics of ISDN and other switched WAN services to create large virtual WAN pipelines.

Because it exploits existing telecommunications services and can tunnel multiple LAN/WAN protocols, multilink PPP offers corporate network architects a powerful, practical tool for melding existing LANs, WANs, and dial-up links into an interoperable, high-bandwidth enterprise-wide network. Along the way, multilink PPP offers the capability to transcend bandwidth restrictions at all but the local level.

Quality of Service

Multilink PPP extends standard PPP to bundle multiple logical data links, including services such as ISDN simultaneous channels, into a single large virtual pipeline. Unlike the `BONDING` capability proposed for inclusion in ISDN, multilink PPP can be implemented solely in software. The result is bandwidth on demand, with traffic fees imposed only as a consequence of actual usage.

Bandwidth on demand significantly extends the usefulness and throughput of existing network equipment without requiring an investment in capacity that is seldom used. For instance, multilink PPP allows the use of a dial-up line with asynchronous modem to augment the carrying capacity of a leased synchronous line.

8.6.1. Operational Concepts

Normal PPP provides a point-to-point link between two peer systems. The initial step is to negotiate and configure the data link using the Link Control Protocol. The peers can negotiate compression schemes at the PPP link level without worrying about potential compression issues arising from different media layers. PPP also offers encryption services as well. An authentication phase follows, during which the peers on the link establish the identifiers to be associated with each other. PPP has been extended to work over a wide variety of WAN services, including ISDN, Frame Relay, X.25, Sonet, and HDLC framing.

Multilink PPP provides a means to coordinate data links between a fixed pair of systems. The resulting bundle is given a unique identifier, derived from the system identifiers, and can be treated by higher-layer protocols as a single virtual link of large bandwidth. The bundle can contain multiple asynchronous dial-up lines, virtual channels carried by multiplexed services such as ISDN, X.25, Frame Relay, or any combination of the above.

Multilink PPP sits between the standard PPP data link layer and the network layer in the protocol stack. It also negotiates configuration options, with the difference being that during the negotiations to establish a link, one router or access device indicates to the other peer that it is willing to bundle multiple connections into a single pipe. This is accomplished using a multilink option as part of the Link Control Protocol exchange.

When the multilink session has been established, the sending MPPP process accepts datagrams from the network layer process. It then fragments the datagrams into smaller packets, encapsulates them in an MPPP header, and distributes them over the bundled links to transmit in parallel with one another. The receiving MPPP process accumulates the fragments, which may have arrived out of sequence due to differences in pathway or in link speed, and reassembles the original datagram.

MPPP supports network administration in several ways. MPPP is not limited to shuffling datagram segments indiscriminately across all links in a bundle; transmission is usually scaled to link capacity and may be further constrained by data link–layer protocol, originating application, and so on. In addition, MPPP allows the network administrator to establish thresholds of activity below which individual links are deallocated, so as to minimize connect time charges.

8.6.2. MPPP Encapsulation

Packets to be transmitted over a multilink bundle are encapsulated according to the rules of standard PPP. The following PPP options must be chosen for the PPP implementation that will support multilink bundling:

- No Magic Number
- No Link Quality Monitoring
- Use Address and Control Field Compression
- Use Protocol Field Compression
- No Compound Frames
- No Self-Describing Padding
- No Async Control Character Map

RFC 1661 allows PPP implementations latitude to enforce various byte boundary alignments, but MPPP implementations must be able to reliably reassemble datagrams despite alignment choices.

Link Control Protocol negotiations may not be carried out on the bundle itself. Configuration requests, acknowledgments, and so on are ignored if sent over a multilink. Individual links must be configured prior to bundling.

MPPP headers include two different sequence numbers: one that indicates relative position within the original datagram and another that indicates transmission sequence over a specific data link. The header also may contain flag bits indicating the beginning or ending fragments associated with a datagram. The standard PPP header, appropriate to the data link–layer options chosen, is wrapped around the MPPP header and the datagram as forwarded by the network layer protocol process.

Fragment link sequence numbers must be contiguous and increasing over a given link within the bundle. This allows the receiving MPPP to detect lost fragments and request retransmission.

Quality of Service

8.6.3. Link Control for MPPP

MPPP extends the standard Link Control Protocol to include negotiation of several additional configuration options, including the following:

- Multilink Maximum Reconstructed Unit—Indicates that the sender implements the MPPP; if accepted, the receiver will construe packets on this link, as associated with those on all other links, with the sender for which this option has been specified.

- Multilink Short Sequence Number Header Format—Advises the peer that the sender wishes to receive fragments with a shortened, 12-bit sequence number; if accepted, the peer will use short sequence numbers on all links within the bundle.

- Endpoint Discriminator—Identifies the sender as potentially terminating a bundle rather than a single link; used to add new links to a bundle or to force a new bundle, depending on the results of authentication.

Individual links within an MPPP bundle can be established or terminated without prejudice to the bundle as a whole. State information regarding the bundle persists as long as at least one link is active within it.

RFC 1990 details option formats and subfield code values for the MPPP header and associated LCP extensions.

8.7. TCP/IP and Broadband Transmission Services

The original TCP/IP protocols, including related asynchronous protocols such as SLIP and PPP, were developed at a time when all long distance transmission lines, and especially switched telephone circuits, operated on an analog basis only.

Over the last decade, digital line services (and interfaces between the telephone network and data terminal equipment) have become increasingly available and cost-effective. The remainder of this chapter looks at the interaction between TCP/IP and its related protocols, and emerging broadband digital transmission services.

8.7.1. Broadband Concepts

Analog switched circuits must allocate a fixed transmission capacity for each link that is established, for example by a voice conversation. Broadband packet-switched networks, on the other hand, dynamically allocate capacity on the telecommunications grid in response to the flux of transmission requirements generated by voice and data sources alike.

Standard T-1 lines can be multiplexed, or shared, on a time division basis. The resulting fractional T-1 services support synchronous protocols such as X.25 and SNA efficiently and effectively, providing the company leasing the fractional line has sufficient traffic to warrant the commitment.

Packet-based multiplexing supports broadband transmission of varying amounts of data on a demand basis. Although it imposes overhead in order to manage the flow of packets, packet-based multiplex techniques provide great flexibility and efficiency in the mapping of physical network resources to a varying demand. Because of this mapping, packet-based multiplexing is also called statistical multiplexing.

Packets must be constructed by fragmenting and encapsulating user data in order to attach the information necessary to route and reassemble the data. Two different approaches exist to accomplish this task: variable-length frames (utilized in Frame Relay) and fixed-length cells (utilized in Asynchronous Transfer Mode, or ATM).

8.7.2. Integrated Services Data Network (ISDN)

Although it generalizes to a wide variety of media and data-link protocols, Multilink PPP was originally proposed to take advantage of a pioneering digital service, namely Broadband Integrated Services Data Network (B-ISDN). B-ISDN provides both circuit mode and packet mode services.

ISDN offers a variety of distribution services, both connection-oriented and connectionless, and can carry either constant or variable bit rate traffic. Where connection-oriented services are chosen, the virtual circuit can persist permanently between two designated endpoints or it can be switched (that is, so named by analogy to dialing an analog connection). Network architects have traditionally allocated permanent virtual circuits over ISDN lines for WAN connections. Because PPP can function above most WAN protocols, MPPP can be used to dynamically acquire bandwidth as needed from switched virtual circuits. MPPP, in turn, can carry IP and TCP above it, thereby yielding a flexible, extensible enterprise network.

8.7.3. Frame Relay

Frame Relay takes its name from its use of variable-length frame packets. The protocol defines how the telecommunications network and the data terminal equipment (computers) interface.

Frame Relay achieves high throughput at the expense of a certain flexibility. The protocol carries only data and requires connection-oriented transmission service.

Quality of Service

In exchange, Frame Relay provides bandwidth on demand and highly efficient sharing of access lines. Although the standard was designed to support either permanent or switched virtual circuits (VCs), only permanent VCs are supported at present. Because a permanent VC allocates all the bandwidth on the physical path to a given packet for the duration of the frame, Frame Relay imposes very little overhead during packet switching. The primary overhead load is incurred when the information is segmented and encapsulated on the sending side and reassembled at the receiving end.

Frame Relay does require the use of specialized interfaces between computers and the network, as does ISDN. One physical access to a Frame Relay-enabled line can support up to 1,024 logical connections.

Different frame encapsulations are used for packets that will be bridged versus those that must be routed. In either case, the packet's payload includes the original IP datagram on TCP/IP networks. Once the frames have been reassembled into the datagram, IP processes it in the normal fashion.

8.7.4. Asynchronous Transfer Mode (ATM)

ATM is a cell-oriented, statistical multiplexed transmission service. It supports data, voice, and multimedia streams simultaneously, each with different transmission and quality of service requirements.

Digital data (including digitized voice) must be encapsulated into ATM cells before being transported. The software/firmware modules that accomplish this task are referred to as the ATM Adaption Layers (AAL). An AAL must also reassemble datagrams once they are successfully received. Encapsulation takes several forms, depending on the media in use and the services being provided.

Every ATM cell is a fixed-length (53-byte) packet. ATM cells from different sources are inserted into the transmission stream on a time-slot basis. Because allocation of time slots to various source-destination pairs is done on a demand basis, rather than by rotation, this is an asynchronous transfer technique.

The AALs serve as interfaces between transmission media and the network protocol stack. A given site will generally implement only one AAL, depending on the ATM services procured. Of course, where multiple ATM services are procured, the corresponding AALs must also be activated.

ATM layered over Broadband ISDN provides a flexible capability. At the same time, ATM requires a significant investment in hardware on the part of both the network provider and the customer. For this reason, and because of the relative scarcity, until recently, of protocols that enable interoperability of private and public networks, ATM is just beginning to be adopted for large-scale use.

In addition, the flexibility and power of ATM comes at the predictable cost of significant conceptual complexity. At least five AALs, representing various combinations of constant versus variable-bit rate, connection-oriented versus connectionless transfer, and permanent versus switched virtual circuits, have been defined. Others are possible and may emerge as multimedia, multicast, and related application requirements mature.

IP datagrams carried within ATM cells are encapsulated by AAL5, also known as the Simple and Efficient Adaption Layer (SEAL). RFC 1577 defines the SEAL-encapsulation format.

AAL5 supports connection-oriented, variable-bit rate services. As with all ATM services, different packet formats are defined for bridged and routed packets.

In addition, AALs implement several different sublayers of transmission. The convergence sublayer encapsulates the IP datagram and passes it to the segmentation and reassembly sublayer, which fragments it into payloads for ATM cells.

IP datagrams can also be encapsulated within a frame relaying–specific convergence sublayer. FR–SSCS passes this packet to the standard convergence sublayer for ATM fragmentation and delivery. In this way, Frame Relay connections can be established over ATM networks, along with voice traffic and mixed transmissions.

8.8. Summary

Early packet-switched networks were designed primarily to provide reliable delivery and to be robust in the face of failures in some part of the communications grid. Robustness included data-flow control to manage congestion and reduce unnecessary packet retransmissions.

The responsibility for ensuring this quality of service was given primarily to the transport layer in the protocol stack. TCP has extensive capabilities, including session negotiation, acknowledgment schemes, and transmission window management, to accomplish these services on behalf of the application software whose information is being transported across the network.

A second major design goal of the TCP/IP protocol stack was to allow interoperation of diverse networks, without regard to the (usually) proprietary LAN or other protocols on which they are based. Segregation of the media access control and data link layers from the network layer protocols accomplishes this goal and allows dial-up access by SLIP or PPP connections to TCP/IP–based servers.

This capability has been further extended by PPTP, which supports the tunneling of LAN and WAN protocols across the public Internet or a corporate packet-switched intranet. PPTP thus allows the use of the public Internet to provide

Quality of Service

remote access to private networks, thereby significantly extending the useful life of existing investments in equipment, software applications, and database architectures.

However, the rapid maturing of multimedia applications has led to increased demand for network services that TCP and its related protocols do not easily provide. Interactive multimedia applications, such as video-conferencing over the Internet, require networks to provide differing and dynamically adjusting levels of service for different media streams simultaneously. The need for stream-oriented services to be provided by an essentially packet-based protocol stack has led to the emergence of several new and proposed protocols that extend the traditional TCP/IP model in several different ways.

These protocols include RTP, for transmission of audio and video datastreams, and RSVP, an innovative mechanism for reserving network resources on an as-needed basis. RTP and RSVP, when combined with multicast extensions to IP, lay the groundwork for realizing the true promise of the Internet by extending the kinds and degree of service quality that can be provided to application software.

Innovations are occurring at the media access level as well. Telephony suppliers have offered a series of digital data services, including Broadband ISDN, Frame Relay, and ATM. Frame Relay over B-ISDN has been the workhorse of packet-switched networks, public and private, during the 1990s. ATM provides a richer set of services that scale well to varying service demands placed by different kinds of datastreams.

Thus, with RTP and RSVP from above and ATM services below, the Internet Protocol now finds an increasingly flexible and powerful context within which to route information across networks.

As exciting as the emerging interactive and multimedia applications may be, however, the vast majority of all network traffic continues to serve transaction and text-oriented applications. As ATM and other broadband services allow bandwidth on demand, thereby lowering transmission costs for casual (as opposed to dedicated) connections, corporations are increasingly looking to TCP/IP–based networks to link the information resources across the entire enterprise. Modest extensions of the traditional TCP/IP protocol family that facilitate an incremental migration, such as T/TCP and Multilink PPP, may prove to be decisive factors accelerating the adoption of advanced internetworking technologies.

9.   Introduction to the Application Layer

10. Support Services

11. Application Services

12. Naming Services

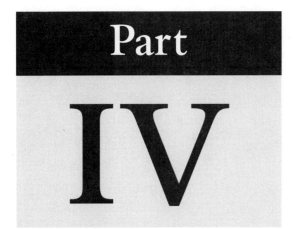

Part

IV

Application Layer

9.1. The TCP Application Interface Model

9.2. TCP/IP Applications in the UNIX Environment

9.3. TCP/IP Applications in the Microsoft Windows Environment

9.4. Summary

Chapter

9

Introduction to the Application Layer

by Robin Burk

In the previous chapters, you looked at the lower layers in the TCP/IP protocol stack. You've seen how the Internet Protocol sits above the physical transmission media and the data-link protocols to provide packet routing and delivery.

Chapter 8 examined the concept *Quality of Service* as a key mission for the transport layer protocols. The original transport protocols, TCP and UDP, and emerging protocols such as RTP and RSVP are designed to provide differing degrees of performance, reliability, and flexibility to best provide transmission of varying kinds and amounts of application information. The separation of transport protocols from IP and the data link and media access control layers allows the most efficient support for application programs, whose data transport needs may range from short datagrams transported by UDP through longer datastreams best transported by TCP to the rigors of high-volume, real-time interactive audio/visual multicasts.

Part IV, "Application Layer," turns our attention to the application programs whose data flows provide the requirements and the rationale for the lower TCP/IP protocol stack. This chapter introduces the application layer interface by means of which user programs can request and receive network transmission services. Chapter 10, "Support Services," examines the foundation service applications that extend the operating environment with network-oriented support. Chapter 11, "Application Services," describes the other commonly used network-oriented applications, and Chapter 12, "Naming Services," is devoted to the naming services that simplify administration of a TCP/IP–based network.

9.1. The TCP Application Interface Model

TCP is the workhorse transport protocol of the TCP/IP family. The designers of TCP consciously adopted an operating and organizational model for TCP that mirrors other basic information management and access facilities in standard operating system environments.

Unlike UDP, which is designed for the exchange of small, asynchronous datagrams, TCP is organized around the idea of a simplex *datastream*, or extended, continuous flow of bytes.

> **NOTE** Although a TCP connection supports duplex communications—that is, simultaneous traffic in each direction—the information exchanged over each side of the duplex connection is (from TCP's point of view) wholly independent from the other side. The only overlap occurs in the use of the TCP header to acknowledge receipt of packets and to advertise window space.

The authors of RFC 793 use the analogy of file management systems when describing TCP. By this analogy, you can expect that

- TCP is able to make varying amounts of data available to the requesting/receiving application program (corresponding to data files)

- This data is stored and transferred in relatively small physical segments (corresponding to disk sectors)

- The application itself views the data as divided into logical segments (corresponding to database records) with which the transport or access service is not directly involved.

The analogy to disk file access will help to make the TCP model for application support more intuitively obvious. Such a model is inherently necessary because of the unique role of a transport protocol in the protocol stack. Transport protocols such as TCP have an interest in both the world of network transmission and routing, on the one hand, and application programs on the other hand.

NOTE   A *socket* is defined by the combination of IP address for a given host plus the logical port number associated with a given application. At any given time on the network, this combination (and hence the socket itself) must be unique.

However, a given socket may be paired with multiple other sockets to define multiple, pairwise connections. This is how the `ftp` process on a repository server can accommodate multiple file transfer requests at the same time, for instance.

A connection may be opened between two sockets, used to transfer information, and then closed. If the same two sockets wish to transfer information later, they must negotiate the connection again. This is referred to as a new *incarnation* of the connection. The TCP protocol definition specifies wait periods, beginning sequence numbers, and other mechanisms to ensure that datagrams lingering from an old incarnation are discarded when a new incarnation of the connection is established. Applications that use TCP for information transport should retain connections long enough to transfer all the information associated with a given logical operation or user session, closing the connection when it cannot predict the likelihood of needing additional data transport any time soon.

File management systems play a similar role with regard to information stored on magnetic media. The file system must know about, but not directly manage, physical media layout and I/O. It must accommodate applications' needs regarding the creation and retrieval of data files without knowing what those files contain.

Just as a file system bridges the data storage and application "layers," TCP bridges the transmission layers of the protocol stack and application programs that request network transport of their information. TCP relies on IP and the lower-level protocols to do the physical "reads" and "writes" across the network, just as the file system relies on device drivers. And like a file system, TCP is not concerned with the information content of the data that is being transported.

What TCP does do is manage network connections between sockets on two network hosts. Just as applications request file-oriented services such as OPEN, READ, WRITE, and CLOSE, so can application programs request similar services regarding network connections.

9.1.1. TCP Connection States

To understand the requests that an application can make of TCP, it is useful to understand the various states that might describe the status of a TCP connection. RFC 793 gives TCP software implementers a detailed state transition description to guide the logic flow of the protocol handler. We won't go into that level of detail here. However, understanding the basics of the TCP state model will help you make sense of TCP/IP dumps, especially in multiprotocol networks. Excessive retransmissions, delivery failures, and other potential administrative concerns will often be caused in one layer of the protocol stack, but force abnormal action in other layers as well. If you are familiar with the state transition model of TCP, you will be able to diagnose when the problem originates at the transport layer and when TCP's actions are secondary results of network and lower protocol actions.

At any given time, a connection is said to be in one of a number of possible states. A specific state represents the results of recent history regarding the connection and determines the response that will be made to subsequent events such as application requests, packet delivery, or network errors.

RFC 793, the IETF Standard that defines TCP, identifies the following possible states for a TCP connection:

```
LISTEN
SYN_SENT
SYN_RECEIVED
ESTABLISHED
FIN_WAIT_1
FIN_WAIT_2
CLOSE_WAIT
CLOSING
LAST_ACK
TIME_WAIT
CLOSED
```

These are listed in the order in which they occur during the standard lifetime of a connection incarnation, including orderly termination of the connection.

NOTE Note that Figure 9.1 shows only one typical scenario. Both ends in a TCP connection may actively open the connection, and a passively opened half of the connection may be converted to active open status once the receiving application has a specific socket to request.

Similarly, either side of the connection may actively initiate a CLOSE operation.

Figure 9.1 shows an overview of the state transitions that occur during a TCP connection's life. The left side of the flow represents a typical user application, which initiates a connection and terminates it when the user ends the application session. The right side of the flow represents a typical server-based service that accepts requests from previously unknown sockets, subject to security and authentication measures.

Each side of the connection must take steps to establish the connection before it may be used to transfer application information.

Figure 9.1.

A typical TCP state transition scenario for local and remote processes.

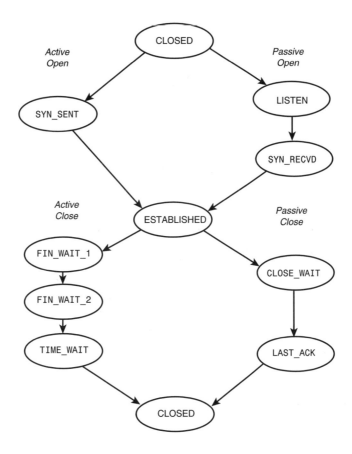

An application may actively open a connection to a specified remote socket or indicate its willingness to passively accept a connection with requesting, but currently unspecified, sockets.

If the application process has requested an active OPEN, TCP will then proceed to send a SYN packet to the specified remote socket. This begins negotiations toward establishing the connection. From the point of view of the local TCP process, the connection is now in a SYN_SENT state and is waiting for a matching request from the remote socket.

If the application process requested a passive OPEN, it is willing to accept a connection from any remote socket that requests one, and the connection is placed into the LISTEN state. No SYN packet will be sent from the local socket until such a request has been received, at which point the TCP process then advances the connection to the SYN_RECEIVED state.

When both the local and remote TCP processes have completed their respective three-way handshakes, the connection is said to be *synchronized* and enters the ESTABLISHED state. At this point, the connection is open and can be used to exchange datagrams. Both the local and remote TCP processes will maintain a transmission control block (TCB) for this connection, which will be used to keep track of the window, sequence, acknowledgment, and buffer information.

Orderly termination occurs when one of the TCP processes initiates a FIN packet. The FIN packet signals that the local application has completed its use of the connection and would like to complete all outstanding transfers. Then the connection enters the FIN_WAIT_1 state *on this system*. The connection enters the FIN_WAIT_2 state when its own FIN has been acknowledged, but it has not received a corresponding FIN from the remote system. The connection is said to be in a half-closed condition at this point.

Upon receipt of the remote system's FIN, the local TCP responds with an acknowledgment and places the connection into the TIME_WAIT state. The connection will remain in this state for a minimum of twice the maximum segment lifetime (MSL), which has been specified in the TCP implementation. The MSL is the maximum time a packet may exist within the network before it is discarded. By waiting a sufficient time for a round trip through the network, the actively closing TCP assures that no packets from this incarnation arrive mistakenly at a new incarnation of the same connection. Once this period has completed, the connection enters the CLOSED pseudostate, so called because no TCB is maintained once this state is attained.

The peer that initiates connection termination is said to perform an *active close*. The other peer must then passively respond by closing its half of the connection. When the remote TCP process has received a FIN packet, it must passively initiate a corresponding close of its half of the duplex connection. It begins by notifying the application that the other system is closing the connection and places the connection in the CLOSE_WAIT state. Upon response by the application, the TCP process then sends its own FIN packet and moves the connection into the LAST_ACK state. When the final acknowledgment of the concluding FIN packet is received, that process considers the connection CLOSED.

An application can force the abort, or reset, of the connection rather than perform an orderly termination. This is done by sending a RST packet rather than a FIN. When the local TCP process receives the application request to abort the connection, it must discard any data remaining to be transferred. The remote system that receives a RST packet is then free to take whatever diagnostic, reporting, or other action is appropriate, in addition to passively closing its own half of the connection.

9.1.2. Application Requests to TCP

As is evident from the preceding section, a TCP process initiates action based on external events, including timer interrupts, the receipt of datagrams, and application service requests.

RFC 793 offers a logical model for the application service requests (called *user commands*) a TCP process should accept. This model derives from early implementations of TCP, primarily in UNIX environments, and the commands are presented as procedure calls. Actual TCP implementations need not follow these procedure names or sequences, but must offer equivalent functionality.

The user commands to be supported by TCP are

> OPEN
> SEND
> RECEIVE
> CLOSE
> ABORT
> STATUS

The TCP process will typically issue a `proc` return as soon as the call has been received and an action is initiated in response. TCP may also provide a delayed response to user commands in the form of a pseudointerrupt. TCP returns error notification in the form of error message strings.

The calling sequences of the user commands are given in the following list, along with a brief summary of the response that TCP makes to each command:

- OPEN *(local port, foreign socket, active/passive[, timeout] [, precedence] [, security/compartment] [, options]) -> local connection name*

  An application must request that a connection be opened, and it may specify a given remote socket as the other connection participant. Typically, the application has previously accessed a naming service to determine the desired IP address and can use a Well Known Port Number to complete the socket specification.

  If the active/passive flag is set to passive, no remote socket identifier is required, and the TCP process moves the potential connection into a LISTEN state.

  A TCB is created when this command is received.

  When the OPEN is successful, the TCP process returns a local connection name by which the application will specify this connection in subsequent commands.

- SEND *(local connection name, buffer address, byte count, PUSH flag, URGENT flag [,timeout])*

  When an application wants to send information across the network, it begins by placing the data into a buffer within its own address space. The SEND call then causes TCP to break the information into segments, encapsulate it, and pass the resulting datagrams to IP (or another network-layer protocol) for routing and transmission.

The PUSH flag causes TCP to force transmission of this and any previous information in its buffers (for this transmission) without waiting to fill the maximum data segment space. The receiving TCP also passes this and any prior information that may still be in the receive buffers to the application.

The URGENT flag requires the receiving TCP to pass the data to the remote application and to note its urgent status. Typically, this flag indicates a system shutdown in progress or some other event that requires timely response in order to preserve full information integrity.

In addition to known sockets, RFC 793 also provides for the use of an implied foreign socket to establish connections from the LISTEN side. This facility allows applications to open connections without ever explicitly knowing the foreign socket address. A passively opened side of the connection can send data as soon as the implied foreign socket has sent at least one packet to it.

■ RECEIVE *(local connection name, buffer address, byte count)*
  -> byte count, URGENT flag, PUSH flag

The RECEIVE command instructs the TCP process to allocate a receiving buffer for the specified connection. Whenever data is received over the connection, it is placed into the buffer, and the application is notified of the amount of data received and the state of the status flags for the transmission.

It is common for both TCP and applications to be implemented such that the application may have more than one RECEIVE buffer outstanding. In this case, the buffer address and the byte count are returned.

■ CLOSE *(local connection name)*

This command indicates that the connection should be closed as soon as previously requested transmissions are complete; a PUSH is implied.

However, the application should continue to RECEIVE data until it is notified that the other peer has also closed its half of the connection.

Note that an application may be prompted to request a CLOSE by TCP itself, especially in the case where the other peer has initiated an active CLOSE on its side of the connection. Wherever possible, the application will close buffers, completely push out any remaining information to the network, and terminate the application session gracefully before closing the network connection from its end.

■ STATUS *(local connection name)* -> *status data*

> This is an implementation-dependent operation. If implemented, it
> returns the following information:
>
>> Local socket
>> Foreign socket
>> Local connection name
>> Receive window
>> Send window
>> Connection state
>> Number of buffers awaiting acknowledgment
>> Number of buffers pending receipt
>> Urgent state
>> Precedence
>> Security/compartment
>> Transmission timeout
>> Only the application process that is authorized to use this
>> connection may receive status information.

■ ABORT *(local connection name)*

> Unlike the CLOSE command, the ABORT command causes all pending
> SENDs and RECEIVEs to be ignored and a special RESET message to be
> sent to the TCP on the other side of the connection.

9.1.3. TCP-to-Application Messages

TCP processes must be able to asynchronously signal (interrupt) the application
program. This facility is used to notify the application when data has been
received and transmitted in certain termination and error conditions.

TCP always passes the local connection name and a response message string to
the application. It may also pass command-related information such as the pointer
and count information associated with a RECEIVE operation.

9.2. TCP/IP Applications in the UNIX Environment

TCP and IP protocol handlers are typically compiled into the kernels for most
UNIX implementations, extending the operating system with these network
facilities.

Early versions of TCP/IP in the UNIX environment expected the foundational application servers such as Telnet and FTP to be launched at boot time so that they would be available in case remote requests were made to their well-known ports.

9.2.1. The Internet Daemon and Service Processes

Subsequently, however, the Internet Daemon `inetd` was developed. `inetd`, like all daemons, is a background process that runs without user initiative or interaction. Its purpose is to create and destroy server daemons as required by requests received via TCP.

The processes that `inetd` is authorized to create are specified as part of the UNIX configuration process. Depending on the implementation, some foundational services such as `rlogin` may be provided as part of the `inetd` code itself.

9.2.2. Service Configuration in BSD UNIX

The first step in configuring TCP/IP services and related applications on a BSD UNIX machine is to compile a suitable kernel. Most UNIX implementations based on 4.3BSD come with a generic kernel that is preconfigured to support the TCP/IP protocol stack. If you wish to set any specific options, you may rebuild the kernel. Be sure you specify the following, no matter which other options you include:

- `options INET`—Forces the inclusion of handlers for TCP, IP, ICMP, UDP, and ARP

- `pseudo-device loop`—Creates header file `loop.h` in the kernel directory

- `pseudo-device ether`—Includes Ethernet support (if required)

- `pseudo-device pty`—Includes virtual terminal support for rlogin, Telnet, and similar applications

- `device {device type}`—For a specific network interface hardware on the system

The following options should be set to reflect your network use and topology:

- `IPFORWARDING`—Specifies whether this host will forward messages to other IP nodes from third-party hosts:

    1 = Always forward

    0 = Default

    –1 = Never forward

- **IPSENDREDIRECTS**—Controls whether ICMP will redirect messages when a more efficient path exists for a message routed through this host:

  1 = Redirect

  0 = Do not redirect

- **SUBNETSARELOCAL**—Controls the message size that will be established for local traffic:

  1 = Use the MTU of the local net to send packets

  0 = Use the default MTU to avoid fragmentation

- **BROADCAST**—Controls the capability to broadcast IP packets:

  1 = With **IPFORWARDING**; allows routing of broadcast packets

  0 = No broadcast to be supported

When the kernel is built and the system is rebooted, `inetd` will read its own configuration instructions from the file `/etc/inetd.conf`. This file contains one entry for each application service that `inetd` will manage.

Configuration entries use the following syntax:

```
<name> <type> <protocol> <wait_status> <UID> <server>
➥<arguments>
```

- **name**—The name of the service as found in the `/etc/services` file (`ftp`, `telnet`, `finger`, and so on).

- **protocol**—The transport protocol used by this service:

  `tcp`
  `udp`

- **wait_status**—Specifies whether `inetd` must wait for the service to release a socket before it listens for a message from that service again.

  `wait` is usually used by UDP-based services.

  `nowait` is used by servers that dynamically allocate sockets in order to support datastreams.

- **uid**—User ID for the server.

  `root` is used for most services.

  `nobody` or `daemon` is usually used for finger as a security measure.

  `UUCP` is for the UUCP service.

- **server**—Full pathname of the executable for this service.

  internal means the service is provided by **inetd** itself.

- **arguments**—The command line used to invoke the server.

Services may be dynamically disabled by commenting out the appropriate line in the **inetd** configuration file, then passing a hang-up signal to **inetd**. This will cause the Internet Daemon to reconfigure itself without rebooting UNIX.

9.2.3. The BSD Socket Model

BSD UNIX includes constructs known as sockets. A socket is a way for processes to communicate with one another. In the early 1980s, the Defense Advanced Research Projects Agency (DARPA) contracted with the Berkeley UNIX team to extend the BSD socket support to include sockets that would communicate with remote processes in support of the TCP/IP stack.

TCP sockets were first released for general use in 4.2BSD UNIX. Since then the BSD reference model for TCP/IP support has included the socket construct, which has spread to a variety of operating system environments.

The BSD socket model includes a small number of basic functions to establish, use, and destroy sockets. These include

- The **establish** function—Creates a new socket for a given host/port combination with addressing=Internet and transfer type=connectionless (datagram/UDP) or connection-oriented (datastream/TCP)

- The **connect** function—Attempts to initiate connection with another socket (remote process)

- The **accept** function—Accepts a connection from another socket (remote process)

- The **read** function—Receives data from the remote process

- The **write** function—Sends data to the remote process

- The **close** function—Terminates the connection with a specific process

The BSD socket model has been extended by third parties to provide hardware- and software-specific support for a wide variety of network equipment and LAN/WAN protocols; to integrate it into a various operating system environments; and to encapsulate it within various application programming interfaces (APIs).

9.2.4. Service Configuration in System V UNIX

Unlike BSD UNIX implementations, the AT&T System V version of UNIX does not provide a generic kernel, so a build must always be configured and compiled.

System V does not use options to control the build. Instead, a configuration entry is required for each of the following capabilities:

```
arp
arpproc
cp
ICMP
ip
llcloop
socket
tcp
ttyp
udp
vty
```

9.2.5. Security Considerations

NOTE

The specifications for TCP arose in a BSD UNIX environment and assume the use of the BSC socket facility. Because System V is datastream-oriented throughout the operating system, a `socket` entry must be specified to force the inclusion of an equivalent support for TCP and UDP within System V.

The remote access applications require careful setup to avoid compromising system security. These applications include the following:

- `rlogin`—Interactive remote login
- `rcp`—Remote file copy
- `rs`—Remote shell execution

Several security strategies are possible with regard to these UNIX-specific services:

- Delete them from the `inetd` configuration file, which prevents their use.
- Force password protection by deleting the `/etc/hosts.equiv` file.
- Force password protection by disallowing `~/.rhosts` files for users.

The file `/etc/hosts.equiv` defines hosts that are to be trusted throughout this system. The `~/.rhost` files define trusted hosts for specific users.

9.3. TCP/IP Applications in the Microsoft Windows Environment

Microsoft Corporation has developed a series of extensions to its Windows products in support of the TCP/IP protocol stack and network-related applications. In general, as the capabilities of the Windows products have evolved from Windows 3.1 to Windows 95 and Windows NT, so have the facilities that enable application programs to access TCP/IP services.

9.3.1. The WinSock API

The first major Internet-related facility offered by Microsoft was the 16-bit Windows Sockets (WinSock) interface for Windows 3.1. Extending the UNIX notion of sockets, WinSock represents an API that connects applications with TCP and the lower protocols. WinSock continues to be supported in Windows 95 and Windows NT, although as you'll see later in the chapter, those operating systems layer higher-level APIs above WinSock. These interfaces are more powerful and hide the operations of TCP; as a result, they are more likely to be used by developers who are designing for the 32-bit Windows environment alone.

By standardizing this interface, the WinSock model guarantees that applications can run above any conforming protocol stack. Rather than limiting either the stack or application programs to Microsoft offerings, the WinSock model encouraged hardware interface manufacturers and LAN/WAN vendors to provide suitable stacks for their protocols and equipment, thereby extending the usefulness and attractiveness of Windows as an operating environment.

However, the primary network protocols supported by the WinSock interface are those included in Internet Protocol Suite (IPS), namely the following:

ARP
ICMP
IP
RARP
TCP
UDP

In addition to the standard BSD socket functions, WinSock includes functions that allow application programmers to utilize the Windows messaging architecture as well as the socket construct. Windows messages are used to exchange information and signal events between processes. By combining both constructs, the

WinSock specification encourages Internet-related applications to embed themselves within the Windows environment and exploit Windows-specific features.

Run-time routines for 16-bit Windows Sockets are provided by `WinSock.dll`. Support for 32-bit Windows Sockets under both Windows 95 and Windows NT is provided by `wsock32.dll`. Apart from the wider data-word width, these DLLs support the same functionality.

The Microsoft Foundation Class includes two classes for developing WinSock-based applications in the C++ language. Class `CAsyncSocket` contains the WinSock API and gives access to low-level network functions. Class `C socket` provides a higher-level interface to WinSock. Both classes support TCP-style byte streams and UDP-style datagram communications.

9.3.2. The WinInet API

With the successful adoption of the 32-bit Windows 95 and Windows NT systems, Microsoft Corporation has also introduced a higher-level API to allow user programs to make use of network services.

Just as the WinSock API hides the details of the TCP and IP operation, the WinInet API hides the details of the WinSock interface. The intent of the WinInet API is to allow application developers to standardize program architectures despite rapidly evolving Internet protocols and network-related services.

WinInet supports not only the standard transport and lower-level functions, but also foundational Internet applications "protocols" such as FTP, Gopher, and HTTP. By grouping these services with transport and transmission services, Microsoft is encouraging developers to provide applications, such as browsers, that offer integrated access to Internet and intranet information.

Unlike the WinSock API, which contains specific functions to synchronize process execution threads and avoid resource deadlocks, the WinInet API is inherently multithread safe. WinInet also manages data caching for applications. WinInet functions closely resemble the Win32 API in their style and functionality.

The WinInet general purpose functions include calls to perform such operations as

- Open an Internet connection

- Initiate an FTP, Gopher, or HTTP session

- Read data from or write to the handle associated with these sessions

- Construct and manipulate Universal Resource Locator (URL) tags

In addition, WinInet supports FTP functions to manage directories and files on remote FTP servers. Data transfer from these files is provided by the general purpose functions.

Similarly, WinInet supports the primary functions a developer would like to have in order to program a Gopher client or manage HTTP-based documents. As you might suspect, these functions underlie Microsoft's own Internet-related products. They also, however, are available to third parties for use in Web browsers, search engines, and other Internet-related application programs.

Run-time routines for WinInet functions reside in `wininet.dll`.

The Microsoft Foundation Class 4.2 introduced wrapper classes that encapsulate the WinInet API, thus providing a higher level of abstraction even than WinInet itself. MFC 4.2 offers four basic connection classes, several file classes, and methods for managing sessions, files, and Web resources.

With the introduction of these foundation classes, Microsoft has insulated Internet-related applications from both the details of TCP/IP and from the evolution of new Internet protocols and capabilities.

9.3.3. Server Facilities in Windows NT

The WinSock and WinInet APIs and the Internet Protocol Suite are client-side capabilities. Microsoft has also introduced server-side functionality on top of the TCP/IP protocol stack.

The Microsoft Internet Information Server (IIS) sits on top of the Windows NT Server and provides Web host services. Microsoft has also provided a new Internet Server API (ISAPI) to allow new server functionality to be added to an IIS environment, thereby encouraging the migration of new technologies such as interactive audio and video multicasting to receive early and stable support on NT-based servers. As with the other Internet-related APIs in the Windows suite, ISAPI is wrapped by MFC classes for robust, object-oriented application development.

9.4. Summary

Application layer programs provide user-oriented capabilities and call upon the transport layer protocols to exchange information with remote application programs.

The transport layer in the protocol stack must bridge the conceptual and operating gap between the network communications-oriented protocols below it and the user information-oriented application above it.

The primary transport protocol, TCP, extends the concepts and intermediary role of a file system to the network and remote resources. Instead of a disk or CD-ROM file and its data contents, TCP manages network connections and transports network data. RFC 793, the IETF Standard that defines the core TCP protocol, identifies a logical model of services that TCP implementations must provide, such as OPEN, SEND, RECEIVE, and CLOSE. Just as a file system does not interpret the information or data structures contained in disk files, so is TCP not concerned with the information content of the application data it transports across a TCP/IP network.

The TCP protocol is specified in terms of connection states and the events, including application program commands, that trigger state changes. Understanding the TCP state model can aid a network administrator in interpreting TCP dumps.

Another key concept inherent in the interface between the transport layer and the application layer is that of sockets. Originally constructed as an interprocess communications mechanism within the BSD UNIX operating system, the socket construct was extended to include interprocess communications across network connections.

The Internet Daemon or inetd is a "superservice" that optimizes UNIX system resources by creating foundational Internet-related application processes in response to requests from remote systems. Although the TCP/IP protocol stack is conceptually independent of the operating system at all but the media access control layer, in practice both TCP and IP, along with application control mechanisms such as inetd, are often tightly integrated into the operating system itself. Such integration provides efficient network communications with the lowest processing overhead.

The BSD socket model has been extended and applied in a wide variety of operating system environments and protocol stack implementations. Among these are the Microsoft application programming interfaces (APIs) and foundational development class libraries that support TCP/IP communications and application development in Windows 3.1, 95, and NT client systems.

The Windows Sockets API extends the BSD model to integrate the socket concept into the Windows messaging model. A subsequent level of abstraction is provided to application programs in the form of the WinInet API. This interface essentially hides the specifics of network communication entirely, treating remote systems as if they were logical resources available to local applications.

The WinSock and WinInet APIs, and their encapsulation within Microsoft Foundation Classes, are another instance in which the TCP/IP protocol stack (including the application layer itself) is tightly coupled with the operating environment. Compared to the integration of the lower protocols and the

Introduction to the Application Layer

Internet Daemon into BSD UNIX, however, the Microsoft APIs provide integration of the TCP/IP stack at a much higher level of abstraction.

Such abstraction removes application programs from considerations of network transmission and data transport. These interfaces have the effect of providing a stable environment for application programs despite the rapid evolution of transmission, routing, and resource management mechanisms to support advanced application needs such as interactive audio and video, multicasting, and related functions. The introduction of APIs between the TCP/IP protocols and application programs provides an efficient, stable base for network application development and execution.

10.1. Timing Services: NTP and SNTP

10.2. Management Services: SNMP

10.3. File Services: NFS

10.4. NetBIOS Over TCP/IP

10.5. Summary

Chapter

10

Support Services

by Robin Burk

In this chapter you'll take your first look at the application layer on a TCP/IP protocol stack. Application programs are not part of the network communications services directly. Rather, they make use of the transport, network, and data-link services provided by the lower layers to accomplish user-oriented tasks.

User applications in any computing environment serve a variety of functions. Some (such as spreadsheets, word processors, and custom database programs) are solely concerned with the user's high-level workflow. Others, however, allow the user to manage the computing environment, access information and hardware resources, and otherwise initiate housekeeping functions.

This chapter takes a look at several of the protocols that support these management functions. Each of them extends the transport and lower levels of the TCP/IP protocol stack to enrich the services that the lower layers can provide to end-user applications.

The services supported by these protocols fall into several categories:

- Timing services—Allow synchronization of TCP/IP-based networks

- Network-management services—Support network administration

- File-management services—Extend user access to remote files

- Network-integration services—Support the integration of LANs and WANs into TCP/IP–based networks

In the protocol stack model for network communications, the application layer need not be flat—that is to say, it is quite permissible for some applications to nest on top of others and use their services. As you will see in the remainder of this book, the protocols discussed here provide core services to a variety of administrative and end-user application programs.

By extending the protocol stack through the application level, these support-service protocols extend the capability to create TCP/IP networks that remain open across multiple hardware and software platforms. The capability, for instance, to access files on a TCP/IP server from a user's client machine, despite differing operating system versions or host hardware, extends the usefulness of the network itself. This in turn encourages the adoption of TCP/IP for use in corporate enterprise networks as well as in the networks that interconnect to form the public Internet.

10.1. Timing Services: NTP and SNTP

Accurate, precise time is a valuable resource in a distributed network architecture. Timestamps identify and sequence packets, determine when a packet has aged while being routed, and are used as pseudo-random keys for encryption and other dynamic information-encoding schemes.

In addition, system time and the ability to generate timer-based interrupts with substantial precision are central to the protocol implementation of several layers of the TCP/IP stack.

To meet this need, the U.S. Defense Department devised a robust, high-precision Network Time Protocol (NTP), now in its third version as defined by RFC 1305. In addition, a Simple Network Time Protocol (SNTP) is defined by RFCs 1361 and 1769. SNTP is a subset of NTP that is suitable for end client machines such as user PCs.

Support Services

10.1.1. NTP

The Network Time Protocol provides a crucial service within TCP/IP networks: It allows a group of network nodes to maintain clock synchronization with accuracy in the range of 1–50 milliseconds. In keeping with the original purpose of the ARPANET—namely the creation of a network that could support mission-critical military use in the face of unreliable communications links and changing network topology—NTP offers both reliable and precise time services at the expense of considerable protocol and implementation complexity.

> **TIP**
>
> Many people confuse accuracy and precision.
>
> A time server is *accurate* if the value it presents is very close to the "true" time.
>
> *Precision* has to do with the size of the units in which a measurement is taken and reported. For instance, the time measurement "3 hours and 40 minutes" is less precise than the measurement "3 hours, 39 minutes, and 47 seconds."
>
> Do not confuse these two attributes of a time or other measurement! The more precise measurement is not necessarily more accurate.

The design of NTP assumes that various peers on the network may or may not be reliably synchronized to the true standard time. If several NTP servers disagree regarding what that time is while claiming to know it, one or more of them must be broken and unreliable. NTP does not concern itself with synchronizing network time servers with one another, but rather aims at propagating correct time synchronization throughout the network, beginning with a trusted external time source. The time value returned by that source is called the *Universal Coordinated Time* (UCT).

Hence, multiple time servers within a TCP/IP network will return very similar time values, not because they are synchronized with one another, but because each server is synchronized to a trusted time source directly, or to one or more reliable servers that themselves are close enough to that source to be accurate.

Servers that receive their time information directly from a trusted external UCT source are referred to as *Stratum Two servers*. Those that synchronize to Stratum Two servers are referred to as *Stratum Three servers*, and so on. The NTP protocol definition allows for a maximum of 15 time-server strata.

Ultimately, the accuracy and precision of the time values propagated through a TCP/IP network using the NTP protocol depend on the external source that serves as Stratum One. For the ARPANET and the public Internet, a variety of radio-based time sources are available.

For example, some networks use the Global Positioning Satellite (GPS) system. GPS provides both public (lower accuracy) and military (very high accuracy) latitude and longitude positioning that is derived from triangulation on a constellation of 26 geosynchronous satellites. These satellites, whose orbits keep them over defined places around the Earth, beam a constant flow of orbital location information, with timestamps whose accuracy approaches that of atomic clocks and that are regularly adjusted by Department of Defense ground-based systems of very high accuracy and precision. GPS receivers deduce their relative distances from multiple satellites across the sky and, because the speed of radio transmission is known, deduce the latitude and longitude at which the reading was taken.

The highest-precision military information band is encrypted and is not available for general civilian use. Nevertheless, because of the accuracy and precision of the timing information that is available on the civilian band, surveying equipment (which can take a series of readings while remaining stationary on the ground) is able to achieve location measurements that are accurate to within centimeters by measuring the Doppler effect of the military beam coming through the atmosphere!

Other sources of trusted timing information exist. Several countries have central standards bodies that provide wire- or radio-based time signals of equivalent usefulness. Time services used in the United States include the Geostationary Operational Environmental Satellite, the Loran–C radio navigation system, VLF radio sources such as OMEGA, and numerous computer-oriented systems such as the Digital Time Synchronization Service.

NTP Server Selection

The higher the stratum level at which a time server exists, the more danger there is of inaccuracies and desynchronization with peer servers. In general, then, each server would like to take its own time from the lowest-stratum server to which it has access. However, NTP operates under the assumption that every server must be viewed with a certain degree of distrust. As a result, NTP prefers that each time server has access to several sources of lower-level strata time values. If three or more such servers are available, well-known algorithms can be used to determine if one of the sources is significantly incorrect.

The normal selection algorithm is to choose the best of the agreeing servers, where "best" is determined by such factors as lowest stratum, closest in network topology, and highest claimed precision.

NTP Subnet Configuration and Association Modes

> **NOTE** When talking about the Network Time Protocol, a *subnet* consists of some part of the timing server (synchronization) tree. This need not be the same thing as all the nodes on the TCP/IP network; however, the tree will usually contain all the backbone nodes and most major nodes in the physical network.

Each node on the network that runs an NTP process must be configured with regard to both the other servers with which it is associated in a subnet and the mode of association it will have with each server.

Most implementations of NTP require a configuration file to be maintained on the server. This file identifies the adjacent nodes (higher, peer, and lower) on the timing server tree—that is, the synchronization subnet for this server.

Along with the server's network address, the configuration file must specify the mode of association that this server will have with the specified node. NTP offers a richly nuanced set of potential associations. Among the more commonly used ones are

- Symmetric-active mode

- Client/server mode

- Broadcast and multicast modes

Two timing servers that are in *symmetric-active* association with one another are peers. At NTP process time, each peer server contacts the other peer server, stating both that it wants to receive timing information from the other server and that it is willing to supply timing information as well. This association is used to create a set of redundant servers, generally reached by different network paths so as to provide fault tolerance and robustness as well as to minimize timer bias due to network path length. Note that most servers at Stratum Two on the public Internet are configured in symmetric-active associations with other servers.

A server may request a *client* association with another server. This mode signals the client's desire to receive timing information from the other server and the client's unwillingness to provide timing information. This mode is used by end-node machines such as PCs that desire a client relationship with a file server or network gateway. Note that a node that is in client association with all other servers in its subnet must not provide timing information to any other machine or process.

The *broadcast* and *multicast* modes provide the least accuracy and reliability, but impose the lowest maintenance overhead. A node that requests a broadcast and/or multicast association need not be configured with specific subnet relationships. Because broadcast messages are not propagated by routers, the assumed synchronization subnet will consist of the set of timing servers that reside within the local physical subnetwork, as bounded by a router. Therefore, broadcast association modes require the presence of a broadcast timing server on the same physical subnet, and multicast associations require both support for multicast IP on the client and access through this server to a multicast server farther on in the network.

NTP Datagram Format

NTP makes use of the UDP transport protocol. Figure 10.1 shows the format of the NTP synchronization message.

Figure 10.1.

NTP datagram format.

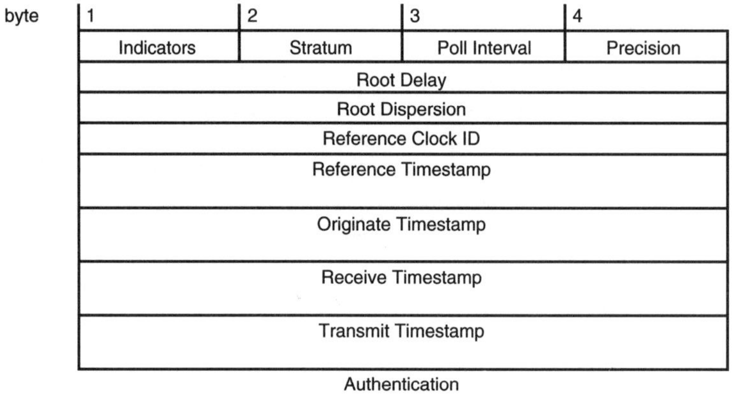

byte	1	2	3	4
	Indicators	Stratum	Poll Interval	Precision
	Root Delay			
	Root Dispersion			
	Reference Clock ID			
	Reference Timestamp			
	Originate Timestamp			
	Receive Timestamp			
	Transmit Timestamp			
	Authentication			

The datagram fields have the following meanings and uses:

Leap Indicator (LI)—2-bit code; warns of an impending leapsecond to be inserted/deleted in the last minute of the current day. It has the following values:

0	No warning
1	Last minute has 61 seconds
2	Last minute has 59 seconds
3	Alarm condition (clock not synchronized)

Version Number Indicator (VN)—3-bit integer indicating the NTP version number, currently three (3).

Mode Indicator—3-bit integer indicating the association mode, with values defined as follows:

0	Reserved
1	Symmetric active
2	Symmetric passive
3	Client
4	Server
5	Broadcast
6	Reserved for NTP control message
7	Reserved for private use

Stratum—8-bit integer indicating the stratum level of the local clock, with values defined as follows:

0	Unspecified
1	Primary reference (for example, radio clock)
2–255	Secondary reference (via NTP)

Poll Interval—8-bit signed integer; indicates the maximum interval between successive messages, in seconds.

Precision—8-bit signed integer; indicates the precision of the local clock, in seconds.

Root Delay—32-bit signed fixed-point number; indicates the total round-trip delay to the primary reference source, in seconds.

Root Dispersion—32-bit signed fixed-point number; indicates the maximum error relative to the primary reference source, in seconds.

Reference Clock Identifier—32-bit code; identifies the particular reference clock. The format of this field varies depending on the value of the Stratum field, as follows:

Stratum = 0/1	Four-octet, left-justified, zero-padded ASCII string
Stratum = 2	Four-octet Internet address of the primary reference host

Reference Timestamp—64 bits; the local time at which the local clock was last set or corrected.

Originate Timestamp—64 bits; the local time at which the request departed the client host for the service host.

Receive Timestamp—64 bits; local time at which the request arrived at the service host.

Transmit Timestamp—64 bits; local time at which the reply departed the service host for the client host.

Authentication—Optional; for use if the NTP authentication mechanism is in force.

Support Services

For more details regarding NTP protocol operations, NTP control messages, and authentication disciplines, see RFC 1305.

10.1.2. SNTP

NTP is a robust, rigorous timing protocol capable of maintaining synchronized times with accuracy of 1–50 milliseconds. To accomplish this, it requires a complex exchange of messages among nodes within and across subnets.

This rigorous complexity is both appropriate and cost-effective on network servers. It is, however, expensive to operate on an end network node such as a client PC. To ease the overhead burden for client PCs and other end nodes, the Simple Network Time Protocol was defined in RFC 1361.

SNTP does not require any changes to NTP message formats or the NTP specification. Instead, SNTP defines an implementation approach and feature subset that, if implemented on end nodes only, delivers time accuracies to within 1 second while imposing a much smaller overhead requirement on the client machine and on the local time server.

SNMP requests for time information are conceptually like stateless Remote Procedure Calls to the local time server. The client passes an NTP message that is empty except for the Mode field, which is set to **3** (client) and the Version Number field. The server will reply with a filled message, of which the Transmit Timestamp is the meaningful field.

RFC 2030 extends the SNTP protocol to encompass the IPv4, IPv6, and OSI network environments.

10.2. Management Services: SNMP

The Network Time Protocols function more or less invisibly to network administrators under normal conditions. This section takes a look at a protocol that more directly supports administrative functions.

The Internet Activities Board recommends that all TCP/IP software allow network management functions within a common framework. There are two legs to this strategy: a common information database and a management protocol. RFC 1156 defines the Internet Management Information Base, which satisfies the first requirement. The protocol used to address the second requirement is the Simple Network Management Protocol (SNMP), defined in RFC 1157. Together they underlie most commercially available tools for managing TCP/IP networks.

As might be expected, it proved much easier to devise a protocol for network management than to pin down the appropriate information to be collected and exchanged for that purpose. RFC 1156 itself replaced an earlier attempt, documented in RFCs 1065 and 1066. These documents were intended to provide a compatible migration path to OSI-compliant network management. However, initial attempts at dual-stack management showed that this goal would be more difficult to attain than was previously anticipated. Therefore, the information base described by RFC 1156 was designed to support TCP/IP stacks and SNMP only. It was shortly updated in RFC 1158 and again in RFC 1213, which remains the information base standard for Version 1 of SNMP.

10.2.1. SNMP Operations

SNMP operates by inspecting and altering the values of variables that are distributed throughout the network. These variables are maintained as objects by the system (host, router, and so on) whose activities they describe. Together, the distributed variables make up the Management Information Base (MIB) for the network.

Note that SNMP does not provide commands or other means by which a remote system may be induced to perform some action, other than resetting a variable's value. However, it is likely that some variable resets will be followed by predictable actions on the part of the complying system. The result is a network-management protocol that imposes a low overhead cost, scales well to various network complexities, and can be implemented across a wide variety of host hardware and software environments.

SNMP operates through the exchange of protocol messages between nodes using the UDP transport protocol. UDP, you will recall, is both connectionless and unreliable—no network or host resources are used to maintain a communications relationship over time, and unfulfilled requests are not retransmitted. However, this does not limit the usefulness of SNMP as a management protocol. Both status information and control are distributed throughout the network, and every message exchange is an independent event.

Central to SNMP operations are a set of administrative relationships that are defined between entities that participate in the protocol. SNMP *application entities* are the systems, such as network-management stations and network nodes, that communicate using the protocol. In addition, the protocol defines peer processes that implement the protocol and hence support the application entities; these are termed *protocol entities*.

Application entities are grouped into arbitrary sets called *communities*, each of which is named as a whole. Only SNMP messages originated by community members are considered authentic; authentication schemes are an important part of any network-management program that relies on the SNMP protocol.

A community's access policy consists of that subset of the MIB that applies to a network element, combined with the access permissions granted for each variable within that MIB view. This access policy guides the actions that will be taken by the protocol entity in response to SNMP requests that concern the application entity at hand.

Thus, administrative relationships in SNMP are organized around policies that determine the access afforded other community members to a system's information.

SNMP also allows the creation of proxy access policies for network elements such as modems that would not otherwise support an SNMP protocol process of their own. This feature of the SNMP protocol allows a single network-management framework to address the widest variety of network elements.

Object instances are named by the concatenation of the object type (identifier) with a unique name or other means of differentiating this instance of the object from all others in the community. The format of these names differs among the different object types.

SNMP messages are transmitted as UDP datagrams. Each message contains a protocol version number, the SNMP community name, and one of five generalized *protocol data units* (PDUs), all represented in the form of ASCII strings. You can think of the PDU as a remote procedure call, combining an action with the specific variable identifiers to be acted on. Once the PDU is created, it is passed to an authentication service along with the community name, its source transport address, and the destination transport address. The protocol entity receives back a new message, perhaps encrypted, which is then passed to the transport (UDP) layer for transmission.

Receiving protocol entities parse the incoming datagram, send it to the authentication service, and receive the original format message.

Table 10.1 shows the PDU types defined for Version 1 of SNMP.

Table 10.1. SNMP PDU types.

PDU Type	Purpose
GetRequest-PDU	Requests the value of one or more variables.
GetNextRequest-PDU	Requests a successive value; used to access table entries.
SetRequest-PDU	Requests that a variable be set to a new value.
GetResponse-PDU	Causes the protocol entity to send the GetRequest, GetNextRequest, or SetRequest PDU to the application entity.

PDU Type	Purpose
SetResponse-PDU	Notifies the requester whether a variable has been modified.
Trap-PDU	Used by the local application entity to force restarts, initialization, and so on.

Although the distinction between the application entity and the protocol entity seems forced, it allows the use of proxy relationships and hence the management of diverse network resources that do not themselves host an SNMP protocol process.

10.2.2. SNMP Management Information Base

The Management Information Base (MIB) is a virtual database consisting of objects that reside on each network entity under management. MIB objects are identified as belonging to one of the several groups organized around a protocol, a service, or the network entity (system) itself. All the objects in the group either must be present or are irrelevant to an implementation. Generally, a group is irrelevant if it refers to a protocol that is not implemented in a given system. The groups provide a framework for information object naming and also cluster objects for implementation decisions.

The following groups are defined in RFC 1213:

- The System Group

- The Interfaces Group

- The Address Translation Group

- The IP Group

- The ICMP Group

- The TCP Group

- The UDP Group

- The EGP Group

- The Transmission Group

- The SNMP Group

The first five groups are mandatory; the rest need be implemented for a given node (system) only if the relevant protocol is implemented. As with all object models, MIB objects are in some cases composite. To illustrate the kinds of

Support Services

information that comprise the SNMP information base, Table 10.2 describes the high-level object types that are mandatory for all systems. For detailed description of object formats, see RFC 1213 and its predecessors.

Table 10.2. Mandatory SNMP MIB objects.

Object	Purpose
The System Group	
sysDescr	Identification of the system's hardware, operating-system, and networking software
sysObjectID	Vendor's identification of the network management subsystem
sysUpTime	Time (in hundredths of a second) since the network-management subsystem was last reinitialized
sysContact	Point of contact and contact information for this managed node
sysName	The node's fully qualified domain name
sysLocation	Physical location of this node
sysServices	A composite number indicating the set of services that this entity primarily offers
The Interfaces Group	
ifNumber	Count of network interfaces present on this system
ifTable	Entries for each interface on this system
ifEntry	One interface entry
The Address Translation Group	
atTable	Maps NetworkAddresses to physical address equivalencies.
atEntry	One such mapping entry
The IP Group	
ipForwarding	Flag indicating whether this entity is acting as an IP gateway with regard to forwarding datagrams
ipDefaultTTL	Default Time-To-Live for IP datagrams originated at this system
ipInReceives	Count of input datagrams received by this system
ipInHdrErrors	Count of input datagrams discarded due to header errors

Object	Purpose
ipInAddrErrors	Count of input datagrams discarded due to a destination address that is not valid for this system
ipForwDatagrams	Count of input datagrams for which this system was not their final IP destination
ipInUnknownProtos	Count of correctly received datagrams discarded because they specified an unknown or unsupported protocol
ipInDiscards	Count of input IP datagrams that were discarded for lack of buffer space
ipInDelivers	Count of input datagrams delivered to IP user protocols
ipOutRequests	Count of IP datagrams supplied locally to IP for transmission (excluding forwarded datagrams)
ipOutDiscards	Count of output IP datagrams that were discarded for lack of buffer space
ipOutNoRoutes	Count of output IP datagrams discarded because no route could be found to transmit them to their destination
ipReasmTimeout	Maximum time (in seconds) that a received fragment will be held while awaiting reassembly
ipReasmReqds	Count of IP fragments received that required reassembly
ipReasmOKs	Count of IP datagrams reassembled
ipReasmFails	Count of IP reassembly failures
ipFragOKs	Count of IP datagrams that have been fragmented
ipFragFails	Count of IP datagrams that needed fragmentation but were marked Don't Fragment
ipFragCreates	Count of IP datagram fragments that have been created
ipAddrTable	Addressing information relevant to this system's IP addresses
ipRouteTable	Contains all IP routes currently known to this system, including path metrics

Support Services

continues

Table 10.2. Continued.

Object	Purpose
ipNetToMediaTable	Maps IP addresses to physical addresses
ipRoutingDiscards	Count of valid routing entries that have been discarded to free up buffer space
The ICMP Group	
icmpInMsgs	Count of ICMP messages that the system has received
icmpInErrors	Count of received ICMP messages that had ICMP-specific errors
icmpInDestUnreachs	Count of ICMP Destination Unreachable messages received
icmpInTimeExcds	Count of ICMP Time Exceeded messages received
icmpInParmProbs	Count of ICMP Parameter Problem messages received
icmpInSrcQuenchs	Count of ICMP Source Quench messages received
icmpInRedirects	Count of ICMP Redirect messages received
icmpInEchos	Count of ICMP Echo (request) messages received
icmpInEchoReps	Count of ICMP Echo Reply messages received
icmpInTimestamps	Count of ICMP Timestamp (request) messages received
icmpInTimestampReps	Count of ICMP Timestamp Reply messages received
icmpInAddrMasks	Count of ICMP Address Mask (request) messages received
icmpInAddrMaskReps	Count of ICMP Address Mask Reply messages received
icmpOutMsgs	Count of ICMP messages that this system attempted to send
icmpOutErrors	Count of ICMP messages that this system did not send due to lack of buffer space or similar problems within ICMP
icmpOutDestUnreachs	Count of ICMP Destination Unreachable messages transmitted

Object	Purpose
icmpOutTimeExcds	Count of ICMP Time Exceeded messages transmitted
icmpOutParmProbs	Count of ICMP Parameter Problem messages transmitted
icmpOutSrcQuenchs	Count of ICMP Source Quench messages transmitted
icmpOutRedirects	Count of ICMP Redirect messages transmitted
icmpOutEchos	Count of ICMP Echo (request) messages transmitted
icmpOutEchoReps	Count of ICMP Echo Reply messages transmitted
icmpOutTimestamps	Count of ICMP Timestamp (request) messages transmitted
icmpOutTimestampReps	Count of ICMP Timestamp Reply messages transmitted
icmpOutAddrMasks	Count of ICMP Address Mask (request) messages transmitted
icmpOutAddrMaskReps	Count of ICMP Address Mask Reply messages transmitted

10.2.3. SNMPv2

Implementation experience with SNMP, along with the adoption of IPv6 and the ongoing desire to reconcile TCP/IP network management with OSI networks, motivated the definition of Version 2 of SNMP. The protocol definition is found in RFC 1905. Associated MIB changes are dispersed among several RFCs, including 1902, 1903, and 1907.

SNMPv2 clarifies the relationships among community entities by distinguishing between manager and agent roles. Message interactions then fall into one of three categories:

- Manager-to-agent request-response interaction, in which a manager requests information or that a variable be set for a device under management, and the device's agent responds.

- Manager-to-manager request-response interaction, used to notify other managers of the status of devices.

- Unconfirmed interaction, in which an agent sends a unsolicited trap message to inform the manager of a new event or status.

SNMPv2 proposes an extended set of PDU types, as follows:

```
GetRequest-PDU
GetNextRequest-PDU
GetBulkRequest-PDU
Response-PDU
SetRequest-PDU
InformRequest-PDU
SNMPv2-Trap-PDU
Report-PDU
```

The `Response-PDU` includes the PDU identifier of the request to which this message is responding and therefore generalizes responses to all requests.

The `GetBulkRequest-PDU` allows for maximally efficient retrieval of large objects such as IP routing tables.

The `InformRequest-PDU` is used to exchange management information with an entity that is remote to the community in which the information is generated.

The `Report-PDU` does not have a defined structure at present. Implementers may use this PDU type to add functionality to their products.

The definition of SNMPv2, along with that of IPv6, indicates the emerging maturity of the TCP/IP protocol stack and the public Internet. Together they provide both the routing facilities and the network administration and management services needed for the integration of TCP/IP–based networks into global enterprise computing and the public adoption of the Internet as a major information and communications resource.

10.3. File Services: NFS

The Network File System (NFS) was designed by Sun Microsystems to allow its UNIX-based workstations to access remote files and directory structures as if they were local resources. NFS was made available for industry adoption and documented in RFC 1094. Version 3 of the protocol is in widespread use today across a variety of hardware, software, and network environments; it is defined in RFC 1813. The protocol continues to be updated and extended as TCP/IP–based networks, LANs, WANs, and other distributed computing and communications environments proliferate in general and corporate use. Version 3, for instance, supports larger file-addressing schemes, extends access security mechanisms, and is backward compatible with previous versions.

To provide hardware and software independence, the Network File System is designed around two core concepts: Services are requested by application programs through the use of *Remote Procedure Calls* (RPCs); software and machine independence are accomplished by passing input and output parameters in a set of common formats called the *eXternal Data Representation* (XDR). The RPCs for a given version of NFS are described in the protocol definition document for that version. XDR is described in RFC 1014 and is similar to the OSI approach for shared data.

10.3.1. NFS Operations

Access to remote file resources begins with the MOUNT operation. This operation associates a remote directory and file tree with a stub on the local directory tree, effecting a temporary logical "graft" of the remote files and directories into the local structure. Once mounted, these directories and files can be manipulated with RFCs in ways that parallel operations on local disk information.

In addition to the NFS protocol itself, which consists of the file-manipulation RPCs, NFS includes two support protocols. The MOUNT protocol manages the mounting process, including enforcement of remote access privileges to other users. The Lock Manager provides support for file locking and manages file states to allow shared read and write access to a given file.

There are three types of agents in an NFS operation. A *server* provides resources to the network. A *client* accesses resources over the network. A *user* is a person logged in on a client, running an application.

RPCs provide a procedure-oriented interface to remote file services. A given RPC process is completely specified by the combination of host address, program number, version number, and procedure number; multiple versions of the protocol can be supported by the same server without conflict.

Unlike those applications that occupy a fixed port assignment, RPC-based protocols such as NFS register a 32-bit program number and an assigned port with the port map service on the well-known port 111. NFS servers generally register as port 2049.

As a LAN protocol, NFS is generally implemented on top of UDP. However, Version 3 of NFS is well suited to function on top of TCP for more reliable transmission across public networks. In either case, NFS is designed to function over various transport protocols and, because it is a stateless protocol, it is not dependent on reliable message transport to function correctly or manage file access. The special case of file locks for multiaccess resources is managed by the Lock Manager, which is associated with (but separate from) NFS itself. As a result, it is possible to implement a small, efficient NFS protocol program without the complexities of recovery mechanisms, in environments or even in specific applications where multiuser database access is not required.

Support Services

Every RPC has a slot for authentication parameters. The values passed for authentication are determined by the type of authentication, if any, that is supported by a given client and server. Servers may support multiple authentication schemes, thereby facilitating mixed network environments. Among the authentication flavors available to a server are the following:

- `AUTH_NONE`—No authentication

- `AUTH_UNIX`—UNIX-style user ID, group ID, and groups

- `AUTH_DES`—DES public-key encryption

- `AUTH_KERB`—DES encryption using Kerberos secret keys

The NFS server applies access control based on credentials passed as RPC authentication parameters on each RPC call. Depending on the authentication scheme chosen, there may be administrative configuration required to correlate authentication information. The encrypted schemes require less administrative burden and are more secure, but impose a greater processing load during network operations.

Once access is permitted, the burden falls on the client (not the server) to translate generalized access into specific file retrievals and updates. In particular, some RPC features may be meaningless within the context of a given server's operating environment. In such a case, the server returns an error code, and the client must decide what steps to take in response. This allows the server to maintain the stateless design of NFS, increasing the protocol's efficiency wherever possible.

In order to ensure reasonable file integrity within this stateless approach, the majority of NFS functions that modify files and directories are *synchronous*; that is, the operation has completed before the caller receives a response. NFS servers must update data blocks, file system information blocks, and file attribute information and flush these sectors to disk before returning from the RPC. In addition, Version 3 of the NFS protocol allows safe asynchronous writes on the server when the `WRITE` procedure is used in conjunction with the `COMMIT` procedure. The `COMMIT` procedure causes the server to flush data from previous asynchronous `WRITE`s to disk (or other stable storage) and to detect whether it is necessary to retransmit the data.

10.3.2. NFS RPCs

NFS provides a full set of file-level services. The protocol also includes directory-related services.

Table 10.3 lists the RPCs supported in Version 3 of NFS. (See RFC 1813 for extended calling sequences and XDR formats for these procedures.)

Table 10.3. Network file system RPCs.

RPC Name	Function
Null	Does no work; used when testing server timing
GETATTR	Retrieve the attributes for a file system object
SETATTR	Set the attributes for a file system object
LOOKUP	Look up a filename
ACCESS	Check access permission
READLINK	Read from symbolic link (pointer to another file)
READ	Read from a file
WRITE	Write to a file
CREATE	Create a file
MKDIR	Create a directory
SYMLINK	Create a symbolic link
MKNOD	Create a special device (including pipes)
REMOVE	Remove a file
RMDIR	Remove a directory
RENAME	Rename a file or directory
LINK	Create a (hard) link to an object
READDIR	Read from a directory
READDIRPLUS	Extended read from directory
FSSTAT	Get dynamic file system information
FSINFO	Get static file system information
PATHCONF	Retrieve POSIX information
COMMIT	Commit cached data on a server to stable storage

Support Services

10.3.3. WebNFS

The rise in popularity and use of the World Wide Web, and similar multimedia capabilities on TCP/IP–based intranets and extranets, places additional demands on the NFS protocol. Web pages, for instance, can consist of many files, each of which must potentially be mounted, opened, and read whenever the Web page is displayed.

RFCs 2054 and 2055 describe a lightweight binding mechanism that Sun Microsystems has devised to support efficient file access in a Web environment. This is accomplished by replacing the `MOUNT` call with the use of a public file handle. Once acquired, the file handle allows immediate access to the resource in question without forcing a longer-lived association of the source directory structure and the client's own file system. The protocol documents provide implementation guidance to ensure that WebNFS accesses are accomplished in the most efficient manner possible.

10.4. NetBIOS Over TCP/IP

NetBIOS was originally designed and implemented by IBM Corporation and Sytek in 1984. It quickly became the interface of choice for applications that wanted to exchange information over LANs, and it remains the predominant transport protocol for PCs.

Strictly speaking, NetBIOS defines a software interface to selected services and not a communications protocol. Protocols implementing NetBIOS services have been implemented on different operating-system, hardware, and network platforms; however, compatible protocols are required if systems are to interoperate.

With the rise of enterprise networks based on TCP/IP, new attention has been given to providing NetBIOS services across a TCP/IP network. RFCs 1001 and 1002 define the mechanisms for providing these services. RFC 1088 describes the reverse service—namely, transporting IP datagrams over NetBIOS networks.

10.4.1. NetBIOS Operations

NetBIOS was devised to allow groups of PCs to communicate over a broadcast-oriented network, such as a LAN, based on Ethernet or Token Ring protocols. NetBIOS offers both connection (session) and connectionless (datagram) services. Unlike in the TCP/IP environment, messages cannot be switched; all participants on the network are identified by names that do not necessarily map into delivery paths. These names are assigned dynamically across the network, with the result that name collisions can occur.

Applications use NetBIOS services to locate resources, establish connections, send and receive data with an application peer, and terminate connections. The NetBIOS specification is indifferent to implementation choices regarding the encapsulation of these services as a distinct layer of processes or their integration into applications or the operating system.

NetBIOS services fall into three categories:

- Name services

- Session services

- Datagram services

Name services are used to acquire and relinquish resource identifiers. Unlike IP addresses, in which the host identifier modifies the wider network identifier, the NetBIOS name space is flat—there are no facilities for grouping names in a manner that associates them with some physical subset of the network as a whole.

Applications bid for use of a name by attempting to register it. If no objections are received by other network applications within a specified time, the name is implicitly approved. Names may refer to a single resource or to a group resource. Nothing in the name or in its treatment by the service provider distinguishes these two cases. Unique names, therefore, refer to a single workstation on the LAN. Group names are held in common and equally by multiple stations.

The following name services are provided:

- Add Name—A bid for exclusive use of the name

- Add Group Name—A bid for use of the name on a possibly non-exclusive basis

- Delete Name—Graceful relinquishment of the name

A *session* is a full-duplex, sequenced, and reliable exchange of messages between a pair of NetBIOS applications. No NetBIOS facility exists to expedite urgent data during a session. A pair of peers may have multiple sessions open at once, and the peers know who each other are by name. Sessions involving a group name are presumed to accept any member of the group as the terminating peer.

The NetBIOS session services are

- Call—Initiate a session with a named process, assuming it is listening

- Listen—Accept a session from a specific caller (if specified) or any caller

- Hang Up—Gracefully terminate a session after completing the transfer of pending data

- Send—Transmit one message

- Receive—Accept data

- Session Status—Pass locally available status information to the application

Support Services

The NetBIOS *datagram services* provide unreliable, non-sequenced, connectionless transmission to specifically named destinations or as a broadcast. Both peers know the name of the other.

The datagram services are as follows:

- Send Datagram—Transmit an unreliable datagram to a specified name

- Send Broadcast Datagram—Transmit an unreliable datagram to any application with a Receive Broadcast Datagram posted

- Receive Datagram—Receive a datagram sent by a specified originating name to this name (or by any sender)

- Receive Broadcast Datagram—Receive a datagram sent as a broadcast

Individual implementations of NetBIOS may support additional miscellaneous administrative services as well.

10.4.2. Supporting NetBIOS Over TCP/IP

NetBIOS operations over TCP/IP rely on the concept of a NetBIOS scope. A *scope* is the group of computers across which a given name is known. Each scope has its own identifier. End nodes within a scope support the NetBIOS services and the applications that use them, and are distinguished by the type of communications relationship each supports: Point-to-Point (P), Broadcast (B), and Mixed (M). For efficient network utilization, it is recommended that no scope contain both B and M nodes; that is, a scope should either model a collision-based LAN or an IP-style network, but not both at once.

The two types of servers that exist in a NetBIOS over TCP/IP environment are the NetBIOS Name Server (NBNS) and the NetBIOS Datagram Distribution (NBDD) server. The NBNS manages name reservation and conflicts with as active or passive a stance as the implementation may desire. The NDDS nodes distribute NetBIOS datagrams into and across the TCP/IP network.

NetBIOS messages are encapsulated for travel across the switched IP network. Each exchange of datagrams is called a *transaction* and carries a unique transaction identifier.

The NDDS provides services that parallel those of NetBIOS itself for sending and receiving messages. Internal to the protocol's implementation, these logical sends and receives are translated into TCP/IP or UDP/IP packets that are transmitted across the TCP/IP network using standard IP routing. Routing translation is provided by the NBNS, which must map NetBIOS style names into IP addresses for this purpose.

10.4.3. Datagram Formats

The NetBIOS name service packets comply with the packet structure defined in the Domain Name Service (DNS) RFC 883. Additional types and codes have been added to the DNS format to support NetBIOS details. Name service packets are preceded by a 16-bit unsigned integer field containing the length of the name service packet.

The NetBIOS names are modified by their scope identifier, separated by a period, to render them as a valid domain system name to DNS. Names are also encoded in DNS format. In addition to the standard DNS services, however, the NBNS must also support additional entry attributes and provide an additional set of transactions, including

Dynamic addition of entries
Dynamic update of entry data
Support for multiple instance (group) entries
Support for entry Time-To-Live values and ability to accept refresh messages to restart the Time-To-Live period

RFC 1002 defines the detailed formats for NBNS datagrams. Note that datagrams have nested formats; that is, many fields are themselves complex and variable records.

Session service packets are sent over a TCP connection. Session service packet codes and types include

00	SESSION MESSAGE
81	SESSION REQUEST
82	POSITIVE SESSION RESPONSE
83	NEGATIVE SESSION RESPONSE
84	RETARGET SESSION RESPONSE
85	SESSION KEEP ALIVE

As with the name service messages, session service packets consist of nested formats containing variable information whose interpretation depends on the topology of the NetBIOS scope under management. Detailed packet formats are described in RFC 1002.

10.4.4. IP Over NetBIOS

The usefulness of transporting NetBIOS traffic across a TCP/IP link is intuitively obvious. Less obvious, but equally important for the mature adoption of TCP/IP-based networks, is the capability to transport traffic in the opposite direction.

RFC 1088 describes the mechanisms for encapsulating IP datagrams within NetBIOS datagrams and assigning IP numbers to the hosts on a NetBIOS network. This facility extends the interoperability of private LANs and IP-based public and private networks.

Support Services

10.5. Summary

This chapter looks at those applications that provide network-related services to other applications on the TCP/IP stack.

Accurate and reliable time services are critical to operation of the complex public Internet, as well as to more localized networks. Both the data link–layer protocols and some transport protocols in a TCP/IP stack rely on time-out/retransmission mechanisms to maintain reliability and integrity. In addition, an agreed time basis is necessary in order for the stack's embedded mechanisms to discard obsolete frames and messages at both the data link and transport layers.

The Network Time Protocol (NTP) is the result of significant theory, analysis, and practical experience in synchronization of time information across a complex, dynamically changing network. NTP does not attempt to directly synchronize network nodes to one another. Instead, it layers the nodes in the network, synchronizing the first stratum to a trusted source, the second stratum to the first, and so on. The full protocol provides substantial mechanisms for identifying untrustworthy time servers. Use of NTP across a complex network such as the public Internet has resulted in synchronization accuracy of 1–50 milliseconds, due to the design of the protocol and the use of sufficiently precise and accurate trusted sources.

Trusted sources may be accessed by radio or wire. Numerous sources are available for use, some of them providing atomic-clock accuracy and precision.

SNTP provides a less rigorous, less expensive time service to client workstations. It delivers time accuracies of approximately 1 second, sufficient for such purposes as setting CMOS clocks on PC motherboards and timestamping files on shared servers.

A second major service that is useful on TCP/IP networks is a common scheme for network administration and management. The IAB does not impose a detailed scheme for Internet management. Instead, it encourages the development of network-management application tools by defining a SNMP on which such applications may be based.

SNMP is based on a distributed, virtual Management Information Base consisting of objects that contain network operational information for the node on which the object resides. Management stations may request (but not demand) that these objects report their values and reset themselves. Authentication and encryption schemes may be applied to protect the network from hostile or inadvertent manipulation.

SNMPv2 extends the existing SNMP protocol to support multiversion IP networks and to further the IAB's original goal for network management, namely that it converge in the foreseeable future to interoperability with OSI-based network schemes.

One primary reason for implementing a network of any kind is to share information among distributed computers and users. The Network File System was devised by Sun Microsystems to allow remote access to file and directory structures as if they were local. NFS has evolved over more than a decade's use. Its design is well suited to TCP/IP environments, because it does not require that resource providers maintain and restore file state information when networks, servers, or clients fail.

To accomplish this support, NFS is organized around the model of Remote Procedure Calls (RPCs). Each RPC must be able to trigger execution of an associate set of code on a remote system, possibly differing in hardware and operating environment from the caller. To facilitate this, RPC parameters are encoded in the eXternal Data Representation (XDR) formats.

Although originally developed as a proprietary software offering, NFS has been opened by the developing company for general adoption. More recently, Sun Microsystems has introduced an extension to the Network File System that is better suited to efficient transfer of files over the Internet. Dubbed WebNFS, this protocol allows for the use of file handles to specify shared file resources, thereby lowering the overhead required to download the many files that constitute a World Wide Web page, among other Internet structures.

With the introduction of loose binding (that is, of using transient access to file handles), NFS moves beyond the UNIX file-structure model on which it was originally based. However, the original NFS facilities to mount a directory tree and bind it into the local file structure of a client machine remain in force. With the additional support of services that enforce shared access permissions and multiaccess locking mechanisms, NFS provides an efficient, robust, and flexible facility for the distribution and access of shared and remote information resources across complex networks. By extending the environment within which NFS functions beyond local area networks to the public Internet and across corporate gateway computers, practical adoption of NFS as an (unofficial) Internet standard adds to the rich possibilities for open systems as elements of a TCP/IP–based network.

Support Services

But TCP/IP protocol stacks are not the only (or even the predominant) network model currently in place on computers around the world. The NetBIOS model for communication among peers on a LAN has proliferated as a true standard across the world of desktop computing. The current investment in software, LAN hardware, and user applications that are NetBIOS aware makes it cost-effective to consider ways to transport NetBIOS traffic across TCP/IP backbones.

In keeping with the goal of open systems and interoperability on TCP/IP–based networks, the IETF has adopted protocol definitions for this purpose. Recently, the reverse transport has been defined as well: TCP/IP traffic carried on a NetBIOS connection. These tools also facilitate the interconnection of corporate, private, and public networks, thereby enriching the usefulness and flexibility of each arena.

As this chapter shows, the application layer of the TCP/IP stack is more than a polite fiction. The network-oriented application layer services significantly extend the power and usefulness of the Internet and other TCP/IP–based networks. This extensibility is a key feature of the layered stack approach that underlies TCP/IP as a whole.

11.1. Telnet

11.2. FTP

11.3. SMTP

11.4. HTTP

11.5. Summary

Chapter

11

Application Services

by Thomas Lee

As noted in Chapter 2, "A Close Look at IPv4 and IPv6," the application layer is the topmost layer in the TCP/IP protocol model. For many users, the application layer *is* the Internet, because it contains the key protocols associated with the Internet, such as news (NNTP), e-mail (SMTP), and the World Wide Web (HTTP).

This chapter looks at four key application protocols:

- Telnet—Used to create remote terminal sessions across a network.

- FTP—Used to transfer files to and from an FTP server. Some Web servers utilize FTP to upload Web pages.

- SMTP—The Simple Mail Transfer Protocol is used between mail servers and, in some cases, between mail clients and servers.

- HTTP—This protocol, Hypertext Transfer Protocol, is used by WWW browsers to get WWW pages from a Web site.

Each of these protocols is a client/server protocol by which a client application talks to a server-based application. The detailed content of the conversation that a client has with the server and vice versa is strictly defined in the protocol. In most cases, an end user will be running the client application, such as Microsoft's Internet Explorer or Netscape's Navigator. This client application will use the underlying protocol (HTTP in the case of these two Web browsers) to communicate with the server. In some cases, the client application is able to speak multiple protocols; Turnpike, for example, handles both news and mail (NNTP and SMTP/POP3) in an integrated fashion.

As long as both the client and server applications implement the relevant protocol, they do not need to be matched (that is, be from the same vendor). Thus, a freeware or shareware FTP client, such as `CuteFTP32` or `WS_FTP32`, can happily be used to access virtually any FTP server on the entire Internet, including those found on UNIX systems and on Windows NT.

11.1. Telnet

Telnet is a protocol used to implement a remote login facility on virtually any host computer from a remote terminal. The idea is that a terminal, which can be as simple as a Teletype machine or as complex as a powerful PC, creates a session on a remote server anywhere on the internetwork—this can be a private network or the worldwide Internet. Because terminals and hosts can vary in terms of the functionality provided, the Telnet protocol was also designed to enable the host and terminal to negotiate additional options to augment the facilities offered to the user.

Figure 11.1 shows a typical Telnet session. The Telnet client, running on the workstation on the left side of the diagram, utilizes the underlying network to make a TCP connection to the NT server called `HILO`. This server is running the Windows NT TelnetD Server and is able to process all the Telnet commands sent by the client.

Figure 11.1.

A sample Telnet session.

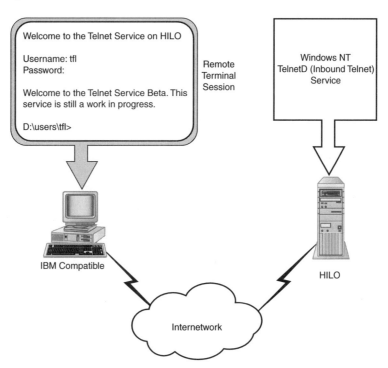

NOTE While the primary purpose of Telnet clients is to use the Telnet protocol to create a remote terminal session, they can also be used to set up a TCP connection over IP to other server processes, such as FTP or SMTP. This can be very useful; for example, you could use a Telnet client to connect to an NNTP or SMTP port on a remote machine and act as an NNTP or SMTP client. An unscrupulous individual might use a Telnet client to forge e-mail or news articles this way. A more legitimate use of this feature that some news administrators take advantage of is to Telnet to the NNTP port and issue NNTP commands. This can be helpful for troubleshooting or testing POP3 servers.

The Telnet protocol was defined in RFC 854, which describes the three main ideas underlying the protocol:

- The Network Virtual Terminal, or NVT—When both the client and server start up, all they can assume is that both sides are capable of supporting a very basic terminal type (that is, the NVT).

- Negotiated Options—Because the NVT is such a simple device, each side can request the other to use more sophisticated features, or options. Each side is free to request that the other use one or more options and is also free to reject an offered option. All clients and servers must support the NVT; the other options are a matter for the designers of client or server product(s).

■ A symmetrical view of terminals and processes—The negotiation of options can be initiated by either side. Both sides are free to attempt to negotiate or to decline any offered option.

11.1.1. The NVT

The NVT is little more than an electronic version of the Teletype, a fictional bi-directional character-based device with a printer and a keyboard. Both the Telnet server and client processes must convert whatever underlying representation exists in the physical terminal, or the server, to the NVT, unless different options are negotiated.

The printer portion of the NVT is used to display incoming characters, and the keyboard is used to send characters out. These outgoing characters can also be echoed to the printer. It is an assumption that, initially, character echoes are only done at the client end and do not traverse the network. This can, of course, be negotiated. The NVT uses the 7-bit USASCII code in an 8-bit field, although a more complex character set can be negotiated.

The NVT printer has an unspecified carriage width and page length and, by default, can support all 95 of the USASCII characters (codes 32 through 126). Of the 33 USASCII Control Codes (values 0 through 31), only those shown in Table 11.1 are supported by the NVT.

Table 11.1. USASCII codes supported by the NVT.

Name	Code	Meaning
Null (NUL)	0	No operation.
Line Feed (LF)	10	Advances the printer to the next print line, keeping the same horizontal position.
Carriage Return (CR)	13	Moves the printer to the leftmost margin of the current line.
Bell (BEL)	7	Produces an audible tone (or some visible signal) but does not move the print head.
Back Space (BS)	8	Moves the print head one space toward the left margin.
Horizontal Tab (HT)	9	Moves the printer to the next horizontal tab position.
Vertical Tab (VT)	11	Moves the printer to the next vertical tab position.

Name	Code	Meaning
Form Feed (FF)	12	Moves the printer to the top of the next page, keeping the same horizontal position.

All other codes have no defined action, other than causing the character to be printed. The NVT must implement the first three of these codes (NUL, LF, and CR), while the others are optional. Neither side can make any assumptions about the effect of the transmission of these optional characters. In addition, it is up to the client and server as to exactly what action, if any, is taken by the VT and HT commands.

The sequence CRLF (or LFCR) will cause the printer on NVT to position the print head at the leftmost margin of the next line on the printer. In some systems, this can cause problems, because these commands are not independent. Therefore, the sequence CRLF is always used when the combined action is required. If just a carriage return is required (for example, on a real printer where multiple typing is used to simulate bold), the sequence CR NUL is used.

11.1.2. Option Negotiation

NOTE Most well-behaved Telnet clients will only attempt to negotiate options when connecting to a true Telnet server (that is, TCP port 23). Because a Telnet client can be used simply to create a TCP connection to some other port, the client should *not* negotiate options when connected to a TCP port other than 23.

An example of option negotiation is using a Telnet client to connect to a POP3 server to check on waiting e-mail or to connect to an SMTP server to carry out some troubleshooting. If the Telnet client attempts to negotiate options in this situation, it may result in the POP3 server failing to accept the password. If you are going to use a Telnet client for other than connection to a Telnet server, check that it can negotiate options properly—and note that some can't!

Most Telnet clients and servers will want to implement a device more complex than the NVT. This is accomplished by *option negotiation*, set out in RFC 855, which allows each side to offer or request an extension to the basic NVT specification.

Because both sides can symmetrically attempt to negotiate options, there are certain rules to prevent acknowledgment loops:

- Either side may only send a request to change an option; they must not send out a "request" just to announce a mode they are using.

- If either side receives a request to enter a mode it is already in, that request must not be acknowledged. This is vital to avoid endless acknowledgment loops.

- When either side sends an option request to the other, and the use of that option will have an effect on the processing of the datastream being sent, that command must be inserted into the datastream at the point where it is to take effect. Because it might take some time for the option to be acknowledged (or refused), the side sending the option should buffer data until the acknowledgment is received.

Application Services

When a Telnet session is first established, it is quite likely that option requests will be sent back and forth as both sides attempt to negotiate the highest level of service possible. Subsequent option negotiation, while less likely, can happen if either side wants to change the options in effect.

11.1.3. Specifying Options

A Telnet session begins with the Telnet client making a TCP connection to the server's Telnet port. At this point, both sides can only assume that the other side supports an NVT. Both the client and server typically begin the process of option negotiation.

To negotiate an option, either side may send one of four option requests:

- WILL—The sender wants to set an option.

- WONT—The sender wants to disable the option.

- DO—The sender wants the receiver to set the option.

- DONT—The sender wants the receiver to disable the option.

In option negotiation, both sides are free to accept or reject a request for an option (WILL, DO), but must always honor a request to disable any option. Thus, there are six separate, valid exchanges, as shown in Table 11.2.

Table 11.2. Option negotiation exchanges.

Sender sends	Receiver sends	What this means to sender/receiver	Result on data stream
WILL	DO	Sender wants to enable the option. The receiver agrees.	Option is enabled.
DO	WILL	Sender wants receiver to enable the option. The receiver agrees.	Option is enabled.
WILL	DONT	Sender wants to enable the option. The receiver disagrees.	Option is *not* enabled.
DO	WONT	Sender wants receiver to enable the option. The receiver disagrees.	Option is *not* enabled.
WONT	DONT	The sender wants to disable the option.	Option is disabled.

Sender sends	Receiver sends	What this means to sender/receiver	Result on data stream
		The receiver must agree.	
DONT	WONT	The sender wants the receiver to disable the option. The receiver must agree.	Option is disabled.

As you can see from this table, either side may request an option. The receiver may or may not accept this. If either side disables the option, the receiver must disable the option.

The option-negotiation process is indicated by the insertion of certain control characters into the datastream. The start of option negotiation is noted by an IAC (Interpret-as command) escape character followed by the command WILL, WONT, DO, or DONT and finally by a code indicating what option the sender is trying to negotiate.

In some cases, a more complex option negotiation process is required, for example, to alter an established line length. This is called *sub-option negotiation* and is initiated first by the normal WILL/DO, DO/WILL to ensure that both parties can understand the option; this is followed by a more esoteric syntax for the actual negotiation of the option details.

The sub-option negotiation is indicated by the insertion of the SB command into the datastream, followed by the details of the option and terminated by an SE (End of Sub-Option negotiation parameters) command.

The sub-option negotiation characters have the ASCII values shown in Table 11.3.

Table 11.3. ASCII values of Telnet negotiation commands.

Command	ASCII Value
WILL	251
WONT	252
DO	253
DONT	254
IAC	255
SB	250
SE	240

Application Services

The details of option specification are set out in RFC 855. A large number of options were in effect at the time RFC 855 was written or have been added since. These options have been defined formally in RFCs and other documents, as shown in Table 11.4. Note that the most up-to-date list of Telnet options can be obtained from the URL `ftp://ftp.isi.edu/in-notes/iana/assignments/telnet-options`.

Table 11.4. Telnet options.

Option ID (Decimal)	Option Name	Defining RFC
0	Binary Transmission	856
1	Echo	857
2	Reconnection	See Note 1
3	Suppress Go Ahead	858
4	Approximate Message Size Negotiation	See Note 2
5	Status	859
6	Timing Mark	860
7	Remote Controlled Trans and Echo	726
8	Output Line Width	See Note 1
9	Output Page Size	See Note 1
10	Output Carriage—Return Disposition	652
11	Output Horizontal Tab Stops	653
12	Output Horizontal Tab Disposition	654
13	Output Form Feed Disposition	655
14	Output Vertical Tab Stops	656
15	Output Vertical Tab Disposition	657
16	Output Linefeed Disposition	657
17	Extended ASCII	698
18	Logout	727
19	Byte Macro	735
20	Telnet Data-Entry Terminal (DODIIS Implementation)	1043, 732

Option ID (Decimal)	Option Name	Defining RFC
21	SUDUP	736, 734
22	SUDUP Output	749
23	Send Location	779
24	Telnet Terminal Type	1091
25	Telnet End of Record	885
26	TACACS User Identification	927
27	Output Marking	933
28	Terminal Location Number	946
29	3270 Regime	1041
30	X.3 PAD	1053
31	Window Size	1073
32	Terminal Speed	1079
33	Remote Flow Control	1372
34	Linemode	1184
35	X Display Location	1096
36	Environment Option	1408
37	Authentication Option	1416
38	Encryption Option	See Note 3
39	Environment Option	1572
40	TN3270E	1647
41	XAUTH	See Note 4
42	CHARSET	2066
255	Extended Options List	861

Notes:

1. Defined in DDN Protocol Handbook, "Telnet Reconnection Option," "Telnet Output Line Width Option," "Telnet Output Page Size Option," NIC 50005, December 1985.

Application Services

2. Defined in *The Ethernet, a Local Area Network: Data Link Layer and Physical Layer Specification*, AA-K759B-TK, Digital Equipment Corporation, Maynard, MA. Also as "The Ethernet—A Local Area Network," Version 1.0, Digital Equipment Corporation, Intel Corporation, Xerox Corporation, September 1980 and "The Ethernet, A Local Area Network: Data Link Layer and Physical Layer Specifications," Digital, Intel, and Xerox, November 1982. Also, "The Ethernet, A Local Area Network: Data Link Layer and Physical Layer Specification," X3T51/80-50, Xerox Corporation, Stamford, CT., October 1980.

3. Defined by Dave Borman, `dab@cray.com`, January 1995—but no formal document reference is listed by IANA.

4. Defined by Rob Earhart, `earhart+@cmu.edu`, April 1995—but no formal document reference is listed by IANA.

RFC 1416 added the concept of authentication types, of which several are now defined, as shown in Table 11.5.

Table 11.5. Telnet authentication methods.

Type	Description	Defining RFC
0	NULL	1416
1	Kerberos V4	1416
2	Kerberos V5	1416
3	SPX	1416
4, 5	Unassigned by IANA	
6	RSA	1416
7-9	Unassigned by IANA	
10	LOKI	1416
11	SSA	See Note 1

Note:

1. Defined by Steven Schoch, `schoch@sheba.arc.nasa.gov`—but no defining document listed by IANA.

As you can see from these tables, a large number of potential options exist for a client or server to implement. Not all will be implemented in any given Telnet client or server; indeed, most clients and servers will only implement a small number of these, such as Echo, Suppress, or Go Ahead. The option-negotiation process, nevertheless, enables good interoperability between diverse Telnet clients and servers.

11.1.4. Control Functions

In the implementation of a Telnet client or server, there are a few control functions that are required. The most common are Interrupt Process (IP), Abort Output (AO), Are You There (AYT), Erase Character (EC), and Erase Line (EL).

The IP function requests that the Telnet server abort the currently running user process. IP is usually invoked by a user when the process appears to be looping or if the user has accidentally requested the wrong function or specified the wrong option. This function only terminates the running process, not the entire remote terminal session.

The AO function is used when a user process on the server has generated output the user does not want to see. This is similar to the IP function, except that AO will not abort the user process—it only requests no further output from the process. The AO function will also clear any output that has been generated but not yet been output—that is, buffered output.

The AYT facility enables a user to determine whether the server is still active. This can be useful when a long-running user process is silent (that is, it is still running, but not producing screen output) and the user just wants to check that the server is still alive.

The EC function is used to delete the last preceding undeleted character transmitted. This is most often invoked as a result of a typing error.

The EL function is used to delete an entire line of input. If the Telnet server offers a line-editing feature (which would be outside the scope of the formal Telnet specifications), the EL function would be used to invoke it.

IP and AO functions are useful when a user process appears to be looping endlessly. This can often happen during program development. However, when these commands are buffered via a large internetwork (for example, the Internet), it can take some time for transmitted information to get to and from the server. To counter this difficulty, the Telnet specification offers the SYNCH mechanism. The SYNCH command is signaled by the Data Mark (DM) Telnet command sent in a TCP segment with the Urgent flag set. The Urgent flag indicates to the Telnet server that this command should be scanned more quickly than would normally happen with buffered input. Generally, the SYNCH causes all buffered input to be ignored up to the point of the SYNCH.

As an example of how this mechanism works, when an AO signal was sent by the user to a server, the server would discard all remaining output and then send a SYNCH back to the client.

The control functions are represented by a simple code, as shown in Table 11.6.

Application Services

Table 11.6. Option values.

Function	Code
IP (Interrupt Process)	244
AO (Abort Output)	245
AYT (Are You There)	246
EC (Erase Character)	247
EL (Erase Line)	249
DM (Data Mark)	242

11.2. FTP

The File Transfer Protocol (FTP) provides a common approach to transferring files between heterogeneous clients and servers. Although being overtaken by the WWW, FTP has been one of the most heavily used functions on the Internet over the years.

Most of this book, for example, was transmitted from the author to the publisher using FTP. Most computer hardware and software vendors have an FTP site on the Internet (for example, FTP.MICROSOFT.COM, FTP.HP.COM, FTP.DELL.COM) for the distribution of software updates or additional documentation. Although the use of FTP is, in some cases, giving way to the WWW as the means of such distribution, FTP remains an important part of an Internet user's toolkit.

FTP, like Telnet, is a client/server protocol. An end user will invoke an FTP client, which may be a dedicated FTP client or an integrated product such as a WWW browser, to enable the user to receive and send files from and to a remote FTP server. Most TCP/IP stacks are shipped with a basic FTP client. Many server operating systems also include an FTP server capability. Microsoft, for example, includes a command-line FTP client as part of its TCP/IP stack for Windows 95 and Windows NT as well as an FTP server offering with both Windows NT Workstation and NT Server. FTP server-and-client capability is also built into most UNIX systems. Derivatives and freeware or shareware clients and servers are readily available.

While Microsoft and other OS vendors do include an FTP client with their systems (that is, Microsoft includes one for Windows 95 and Windows NT), these are often console based. These tools can be cumbersome and awkward to use—and there are much better tools available, especially for the Windows environments. For example, I use the excellent freeware WS_FTP 32 and shareware CuteFTP programs for Windows 95 and Windows NT. Both these products can be found on most Internet shareware sites, such as ftp.cica.ui.edu. The CuteFTP home page is found at http://papa.indstate.edu:8888/CuteFTP/.

Please: If you do obtain these products, be sure to read and comply with the licensing restrictions for them.

In discussing FTP, it is also important to make the distinction between the FTP file-transfer protocol and networked file access. Facilities such as NFS or Microsoft's and Novell's networked file sharing (as described in Chapter 9, "Introduction to the Application Layer") allow an end user to mount a directory on the file server as though it was local and to access files through the mechanism of an underlying file-sharing protocol (such as NFS, SMB, or NCP). FTP, even though it does allow file transfer, is quite different from these file-sharing protocols.

The FTP protocol is defined in RFC 959, "File Transfer Protocol." Some updates to FTP are documented in RFC 1639, "FTP Operation Over Big Address Records" (FOOBAR), although not all FTP clients are capable of utilizing FOOBAR.

A separate protocol, TFTP, has also been defined (RFC 1350 and updated by RFCs 1782, 1883, 1784, and 1785). TFTP, as the name implies, is a simplified version of FTP that runs over UDP instead of TCP. TFTP is often used by diskless devices, in conjunction with BOOTP, to download a boot image. TFTP servers and clients also exist for most popular operating systems and can be used in preference to full FTP. They can be useful in batch scripts, for example.

FTP is different from most other application protocols in that it uses two separate TCP connections between FTP client and FTP server. The first connection, which is active for the duration of the FTP session, is for FTP control information. The other connection is only made when any data is to be transferred. The control connection can enable the client to send commands to the server and for the server to signal the result of the command, while a separate data connection is made each time a file is to be transferred.

The basic client/server model for FTP, based on RFC 959, is shown in Figure 11.2.

Application Services

Figure 11.2.

The FTP client/ server model.

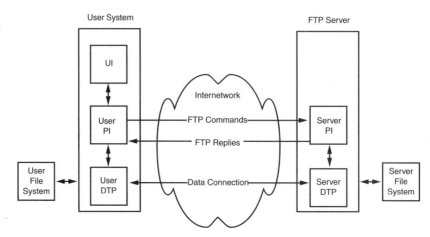

In this model, the FTP client consists of a user interface (UI), which can be command-line–driven or based on some underlying windowed architecture (for example, Windows NT or X Window). The end user sees all FTP operations via this UI. The other two components of the FTP client are the User Protocol Interface (PI) and the User Data Transfer Process (DTP). Depending on the client, these may be separate processes, different threads, or just a single process.

On the server side, there are two main components: a Server Protocol Interpreter and a Server Data Transfer Process. As on the client side, these may be one process, multiple processes, or multiple threads.

When the user starts up the FTP client, the client obtains the name or IP address of the FTP server from the user. This could be via some stored list, from the command line, or via direct user input. The client PI will then make a TCP connection to the FTP server's well-known port 21, which connects it to the server PI.

The FTP server PI, when the FTP server is started up, passively opens TCP port 21 and waits for the control connections from user PIs. This control connection is used by the user PI to send commands to the server PI and for the server PI to send status responses back to the user PI, which can then display them via the UI.

All commands and responses sent over the control connection are transmitted in NVT ASCII. The first commands sent from the client to the server are user authentication—that is, a user ID and a password.

When the FTP client wants to transfer from the FTP server to the client, the FTP client will open a local TCP port and pass the IP address and TCP port number to the FTP server, which can then use that port to achieve the data transfer. This is described in more detail in the next section.

11.2.1. FTP Sessions

An FTP session begins when, based on instructions from the client UI, the client PI makes a TCP connection to the server PI. Once this connection is established, the client will log on to the server. When this is completed, the client can issue file transfer commands, which typically involves navigating the FTP server's directory structure and sending or receiving files. The session is terminated when the TCP connection is terminated between the client PI and user PI, typically as a result of the QUIT command.

In the following code, an example of the start of an FTP session is shown. This was generated by using a command-line–based Telnet client to make a connection from a Windows NT Workstation system to a well-known FTP server in the UK, ftp.demon.co.uk. The text in bold italic was typed by the user; the rest was transmitted from the FTP server to the Telnet client:

```
220-
220-   Welcome to Demon Internet's ftp archive.
220-
220-      Files for accessing Demon are now stored under /pub/
       ➥demon/
220-
220-      /pub/unix is currently being reorganised
220-
220-      Demon customer web pages should be uploaded to
       ➥homepages.demon.co.uk
220-      not this server.
220-
220-
220-
220 disabuse.demon.co.uk FTP server (Demon/Academ/WU [1]
       ➥ Aug 9 13:24:24 BST 1996) ready.
USER FTP
331 Guest login ok, send your complete e-mail address as
       ➥password.
PASS tfl@psp.co.uk
230-Welcome fellow Demon Internet user, psp.demon.co.uk.
230-
230-The local time is Fri Jan 17 00:08:41 1997.
230-
230-Material on this system is provided without warranty or
       ➥guarantee and under
230-the condition that no liability for any situation or event
       ➥directly,
230-indirectly or otherwise caused by access to this system is
       ➥assumed by the
230-operators. It is the responsibility of the downloader to
       ➥ensure any
230-material downloaded is suitable and may legally be pos-
sessed in your
```

```
230-country or establishment.
230-
230-There are currently 24 anonymous Demon hosts using this
    ➥server.
230-
230-Your WWW homepages are not held on this server, they
    ➥should be uploaded
230-to homepages.demon.co.uk
230-
230 Guest login ok, access restrictions apply.
PWD
257 "/" is current directory.
```

As you can see, as soon as the client PI connects to the server, the server generates an initial greeting. The client PI may or may not pass this greeting on to the user interface, depending on the design of the UI. The next step is to log in using the **USER** and **PASS** commands. If successful, this generates a further set of messages back from the server to the client.

At this point the client is logged in. The client PI can then begin issuing commands, such as **PWD** (to display the current directory for the server), that may generate responses.

NOTE   One of the often-noted weaknesses of FTP is that the user ID and password are both sent in clear text, so anyone using a packet-capture utility, such as **TCPDUMP** or Microsoft's Network Monitor, can observe both the user ID and password. For this reason, most major FTP servers utilize what is known as anonymous FTP. This involves transmitting the user ID of "anonymous," plus any password. By convention, this password is the user's e-mail address (for example, tfl@psp.co.uk). To simplify matters, many FTP servers will also accept FTP as a shortcut for anonymous (which some folks can have trouble spelling, especially late at night—a popular time for downloads!).

Anonymous FTP is thus open to anyone in the entire world with a suitable Internet connection. To slightly improve security, some FTP servers insist on being able to do a reverse DNS name lookup on the IP address making the initial TCP connection before the greeting message is displayed. If this reverse DNS fails (typically due to the IP address not being properly registered in DNS), the connection will get dropped. The FTP server ftp.demon.co.uk works this way, as do many others.

For the client or server to transfer any actual data, including the list of files within a directory, a separate connection must be made between the FTP client and FTP server.

The session involves the transfer of commands from the client PI to the server PI. These commands are generated by the user interface and are not usually entered directly by the user; they are described in the "FTP Commands" section of this chapter. Some of these commands will take one or more parameters (for example, the USER and PASS commands), while others do not. All commands and parameters are transferred in clear text using the NVT ASCII character set specified by the Telnet protocol.

Before any data transfer between the FTP client and server, it is necessary for a second TCP connection to be established between the client DTP and the server DTP. This connection is initiated by the client, which will do a passive TCP open on an ephemeral (local) port. The client PI will then use the **PORT** command to send this port number to the server PI across the control connection. The server DTP then does an active open to that port. The FTP server will always use the well-known TCP port 20 on the server for the data connection. Once this connection is established, the client PI can issue a data transfer command, and the resulting data is then transferred over the data connection. Once the data has been transferred, the server usually does an active close on the data connection, thus forcing the client-side connection to be dropped.

If a long FTP session occurs, this may result in numerous data connections being established and then dropped. This is a bit wasteful of bandwidth, as there is some connection startup and shutdown overhead, but in comparison to the data typically transferred between FTP client and server, this is relatively trivial.

11.2.2. FTP Commands

NOTE — The commands shown in this section are those passed between the PI components of the FTP client and server and are distinct from those issued to the FTP client's user interface. To see the protocol commands, you will need to use a packet sniffer or an FTP client that displays them.

The commands sent from the FTP client to the FTP server are all three or four characters long, and some will have one or more additional parameters. RFC 959 defines a large number of commands that are passed from the user PI to the server PI (as shown in Figure 11.2), many of which are not used or implemented by most modern FTP clients or servers. The more commonly used protocol commands are described in the following sections. Each of these commands is shown with the command and any optional parameters.

Access Control Commands

These commands, shown in Table 11.7, are used as part of the FTP authentication process.

Table 11.7. FTP access control commands.

Command	Parameter(s)	Effect
USER	*<username>*	This command identifies the user of the FTP session.
PASS	*<password>*	The password associated with the user, specified in the USER command.
CWD	*<directory>*	Changes the directory on the server to that specified in the *<directory>* parameter.

continues

Application Services

Table 11.7. Continued.

Command	Parameter(s)	Effect
CDUP		A special case of the CWD command; moves the directory tree one level up. Equivalent to CD .. in DOS, Windows 95/NT, and UNIX.
QUIT		Terminates a user and, if a file transfer is in progress, aborts the file transfer.

The FTP session normally begins with the FTP client passing the username and password to the server. The session then tends to involve some navigation of the FTP server's file store, plus some transfer commands (described in the next section). The FTP session is terminated by the QUIT command.

Data Transfer Commands

These commands are used to actually transfer data between the FTP client and server. The commonly used commands are shown in Table 11.8.

Table 11.8. FTP data transfer commands.

Command	Parameter(s)	Effect
PORT	h1, h2, h3, h4, p1, p2	This command tells the FTP Server PI which port on the FTP client will be used to receive or send data.
RETR	<filename>	Requests the FTP server to send the FTP client the specified file via the port specified in the PORT command.
STOR	<filename>	Tells the FTP server to get a file from the FTP client and store it in the filename specified.
RNFR RNTO	<old name> <new name>	These commands, which follow each other, request the FTP server to rename the file <old name> to <new name>.
ABOR		Tells the file server to abort the file transfer in progress.
DELE	<filename>	Requests the FTP server to delete the file <filename>.

Command	Parameter(s)	Effect
MD	*\<directory>*	Asks the FTP server to create a new directory, *\<directory>*.
RMD	*\<directory>*	Requests the FTP server to delete the directory, *\<directory>*.

Once the user is logged in and has navigated to the right place in the FTP server's file store, the RETR (get a file) and STOR (upload a file) commands can be used to transfer files. The RNFR and RNTO commands allow the user to rename a file, DELE will delete a file, and RMD and MD allow the user to remove or make a directory.

It is important to note that all the main data-transfer operations, while signaled between the client and server PIs, actually are accomplished over the DTP port. On the server side, this will be the well-known TCP port 20. On the FTP client side, this port is an ephemeral port, passively opened by the FTP client, as noted earlier.

Before the data-transfer commands can be utilized, the client must have opened this port and notified the server via the PORT command. The PORT command takes six parameters, as shown in Table 11.6. The h1, h2, h3, and h4 parameters represent the four octets of the client's IP address; b1 and b2 represent the ephemeral DTP port number on the client. The actual port number is 256*b1+b2 at the IP address specified.

As an example, if the client was at IP address 193.195.190.200 and the DTP port to be used for the transfer was ephemeral port 1254, this would be specified by sending the following PORT command:

```
PORT 193,195,190,200,4,230
```

In theory, the PORT command could be used to request the FTP server to send output to a port on a different machine; thus the FTP client could be acting as an agent between two other servers. While this is catered for in the FTP RFCs, and possibly for some FTP servers, most FTP clients only send PORT commands based on the IP address where the client is running.

Other Commands

The final set of commands, shown in Table 11.9, are more general in nature and assist the client in using the FTP server.

Table 11.9. Other FTP commands.

Command	Parameter(s)	Effect
PWD		Asks the FTP server to list the files in the current working directory; the list is sent to the port specified with the PORT command.
SITE	<parameters>	Used to provide server- or site-specific functions. Can have multiple parameters specified.
STAT		Asks the FTP server to send a status report over the control connection.
HELP		Used to obtain a list of the PI commands supported by the server.

The current working directory can be displayed, via the control connection, with PWD. The currently supported commands can be shown with the HELP command. The STAT command will print out a current status report.

The following is an example of the output of the STAT command when using Windows NT 4.0:

```
211-lapguy Microsoft Windows NT FTP Server status:
    Version 2.0
    Connected to TALLGUY
    Logged in as tfl@psp.co.uk
    TYPE: ASCII, FORM: Nonprint; STRUcture: File; transfer
➥MODE: STREAM
    No data connection
```

11.2.3. FTP Response Messages

The commands noted in the previous section are sent from the FTP client PI to the FTP server PI. The FTP server PI interprets these commands and carries out the action(s) relating to that command (for example, begin the transfer of a file, pass a directory listing to the client). The server PI will then pass back one or more status messages to the client via the control connection, indicating the success or failure of the requested action. These status messages are all three numeric characters long and can be appended by additional text.

The response message IDs are all of the form XYZ. The value of X determines the general type of the reply, Y indicates what type of reply, and Z gives more details.

The possible values for X are

1. Positive reply—This is a preliminary reply, and more replies are expected.

2. Positive reply—This indicates the completion of some action and another command.

3. Intermediate reply—The command has been accepted, but no more commands may be sent (that is, until a 2nn command is received).

4. Negative reply—This indicates some sort of transient error, and the client is probably free to retry the command.

5. Negative reply—This indicates that a more serious error has occurred and the command was not accepted. A 5xx message suggests there is no point retrying this command (at least at this time).

The possible values for Y, which gives more details of the command, are

0. Syntax—This is usually due to a syntax error in the command.

1. Information—This is a general information category.

2. Connections—This relates to the connection between the FTP client and FTP server.

3. Authentication—This class of errors relates to problems with authentication.

4. Unspecified—This category is not specified in the RFC.

5. File system status—This relates to problems with the server's file system.

The Z value is used to give more detail about the reply; and Z values are not specified in the RFC.

These three-digit XYZ reply codes are meant to be understood by the PI and thus are cryptic to the end user. For ease of use, they are usually accompanied by more readable text. The actual format of this text is implementation dependent.

Following are some typical replies given by Microsoft's FTP server supplied in Windows NT 4.0:

Event: At login.

Reply: `220 Lapguy Microsoft FTP Service (Version 2.0)`

Event: In response to an anonymous user specified by USER command.

Reply: `331 Anonymous access allowed, send identity (e-mail name)`
`as password.`

Event: After successful login.

Reply: `230 Welcome to Lapguy's FTP Service`
`230 Anonymous user logged in.`

Application Services

Event: After `DIR` command sent (along with the `PORT` command to specify where the output is to go to).

Reply: **200 PORT command successful.**
150 Opening ASCII mode data connection for /bin/ls.

Event: After the output is received.

Reply: **226 Transfer complete.**

Event: In response to the request to change the directory to `XXX` (which does not exist).

Reply: **550 XXX: The system cannot find the file specified.**

Event: In response to change the directory to one that does exist.

Reply: **250 CWD command successful.**

Event: In response to the `QUIT` command, NT sends a rather terse reply.

Reply: **221**

For the most part, the actual response numbers and text are of little use to most users. The FTP client will read and interpret those messages, displaying a more meaningful message to the user as necessary. In some point-and-click windowed FTP clients, the end user may not even be aware of these messages being issued. However, if errors are encountered with the FTP server, support staff will need to know the actual error number in order to carry out fault diagnosis and repair.

11.2.4. FTP Data Transfer

RFC 959 names a number of defined types of files that could, in theory, be transferred between client and server files. These are files in different formats and with different file structures. The RFC also indicates different modes of transfer that could be adopted; it was attempting to reach a very wide audience of potential users.

The defined types of files, per RFC 959, are ASCII, Image (or binary), EBCDIC, and what is called a *local file type* (used to transfer files between hosts with different numbers of bits/bytes). Most FTP transfers today involve either ASCII or binary files.

When transferring ASCII or EBCDIC files, RFC 959 allows for three different file formats: Non-Print, Telnet Format, and FORTRAN carriage control. Non-Print, which is the default, contains no vertical formatting information, whereas the Telnet Format contains standard Telnet vertical format controls. In FORTRAN carriage-control format, the first character of each line contains a FORTRAN format-control character.

RFC 959 also defines different file structures that could be transferred, including a standard file, a record-structured file, and a page-structured file.

The defined transfer modes between FTP client and server include stream, block, and compressed.

Although RFC 959 defines what should happen for all possible combinations of these options, most of the combinations are simply never used and are not implemented within the FTP servers or client products. Virtually all FTP operations today involve the transfer of either ASCII or binary files, in Non-Print format, using standard file structures and transmitted in stream mode. Naturally, there are exceptions to this in some circumstances.

11.3. SMTP

> **NOTE** As noted, for many professionals e-mail is one of the "killer apps" on the Internet—one that makes having Internet connections worthwhile. There are many reasons for this. First, e-mail is simple. A few keystrokes can send an e-mail halfway around the world in a matter of minutes. This makes communications with people simple and easy. Second, it's cheap. With the Internet, you can simply make a local phone call and send e-mail to anywhere in the world, including to your little sister at the university and your aunt on safari in India, as well as to work colleagues just a few miles away. But for me, the real advantage is the leverage it gives you. You can compose and send e-mail messages at any time of the day or night, and often can reach people faster and easier than with any other form of modern communication.
>
> A recent report by Forrester Research (*Investor's Business Daily*, January 15, 1997, A6) suggested that today, around 15% of Americans use e-mail, up from 2% in 1992. They predict that within 5 years, this will grow to 50%. Some might suggest that this report underestimates the impact of electronic mail, with the 5-year number likely to be far higher!

E-mail is the "killer" Internet application, as far as many people are concerned. Many professionals, particularly in the computing world, literally exist on a large diet of e-mail. I regularly receive upwards of 100 e-mail messages per day. During the writing of this chapter, e-mails to and from colleagues, the publisher, co-authors, and other sources averaged between 20 and 30 per day.

The overall architectural model of an e-mail system is defined in RFC 821 and is depicted in Figure 11.3. In this figure, the end user uses a User Agent, a program for reading incoming mail and preparing outgoing mail. A separate program, the Mail Transfer Agent (MTA), will then send mail to and receive mail from other MTAs. In some cases, there may be multiple intervening MTAs involved in the transfer of an item of e-mail from one user to another.

Application Services

Figure 11.3.
An overall architectural model for e-mail.

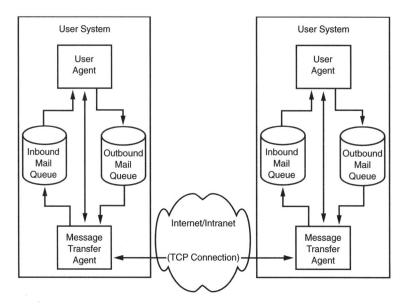

While writing this chapter, I posted a message in a few local newsgroups asking people what they use to read mail and why. Virtually everyone who responded quoted a different product, each of which was cited as being "the best." The degree of passion used to express the choice of e-mail client borders on religious fervor. Clearly, the choice of mail client (and MTA) will depend on the platform—Turnpike and Agent, for example, are not available on UNIX. The results of this mini-survey indicate that there is no such thing as a perfect mail client, although most people prefer paying as little as possible. The closest thing seems to be the one you are currently using, and even that needs just one or two little improvements. And if you want to start an international incident, post a Usenet article suggesting that some mail client is worthless!

For the most part, only the communication between MTAs utilizes SMTP. The protocol that most user agents utilize is typically the Post Office Protocol (POP3), although some user agents do make use of SMTP.

I use an integrated e-mail and news suite called Turnpike, a UK product (see `http://www.turnpike.com` for more information). The Turnpike suite has two separate programs: Offline, which is used to manage the local copy of the news spool, and a separate program (that is, the user agent); and Connect, which manages the connection to the Internet and the transfer of mail between our Internet service provider and the local mail spools (that is, the MTA). Turnpike is among the few that can talk both SMTP and POP3 between user agent and MTA components, which some regard as useful.

Other popular MTAs for the Windows environment include Pegasus, Agent, Lotus cc:Mail, Microsoft Outlook, and Eudora. In the UNIX world, there are also a large number of user agents, including Pine, Elm, MH, Emacs, and MUSH. The design and features of the user agent and the design of protocols used between user agent and MTA are hotly debated by end users, but they are both outside the scope of this book.

As you saw in Figure 11.3, the mail messages are passed between MTA via a TCP connection. This is not dissimilar to the FTP transfers you saw in the "FTP" section. When an MTA wants to exchange mail with another MTA, it will make a connection to the other MTA's well-known TCP port 25 and begin the transfer. Once the TCP connection is established, the MTAs communicate using SMTP.

The emphasis in SMTP, as defined in RFC 821, is on *simple*. A basic SMTP implementation uses just eight commands, as opposed to far more for FTP. These commands are discussed in the "FTP Commands" section. The format of the mail message as it is transferred across the Internet or an intranet is also simple; this is described in more detail in section 11.2.2 as well.

It must be noted that the diagram shown in Figure 11.3 shows a simplistic view of mail transfer—that is, between the two MTAs directly utilized by the user agents. In today's Internet and in most corporate intranets, the actual transfer often involves more complex transfers. This is described in the "FTP Response Messages" section.

11.3.1. SMTP Commands

SMTP uses a client/server approach to sending mail, although both client and server are MTAs. When one MTA (that is, a client) wants to send mail to another (that is, the server), the client MTA makes the TCP connection from itself to the server MTA. Then, in a manner similar to that adopted by the client PI and server PI in FTP, the client MTA will send a series of commands and possibly data (for example, mail messages) to the server MTA. The server MTA responds by using simple messages of the type used in FTP.

The main messages used in mail transfer are shown in Table 11.10.

Table 11.10. SMTP commands used in mail transfer.

Command	Parameter(s)	Effect
HELO	`<domain>`	This command identifies the client MTA's domain to the server MTA.
MAIL	FROM: `<reverse path>`	Used to initiate a mail transfer from the sender identified in `<reverse path>`.
RCPT	TO: `<forward path>`	Identifies that the mail message is to be delivered to the mailbox identified by `<forward path>`.

continues

Table 11.10. Continued.

Command	Parameter(s)	Effect
DATA		This indicates the data portion of the e-mail message. It is followed by a number of lines consisting of the mail message and terminated by a line consisting of just a full stop and a CRLF.
VRFY	<string>	Requests the server MTA to confirm that the recipient, named in <string>, exists.
EXPN	<string>	Gets the server MTA to expand the mailing list named in <string>.
QUIT		Terminates a mail session and may close the TCP connection.
TURN		Allows the client and server MTAs to reverse roles and send mail in the opposite direction.
NOOP		This is a NO-OP (no operation) and does not affect the mail transfer.

All these commands are terminated by a CRLF sequence, and where multiple arguments are shown, each is delimited by at least one space character.

RFC 821 defines a number of additional commands, but the minimum set that must be implemented by all MTAs are HELO, MAIL, RCPT, DATA, RSET, NOOP, and QUIT.

After the TCP connection is made between the MTAs, and a mail session is started by the HELO command, mail transfers can commence. The basic transmission of a single e-mail message begins with a MAIL command, which identifies the sender of the mail. This is followed by one or more RCPT commands to identify who is to receive the mail (there can be multiple recipients of a mail message). Once all the recipients are identified, the DATA command is sent, followed by the actual body of the mail message. The mail message is sent as a series of lines and is terminated by CRLF. The end of the actual message is terminated by a line containing just a full stop character (.) followed by a CRLF. A typical mail session will involve transmission of several mail messages and is terminated by QUIT.

This simple mail session and the transfer of a single mail message are demonstrated by the following Telnet session log:

```
Telnet: post.demon.co.uk:SMTP
220 post-1.mail.demon.net Server SMTP (Complaints/bugs to:
➥postmaster@demon.net)
>HELO tallguy.psp.co.uk
>250 Good afternoon, pleased to meet you
>MAIL FROM: tfl@psp.co.uk
>250 OK
>RCPT TO: tcp-book@psp.co.uk
>250 Recipient OK.
>DATA
>354 Enter Mail, end by a line with only '.'
>this is a test mail message.
>This is the 2nd line of the test
>and this is the last
>.
>250 Submitted & queued (18/msg.aa513240)
QUIT
221 post-1.mail.demon.net says goodbye to max099.frontier-
➥networks.co.uk at SUN Jan 19 13:04:34
```

After transmission, this mail message was eventually received by my user agent; it looked like Figure 11.4.

Figure 11.4.

An e-mail received by Turnpike.

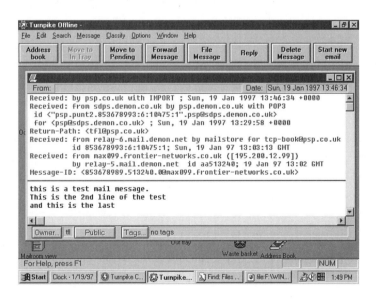

Application Services

You will note that there are some lines in the e-mail shown in Figure 11.4 that do not appear in the Telnet session. These header lines were added by the MTA and are discussed in more detail in the section "SMTP Mail Format."

The parameters to the `MAIL` and `RCPT` are more complex expressions, known as a *reverse path* and a *forward path*, respectively. In this Telnet session, they are simple e-mail addresses of the type commonly seen. They can be more complex.

RFC 821 notes that the reverse path can contain "a reverse source routing list of hosts and source mailbox." Likewise, the forward path can contain "a source routing list of hosts and the destination mailbox." The RFC also presents a detailed description of how to parse these expressions. Fortunately, most users do not need to know the intricacies of these expressions; those who do are well advised to read the relevant RFCs carefully, as well as to study some reference code implementations in detail.

11.3.2. SMTP Reply Codes

As noted in the previous section, the client MTA makes the connection to a server MTA and sends a series of commands plus the actual mail messages. The server MTA acknowledges these commands by a series of status codes. This is very similar to the approach taken by FTP, although with SMTP, there is only one TCP connection between the client and the server.

The transfer of mail is a state-full process—that is, one with a series of specific states, with commands being needed to modify the states or to move between these states. For proper working, these commands must be entered in the right order. RFC 821 describes these state transitions in considerable detail. The reply codes assist the MTAs in ensuring that the necessary synchronization of request and actions occurs, and that the client MTA knows what state the receiver MTA is in. Each command sent by a client MTA will generate exactly one reply.

An SMTP reply consists of a three-digit reply code followed by extra ASCII text. This number is a formal statement of the reply and is intended to be used by the MTA to determine the next state to enter. The extra ASCII text helps users to understand what the codes mean, although most end users will not see them. They are typically most useful to support staff or implementers of mail clients.

The replies are all of the form `XYZ` and are similar to those produced by the FTP server. The value of `X` determines the general type of the reply, `Y` indicates the specific type of reply, and `Z` gives more details as defined in the following.

The values of X are as follows, as noted from RFC 821:

1   Positive preliminary reply—The command has been accepted, but the server MTA is waiting for some additional information. The client MTA should send some more information as to whether to continue or abort. Note: This value of X is specified in RFC 821, but no actual codes are defined. Also, there are no continue or abort commands provided.

2   Positive completion—The requested action has been completed, and a new request may be initiated.

3   Positive intermediate reply—The command has been accepted, but the requested action has not yet been completed. The client MTA can now send further commands.

4   Transient negative completion reply—The command was not accepted, and the requested action did not occur. The error is probably temporary, and the action may be requested again.

5   Permanent negative completion reply—The command was not accepted, and the requested action did not occur. The error here is more serious, and in general, the client MTA should not attempt it.

The second digit of the reply code, Y, is used to give more detail to these general replies, as follows:

0   Syntax—This relates to the syntax of the received command.

1   Information—General information.

2   Connections—This reply relates to the transmission channel.

3, 4 Unspecified.

5   Mail system—This indicates the status of the server MTA, with respect to the requested command.

The third digit, Z, is used to break down the more general information provided by X and Y and to provide more details on the specific response.

The following Telnet session, which simulates an SMTP session, demonstrates some of these replies:

```
220 post-2.mail.demon.net Server SMTP (Complaints/bugs to:
↪postmaster@demon.net)
helo psp.co.uk
250 Good afternoon, pleased to meet you
testing
500 Unknown or unimplemented command
mail ddd
501 No sender named
mail from: tfl@psp.co.uk
250 OK
data
```

Application Services

```
503 No recipients have been specified.
rcpt tfl@psp.co.uk
501 No recipient named.
rcpt to: tcp=bool
550 Unable to parse address
rcpt to: tcp-book@psp.co.uk
250 Recipient OK.
data
354 Enter Mail, end by a line with only '.'
testing more and more
all dond
.
250 Submitted & queued (21/msg.aa622613)
help
214-The following commands are accepted:
214-helo noop mail data rcpt help quit rset expn vrfy
214-
214 Send complaints/bugs to:  postmaster@demon.net
quit
221 post-2.mail.demon.net says goodbye to max090.frontier-
➡networks.co.uk at Sun
Jan 19 16:32:12.
```

In this Telnet session, I sent some valid and invalid commands, each of which generated a single response (except the HELP command, which generated several lines of output). A mail message was sent, complete with a typographical mistake.

11.3.3. SMTP Mail Format

In the sections "SMTP Commands" and "SMTP Reply Codes," I described how MTAs use the SMTP protocol to transfer messages. In essence, a mail message consists of three distinct components:

- The SMTP envelope

- Mail headers

- The mail body

The SMTP envelope is generated as a result of the MAIL and RCPT commands and indicates who sent the message and who is to receive it. The mail headers and body are data sent between the client MTA and server MTA as part of the mail data. These are lines of text, sent after the DATA command, and are terminated by a line containing just a full stop (.) and a CRLF.

The header lines each consist of a header name, followed by a colon (:), a space, and a header value. Once the mail message is delivered to the final destination, the SMTP envelope is lost. This can make troubleshooting more difficult, especially if the contents of the headers within the mail message itself are different than what is specified in the SMTP envelope. This can occur due to errors in mail clients or servers, or can be done deliberately. Much "junk" e-mail is generated in this way, with the headers deliberately forged to make the messages look like they came from someone other than the real sender. Thus the mail user agent only has the content of the header line to use in constructing what the user sees.

A genuine e-mail message, with full headers, is shown here:

```
Received: from sdps.demon.co.uk by psp.demon.co.uk with POP3
 id <"psp.punt1.853167785:9:00902:14".psp@sdps.demon.co.uk>
 for <psp@sdps.demon.co.uk> ; Mon, 13 Jan 1997 15:06:43 +0000
Return-Path: <mbligh@sequent.com>
Received: from relay-9.mail.demon.net by mailstore for
➡tfl@psp.co.uk
          id 853167785:9:00902:14; Mon, 13 Jan 97 15:03:05 GMT
Received: from gateway.sequent.com ([138.95.18.1]) by relay-
➡10.mail.demon.net
            id aa1012851; 13 Jan 97 15:02 GMT
Received: from uksqnt.uk.sequent.com (uksqnt.uk.sequent.com
➡[158.84.84.5]) by gateway.sequent.com
(8.6.13/8.6.9) with ESMTP id HAA09096 for <tfl@psp.co.uk>;
➡Mon, 13 Jan 1997 07:02:44 -0800
Received: from ukgw.uk.sequent.com (ukeugw0a.uk.sequent.com
➡[158.84.9.10]) by uksqnt.uk.sequent.com
(8.6.12/8.6.9) with SMTP id PAA13402 for <tfl@psp.co.uk>; Mon,
➡13 Jan 1997 15:00:44 GMT
Received: by ukgw.uk.sequent.com with Microsoft Mail
     id <32DA4EE5@ukgw.uk.sequent.com>; Mon, 13 Jan 97 15:04:05
➡GMT
From: "Martin Bligh (mbligh)" <mbligh@sequent.com>
To: Thomas Lee <tfl@psp.co.uk>
Subject: RE: TCP/IP book - chapter 2
Date: Mon, 13 Jan 97 15:00:00 GMT
Message-ID: <32DA4EE5@ukgw.uk.sequent.com>
Encoding: 3 TEXT
X-Mailer: Microsoft Mail V3.0


Testing your mail address ...
```

Application Services

This example shows a genuine e-mail message sent between two of the main authors of this book to test out the mail connection. The headers include details of who the message is from and to, details about the path the message took in its journey from sender to receiver, the date the message was composed, plus other fields useful for debugging or for client display (for example, the Message-ID and X-Mailer header lines). In this case, the actual message was a mere one line long.

The mail message, as transmitted by the DATA command, consists of the headers and actual message body. These messages are all sent as normal ASCII and are delimited by a normal CRLF sequence. SMTP, as a message transport protocol, cares little about the contents of the actual message, leaving it largely up to the user agents to define the contents.

The detailed format of mail messages is defined by RFC 822. This RFC has been updated by both RFC 987 and RFC 1327. The contents of an e-mail message are similar to that of a Usenet news message, as described in RFC 1036, and what is often referred to as "son of 1036" is used as a more recent and detailed description by many implementers. This later document can be found at ftp://ftp.zoo.toronto.edu/pub/news.ps.Z. While Usenet messages are different from e-mail messages, many mail client implementers consider it prudent to at least be aware of Usenet message formats.

These message format descriptions, some of them going back 10 years or more, define what are essentially text-based messages. Since then, e-mail has gone universal, and USASCII is simply inadequate today. The transmission of European and Asian languages is one significant problem area, particularly for transnational enterprises.

Additionally, the huge set of new technologies that have been developed since RFC 822 was written have given rise to the use of e-mail to distribute all manner of objects—such as word processing documents, spreadsheets, sound/video clips, and so on—that were unforeseen at the time RFC 822 was written.

There are several solutions to this problem. With the UUENCODE and UUDECODE facilities, a user agent can convert standard binary files to ASCII for transmission. Upon receipt, these can be converted back to binary by the receiver's user agent. Most modern e-mail clients handle this conversion with ease and often without the user being aware of it.

Another solution to the problem of sending application data through an ASCII transport is MIME (Multipurpose Internet Mail Extensions), which is well suited to handling languages other than English. The basic MIME format was described, most recently, in a series of RFCs: 2045, 2046, 2047, 2048, and 2049. Essentially, these documents define the header and content details that enable a user agent to turn complex objects into ASCII for transport over SMTP.

The problems involved with the transport of complex objects through a simpler and underlying protocol are also seen in the WWW area. WWW browsers are used to display all manner of media, including a wide variety of complex document types (spreadsheets, graphics, word processing, and so on) as well as a vast array of audio-visual material. MIME is also used for these purposes.

11.3.4. **SMTP in the Enterprise**

The preceding discussion of SMTP concentrates on the simple transfer of e-mail, possibly highly structured through the use of MIME or UUENCODE/UUDECODE. The diagram shown in Figure 11.3 shows only two MTAs involved in this transfer. In larger organizations (and most specifically, on the Internet), the mail-transfer process typically involves a single message passing through multiple MTA (or *relay*) agents.

The headers of the sample e-mail message in the section "SMTP Mail Format" indicate that several MTAs were involved, including `ukgw.sequent.com`, `uksqnt.uk.sequent.com`, `gateway.sequent.com`, `relay.9.mail.demon.net`, and `sdps.demon.co.uk`. While some of this will relate to the mail policies of a given company, Sequent and PS Partnership, in the example, this also can reflect on how mail is transferred on the Internet. It is interesting to note that the entire journey made by the e-mail message took a mere six minutes!

As e-mail scales from a simple two-MTA scenario presented earlier in this chapter to the more complex and real-life example discussed, there is a need for the mail transfer agents to handle more complex mail routing. This routing is not really a function of the SMTP protocol itself; rather, it relates to the design of the mail transfer agents. Additionally, MTAs are able to take advantage of the features of DNS (described in Chapter 11, "Application Services") in particular the use of the MX record.

11.4. **HTTP**

NOTE	Many people confuse the

Many people confuse the underlying Hypertext Transfer Protocol (HTTP) with the HTML markup or layout language for use in WWW browsers. HTTP is a client/server transport protocol used between a WWW browser client, such as Internet Explorer or Netscape Navigator, and a WWW server, such as Apache or Internet Information Server. HTTP is mainly used to transfer files containing HTML or graphics between the server and client. The browser then interprets the contents of that HTML and graphic files to produce the images you see within the browser.

The HTML that is transferred can contain both "standard" HTML and browser-specific (that is, "nonstandard") HTML, as well as more sophisticated objects including Java and Microsoft's ActiveX and the associated scripting commands needed to activate those objects. Like HTTP, the details of HTML are also in a high state of flux as the key vendors constantly update their offerings.

HTTP is the underlying protocol for the transfer of hypertext and is the foundation for the World Wide Web. First published in the early 1990s, HTTP was the basis for a simple, text-based Web of *hyperlinks*, pieces of text that could be clicked on to take the user to some other document somewhere out in hyperspace. This simple concept, a natural extension to the Gopher protocol described in RFC 1436, has captured the imagination of both the public and the vendors alike. Both groups have embraced these basic concepts and are pushing hard to utilize them to the full, as well as to extend them at a significant rate.

Application Services

It is probably an understatement to say that the technologies within the WWW are in a state of rapid development. The so-called "browser wars" and "server wars" being fought at the time of this writing have seen very rapid advances in the technology, with Microsoft, Netscape, and others all scrabbling almost desperately for market share. To write any sort of definitive view of the HTTP protocol that will stand up to examination even six months later is a very tall assignment.

RFC 1945 defines the basic Hypertext Transfer Protocol, HTTP 1.0. An updated RFC, RFC 2068, was more recently released, and it describes HTTP 1.1. At present, both RFCs are considered informational, although vendors are using elements of them in product offerings. Certain features of HTTP 1.1 are already in use by some clients and some server products.

This chapter looks at the basics of HTTP 1.0 and briefly mentions the extensions defined in RFC 2068. It does not enter into any debate as to the relative value of the various approaches being taken by the key vendors, and avoids discussing the details of HTML. It is hoped that the basics of HTTP will remain broadly the same, whichever Web browser and Web server you use.

HTTP is a more modern protocol than Telnet, FTP, and SMTP, and the writing style of the RFCs that define HTTP is different from that of the other protocols defined in this chapter. But the general structure of HTTP is in many ways a logical progression from the earlier work, and the strong foundation of the earlier protocols is clearly evident.

HTTP, like the other protocols discussed in this chapter, is a client/server protocol, with a user agent—typically a WWW browser such as Microsoft Internet Explorer or Netscape Navigator—making requests from or sending information to a WWW server. Like SMTP, HTTP is simply a transport mechanism and avoids dealing with the message content. The content of a Web page is defined by Hypertext Markup Language (HTML). Like HTTP, HTML is also evolving rapidly with many vendor extensions being added into the language.

With HTTP, the user agent creates a TCP connection to the HTTP server and issues a request that generates a response. This is similar to the FTP and SMTP protocols. The TCP connection is made to the well-known TCP port 80. HTTP could operate over other transport protocols, although so far, the main implementations use TCP.

The HTTP request is a structured ASCII text message consisting of the following:

- A method—This is an action for the server to perform. Methods are defined in more detail in the section "HTTP Methods."

- A request URI (Uniform Resource Identifier)—This identifies an object that the method relates to.

- The HTTP version identifier—This is a string used to identify the version of the HTTP protocol. RFC 1945 defines this string as "HTTP/ 1.0." for HTTP version 1. Version 1.1 of HGTTP is identified by the string "HTTP/1.1".

- The request header information—This is additional information that the client can send to the server.

A typical HTTP request might consist of the GET method, requesting the server to return a specific document (for example, an HTML file), which it identifies by a URI. The HTTP server will then act on that request and return a response to the client. The request header information passed by the HTTP client contains a number of individual header lines, separated by CRLF strings, that further qualify the request. The entire request message is terminated by two CRLF strings.

The URI identifies the object that the request relates to. If the request method is GET, the URI identifies the file that the HTTP client wants to get from the HTTP server. (The format of the URI is explained in the section "Response Codes.")

The response message, sent back to the HTTP client, consists of the following:

- The HTTP version identifier—To identify the version of the response. Usually, this will be the same as for the request.

- The response status—A three-digit response code, similar to those generated by FTP and SMTP, plus textual information. Response codes are discussed later in this chapter in the "HTTP Futures—HTTP 1.1 and Beyond" section.

- The entity body—Data being returned back to the HTTP client. Not all responses will return data, thus this component of the reply is optional.

If the request sent to the server was a GET for a document (for example, INDEX.HTML), the response would indicate whether that document was available (indicated by a status code of 200, plus the string OK) followed by the contents of the document INDEX.HTML. The entity body is separated from the remainder of the response by two occurrences of a CRLF string. The response is terminated with two further CRLF stings. The response codes are described in more detail in the section "Response Codes."

The way that an HTTP client typically creates a single TCP connection for a request has certain inherent flaws. When the reply, which may include a requested document, has been transmitted, this connection is dropped. This was adequate for a simple, text-based WWW implementation, but as HTML documents have evolved and have become richer and more complex, it can often consist of a number of embedded objects (graphics, audio-visual elements, and so on). Therefore, the rendering of a single document by a WWW browser can generate multiple connections.

Application Services

This approach of one TCP connection per request can be very wasteful of connection resources; a busy server can have a large number of ports more or less constantly in a `CLOSE_WAIT` state. Because most individual documents tend to be quite small, this approach also means that many, if not most, HTTP transactions are transmitted via TCP while the TCP connection is still in a slow start mode, so users often see slower performance than might otherwise be possible. Finally, because all the congestion and flow information relating to the path between the HTTP client and server is effectively thrown away each time the connection is dropped, neither end, nor the intervening network, is able to do much optimization of data flows.

HTTP is also based on the notion that the client, while making the request to a server, might have that request actually fulfilled by an intermediate system: a cache or a proxy. As the Internet has embraced the WWW as a virtual standard, the limitations of HTTP, with respect to caching, have become evident.

HTTP 1.0 also provides a simple authentication mechanism to provide more secure access to a WWW site. A WWW server can use this mechanism to challenge a client request. The WWW client can then respond to this challenge with suitable authorization information.

HTTP 1.1 contains several features to reduce these problems by allowing the server and client to reuse the TCP connection for further messages as well as improving the caching facilities of the underlying HTTP protocol.

11.4.1. HTTP Methods

As noted earlier, each HTTP request includes a method or function to be performed by the request. In HTTP 1.0 there are three defined methods:

- `GET`—To enable information to be retrieved

- `HEAD`—Similar to `GET`, except that only header information is returned

- `POST`—Used to transmit information from the client to the server

When an end user is using a WWW browser, most HTTP requests are sent using the `GET` method, requesting either an HTML document or an element to be displayed or used within the HTML page. The `POST` method allows the browser to return information back to the server for server-side processing. The `HEAD` method can be used to test hyperlinks for validity or for recent modification.

The `POST` method is mainly used in conjunction with HTML forms. It provides a uniform way for the HTML page designer to capture information, such as survey data or order entry details, from the user and transmit it back to the server for subsequent processing and analysis. The specific action taken by the server on receipt of a `POST` request is server dependent and is not a function of the HTTP protocol. One common way that this can be accomplished is by the server running a *Common Gateway Interface* (CGI) script. A CGI script is a program (possibly a C program, or a script file written in a language such as Perl or REXX.), called by the CGI interface. WWW server vendors have been quick to find new ways to improve on this basic mechanism.

Additional methods have been defined in HTTP 1.1. They are described in the section "HTTP Futures—HTTP 1.1 and Beyond."

11.4.2. HTTP Header Fields

As part of an HTTP request or response, the sender can include additional information in the form of header fields. These provide more information to the receiver and consist of a header field name and value, delimited by a colon and followed by a space. Each header line is delimited by a `CRLF`.

RFC 1945 defines 16 header fields. They are outlined in Table 11.11.

Table 11.11. HTTP 1.0 headers.

Header Field Name	Header Value	Header Function
`Allow`	Method	Lists the methods supported by the URI (for example, `GET`, `HEAD`)
`Authorization`	Credentials	Passes access credentials
`Content-Encoding`	Content-coding	Defines any content encoding applied, typically to the URI
`Content-Length`	Length	Indicates the size of the passed entity (for example, the file)
`Content-Type`	Type	Indicates the type of data that is being passed
`Date`	Date/time	Date/time the message originated
`Expires`	Date/time	Indicates when the entity should be considered stale
`From`	E-mail address	Indicates the e-mail address of the user controlling the WWW browser

continues

Table 11.11. Continued.

Header Field Name	Header Value	Header Function
If-Modified-Since	Date/time	Used in conjunction with the GET method to make it conditional
Last-Modified	Date/time	Indicates when the sender believes the object was last modified
Location	Location	An absolute URI
Pragma	Directive	Passes implementation–specific information between client and server
Referer	URI	Tells where the requested URI is obtained from
Server	Product	Contains information about the server servicing a request
User-Agent	Product	Contains information about the client generating a request
WWW-Authenticate	Challenge	Used to authenticate a request

The Allow header field enables the sender to inform the recipient of the methods that may be associated with the URI. This header field cannot, however, prevent the client from trying other methods. It will also not provide information as to what methods the server actually implements.

The Authorization header enables the user agent to authenticate itself with the server. The client will pass sufficient information to enable this authentication to occur. This field might be sent in response to a WWW-Authenticate challenge issued by a WWW server.

The Content-Encoding, Content-Length, and Content-Type fields are used to tell the receiver what sort of data is being sent, how long it is, and how it is encoded. As for e-mail, HTTP needs to be able to handle non–ASCII data. HTTP, like SMTP, uses MIME for this purpose. These fields are very useful to WWW browsers, for example, to help them determine how to interpret the datastream returned via a GET request.

The `Date` header field is used to inform the recipient when the request was generated, which can have implications when dealing with caches. The `Expires` header field is used to tell how old an object is and whether it is still valid. These fields can be of great use in a proxy situation, where an intermediate proxy can hold a copy of an object until it expires; thus, if the date is greater than the `Expires` value, returning the cached copy will no longer be appropriate.

The `From` header field can be used to transmit the e-mail address of the individual making the request from the client UA to the server. Because this can have profound security implications, RFC 1945 clearly notes that this should never be transmitted without explicit user permission.

The `If-Modified-Since` header field turns a request—for example, a `GET` request—into a conditional one. The object is returned only if it has been modified after the specified date. The `Last-Modified` header field states when the sender believes the object being returned was last modified. Both these fields are useful implementation of caches.

The `Referer` header field is used to enable the client to specify, for the server's benefit, the URI from which the current URI was obtained. Thus if a UA loads an HTML file containing a reference to a `.gif` file, when the UA issues the `GET` to download this file, it can use the `Refer` file to return the context of that `GET` (that is, the HTML page). This can allow a server to generate lists of back links and usage logs as well as to identify out-of-date or broken links.

The `Server` and `User-Agent` header fields are used to identify the products used to make the request and response. This might be useful to help the browsers to interpret the requests and responses.

Some browsers and servers make use of additional, non–HTTP 1.0 header fields. For example, the Microsoft Internet Explorer browser sends nonstandard header fields with each `GET` request, including `UA-pixels`, `UA-color`, `US-OS`, and `UA-CPU`.

In addition, many modern browsers can and do include some HTTP 1.1 header fields. For example, both Internet Explorer 3.01 and Netscape Navigator 3.01 send the `Connection:` header field. This is another example of the rush-to-market syndrome noted in the section "HTTP Methods."

11.4.3. URI Format

The designers of most transport protocols often struggle to ensure that the names of the objects used within the formal protocol definitions, by both the vendors implementing those protocols and the users using those products, are useful and helpful. The language of some protocol-definition documents can sometimes be arcane and stilted. HTTP is no exception.

The HTTP request will generally need to identify some object for transport—typically a WWW page or a component of that page being requested by a GET request or a CGI script being sent by a POST request. HTTP uses the term *Uniform Resource Identifier* to identify this network resource. A URI is either a formal Uniform Resource Name (URN), as defined in RFC 1737, or the more familiar Universal Resource Locator (URL) defined in RFC 1808.

The syntax of an HTTP URL, as set out in RFC 1945, is

```
"http: " "//" <host> [ ":" <port>] [<path>]]
```

> **NOTE**
>
> The URL is an important component of most users' perception and usage of the WWW. *But it is so ugly.* As large companies are embracing the Internet (and more specifically, the WWW) and including URLs in advertising and other corporate communications, these URLs become interrelated to the companies' overall images. While to a technophile a URL makes perfect sense, to the man in the street, it is pure gibberish. Watching or listening to uninitiated TV and radio presenters grappling with these can also be amusing. Quite possibly, the designers of the WWW never intended to expose URLs to the wider public. But many companies are now proudly including URLs as part of their corporate images, so the public, I suppose, will have to just get used to them. In time, they might even become an art form and some day there will be a Berners-Lee Gallery of URLs. Funnier things have happened!

where <host> is any legal Internet host; <port> is the TCP port over which the connection should be made (the default is 80); and <path> identifies a document, file, or object at that host.

A typical URL might be http://www.psp.demon.co.uk/tfl/tfl.htm. This URL is a real Web page; in fact, it is my personal home page.

In some cases, a WWW user might just know the name of a Web site and want to view whatever is at that site. This can be achieved by sending a simpler syntax such as http://www.psp.demon.co.uk/. The URL sent to the server in this case is simply /, which the destination server interprets as a request for the document index.html. It must be stressed that this interpretation of / is server specific and can vary from server to server.

11.4.4. Response Codes

As in FTP and SMTP, when an HTTP server returns a response message to the user agent, it will send a three-character response message along with the other components of the response, as indicated in the section "HTTP Methods."

The first digit of an HTTP response code indicates the class of the response:

1XX	Informational—This class is not used and has been reserved for future use.
2XX	Success—The action was received, understood, and accepted.
3XX	Redirection—The action was received, but some further action must be taken in order to complete the request.

4XX	Client error—The request is either syntactically invalid (as far as the server can determine) or cannot be fulfilled.
5XX	Server error—The request appears to be valid, but the server is unable to fulfill it.

RFC 1945 defines a number of specific response codes, as well as a mechanism for additional extension codes to be defined. The main response codes you are likely to see in practice are shown in Table 11.12.

Table 11.12. HTTP response codes.

Code	Meaning
200	OK
201	Created
202	Accepted
204	No content
301	Moved permanently
302	Moved temporarily
304	Not modified
400	Bad request
401	Unauthorized
403	Forbidden
404	Not found
500	Internal server error
501	Not implemented
502	Bad gateway
503	Service unavailable

Application Services

11.4.5. HTTP Futures—HTTP 1.1 and Beyond

As both vendors and users have embraced the opportunities offered by the HTTP protocol and have delivered products based on it, the limitations of HTTP have become evident. During the writing of this chapter, a revised version of HTTP, HTTP 1.1, was formally published as an RFC (RFC 2068). As noted in the "HTTP Header Fields" section, some components of this later protocol are already being implemented and are being used in products that advertise themselves as HTTP 1.0–compliant. Naturally, the effect of such usage is server- and browser-dependent.

HTTP 1.1 provides improvements over HTTP 1.0 in a number of areas, including additional request methods and header fields, enhanced support for caching, and improved use of the underlying TCP infrastructure. Two key objectives of HTTP 1.1 are to reduce the impact of HTTP on the Internet, thus making HTTP better behaved, and to be as compatible as possible with HTTP 1.0, especially for HTTP clients and servers.

HTTP 1.1 defines four new methods: `OPTIONS`, `PUT`, `DELETE`, and `TRACE`. The `PUT` method allows an object to be transported back up to a server and stored at the URI, while `DELETE` offers delete capability.

HTTP 1.1 also defines many new header fields. Both these new methods and the header fields are in the same format as for HTTP 1.0 to minimize the impact on developers.

At the same time, additional issues relating to HTTP remain unsolved. They include the following:

- Hit counting—The reporting of hit counts can have an impact on the design of caching algorithms, particularly because some servers reduce or eliminate content caching to enable more reliable hit counting. Some work has been done in this area, but more is required.

- A more compressed protocol—The protocol is verbose and lengthy. No doubt some compression could reduce the protocol overheads, especially for small requests.

- Multiplexing of the HTTP stream—This might remove the need for multiple TCP connections, thus improving performance.

- Transparent content negotiation—To improve the nature and method of transporting an ever-increasing range of data types.

These are just some of the areas under discussion, and by the time you read this book, there may well be further developments in each of these areas.

11.5. Summary

In this chapter, we have looked at four key application protocols: Telnet, FTP, SMTP, and HTTP. Each of these protocols is inherently simple. And each is based on, and assumes, a reliable underlying network, provided by the TCP, IP, and the physical network protocols.

We have not, however, examined a number of additional protocols. They include the following (I've indicated where you can get more information about them):

- NNTP—Network News Transfer Protocol, used to transfer Network News (a.k.a. Usenet). NNTP is defined in RFC 977.

- Rlogin—A simplified method of remote logins, not dissimilar to Telnet. Rlogin is defined in RFC 1282.

- Finger—A simple protocol used to transfer user information. Finger is defined in RFC 1288.

- WHOIS—The WHOIS service enables lookup of registered DNS domains and domain contacts. WHOIS servers are provided at all DNS registries, including `ds.internic.net` and `ripe.net`. WHOIS is defined in RFC 1812.

- Archie—Archie provides a method of searching for a file across many FTP file servers around the world. Archie is based on the proprietary Prospero protocol.

- Gopher—Gopher is a distributed document search-and-retrieval protocol. It is very similar to the WWW, but is purely text based. RFC 1436 describes the Gopher protocol.

- WAIS (Wide Area Information System)—WAIS provides for a free text search of databases.

- Veronica—Veronica provides an index to Gopher servers.

Application Services

Chapter

12

Naming Services

by Martin Bligh

12.1. Overview

12.2. DNS Concepts

12.3. DNS Data and Protocols

12.4. Debugging with **nslookup**

12.5. NetBIOS Name Service (WINS)

12.6. Summary

This chapter covers the principles and protocols behind the Domain Name System (DNS). It does not attempt to show you how to set up any specific implementation of DNS, but does use examples from Berkley Internet Naming Daemon (BIND), the predominant implementation, to illustrate particular points. The core protocols of DNS are covered, but the optional extensions have been omitted because they are not normally used.

12.1. Overview

Computers find it easier to refer to things by numbers, but humans are inclined to give them names. So while my computer might be known to other computers by its IP address (178.93.59.21), it is known to human users as Mars.

IP addresses provide a physical grouping for machines; the address that a machine's network interface uses depends on where it is physically plugged into the network. Names provide us with an opportunity to group machines logically, perhaps according to the department to which the machines belong. If a database server is moved to a different location in the building (on a different subnet), we have to change its IP address, but we don't want to have to change the configuration of every client.

These two differences explain why we need names for machines, but having names means that we need some way to provide a mapping between machines' names and their IP addresses.

With a small network, it is acceptable to have a list of names and numbers in a file (normally called hosts) that is updated when machines are added or changed. As the network grows, copying this to every machine becomes impractical, so a more structured system was designed to handle the situation: the Domain Name System.

DNS was designed as a robust, distributed database in which different sections of data could be controlled by different people. The data is held in a tree structure, rather than a simple flat structure. It was also given the capability to hold many different types of data for each name, not just IP addresses.

Each host that wants to act as a DNS client needs a *resolver*—a set of routines or a process whose task is to find out information about particular names for user processes. This information is held on DNS servers (commonly called *nameservers*). Clients communicate with servers, and servers communicate with other servers. This communication is carried out through DNS *queries*.

In a typical scenario (shown in Figure 12.1), a user process asks the host's resolver for the IP address of a particular host (1). The resolver asks the local nameserver for the information (2), and is sent a reply containing a referral to another nameserver (3). The resolver asks the second nameserver (4), and obtains the IP address (5). This address is passed back to the user process (6), which can then contact the desired host.

Figure 12.1.

The information flow for a typical DNS query.

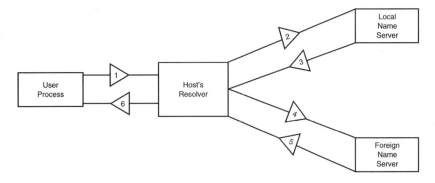

12.2. DNS Concepts

This section describes some of the key concepts behind DNS; the terminology and concepts are keys to understanding the following sections.

12.2.1. The Domain Namespace

The domain namespace is a way of structuring the myriad of names that are assigned to hosts on a large network. The namespace is a tree structure; Figure 12.2 shows an example of a tiny fragment of such a tree.

Figure 12.2.

A fragment of a sample domain namespace.

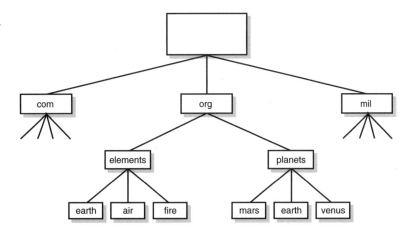

Definition of Domain Name

Both internal and external nodes in the namespace tree are all labeled, often with one word (for example, `planets` in Figure 12.2). The permitted format for labels is a matter of some debate, but if you stick to the following rules, you should avoid problems.

Naming Services

Labels consist of letters (a–z, A–Z), digits (0–9), and hyphens (-). Other characters may work, but this set helps to provide backward compatibility with other systems. Labels are restricted to 63 characters, starting and ending with a letter or a digit and containing at least one letter. Labels are not necessarily unique (for example, there are two nodes labeled `earth` in Figure 12.2), subject to the restrictions described in the "Naming Conflicts" section. Labels are not treated as case sensitive for comparisons, but case is preserved where possible when transferring or storing information.

Each node is referred to by its *domain name*, which is obtained by traversing the tree from the desired node upward, taking a list of labels separated by dots (`.`). Thus the node labeled `air` in Figure 12.2 has the domain name `air.elements.org.` (note the trailing `.` and the fact that the root node at the top of the diagram has a null label).

Internal nodes (for example, `planets.org.`) are usually called *domains* or *subdomains*, depending on the context. External nodes (for example, `air.elements.org.`) are usually called *hosts*.

NOTE	The term *domain name* is used to refer to both internal and external nodes.

A fully qualified domain name (FQDN) is the complete trace through the tree, right up to the root node; it is signified by the trailing `.` at the end of a domain name. A machine may also be referred to in a local context by a partially qualified domain name (PQDN)—for example, `air.elements.org.` could refer to `fire.elements.org.` as `fire.elements` (because both systems are under the `org.` domain) or as just `fire` (because both systems are under the `elements.org.` domain). If in doubt, use the FQDN.

Naming Conflicts

In a simple, flat layout, rigorous controls would be needed over the whole network to make sure that nobody else calls his or her machine `Mars` as I have (otherwise, when somebody tried the command `telnet Mars`, who would he connect to?). Having multiple machines using the same name must be avoided, but this quickly becomes unmanageable once the network becomes large.

The DNS structure allows multiple machines to have the same hostname as long as their domain names are different. In Figure 12.2, you can see that there is a machine called `earth` under both the `elements.org.` and `planets.org.` domains. This is permissible because the machines have distinct domain names (that is, `earth.elements.org.` and `earth.planets.org.`). It is not permissible to have two nodes with the same label under exactly the same parent (for example, two machines with the domain name `earth.elements.org.`).

NOTE   Remember, a domain name is a *unique* identifier for a node in the domain space tree.

By using a tree structure for the domain namespace, different groups can name machines independently of each other (assuming each group has its own domain). Note that although different hosts may not use the same name, one host *is* permitted to use multiple domain names.

12.2.2. Reverse Lookups

Often, it is useful to find the domain name for a given IP address. DNS indexes data by domain name, so it is impractical to try searching through every record, looking for an IP address. A clever solution to this problem has been implemented: Each IP address is turned into a domain name and stored under a special domain.

IPv4

IPv4 stores addresses for reverse lookups under the `in-addr.arpa.` domain. This results in a domain name of the form `x.x.x.x.in-addr.arpa.`. There is a problem, however: IP addresses store their least significant part *last* (for example, in `12.34.56.78`, the `78` part is least significant), whereas domain names store their least significant *first* (for example, in `abc.def.ghi.jkl`, the `abc` part is least significant). The solution? Reverse the IP address—so `12.34.56.78` maps to `78.56.34.12.in-addr.arpa.`. This domain name is shown as part of Figure 12.3, which shows how the `in-addr.arpa.` domain fits into the domain namespace.

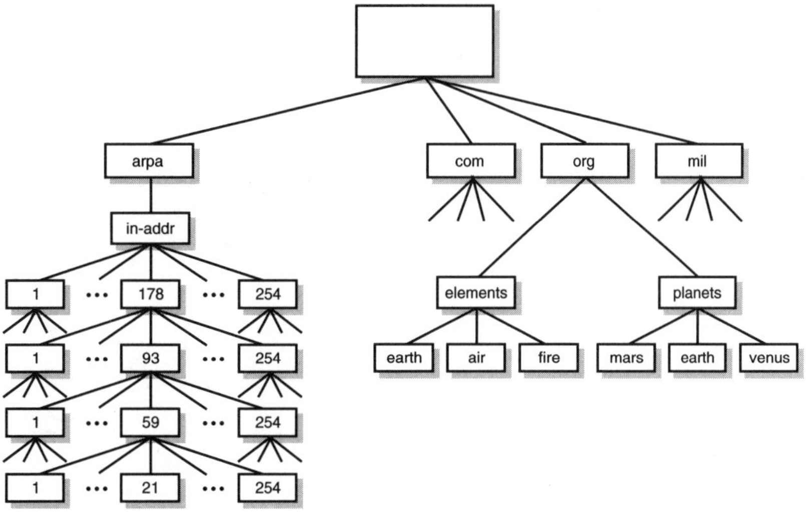

Figure 12.3.
A fragment of the domain namespace showing `inaddr.arpa.`.

Now I can ask for data corresponding to the domain name `78.56.34.12.`
`in-addr.arpa.` and be told that the matching domain name is `foo.bar.com.`.
This means that the (*hostname*, *IP address*) pair is stored in two different places
in the tree. Care must be taken to ensure consistency.

IPv6

Reverse lookups for IPv6 work in a very similar way: The address is still reversed,
and the domain `ip6.int.` is appended to the encoded address. However, instead
of the address being grouped in bytes and expressed in decimal, it is grouped by
nibble and expressed in hex. So the address

    ab9f:1:2:3:4:5:987:248c

encodes to

    c.8.4.2.7.8.9.5.4.3.2.1.f.9.b.a.ip6.int.

12.2.3. Zones versus Domains

DNS uses a distributed database—that is, the information for all the hosts on the
network doesn't reside on one server, but is split up into sections that can be
independently administered. These sections are called *zones*; their scope commonly matches a domain, but they may delegate control of some subdomains to
other zones. Hence a zone's scope can be considered to be "the scope of the
domain, minus any other zones defined under the domain." Zones are named
after the domain from which they are derived.

In Figure 12.4, two zones are defined—the `org.` zone and the `planets.org.` zone.

Figure 12.4.

An illustration of zone structure.

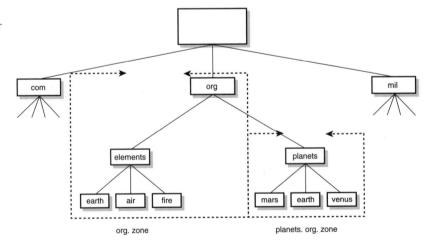

The `planets.org.` zone has no other zones under it; thus the scope of the zone matches the scope of the `planets.org.` domain.

However, the `org.` zone has the `planets.org.` zone defined under it; thus the scope of the `org.` zone is the scope of the `org.` domain *minus* the scope of the `planets.org.` subdomain.

If the information needed isn't on the local nameserver, how do you find it? Nameservers know of other nameservers from NS resource records (see the "Resource Records" section, later in this chapter). If they don't have the appropriate resource record, they can always go up to the top of the tree and work down from there.

All nameservers hold records for the root nameservers.

12.2.4. **Primary and Secondary Servers**

Each zone needs a server to answer questions about the resource records in that zone. But suppose that server goes down? Name resolution is so important that the service's absence would affect many other machines—they wouldn't be capable of finding the IP addresses of any machine in that zone.

The solution is to have more than one server for each zone. The resource records are fed to one server (the primary), and are distributed to other servers (the secondaries) from there. While it is technically possible to have multiple primary servers, this is *not* recommended because it makes it very hard to keep the data consistent. It is an excellent idea to spread out the servers across the network as much as possible—this gives greater protection against network failure.

Both primary and secondary servers are said to be *authoritative* for their zones. A server can serve more than one zone, and can be a primary for some and a secondary for others.

For instance, given three zones (A, B, and C) and three servers (1, 2, and 3), the nameservers could be set up as

1. Primary for A; secondary for B.

2. Primary for B; primary for C.

3. Secondary for A; secondary for C.

A server can also give out non-authoritative information—this means that while it isn't an authoritative server for the relevant zone, it does happen to know the answer to your question (normally because the answer to this question is in the cache).

12.2.5. Iterative versus Recursive Queries

Data is split up into zones. So what happens if I ask my local nameserver for information that isn't held in its zone? The information is on another nameserver, so my local nameserver has a choice of actions. It can do one of the following:

- Refer me to the correct nameserver or to another nameserver that is more likely to know where the information is to be found. This is an *iterative* query; it puts the load onto the client and takes the load off the server.

- Find out the answer to my question and pass the information back to me. This is a *recursive* query, and it puts the load onto the server. It not only puts less load on the client, but also makes the client a lot easier to write and to configure.

There is another advantage to recursive queries: Replies to questions are cached for later use, and if the cache is centralized at the server, it can be shared by everyone. This results in less traffic going offsite (usually this is highly desirable).

12.2.6. Forwarders and Slaves

Some nameserver implementations can be configured with a list of forwarders (DNS servers to which queries should be forwarded). In the event of a query that the server cannot answer from information available locally, it will try the forwarders before going through the normal process of locating an authoritative nameserver.

If all nameservers on a site are set up with the same set of central forwarders, these central nameservers will build up a large amount of cached information, reducing the amount of DNS traffic going offsite through a slow link.

Configuring a server as a slave means that all queries that cannot be answered locally will be sent to the servers listed as forwarders. No other servers will be contacted. This is mainly for sites behind a firewall that cannot contact external nameservers.

12.2.7. Resolvers

The resolver is the DNS client, commonly implemented as a set of library routines (for example, `gethostbyname` and `gethostbyaddr`). The resolver will require some configuration; at the very least it will require the names of one or more local nameservers. The remainder of this section describes some of the options that are configurable in a typical implementation.

If a hostname is given that is not fully qualified, the resolver will attempt to append domain names to give it an FQDN. The list of domain names that will be tried is configurable in most resolvers. The default is normally the host's domain, then the host's parent domain, and so on up the tree to the root node. For example, suppose a host in domain `alpha.beta.gamma.delta.` tries to resolve the name `omega` — the sequence tried would be `omega.alpha.beta.gamma.delta.`, `omega.beta.gamma.delta.`, `omega.gamma.delta.`, `omega.delta.`, `omega.`.

A query for the IP address of a multihomed host (that is, a host with multiple IP addresses) will result in a list of address records being returned. The responsibility for ordering these lies with the resolver (see RFC 1123). This is configurable in some resolvers, but not in others (particularly older versions).

The BIND resolver is controlled by a configuration file, `/etc/resolv.conf`. If this file contains any nameserver directives, DNS lookups will be performed, rather than just using the `hosts` file. In early versions DNS was used exclusively, with no reference to `/etc/hosts`. Later versions are configurable as to which services are accessed and in which order. Consult your vendor's manual pages for details of your particular implementation.

A simple resolver that only issues recursive queries is called a *stub resolver*.

12.3. DNS Data and Protocols

This section provides a more in-depth look at DNS—both the data held by the nameserver and the protocols used to exchange that data.

12.3.1. Resource Records

The main function of the DNS is to store IP addresses for each domain name, but it is also capable of storing far more information. Each snippet of information in the database is held as a *resource record*. The resource record structure described in the following list is taken from RFC 1035:

- Resource Name—The domain name for this resource record.

- Resource Class—The protocol that this record is associated with, represented by a 16-bit opcode. The Internet's class is `IN`; its opcode is 1.

- Resource Type—Specifies the type of information held, represented by a 16-bit opcode. Common types are specified in Table 12.1.

- TTL—Time-To-Live. Each copy of the resource record has a fixed time to live. At the end of that period, the information must be discarded and a fresh copy obtained from an authoritative source. This ensures that stale copies of data do not hang around in caches for too long. A TTL value of `0` indicates that the data must not be cached.

Naming Services

■ Resource Data—The data for the resource record. This starts with an unsigned 16-bit integer specifying the length of the remaining part of the field. The format of the data is type specific (see Table 12.1).

Storage Format of Domain Names

Domain names are stored in messages as a sequence of labels. Each label is represented as an 8-bit length field followed by the label itself. The domain name is terminated by a length field of 0. The high-order 2 bits of every length field must be 0 because labels are limited to 63 characters. For example, mars.planets.org. would be represented as:

```
4 m a r s 7 p l a n e t s 3 org 0
```

To compress messages with repeated domain names, a pointer structure is available. The use of a pointer is indicated by the high-order 2 bits being set to 1. The pointer structure is 16 bits long, with the remaining 14 bits specifying an offset in bytes from the start of the message (pointing to a previous instance of the domain name). This is a real headache when trying to read a DNS protocol trace.

Specification of Resource Record Types

Table 12.1 specifies all of the resource record types in common usage. Much of the information here is taken from RFC 1035.

Table 12.1. Resource record information (by type).

Code	Record type	Description	Data	Example
A	Address record (type code = 1)	Gives the IPv4 address for a host's domain name.	An IPv4 address (32-bit).	earth.planets. org.IN A 1.2.3.4
AAAA	IPv6 address record (type code = 28)	Gives the IPv6 address for a host's domain name.	A IPv6 address (128-bit).	earth.planets. org.IN AAAA ab9f1234598 7248c
CNAME	Canonical name record (type code = 5)	Gives the real canonical domain name for an alias.	A domain name.	ftp.planets. org.IN CNAME mars.planets.org
HINFO	Host info record (type code = 13)	Used to store information about a host.	CPU-type character string, OS-type character string.	earth.planets. org.IN HINFO MagnaCPU MantleOS

Code	Record type	Description	Data	Example
MX	Mail exchange record (type code = 15)	Defines the mail handler for a domain name (host or sub-domain).	Preference (16-bit integer)—lower values preferred (domain name).	`planets.org. IN MX 10 mailgate. planets.org.`
NS	Nameserver record (type code = 2)	Specifies an authoritative nameserver for the domain.	NSDNAME (domain name).	`planets.org. IN NS name server.planets. org.`
PTR	Pointer record (type code = 12)	Provides a pointer to another domain name (commonly used to find a domain name from an IP address).	PTRDNAME (domain name).	`4.3.2.1.in-addr.arpa. IN PTR jupiter. planets.org.`
SOA	Start of authority (type code = 6)	Used to indicate the start of a set of authoritative data.	MNAME (domain name)—name of zone's primary server. RNAME (domain name)—mailbox of zone's admin-istrator. SERIAL (32-bit integer)—serial number of last change. REFRESH (32-bit integer)—time in seconds before refresh. RETRY (32-bit integer)—time in seconds before retry.EXPIRE (32-bit integer)—time in seconds before expiry. MINIMUM (32-bit	`planets.org. IN SOA (1; serial 10800; refresh) 3600; retry 604800;expire 86400; minimum TTL)`

Naming Services

continues

Table 12.1. Continued.

Code	Record type	Description	Data	Example
			integer)—the minimum TTL for records in this zone.	
TXT	Text record (type code =16)	Used for miscella-neous information about the TXT-DATA character string.		earth.planets. org. IN TXT "Location: Solar System"
WKS	Well-known services (type code = 11)	Allows a host to it advertise services it has available— forexample, mail, news, and so on.	ADDRESS (32-bit)— IP address for the host. PROTOCOL (8-bit)—IP protocol number (for example, TCP).BIT MAP (variable length bit map)— specifies services available.	earth.planets. org. IN WKS TCP (ftp telnet smtp)

12.3.2. Glue Records

If you want to delegate a subdomain `solar.planets.org.` from the zone `planets.org.`, you will need to put NS records in the zone files for `planets.org.`. For instance, if `pluto.planets.org.` is a nameserver for the delegated zone, the nameserver record would be the following:

        solar.planets.org.   NS   pluto.planets.org.

To find data in the `solar.planets.org.` zone, the nameserver first retrieves the NS record for `solar.planets.org.` from the `planets.org.` zone. This record specifies that data for the zone `solar.planets.org.` is held by the nameserver `pluto.planets.org.`. The IP address of `pluto` is now needed. This is easy enough because `pluto` is in the domain `planets.org.`.

However, a problem occurs when the nameserver being delegated to is *inside* the zone being delegated. For example, suppose the following:

        solar.planets.org.   NS   neptune.solar.planets.org.

How do we find the IP address of `neptune` now? We know that `neptune` holds the information, but we can't contact it yet! This circular problem can be solved by the use of an additional address record called a *glue record* in the `planets.org.` zone files. The glue record for the example here might be

```
neptune.solar.planets.org.    A    178.93.60.73
```

> **WARNING**   *Don't* use glue records where you don't need them. Having the same information (the delegated server's IP address) stored in more than one place without an automated copying mechanism (for example, a zone transfer) is just asking for consistency problems.

This is a bit strange because we are putting in an address record for a machine in the `solar.planets.org.` zone into the `planets.org.` zone files. It's also an administrative headache. If we change the IP address of `neptune`, we have to remember to change *both* zone files.

Incidentally, glue records are not necessary if the nameserver for the delegating zone is also a nameserver for the delegated zone. For instance, if *all* nameservers for `planets.org.` are secondary nameservers for `solar.planets.org.`;each nameserver already has the IP address for `neptune`.

12.3.3. Queries in Detail

There are a few different types of queries, but the only one in common usage (and the only one that DNS *requires* to be implemented) is the standard query. Hence this section covers only that type, and assumes records of class `IN`.

The structure defined by RFC 1035 is given in this section—it is used for both DNS queries and answers to those queries. The data structure consists of five sections:

- Header
- Question
- Answer
- Authority
- Additional

Domain names stored inside this data structure are encoded as described in the "Storage Format of Domain Names" section earlier in this chapter.

Header

The *header* specifies the format of the message and various message options. It is a fixed-length section (96-bit) that is always present, and it contains the following fields:

- ID (16-bit)—Identifier; numerical tag used to match up answers to queries.

- QR (1-bit)—Query/Response; a flag. Set to 0 for a query, 1 for a response.

- OPCODE (4-bit)—Query type; Standard Query = 0.

- AA (1-bit)—Authoritative answer. This flag is set in an answer if the nameserver is authoritative for the domain name specified in the question.

- TC (1-bit)—Truncation; set if the message is truncated.

- RD (1-bit)—Recursion Desired; this bit is set in a query if the client would like a recursive query. It is copied in the response.

- RA (1-bit)—Recursion Available; set in a response if the nameserver is willing to perform recursive queries.

- Z (3-bit)—Reserved. Always set to 0.

- RCODE (4-bit)—Response code. Indicates any of the following error conditions:

0	No error.
1	Format error—question incorrectly formatted.
2	Server failure.
3	Name error—domain name nonexistent.
4	Not implemented—server does not support this query type.
5	Refused—the nameserver doesn't want to answer the question!

- QDCOUNT (16-bit)—Number of entries in the question section.

- ANCOUNT (16-bit)—Number of entries in the answer section.

- NSCOUNT (16-bit)—Number of entries in the authority section.

- ARCOUNT (16-bit)—Number of entries in the additional section.

> **NOTE** Setting the RD flag does not guarantee a recursive response—the server may be unwilling or unable to do recursive queries.

Question

Each question is a request for information about a particular domain name. The number of questions being asked is specified in the QDCOUNT field. Each instance of the question section contains the following fields:

QNAME (variable length×8 bits)—The domain name.

QTYPE (16 bits)—The query type (see Table 12.1 and the "Zone Transfers" section).

QCLASS (16 bits)—The query class (normally set to 1; class IN)

Answer

Answers contain resource records sent in answer to the query. The number of records in the answer section is specified in the ANCOUNT field.

Authority

The authority section of the query specifies authoritative nameservers relevant to the query. The number of records in the authority section is specified in the NSCOUNT field.

Additional

> **NOTE** The query type can be set to ANY, which will return all records for the given domain name. Sending this query to non-authoritative nameservers can give misleading results, because they will just return whatever is in their cache, which may not be a complete answer.

The additional section contains resource records relevant to the query—for example, address records for nameservers referenced. The number of records in the additional section is specified in the ARCOUNT field.

Queries can be sent either over UDP or TCP, using port 53 in both cases. UDP is more popular because it does not suffer from the stream setup overhead incurred by TCP.

12.3.4. Zone Transfers

Servers keep a copy of the resource records for each zone for which they are a secondary server. This data is obtained from the primary server via a zone transfer. The secondary server obtains the current serial number of the relevant zone's SOA record. If this is greater than the serial number of the copy held locally, the secondary's copy needs updating.

> **NOTE** Microsoft uses a non-standard record type to store information from WINS databases. If the primary server for a zone is a Microsoft DNS server and the zone's secondary server is running BIND, problems may occur. When the zone transfer is done, unrecognized record types will be received. The behavior of the secondary for this case is undefined, but often the records are discarded.

The frequency with which an update is attempted is governed by other parameters in the SOA record (see Table 12.1). *REFRESH* seconds after the last update, a transfer will be attempted. If this is unsuccessful, another attempt will be made every *RETRY* seconds. When *EXPIRE* seconds have elapsed since the last successful transfer, the data is considered to be too old and is discarded.

Zone transfers are always enacted over TCP because they elicit lengthy replies and require a transport with guaranteed reliability. Transfers are initiated by a query with the name field set to the zone name and the type field set to the special value AXFR (opcode 252).

12.4. Debugging with `nslookup`

The `nslookup` tool is extremely useful for debugging DNS setups; it allows you to fire queries at a nameserver of your choice. This section gives an overview of the `nslookup` tool, but is not intended to replace the product's documentation.

12.4.1. Invoking and Setting Options

The `nslookup` utility works in either interactive or non-interactive mode. Simply typing `nslookup` will invoke the interactive mode, which is the more common mode of operation. Invoking `nslookup <domainname>` will give a non-interactive query, suitable for simple lookups or for automation in scripts.

Once in interactive mode, domain names can be resolved by typing only their name—for example, `foo.bar.com` will perform a lookup on that domain name. Reverse lookups can be performed simply by typing the relevant IP address.

The way lookups are performed is governed by which options are currently set. The general form for setting an option is `set <keyword>` or `set <keyword>= <value>`, depending on the option. To display all the options currently set, use the `set all` command. By default, `nslookup` will normally look for records of type A and of class IN.

Calling `nslookup - <nameserver>` will change the default server being queried when `nslookup` is invoked. The command `server <nameserver>` is used to change the nameserver once in interactive mode.

12.4.2. Search Lists

`nslookup` may not expand partially qualified domain names in the same way as the resolver. *Always* use fully qualified domain names if you are unsure.

12.4.3. Zone Transfers

Zone transfers can be performed using the `ls` command—for example, `ls <zonename>`. The output can be redirected to a file by appending `> file` or `>> file` to the command. Several options are available, the most useful being `-t` to specify the type of records desired—for example, `ls -t ANY <zonename>`.

12.4.4. Debugging

When trying to troubleshoot complex problems, it is sometimes useful to see the details of the packets being transmitted. There are two levels of debugging available in `nslookup`: Level one shows the reply packet, while level two shows the query and the reply. The `set debug` command invokes level one, while `set d2` turns on level two.

12.5. NetBIOS Name Service (WINS)

NetBIOS was designed for personal computers operating non-routable protocols over a local area network (LAN). Networks have now grown to such a size that routers are necessary to segment them into manageable parts, meaning that methods that used to work over LANs may not work any more (for example, the use of broadcasts is not practical over a wide area network). Running NetBIOS over TCP/IP means that existing software can be used with few changes using two existing standards, but this incongruous marriage presents a few problems.

On a small LAN, names of systems can be mapped to network addresses by sending a broadcast message requesting the necessary information. However, such broadcasts are normally restricted to the local network, and will not usually propagate through routers. Even if routers are configured to pass certain broadcasts, the traffic levels generated can cause severe problems. Therefore, for NetBIOS to run over a wide area network (WAN) protocol (for example, TCP/IP), broadcasts are not an acceptable method to obtain such data.

NetBIOS nameservers provide a service to manage NetBIOS names via directed unicast messages, rather than relying on broadcasts. Unnecessary network traffic is greatly reduced, and the efficiency of computers on the network is increased.

The predominant implementation of a NetBIOS nameserver is Microsoft's WINS (Windows Internet Name Service). This section focuses on WINS, although the same principles apply to other NetBIOS nameservers.

12.5.1. WINS versus DNS

WINS, like DNS, provides a distributed database for name resource management, but it is important to appreciate that WINS and DNS manage two independent namespaces. WINS deals with the flat namespace of the NetBIOS model; NetBIOS names are commonly used for PC networking (such as connecting network drives under Windows File Manager, or with the `NET USE` command). DNS, on the other hand, deals with the structured tree model of domain names

Naming Services

(do not confuse Windows NT domains with DNS domain names). Domain names are commonly used for applications more traditionally associated with TCP/IP (especially applications from UNIX), such as Telnet, FTP, and HTTP.

Despite the two namespaces being conceptually separate, Microsoft's domain name resolver seems to have a habit (when stuck) of resolving the given domain name as if it were a NetBIOS name. Whether this is a "useful feature" is open to debate. The NetBIOS name resolver can also be set to try resolving the given NetBIOS name as a domain name (if it can't resolve it as a NetBIOS name); this is controlled through the Use DNS for Windows name resolution option under the Network section of the Control Panel (see Table 12.3 later in this chapter).

WINS is designed for PC networks, which tend to be dynamic; PCs are added, moved, and removed on a regular basis. DNS has its roots in relatively static networks of high-end multiuser systems, where systems are rarely changed or powered down. Accordingly, WINS is a the more dynamic system of the two, capable of registering and destroying records in its database automatically. DNS relies upon databases that are normally populated by flat text files and are updated by hand. In BIND (the most common implementation of DNS), a hangup signal needs to be sent to the server after such an update, causing it to reload *all* configuration files. This difference means that the management of WINS databases tends to require less manual intervention than DNS.

The flat namespace used by NetBIOS, where each host is given a simple name, means that each name must be unique. This requirement means that allocation of computer names must be done by a central authority (such as the company's MIS department) if the situation is not to become chaotic. The tree structure used for the namespace of DNS means that name allocation can be split up by zones, with multiple authorities allocating names without fear of conflict (refer to the "DNS Concepts" section earlier in this chapter for details).

12.5.2. NetBIOS Names

Each NetBIOS name is represented by a 16-byte string, of which the last byte is reserved for the service number (see Table 12.2). Names may not start with the asterisk (*) character; it is reserved for broadcasts. Names are padded out with spaces.

Table 12.2. Types of NetBIOS names registered.

Value (Hex)	Name registered	Group or Unique?	Description
00	Computer	Unique	Workstation name
00	Domain	Group	Register as active member of the domain (for browser broadcasts)
01	--__MSBROWSE	Group	Master Browser
03	Username	Group	Messenger Service
03	Computer	Unique	Messenger Service
06	Computer	Unique	RAS server
1B	Domain	Unique	Domain master browser (for remote browsing)
1C	Domain	Group	Domain controllers for the domain (up to 25)
1D	Domain	Unique	Domain master browser (for backup browsers)
1E	Domain	Group	Domain browser (used to select master browser)
1F	Computer	Unique	NetDDE
20	Computer	Unique	Server
21	Computer	Unique	RAS client
BE	Computer	Unique	Network Monitoring Agent
BF	Computer	Group	Network Monitoring Utility

12.5.3. LMHOSTS

Microsoft also uses a flat-file database called LMHOSTS to provide a list of static data about NetBIOS services (akin to /etc/hosts in UNIX). In this database, however, the information needs to be manually updated for every change. Given the highly dynamic nature of NetBIOS networks, this is usually unacceptable as a sole method, although it can provide a useful backup service.

The format of this file is one record per line, with fields separated by whitespace:

```
<IP address>      <NetBIOS Name>      <Optional Keyword>
```

The first two fields are self explanatory, but the optional keyword is more interesting. The #PRE keyword specifies that the entry should be preloaded into the name cache on startup. The #DOM:<domain> keyword informs the client that the record specifies the name of a primary or secondary domain controller for the NT domain <domain>.

You can also specify other LMHOSTS files to be included via the #INCLUDE <filename> statement. A UNC (universal naming convention) filename can be used if the server's address has already been loaded with a previous #PRE entry.

If the LMHOSTS file to be included can be obtained from several alternate servers, the possible #INCLUDE statements can be grouped with #BEGIN_ALTERNATE and #END_ALTERNATE statements. For example:

```
#BEGIN_ALTERNATE
#INCLUDE \\server1\netconfig\LMHOSTS
#INCLUDE \\server2\netconfig\LMHOSTS
#INCLUDE \\server3\netconfig\LMHOSTS
#END_ALTERNATE
```

The # symbol also denotes the start of a comment anywhere in the file (apart from where it might be interpreted as a keyword).

12.5.4. Node Types

Hosts using NetBIOS can obtain name data from a local or a remote source. The local sources are the host's cache of NetBIOS names and the LMHOSTS file. Remote sources of information are contacted by unicasts (to a WINS server) or broadcasts; the choice depends on the local node type.

B-Node (Broadcast) <type = 1>	Will always use broadcasts to manage name data, never unicasts.
P-Node (Point to Point) <type = 2>	Will always use unicasts to manage name data, never broadcasts.
M-Node (Mixed) <type = 4>	Will use both unicasts and broadcasts to manage name data, but prefers broadcasts.
H-Node (Hybrid) <type = 8>	Will use both unicasts and broadcasts to manage name data, but prefers unicasts.

The appropriate policy must be chosen carefully. Broadcasts send traffic unnecessarily to many machines and are not normally suited for communication across routers, whereas a host that only uses unicasts will be crippled if it is unable to contact a nameserver. H-node is the default setting for WINS clients—this keeps traffic down where possible, but the client can still function in a limited capacity without contact with the WINS server. Hosts not using WINS are configured as B-nodes.

12.5.5. NetBIOS Name Service in Action

This section describes the process of registering a NetBIOS name with a server, keeping that name, and releasing it when it's finished.

Name Registration

A host can use multiple names, one for each of several services it provides. Typically, each name will have the same textual part, but a different service number at the end. Each name will be registered separately. Most types of service must have unique names. This is facilitated by name registration; a host must register a name before use to make sure no other host is already using it.

There are two possible outcomes to an attempt to register a name:

■ A positive name registration means that the host has been successful and will continue to initialize the network stack. This is the normal outcome and is transparent to the user.

■ A negative name registration will be reported to the user as a name conflict and will usually stop the network stack from initializing.

For broadcast registration, a host broadcasts a *name registration request*, stating the intent to use the name. A system already using that name will reply with a *negative name registration* broadcast (see Figure 12.5). If no such objections are received within a set time, the host will proceed to use the name.

Figure 12.5.
An unsuccessful NetBIOS name registration by broadcast.

In unicast registration, the host sends a name registration request to its configured WINS server. If the name is not currently in use, the server sends a *positive name registration response* back to the host (see Figure 12.6).

However, if the name is already in use, the current holder is challenged to see whether it is still using the name. If the name is no longer in use, a *positive name registration response* is sent back again. If the holder does not respond, the name is reallocated, and a *positive name registration response* is sent back (see Figure 12.7).

Figure 12.6.

*A successful,
unchallenged
NetBIOS name
registration by
unicast.*

Figure 12.7.

*A successful,
challenged
NetBIOS name
registration by
unicast.*

If the current holder still requires the name, a *negative name registration response* is
sent back to the requester. (See Figure 12.8.)

Figure 12.8.

*An unsuccessful
NetBIOS name
registration by
broadcast.*

Which Type of Name Registration to Use?

Name registration is performed according to node type:

B-node (Broadcast)	Try broadcast registration. If a *negative name registration* broadcast is received, do not initialize.
P-node (Point to Point)	Try unicast registration. If a positive name registration response is not received, do not initialize.
M-node (Mixed)	Try broadcast registration. If a negative name registration broadcast is received, fail to initialize. If no such message is received, try unicast registration. If a positive name registration response is still not received, fail to initialize.
H-node (Hybrid)	Try unicast registration. If a positive name registration response is not received, fail to initialize. If this message is received, try broadcast registration. If a negative name registration broadcast is received, fail to initialize.

Name Refreshes

Both positive and negative responses include TTLs. This means that any name allocation will have a fixed time span and must be renewed after that time.

To ensure that the WINS server is not stuffed full with old data, each name registration has a TTL (Time-To-Live) associated with it. After this TTL has expired, the name is deleted. To make sure a name is not deleted while it is still in use, hosts attempt to refresh their registered names well before the TTL is elapsed.

After initial registration, a refresh is attempted after one-eighth of the TTL has elapsed. If unsuccessful, the refresh will be attempted again after the elapsing of each eighth of the TTL. After half the TTL has elapsed, the client switches to the secondary WINS server. After the first successful refresh, subsequent refreshes are attempted after half the TTL has elapsed and re-attempted every one-eighth of the TTL.

Name Resolution

If a system wants to resolve a NetBIOS name to an address, it can draw on the following sources of information:

- Its NetBIOS name cache
- The LMHOSTS file
- A unicast query to a NetBIOS nameserver
- The results of a sent broadcast for the required information
- The HOSTS file
- The DNS server

Table 12.3 shows in which order the client will use these sources of information in its attempt to resolve a name.

Table 12.3. Order of resolution methods tried for each node type.

B-node	P-node	M-node	H-node
Name cache	Name cache	Name cache	Name cache
Broadcast	Unicast	Broadcast	Unicast
-	-	Unicast	Broadcast
LMHOSTS[+]	LMHOSTS[+]	LMHOSTS[+]	LMHOSTS[+]

continues

Naming Services

Table 12.3. Continued.

B-node	P-node	M-node	H-node
HOSTS*	HOSTS*	HOSTS*	HOSTS*
DNS*	DNS*	DNS*	DNS*

⁺*If the Enable* LMHOSTS *lookup option is enabled.*

If the Use DNS for Windows Name Resolution option is enabled.

(Both these options are set under the Network section of the Control Panel.)

Name Release

> **NOTE** The search will terminate upon a successful query.

A workstation should release its NetBIOS name when it is shut down by using a *name release request* for each name registered. There is a *name release response* message sent in reply, although it is ignored.

Replication

It is important to have more than one server available to each client to ensure resilient operation. For the information kept on these servers to be useful in the event of one of the servers failing, they must feed information to each other. WINS achieves this by a process called *replication*.

Replication works by allowing pairs of servers, called *push* and *pull partners*, to talk to each other. Information flow is from the push partner to the pull partner. Only the changes are transmitted, not the whole data set (as happens in DNS).

Who initiates replication? The pull partner will initiate connection at startup and at regular time intervals. The push partner will initiate connection when a specified number of updates have been made. The administrator can also manually initiate replication.

Proxy Agents

If there is not a WINS server on every subnet, B-node clients (that is, those unable to use WINS) will be unable to resolve names from the WINS server. Thus, it is often useful to have a WINS proxy agent on the subnet to forward name resolution queries to the WINS server.

WINS proxy agents also hold a cache of information to reduce traffic, but they do not forward name-registration requests (this is a problem, because it introduces the possibility of duplicate names across subnets). If the proxy agent is unable to resolve a query, it will not reply to it.

12.5.6. Name Encoding

NetBIOS names are encoded to a domain name format for use over TCP networks. They are then compressed according to the rules of domain name compression (see the previous section, "Storage Format of Domain Names," for details).

Each half byte (nibble) of the NetBIOS name is mapped to one character in the domain name. The numerical value of the nibble is added to the ASCII value of the character A, resulting in a letter from A to P (there are 16 possible values; see Table 12.4). The whole encoded name is thus represented by a 32-character string (for example, FooBar[93h] is 466f6f42617220202020202020202093 in hex, which encodes to EGGPGPECGBHCCACACACACACACACACAJD).

Table 12.4. NetBIOS encoding.

A	B	C	D	E	F	G	H	I	J	K	L	M	N	O	P
0	1	2	3	4	5	6	7	8	9	a	b	c	d	e	f

A trailing dot (.) and the NetBIOS scope ID are appended to the encoded value to complete the domain name.

12.6. Summary

DNS and WINS provide similar services. They approach the problem of naming hosts in different ways, and each has its own advantages. DNS is more powerful and scales better to large systems, while WINS is more dynamic and much easier to configure. Ultimately, the choice of which to use is dictated by which type of system you run.

The integration of the two systems is a difficult and rapidly developing field. It is necessary because hosts that use NetBIOS services will often also need to communicate with hosts that do not—their name needs to be the same in both namespaces. The most significant problem is that WINS is dynamic, while DNS is fairly static. There are many commercial solutions available, each with its own advantages and disadvantages—proposals for dynamic DNS (DDNS) are also being created.

Naming Services

13. Operating and Administering a TCP/IP Network

14. Troubleshooting Common TCP/IP Problems

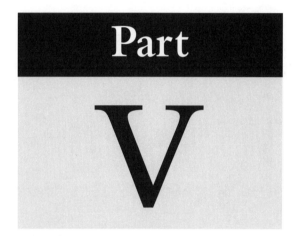

Part

V

Running with TCP/IP

13.1. Designing for Growth

13.2. Design Guidelines

13.3. The Departmental Work

13.4. The Company Backbone

13.5. The Internet Service Provider's Network

13.6. Network Security

13.7. Network Management

13.8. Summary

Chapter

13

Operating and Administering a TCP/IP Network

by Mark Vevers

The key to operating any TCP/IP network is trying to ensure that the network runs itself as far as possible. To this end, it is important to ensure that the design is correct from the outset.

It would be impossible to place enough emphasis on the importance of planning a network thoroughly, especially a TCP/IP network. Too many people have paid the price of building a network, piece by piece, only looking at their current goals. Even the most experienced network managers have looked back and wished they had spent a little more time thinking before acting. Failure to plan will result in a mess that is difficult to administer and virtually impossible to document.

You may not know how large your network is going to grow at the outset. However, with a little forethought and careful design, adding to your network becomes a quick and simple task. The following pages will discuss designing, building, and running a network. The basic principles can be applied to whatever size network you are implementing.

13.1. Designing for Growth

The first stage of design involves specifying a network to match your requirements. You'll need a vision of the purpose of the project. You might be adding IP to an existing network, or you might be installing a brand new network but integrating existing equipment. Questions to ask yourself include the following:

- How is the network going to be used and for what purpose? The graphics design bureau is likely to require more bandwidth per workstation than the administrative office because images are often many megabytes.

- Remember that your total bandwidth is limited by the weakest link in your network. If possible, a server should have a bigger pipe to the network than the workstations it serves. An example might be allocating a single port on a switch to each server, instead of concentrating multiple servers into the same port.

- What security requirements are there, both between users and departments and also the outside world? Is this network likely to be connected to the Internet now or in the future?

- Where can I physically locate my servers? Does this suit the network topology I am proposing?

- What is the projected growth of the network in terms of workstations, data capacity, and transient traffic such as e-mail and Web browsing?

- As for flexibility, your requirements will change over time. Are you choosing components that allow for easy reconfiguration? Can you make peripheral changes to your network design without interrupting service?

Users will expect this new network, or new service you are adding, to work perfectly. Managers, specifically, and other network managers are likely to worry about the impact of adding IP to an existing network. You need to make sure what you propose is cost effective and will be efficient.

13.2. Design Guidelines

The following guidelines are applicable to any type of network protocol; however, only the issues related to an IP network will be discussed in detail. It is assumed that at least part of your network is likely to be multiprotocol. The guidelines start at the workstation level and work outwards to corporate WANs and even Internet service provider (ISP) backbones.

The number of routers/router ports you need depends to some degree on your IP address allocation. Although with IPv6 the lack of IP addresses will be greatly alleviated, the Internet Assigned Numbers Authority (IANA), `http://www.isi.edu/iana/`, will still be careful about how it allocates addresses. IANA wants IPv6 to last! You must be able to show that you are going to use at least a 25% of your allocation immediately.

It might be better to use a proxy server and a private internal addressing range, especially if you are implementing a firewall as well. The private addressing ranges available for use are shown in the following:

Range	Network Class	Quantity
`10.0.0.0–10.255.255.255`	A	1
`172.16.0.0–172.31.255.255`	B	16
`192.168.0.0–192.168.255.255`	C	255

For further details on private address space, see RFC 1597.

If you are buying IPv4 routers, make sure they can be upgraded to cope with IPv6. Check that the upgrade is simple, such as remote flash ROM update, and does not require a site visit by the manufacturer.

Even if you never intend your network to be connected to the Internet, *do not* use somebody else's allocation. The private, nonrouted network allocations should be more than sufficient, even for an international network. Somebody, somewhere, one day will want to connect to the outside world.

13.3. The Departmental Network

Decide on the maximum number of stations per physical segment for each work area type (for example, graphics processing, word processing, and so on). The fewer workstations the better. Remember there is a direct trade-off between the number of workstations/hosts per physical segment and network performance. The following are a few categories and the likely differences in network usage:

- Workstations with applications stored centrally—High peak network usage, but generally low network utilization once running.

- Graphics workstations (CAD/DTP)—Applications are usually stored locally due to their size; however, the document sizes can be very large (can be gigabytes).

- Workstations used for word processing and spreadsheets, with applications stored locally.

- Very low network utilization, generally fairly even during a working day. Small peaks will be seen in the morning, at lunchtime, and at the end of the day.

Once you have categorized your workstations, you will need to work out the likely network utilization and the maximum number of workstations per physical network segment. If possible, visit a number of other sites with networks similar to the one you are proposing and perform some traffic analysis. Software vendors, especially CAD vendors, should be able to give you some idea of the requirements of their products or be able to offer reference sites.

13.3.1. Configuring the Departmental Network

Having defined your design rules, split the network up according to these criteria. Using these criteria, decide where switches and routers are to be placed. The network topology of the ideal IP network may not match the ideal topology for a NetBIOS/NetBEUI or IPX/SPX network; however, you may be able to configure your switches to handle IP in a different manner to other protocols. Figure 13.1 shows how a network can be configured to control data flow—the traffic that is allowed to cross each type of active network component is listed to its right.

Figure 13.1.
An example of configuring your network to control data flow.

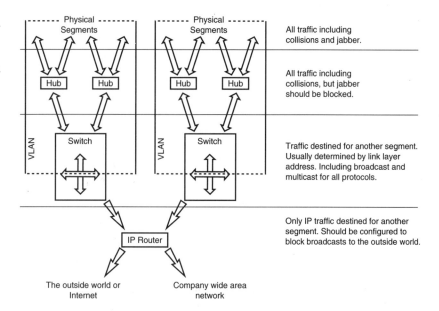

Remember that any workstation generates broadcasts of one kind or another that will cause unnecessary congestion if they reach the company backbone. The basic principle is localization of data: It is desirable to keep the backbone free from intradepartmental traffic. Similarly, try to keep interdepartmental traffic from having to cross a third-party department's network en route. Even if you are building a small network, try to build in a backbone from the start.

Do not attempt to bridge or switch your entire network unless it is very small. Bridging may work well for other protocols, and may seem simple and easy for IP, but you will pay the price later when you need to reconfigure. You may already have a large, switched network in place, so if you can configure it not to switch IP between departments and use routers instead, do so. Some modern switches allow you to configure virtual local area networks (VLANs) for switching, and then route IP between the VLANs internally.

13.3.2. Use of Virtual LANs

Within a switch, any incoming packet is normally directed by its MAC address to the destination segment. A VLAN is simply a logical division within a switch that creates a barrier to network traffic. This has two main uses: The first is to provide security for an area of the network, and the second is to limit the scope of a broadcast packet.

It is quite common then to add a router between the VLANs to provide a controlled path for traffic that is supposed to cross. Remember that most switches only know how to handle the MAC address—the lowest level of addressing within any packet—although it is increasingly common to find switches that have some higher-layer functions.

It may seem more cost effective to place packet filters within the switch on the MAC address of network hosts. Every time you add a host, however, your switch will need reconfiguring. An IP router will look inside the packet at the IP information to determine how the packet should be handled, and hence does not need to be modified to be copied with any additions to the network.

13.3.3. Sizing the Network

In a small- or medium-sized network, it is worth allowing at least 50% over capacity in the number of ports on any switch—that is, order a 24-port switch if you think you need a 12-port switch for your current requirements. For larger networks, 20% over capacity should be sufficient.

Make sure the internal backbone within the switch can handle the required throughput of data. It is often a good idea to attach a server to a dedicated port on a switch, because this will provide the server with the fastest and least congested link to the network possible.

If you are installing new cabling as well, especially if you use structured cabling such as category 5 UTP (Unshielded Twisted Pair), flood the wire if at all possible (that is, install as many ports as you can in as many rooms as you can). Category 5 wiring has the advantage that it can be used for several different network/data types. Examples include (fast) Ethernet, CDDI, and telephony. Do not restrict yourself to the exact requirements. You need a good degree of flexibility here. Remember, modern printers can often have direct network attachments as well, and there are an increasing number of resources that can be attached directly to a network.

13.4. The Company Backbone

How you divide your IP allocation depends on how many hosts there are within each area of your network. This division or subnetting should allow for rapid growth within any department. If a network has to be reconfigured later, although in theory it may be simple, remember no one is perfect; you will make mistakes that will result in downtime on an existing network.

As an example, suppose you are building a company network with 16 major divisions or departments and a total of 1,500 workstations. You are going to use a private Class B IPv4 network range, 172.16.x.x, using a firewall and IP address translation or proxy servers to connect to the outside world. Remember that as far as the addressing scheme is concerned, IPv6 will only really affect the size of the addresses and associated netmask.

How do you divide this? How many routers or router ports do you need? Assuming you are going to give each department its own subnet, the natural way to divide the IP allocation would be using a 20-bit netmask, which would give you 16 subnets. However, this gives us little room to maneuver if a new department is created.

You could use a standard class C, 24-bit netmask; however, this only allows 254 hosts within that segment. Although you have only 1,500 workstations at the moment, one department might grow disproportionately with respect to the others. A good compromise would be a 22-bit netmask, giving us 1,022 hosts per subnet—the number of hosts in a given IPv4 subnet $= 2^{(32-netmask)}-2$. This gives us plenty of scope to grow in the future with little or no reconfiguration of the existing network.

13.4.1. Fault Tolerance

As far as hardware is concerned, a central switch with multiple interface cards would seem to be the most cost-effective way of implementing this scheme. Bear in mind that if a failure occurs here, it could bring down the entire inter-departmental network. The level of fault tolerance you can build in will depend upon your budget.

In Figure 13.2, the use of routers as well as the central switch may seem to be excessive; however, they serve two very useful purposes: They provide departments with independence from the central network, and provide flexibility in allocation of IP addresses and access control.

Figure 13.2.

An example of using routers to provide data localization and security.

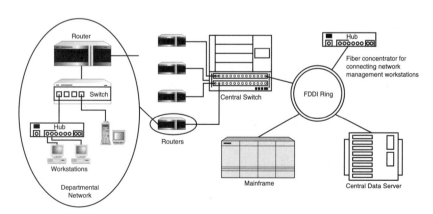

In the event of the switch failing, it could, in this instance, be temporarily replaced by a hub or concentrator, with the only noticeable effect being a loss of performance on connections outside the departmental network. If the routers were not present, it would not be possible to do this because the combined level of broadcasts from a large network would be likely to bring the network to its knees.

The FDDI ring provides an independent fault-tolerant circuit for the core computing equipment, which is insulated from failure in the rest of the network.

13.4.2. Switching versus Routing

For reasons of performance, the central switch will use cut-through switching. This means that the switch will start transmitting the packet as soon as possible on the destination network, in fact before the end of the packet has been sent. This means that there is no error checking on forwarded packets because it is not possible to calculate the checksum until the whole packet has been received. The routers, by contrast, store and then forward a packet depending upon a number of criteria, such as the access control lists and error checking.

As a consequence of this, if a device were to send out a continuous stream of rogue broadcast packets at the MAC address level (to address FF:FF:FF:FF:FF:FF), these would be transmitted from every port of the switch, and if it were not for the store and forward actions of the routers, the whole network would come to a standstill. Troubleshooting an example of this happening is discussed in Chapter 14, "Troubleshooting Common TCP/IP Problems."

Modern IP routers are often multiprotocol and understand protocols such as IPX, in addition to IP. Routers also separate non-routed protocols into discrete domains, allow far greater flexibility in network design, and provide greater security.

The only drawback to routers is that they are not capable of the same throughput as switches. Therefore, where performance is likely to be the real issue, as at the center of the network, a switch will be a more suitable choice.

To summarize, Table 13.1 lists the pros and cons of routers and switches.

Table 13.1. The pros and cons of routers and switches.

Device	Pros	Cons
Router	Better isolation from faulty equipment.	Generally slower than a switch.
	Security is easier to implement.	Hard to configure correctly.

Device	Pros	Cons
Switch	Fast and efficient. Dynamic learning of destination MAC addresses.	Can pass broadcast storms unless carefully configured. Security hard to implement and maintain.

13.5. The Internet Service Provider's Network

As an ISP, you have a somewhat different task to perform. Not only do you have to take into account the preceding network management issues, you need to remember that your customers are paying for bandwidth. If your network acts as a bottleneck, the effect on the customer's connections can be disastrous. If you fail to meet your contractual obligations, especially on a leased-line service, you will be commercially liable.

To this end, technologies that have inherent or built-in fault tolerance, such as a dual-attach FDDI ring, should form the backbone of any network. If at all possible, the network must not have a single critical point. A single, central switch would be a poor choice unless you have a hot standby, and the capability to perform the change over immediately should any failure occur.

Many people will be amazed at how little bandwidth you actually need as an ISP to provide good quality service to your customers. The key, as discussed in the design of a company network, is localization of data. This will reduce the strain on your network, and, should a partial failure occur, it may go almost unnoticed. We will discuss how to achieve this in the "Proxy Hosts" section.

13.5.1. An Example of an ISP's Network

The majority of any ISP's network traffic will be due to Web access or file transfer (FTP). The amount of synchronous (that is, audio and video) traffic on the Internet is still very small compared to the World Wide Web and FTP usage. This means that by providing large and efficient caching proxy servers, you, as an ISP, can cut the bandwidth that you need to the outside world as well as improve your level of service to the customer. As shown in Figure 13.3, it is worthwhile to provide your proxy servers with their own network feed to the backbone.

Figure 13.3.

A possible design for an ISP's network.

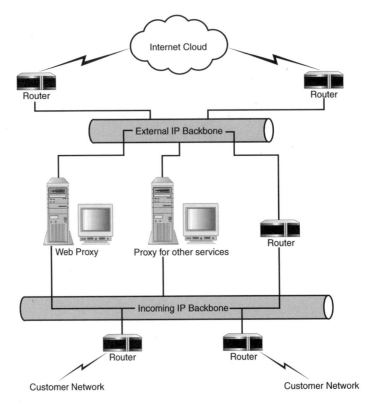

Although Figure 13.3 shows physical backbones, there is no reason, subject to your budget, why these could not be replaced by switches to form a collapsed backbone. Remember to ensure that a hot standby is available should one of these critical switches fail.

Note that the design separates out the traffic to and from the proxy servers, while ensuring optimum access to the Internet for customer traffic for which no proxy is provided. It would also be sensible to connect any DNS or mail servers to both backbones (known as dual-homing), thus reducing through traffic on your internal routers.

You can also see that there are two connections to the "Internet Cloud" that would ideally be through entirely separate access points. You can improve your fault tolerance by adding more links; however, each link introduces a seemingly exponential increase in the complexity of your router configuration. If your routers are programmed correctly, you can improve your efficiency by load-balancing your traffic during normal operation and by providing resilience should a failure occur or maintenance be needed.

13.6. Network Security

An important part of any network design is how you secure it against unwelcome intrusion. The first point to remember is that attack may well come from within your network as well as outside. This may sound a little paranoid, but all too often access is gained from outside the network, due to carelessness or deliberate intent within.

We are going to cover three main technological methods of providing network security: firewalls, IP translation/proxy servers, and logging (for example, TCP wrappers). These, if implemented completely, should be effective barriers to potential hackers.

You will never be able to guarantee that the network is 100% secure; however, if you implement all of the following measures, the leak is more likely to be due to deliberate action within your organization, and, therefore, it is vital to consider the human aspect as well.

13.6.1. Security Policy

At the heart of good network security is a good security policy. This policy forms the basis of a contract between your organization and its staff, in which you define both the users' rights and the expectations of their behavior. It also covers what the users should do in the event that they suspect a security breach, and what you, the network manager, are expected to do in response.

Ideally, certainly in large organizations, users should be made to read and sign the policy before being given access to the network. The vast majority (more than 80%) of network security breaches are due to human error on the part of users or system administrators, not due to the failure of hardware or software.

13.6.2. Passwords

One of the key and usually primary security features of any network is the password. A good password meets the following criteria:

- Is easy to remember—You shouldn't have to write it down.

- Is not obvious—Your car registration plate, cat's name, favorite motorcycle manufacturer, and so on are not good choices.

- Contains no personal information—This includes your date of birth, age, or any of your names (even backwards).

- Is not in a dictionary—Password-cracking programs often start here.

- Is not easily obtained by permuting a dictionary word—For example, *plut0n1um* is as obvious to password-cracking software as the original *plutonium*.

- Has a minimum of six characters, preferably more.

- Is a mixture of lowercase, uppercase, and alphanumeric characters.

Users must be made aware of the importance of keeping their passwords to themselves and that not following the preceding guidelines is a serious breach of the security policy and will result in the removal or disabling of their network accounts.

If a user suspects that his password has been compromised, it is important not only for him to change his password immediately, but also to inform you, the system manager, so you can attempt to trace the security breach.

13.6.3. Router Security

As the network manager, you are equally responsible for the passwords on your routers and other network hardware. These must be secure and fairly cryptic. Unfortunately, router passwords are often infrequently used and consequently forgotten once a network is in place and running smoothly. If you need to write them down, do so in such a way as to disguise what they are and how to extract them, and then place them in a locked cupboard or safe.

Another key feature of router security is often overlooked—access restrictions. Most routers have the capability to be remotely configured. While this is extremely useful for network managers, it presents a fairly major security hole if not protected properly.

You should restrict access by

- Router port—That is, tied down to a specific internal network only.

- TCP/IP address—Only the network manager's workstation(s).

- MAC address (if possible)—Remembering that if there is a gateway/router between the network manager's workstation and the router, the MAC address will be that of the closest gateway or router on the network path.

Figure 13.4 shows a possible network configuration and how you work out the preceding parameters.

Figure 13.4.

*Determining the
router access
security
configuration.*

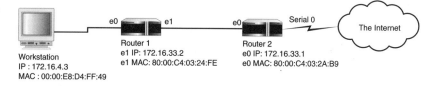

Resulting restrictions on access to configuration on Router 2:
Host must be
1. On interface e0
2. Have IP address : 172.16.4.3
3. Must come from MAC address 80:00:C4:03:24:FE

Most routers also have a local RS-232 serial port for configuration. Indeed, this is usually the only way to initially load the configuration into the router, because when shipped from the manufacturer, all the ports are disabled with no IP addresses assigned.

It makes your life as a network manager a lot easier if you have a small portable PC or palmtop with a selection of serial adapters that fit all your routers and switches set aside for precisely this task. With some simple terminal-emulation software loaded, this should suffice for most of your needs.

13.6.4. Firewalls

What is a firewall? At the heart of any firewall there is a packet filter discriminating between wanted and unwanted packets. The most common form of firewall will be the packet filtering you implement on your routers. A number of uses for a firewall are discussed later in this chapter, but it is important that you first have an understanding of how a firewall works.

We already mentioned that you need to define a security policy. As part of that policy, you will need to decide what level of access across the firewall is appropriate. You also need to know why any restrictions are necessary. You will have to justify any restrictions you impose to your management and your users at some point. It is important to strike a balance between ease of use and security. If the firewall means that the network doesn't meet the original requirements, you have the design wrong.

13.6.5. Packet Filtering

There are a number of criteria by which you may discern welcome packets from unwelcome ones:

- Source Address

- Destination Address

- Port number

- Packet type (TCP or UDP)
- The Acknowledge bit (often known as the Ack bit or TCP Ack)
- The Source Route flag (or in IPv6; the routing header)

In order to make use of these criteria, you need to know how to combine them and which types of packets are wanted and which aren't. It is not possible to give the command lines for your specific router because the programming languages are proprietary and specific to each different manufacturer. However, the resulting table should act as a starting point for your own configuration.

13.6.6. Building a Firewall

The following are a few standard rules for building a firewall:

- Reject all packets to or from a private network—For example, `172.16.x.x`. The Source or Destination Address contains an address within the private addressing ranges.

- Reject all packets with routing information present (source routing)— This can be used to bypass the preceding rule because when the enclosed packet is extracted by the router, it can contain a private network source address that will be used on retransmission from the router.

- Reject incoming packets with Source Addresses within our IP range—A packet received on an external router port with a Source Address that is within our IP allocation. This usually occurs when someone is trying to emulate one of our hosts outside the network. This is more commonly known as IP spoofing.

- Reject outgoing packets with Source Addresses outside our IP range— This is really aimed at stopping people within your network who are attempting to hack other people's networks. It will also prevent packets from misconfigured hosts reaching the outside world.

Having blocked all of these, you now need to define your policy on which services you wish to permit access to and which you should deny. There is always debate over whether to deny only traffic that you know is bad or to permit only traffic that you know is good.

If you are at all concerned about security, you must be paranoid. It will involve more work to control access by permitting only specified traffic, but if you get it right from the start, it can save you a lot of heartache over whether you secured everything correctly.

13.6.7. Configuring Your Firewall

The basic rule of configuring your firewall is that you do not allow the traffic initiator to be outside your network. All TCP/IP packets carry both an IP destination address and a destination port number. This port number defines the TCP socket to which the packet will be sent upon receipt by the final destination.

The TCP packets also contain a source port that will be used as the destination when traffic is returned. For instance, suppose you telnet from `192.9.200.5` to `194.238.48.13`. The following is what you might see in the relevant TCP/IP fields:

Src IP Address	Src Port	Dest IP Address	Dest Port	TCP Ack Bit
`192.9.200.5`	1025	`194.238.48.13`	23	0
`194.238.48.13`	23	`192.9.200.5`	1025	1

13.6.8. Restricting Traffic by Service Type

The source port for any communication will be the socket number allocated to the application when it opens the connection to the remote host. This will usually be greater than 1024 for TCP applications. The destination port is set to the service number for which the packet is destined. The TCP acknowledge bit is set by the remote host whenever it is responding to a request and hence is a useful discriminator for determining which host initiated the current sequence of communication.

Unfortunately, because UDP is a stateless protocol, it has no acknowledge bit, and therefore you should force the use of TCP by blocking UDP in general. One exception to this, however, is DNS (port 53), which requires UDP to transmit domain maps between primary and secondary DNS servers.

You then need to consult a list of services (see Appendix B, "Service Port Numbers"). If you don't know what the service is, don't permit it until you do. This will serve two purposes: Not only will your network be secure, but you will know what is happening on your network. Note that you will need to be responsive to your users here. If they need access to new services, don't just say no. Find out if it will be a real security risk. New services are appearing all the time, including Real Audio, Internet Phone, ICQ, and so on.

There are a few services you will need to permit depending upon whether you have the relevant service providers, such as DNS for a name server, or SMTP for a mail server, and so on:

Service	Description	Port No.	TCP/UDP	Permit Incoming
DNS	Domain Name Service	53	Both	Yes to DNS server only
SMTP	Simple Mail Transfer Protocol	25	TCP	Yes to mail servers only
HTTP	World Wide Web	80	TCP	Yes to Web servers only
Telnet	Remote login session	23	TCP	No
nntp	Network News Transfer Protocol	119	Both	Yes to news servers only
POP3	Postoffice Protocol V.3	110	TCP	Depends but probably no
FTP	File Transfer Protocol	20/21	TCP	Specified hosts only

The list you create forms the basis for your firewall configuration. Notice that where incoming access is permitted, it is permitted only to the hosts that are supposed to deal with that type of traffic, which are known as bastion hosts. In general, no other host should be allowed incoming TCP traffic, which means that you should add a line to your router configuration that rejects all other packets from the outside world without the acknowledge bit set.

13.6.9. Bastion Hosts

These hosts are open to incoming traffic, as permitted by your firewall, and hence will be the first point of attack should someone attempt to break into your network. They are called *bastion hosts* because they are the hosts that you fortify against intruders.

There are a few important rules to apply to bastion hosts:

- Only run/start daemons or services for the protocols that are supposed to be running on these hosts. That is, make sure `fingerd`, `rwhod`, `nfsd`, and so on are not running.

- Do not allow general login access to these hosts from within your organization. Only those people that actually need access to these hosts should have accounts on them.

- Monitoring and security checks should be performed on a regular basis.

- Any password must be secure. (Refer to the section "Passwords.")

It is quite common to place all of these bastion hosts together on a network segment that is isolated from the rest of your main network by firewalls. This provides you with a high level of security for your internal network, while still allowing you some freedom to configure your Internet provision to suit the organization's needs.

Figure 13.5 shows an example of a bastion network, where the hosts that need to interact directly with the Internet are placed on a network isolated from the main network. The bastion network is in effect your castle wall; the overriding principle here is to harden the hosts against attack. If a hacker compromises these hosts, they have a foot in the door of your network, and unless you are very careful, given time, they will gain access to the rest of the network.

Figure 13.5.
Using a bastion network to protect your main network.

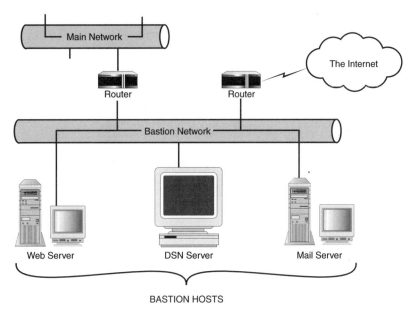

13.6.10. Proxy Hosts

Caching proxy servers have already been mentioned as a way of localizing data to prevent repeated retransmission of frequently used data. They also serve an extremely useful role in securing your network.

In order to add another layer of security, ensure that your confidential data is not available outside your organization, and still provide Internet access throughout your network, you can configure your network using a private IP addressing range and then use proxies to fetch the data for you.

In Figure 13.6, the internal router separates the two networks and hides the rest of the company network from the outside world in the same way as a bastion network does on its own. However, the only traffic permitted to cross the router will either originate from, or be destined for, the proxy. For this to work, the proxy is dual-homed—that is, it has two IP addresses: one internal address, which the internal network sees, and the other real address, used for communicating with the Internet.

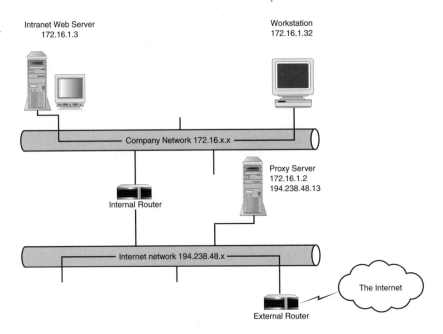

Figure 13.6.

Use of a proxy server to provide secure Internet access.

By adding a specific route to the host `172.16.1.2` for the internal router (shown in the diagram) and then restricting traffic by both port address and Acknowledge bit, you guarantee that the only traffic that will ever reach your company network will be generated by your proxy server. Note that you should *not* enable routing on the proxy server—doing so opens a loophole and could allow a potential hacker to bypass your firewall.

Even if someone does gain access to this host because no one can initiate a TCP connection through the firewall onto your company backbone—assuming the router access and software are secure—nobody from outside should be able to break into your company backbone.

It is a good idea that this host has no login access by anybody other than the system administrators. Preferably, access should be restricted to the console (that is, someone actually sits in front of the machine). As an additional security measure, your external router should also be configured to block unnecessary outgoing packets from this host (for example, any telnet or SMTP communication).

13.6.11. TCP Wrappers

Should a breach of security occur, it is important to be able to identify the breach and trace its source. An effective aid in this is something known as a *TCP wrapper*. When a connection is made to a host, before the service being called is invoked, the TCP wrapper software is invoked instead.

A number of actions can then be taken:

- Reverse and forward DNS lookup to check validity of IP address.

- Logging of connection source, time, and duration.

- Scripting or recording of telnet sessions.

- Fingering the calling host. If the remote host permits the finger protocol and responds, it will show who is logged on.

- Additional security verification.

- Immediate termination of connection if any required conditions are not met.

The flexibility of what you're able to achieve will depend on the operating system and software you use. The greatest flexibility is provided by UNIX operating systems because they can invoke any program or script you choose on receipt of a TCP or UDP connection, as controlled in the configuration file `/etc/inetd.conf`.

One word of warning though: Check that your scripts/wrapper software is secure (that is, users cannot escape out of your script to the OS, and that they cannot invoke other applications or executables). That aside, TCP wrappers provide an extremely flexible and useful verification and logging tool for network activity.

13.6.12. Intranets

An internal Web server, called an intranet server, is shown in Figure 13.7. This server could be used for posting internal information that is not for general issue to the outside world, but is freely accessible to people within the organization.

Figure 13.7.
Using a Web server to provide a secure intranet.

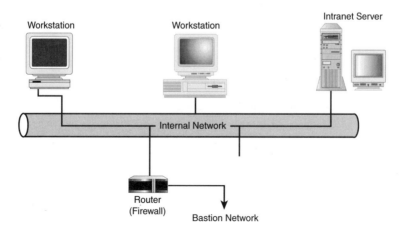

It is estimated that the number of intranet Web servers will eventually outstrip the number of Internet Web servers. There are many uses for a well-designed intranet—everything from fault-reporting forms to the organization's news bulletins.

There is very little difference between an Internet and an intranet Web server—the only real difference being the firewall restrictions on the routers that prevent external access.

13.6.13. Mail Server Security

As an aside, your company mail server will need to be seen by the outside world for incoming SMTP connections to receive mail. Because this server is likely to be a holding point for confidential material, you might consider preventing incoming SMTP directly and then using another server as a mail forwarder or SMTP proxy.

If you make this second server your primary mail exchanger in your DNS tables and configure it to forward all incoming SMTP mail directly to the mail server, there is no need for an MX record entry in your DNS tables for your real mail server. The SMTP proxy should have a minimum configuration, have no user accounts, and should not talk any protocol other than SMTP or DNS.

The mail server can still send mail to the outside world without having to go through the SMTP proxy, as shown in Figure 13.8. You are now able to prevent incoming SMTP connections to your mail server by configuring the router to allow such traffic to go only to the SMTP proxy.

Figure 13.8.
Protecting your mail server with a proxy.

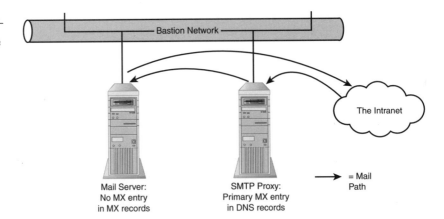

Operating and Administering
a TCP/IP Network

Because SMTP mailers are notoriously bug ridden and have been the source of many security scares, if you use a different mail implementation on the forwarder or proxy, this will prevent anybody from using the same bug twice and therefore should provide you enough time to react when your monitoring software alerts you to the threat.

There are many possible permutations of the preceding configuration, but whatever network design you devise, if you think carefully about which traffic should be allowed across each router on a step-by-step basis, you won't go wrong. Do not be tempted to open any special case security loopholes. If the network administrators require access from home, set up some dial-back modems. Don't open the firewall!

13.7. Network Management

There are two aspects to network management: the technical aspect, in terms of software tools, and the organizational skills that will be needed to keep control of any large or rapidly growing network. It is important to ensure that additions and changes to the network are well thought-out, and that the day-to-day maintenance tasks are not neglected. Chapter 14 deals with maintenance tasks.

Part of a network managers responsibilities include management of the network resources—capacity planning and upgrades to servers, workstations, and network components. A good network manager will know the following information relating to his network:

- Network loading—Collision and error ratios, traffic throughput
- IP allocation—Percentage of utilization per subnet
- Server loading—CPU, memory, and network I/O
- Server response times—Not just ping, but file delivery as well
- Server hard disk capacity

13.7.1. Capacity Planning

As your organization grows, it will gradually use all the available resources. It is important to plan ahead to ensure that you do not run out of any particular resource. You will need to know information such as growth rates and have utilization figures, not only for technical reasons, but for any major upgrades. You will almost definitely need to put a business plan together; you will be required to state why you need such vast sums of money, and how this will benefit your organization.

In order to gain the information you need, you will need to monitor your network. This should not be seen as a secondary task, or even as a spying activity, but as a task of primary importance. Monitoring will not only provide useful information in terms of usage, but may help spot trouble before it strikes. As already mentioned, TCP wrappers are a good example. They can be used to provide both proof and advanced warning of an impending security breach.

Information can be gathered from a variety of sources, but here is an example of the output from `netstat -i` on a UNIX system:

```
Name  Mtu   Network  Address            Ipkts     Ierrs    Opkts     Oerrs  Collis
ef0   1500  <link1>   00:a0:24:47:93:78  49172137  32       36234592  253    4077336
pe0*  1500  <link2>   00:00:00:00:00:00  0         0        0         0      0
xir0* 1500  <link3>   00:00:00:00:00:00  0         0        0         0      0
lo0   1536  <link4>   1815704            0         1815704  0         0
lo0   1536  127       localhost          1815704   0        1815704   0      0
sl0*  308   <link5>   0                  0         0        0         0
ppp0* 1500  <link6>   0                  0         0        0         0
```

These figures can be used to assess the collision ratios, calculated by dividing the number of collisions by the number of transmitted packets (`Opkts`). In the preceding example, the ratio is 11%—too high for an Ethernet segment. This suggests that you need to divide or segment the network attached to `ef0`. The `lo0` interface is the internal loopback, so hopefully no errors should be seen here!

Similar figures can be obtained from most operating systems. The same command works for Windows NT; `netstat -s` is used for Windows 95; and for Novell, you will need access to the console of the server. Note that these figures are only for TCP/IP. If you have other protocols running on your servers and clients, you will need to check the statistics there as well to obtain an overall picture.

13.7.2. New IP Allocations

Assuming that you haven't been fortunate enough to plan from the start the network you now manage or that your initial design was not large enough, at some point you may need a new allocation of IP addresses. There are two ways of approaching this problem: You can either renumber your entire network, releasing your old IP addresses for reuse or add an additional allocation to your existing one.

While it may seem easier just to add an additional allocation to your current addressing scheme, you are unlikely to be able to get the adjacent allocation to the existing one, and hence you will have to think about how you allocate your IP addresses quite carefully. It is very easy to end up with a highly fragmented IP address space. Don't be overambitious though; you will need to justify at least 25% of your allocation request before you will be granted it.

13.7.3. Remote or Satellite Sites

When attaching satellite sites, where you connect them to your network depends upon whether the site is a subset of a department or whether it will need to connect to the company backbone. It may be that there is to be free access from that site to a specific department, with access to and from other areas restricted.

If you wish to add this site to an existing departmental network, it may seem sensible to allocate its IP addresses from within that department's allocation. This, however, will cause you a number of problems unless you are running a more advanced routing protocol than Routing Protocol Information (RIP) because RIP carries no subnet mask information.

Routing protocols, such as Border Gateway Protocol (BGP) and Open Shortest Path First (OSPF), can handle this configuration with little difficulty, although every host that needs to send packets to the satellite site will either need a static route configured (in the correct order) or will need to be running appropriate routing software. A more sensible approach would be to use a block of your unallocated address space and break it into smaller fragments for use in small areas or remote sites.

As an example, suppose you have a department with IP allocation `172.16.8-11.x`, (that is, with a 22-bit network mask), and you want to add a satellite site with approximately 20 workstations to the department's network. If you allocate the satellite site a netmask of `255.255.255.192`, it will have 62 usable IP addresses. That should be sufficient, unless you know of plans to radically alter the remote site.

13.7.4. Software Licensing

Although not directly related to IP, part of your responsibilities as a network manager includes ensuring that all the software on your network is legal and that your usage of the software is within the license agreements relating to that software. You need to guarantee that you have not exceeded any concurrent user license agreements.

Remember that license agreements usually apply to IP monitoring tools as well as to standard application packages, and are often based on the number of clients you are monitoring. You will need to take account of this and order extra licenses as necessary when you add new devices to your network.

13.7.5. Client/Server Backup—Tuning IP Accordingly

As a network manager, you are responsible for the data stored on the servers you manage. It is vital to ensure that you have a proper backup strategy. Even on a small network, the cost of the time to re-enter the data, should failure occur, can bankrupt a company.

Rather than spending large sums of money on standalone tape drives for each server, it may be more cost effective to make use of the network, have a central backup server, and use a client/server backup strategy. This has a number of implications for your network design, and reminds us of the importance of localization of data.

Unfortunately, it will not always be possible to use the optimum solution due to design constraints (for example, the location of the backup server in relation to the data servers).

It is important to ensure that your network is optimized to move the huge amount of data this involves. The following are some issues that will affect you:

- The size of the IP buffers in the respective hosts

- Packet size/maximum transmissible unit (MTU) for the network path

- The number of concurrent backup streams

- The write speed of the archive device(s)

It is important to remember that IPv6 handles the MTU and consequent packet sizes in a different manner from IPv4. All packet fragmenting is done at the source hosts in IPv4, and not by any routers en route to the destination as in IPv6.

This implies that, if you have a network segment with a smaller MTU than the source and destination hosts, there will be a considerable amount of packet fragmentation and reassembly.

Given the scenario in Figure 13.9, to transmit a packet from the host network C to the backup server on network A using IPv4, the host on network C will have to fragment the packet into three smaller packets. Then the host on network A will have to recombine the fragments. If IPv6 were in use instead, the routers would do the majority of the work of fragmenting and recombining packets.

Figure 13.9.

The effect of packet size on performance.

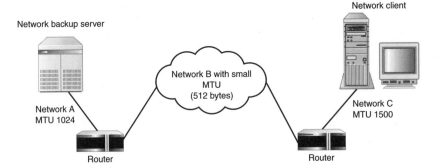

As result, this will increase the load on the two hosts, with a consequent loss in performance. Also remember that the minimum IPv6 header size is a good deal bigger than the minimum IPv4 header size; therefore, you should seek to maximize the MTU as far as possible, but ensure that it is consistent across the whole data path.

You will also need to increase the size of the receive buffer on your backup server and the size of the transmit buffer on the backup clients to achieve optimal throughput. Because the amount of RAM this takes up will be small compared to the RAM in most modern computers, it is well worth increasing the other buffers to ensure good recovery performance.

During the backup, once the network is saturated there is no point in increasing the backup concurrency because doing so will provide no extra benefits. Indeed, with some network architectures, such as Ethernet, it will result in a degradation of performance.

Do not be surprised if the limiting factor is the performance of the tape drives or some other component. Figure 13.10 shows the likely bottlenecks and their causes. With some simple arithmetic and some figures obtained by monitoring your network, you should be able to calculate where the bottlenecks are and eliminate them.

Figure 13.10.

*Possible
bottlenecks and
their causes.*

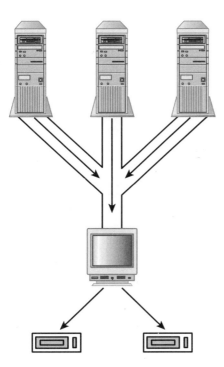

Hosts being backed up.
Limited by I/O
performance — both disk
& network.

Network — limited by
bandwidth available
between host and backup
server.

Backup server—
Limited by CPU speed & I/O
performance (both network
and storage devices)

Tape drives—
Maximum data rate limited
by tape write speed.

Your backup policy, in terms of how much data you back up each night and how often you make complete system dumps, will vary the amount of data you will need to transfer across your network. The details of designing a backup strategy are outside the scope of this book. However, remember that, in general, backups should be taken at slack periods due to the massive impact they have on network performance.

13.8. Summary

Although designing a network from scratch can be quite a daunting task, it is important to reiterate that time spent planning your network thoroughly is extremely valuable. Planning does not just mean designing or even assessing technical feasability; you need to factor in support costs and human factors such as user perceptions as well.

The key steps in designing your network are

1. Decide what you want to achieve. Ensure this meets your organization's *real* needs.

2. Think about the size of the required network—not just for now but plan for growth as well.

3. Choose the right type of network to fit your needs.

4. Ensure that you provide suitable security, including security against failure (for example, backups).

5. Draw up your network plan with all this in mind.

6. Buy/write/think about the monitoring tools you need to ensure that your network continues to meet your requirements.

Only when you are 100% happy with the design should you proceed to implement it. Don't be afraid to let colleagues help, and it often beneficial to let someone external to your organization examine your design (that is, if you are allowed). Remember, networks can be very expensive; think carefully before committing yourself. Sometimes things will go wrong. Don't worry; you should plan some contingency, time, and budget to cover this.

Finally, a good network manager always has a trick or two up his sleeve to impress the users and, more importantly, his boss.

14.1. Analyzers and Sniffers

14.2. Software Tools to Help You Solve Problems

14.3. Windows NT Network Monitor

14.4. Common Problems

14.5. Analyzing Packet Dumps and Examples of Common Sequences

14.6. Summary

Chapter

14

Troubleshooting Common TCP/ IP Problems

by Mark Vevers

We have spent so much time in this book describing how all the different protocols work. Some people may be curious to know what's going on "under the hood," but do you really need to know? Not until something goes wrong. It's all very well to follow the instructions to "point and click," but what if it doesn't work?

This chapter tells you how to find out what is *really happening* on your network. Refer to the earlier chapters on IP protocols to find out what's *supposed to be happening*. Compare the two, and (theoretically) you have your problem. In practice, it can be a bit more difficult than that.

Debugging networks is both an art and a science. Some things only can be picked up through experience, but a logical approach will solve most problems. First, here are a few general principles:

- The error you're seeing is the symptom of the problem. You need to find the cause. They can be a long way apart, and it's often not obvious. Multiple problems that initially appear unrelated often turn out to be caused by the same problem.

- Don't make assumptions or go too far down one path without stepping back to consider the whole picture. Often the problem will turn out to be the most obvious thing.

- When did it break? If it worked fine Monday but not Wednesday, what did you change between then? This is not infallible. Things sometimes break for no discernible reason.

- Try to find a way to reliably re-create the problem. If it's intermittent, it will be much more difficult to diagnose.

- If the problem is intermittent, is there a pattern to when it occurs? When did it start? Does it happen at one particular time of the day, when a certain job is running, or when the network or host is busy?

- Are there error messages in the logs? Seemingly unrelated messages can solve the problem—for example, DNS errors causing backups to fail.

- Is there a pattern of which machine it occurs on? Network diagrams are useful here.

- Does the problem happen only when going to/from a particular machine? Is there another working machine with which you can compare configurations?

- By all means, take a few guesses about what's going wrong. If they're not right, it comes to a point when you'll just have to work through it methodically—what's *meant to be* happening step by step. Check it off against what is *actually* happening.

■ Keep breaking the problem down. Try to replicate the error in a simpler way. If a complex mailing program is producing errors, try sending a mail message to the remote site invoking sendmail by hand. If that doesn't work, try to telnet to the remote machine's SMTP port. If that doesn't work, try pinging the remote machine. If that doesn't work, try pinging your default gateway and every router along the path to the remote host (or use `traceroute`).

■ If there's a chain of commands being executed, look at the output of each command. For example, try changing "foo | bar" to "foo | tee log | bar". This will take a copy of the pipe's contents into a file called *log*.

14.1. Analyzers and Sniffers

At the most basic level, analyzers and sniffers are tools for looking at the packets flying around your network (often referred to as "taking a trace"). Some will monitor any traffic going past on the network, while some are just for watching what's going in and out of the machine on which you are sitting.

In order to monitor the network, you can either use a dedicated device such as network sniffer, or you can use a PC with some suitable software to analyze the traffic. You can see an example of the use of such software in the section "`tcpdump`."

Hardware solutions can cope with higher levels of traffic, but tend to be expensive. Software solutions tend to be fairly basic and unable to give full packet analysis, but are cheap and flexible (you can write scripts to interpret the output).

Looking at the packets going across the network is a brute force approach to solving a problem, but often it's the only way. It's not as bad as it sounds; the main problem is too much information, so you need to filter out exactly what you need.

Most good network analysis tools can filter by criteria, such as:

■ Source IP address

■ Destination IP address

■ Source Port

■ Destination Port

More sophisticated tools can interpret protocols for you, such as:

■ IP

■ TCP and UDP

■ Telnet, FTP, LPD, and so on

The data captured is usually available in a textual or ASCII format. This enables you to run your own processing scripts on it and then print or store the results. Some new WWW-based tools are emerging, which present the output as hypertext so you can more readily navigate and interpret the information.

14.2. Software Tools to Help You Solve Problems

There are a number of standard tools that are available on most systems to help diagnose IP-related problems. In most cases, if the tools are used correctly, you should be able to correct most problems without recourse to more expensive means such as hardware analyzers. The three tools discussed here are `ping`, `traceroute`, and `tcpdump`. They are available on most systems.

14.2.1. ping

If you have a problem contacting another machine, the first thing to try is to ping its IP address. This should tell you whether IP packets are being routed correctly to their destination, by sending an ICMP echo request to the remote end. This will send back an ICMP echo reply.

The output of `ping` varies from system to system, but a typical successful `ping` might say `host is alive` or look like the following:

```
PING earth.planets.org (158.84.70.100): 56 data bytes
64 bytes from 158.84.70.100: icmp_seq=0 ttl=255 time=2.861 ms

 --- earth.planets.org ping statistics ---
1 packets transmitted, 1 packets received, 0% packet loss
round-trip min/avg/max = 2.861/2.861/2.861 ms
```

Meanwhile, an unsuccessful `ping` might bring the error message `request timed out` or give an output like the following:

```
PING 1.2.3.4 (1.2.3.4): 56 data bytes

 --- 1.2.3.4 ping statistics ---
1 packets transmitted, 0 packets received, 100% packet loss
```

Most versions of `ping` also give you the round-trip time to the remote host and back again. This indicates the *latency* of the network, NOT the *bandwidth*. This is an important distinction. If the round-trip time is two seconds, it does not indicate that you cannot send a large amount of data per second over the network.

It is perfectly possible to have a link that will transmit at 10Mbps (high through-put), but data will take 10 seconds to get from one end to the other (high latency). If you were to compare a data link to a water pipe, the bandwidth (throughput) would be the diameter of the pipe, and the latency (delay) would be its length.

14.2.2. traceroute

traceroute is a more sophisticated tool than ping and will record each hop along the route that the packet takes from the local to the remote host. This is a useful tool when the remote host is not on the same local subnet. It is useful in several situations:

- Correcting routing problems

- Identifying the exact route taken (especially useful when you have multiple possible routes between any given pair of hosts)

- Checking connectivity between hosts

traceroute works by sending out a UDP packet destined for the remote host, but with the Time-To-Live (TTL) value initially set to 1. The next gateway in line should decrement this to zero and, because it has not reached its destination, return an ICMP TIME_EXCEEDED error response to the originating host.

The ICMP TIME_EXCEEDED packet will contain the IP address of the router or gateway on which traceroute then does a reverse DNS lookup to obtain the hostname. For each step along the way, traceroute sends three packets and then increases the TTL by one, hopefully eliciting an ICMP error from each router or gateway in turn. The output of traceroute shows the response from each set of three packets with the same TTL:

```
$ /etc/traceroute www.xara.net
traceroute to www.xara.net (194.143.166.2), 30 hops max, 40 byte packets
  1  r19rhe1.sequent.com (138.95.19.122)  3.639 ms  3.221 ms 2.495 ms
  2  r200rhe3.sequent.com (138.95.200.143)  3.675 ms  3.673 ms 2.871 ms
  3  border5-serial2-6.Seattle.mci.net (204.70.233.33)  9.901 ms  9.359 ms
     ➡8.771 ms
  4  core2-fddi-0.Seattle.mci.net (204.70.203.49)  12.454 ms 9.182 ms  9.062 ms
  5  pacbell-nap-atm.SanFrancisco.mci.net (204.70.1.202)  27.609 ms  35.117 ms
     ➡37.041 ms
  6  pacbell-nap-atm.SanFrancisco.mci.net (204.70.1.202)  24.356 ms  42.329 ms
     ➡102.478 ms
  7  pb-nap.agis.net (198.32.128.19)  150.561 ms  28.26 ms 27.616 ms
  8  a5-0.1003.losangeles1.agis.net (206.62.13.246)  66.543 ms 211.793 ms
     ➡61.43 ms
  9  h1-0.30.washington1.agis.net (204.130.243.36)  108.446 ms 111.7 ms
     ➡108.846 ms
```

```
10  me1-e0-meth-lan-mertrs.xara.net (192.41.177.215) 128.167 ms   128.813 ms
    ➥122.71 ms
11  TH1-e0-matm-ptp-ME1.xara.net (194.143.162.93)   203.703 ms
    ➥212.559 ms   211.354 ms
12  TH7-h0-1-xfr-p200-TH1.xara.net (194.143.162.254)  594.113 ms  216.332 ms
    ➥214.324 ms
13  * TH7-h0-1-xfr-p200-TH1.xara.net (194.143.162.254)  214.801 ms  214.243 ms
14  onyx.xara.net (195.224.53.5)  219.383 ms * *
```

For each packet with the same TTL, the round-trip time is shown. If multiple hosts are shown for any TTL value, this indicates that the packets are able to take different routes at that point. If you receive a response of three asterisks in a row, this indicates that the gateway in question either does not send `ICMP TIME_EXCEEDED` packets or that it is returning them with an incorrect value in the TTL field.

If `traceroute` does not return a hostname, but returns just an IP address instead, this indicates that the reverse domain name lookup failed (that is, there are missing PTR records for that router or gateway in the DNS tables for that domain). This is not necessarily a mistake; it is quite often done for security reasons, and may be an attempt to hide the network structure.

14.2.3. `tcpdump`

`tcpdump` is a UNIX tool that allows you to take a trace of IP packets going in and out of a host. If the Ethernet card is put into promiscuous mode (allowing it to pick up all packets on the network, not just those addressed to itself), it can also be used to monitor the network. However, the high levels of traffic this sometimes involves means that data may be lost—a specialist hardware device is better for this type of monitoring. `tcpdump` is a fairly basic tool that doesn't do much analysis for you, but provides you with all the data. This data is often fed into a script to interpret it, or you can do it by hand.

Writing a script to interpret packets is an excellent way to familiarize yourself with the low-level details of TCP/IP. How complex you make the script is up to you. Start with the IP header, and work on to TCP, and then protocols such as Telnet, FTP, LPD, and so on.

`tcpdump` can take packets selectively, and you can determine how much of the packet is saved. To take the whole packet, make sure that you capture at least the MTU size of the interface (for example, normally 1500 for Ethernet).

The following will capture all traffic from the host to the remote host `1.2.3.4`, by dumping in hex (`-x`), using verbose output (`-v`), and capturing up to 1500 bytes of information (`-s 1500`). The output is normally redirected to a file, but it's normally buffered. So when you've finished, kill the process with a hang-up signal (`SIGHUP`) to let it flush the output before exiting. In order to see the output immediately, you can switch the buffering to display the trace line by line by specifying (-1).

You can extract the traffic for a particular host by means of the host filter. For example, for host 1.2.3.4 the command would be

```
tcpdump -x -v -s 1500 host 1.2.3.4
```

You can also filter by network (for example, net 1.2.3) or by port (for example, port 23). There are even more sophisticated filters (see the manual pages), and filters can be combined using the usual boolean operators.

See the "sample packets" section at the end of this chapter to get an idea what some typical packet sequences should look like and how to analyze them.

14.3. Windows NT Network Monitor

The Network Monitor, as provided with Windows NT 4.0 Server (otherwise it is in the SMS bundle), provides a highly useful diagnostic tool for networks in general from a top-level view, shown in Figure 14.1, to packet analysis, as shown in Figure 14.2.

There are a large number of filters for many different protocols, and hence they will give an overall picture of what is happening on your network.

Figure 14.1.

A snapshot of a busy network using Network Monitor.

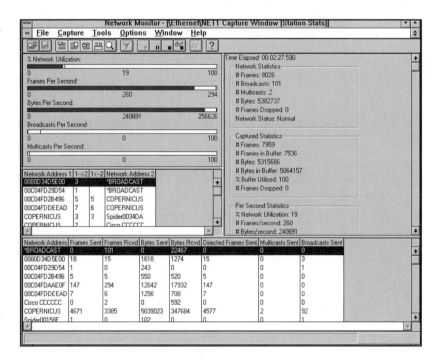

As you can see from Figure 14.1, the network is 10Mbps and is moderately busy, but is running fairly efficiently. One of the useful features of the Network Monitor is that it can extract the hostnames attached to particular network addresses, not only IP, but other protocols as well, such as NetBIOS and IPX. This allows you to see a dynamic picture of the traffic on your network, and can identify at a glance which hosts are talking to which other hosts.

Once a capture is complete, you can then analyze the network, much as you can do with `tcpdump`, except that most of the work is done for you. Note that there isn't a parser available for IPv6 yet; however, it will not be too long in coming. By default, Network Monitor only decodes a limited number of services; therefore, it is well worth having Appendix B, "Service Port Numbers," open while decoding a trace.

Figure 14.2 shows part of an X Windows session (TCP port 6000). Notice that you can inspect the packet in a hierarchical manner, only expanding the parts in which you are interested. The part of the packet you are currently looking at is highlighted in the bottom part of the window; this is quite useful for inspecting the data part of the packet.

Figure 14.2.

Examining packet contents using Network Monitor.

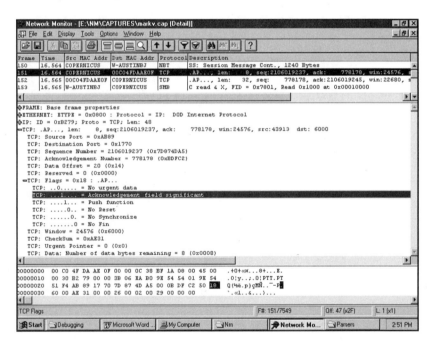

14.4. Common Problems

The following sections illustrate some of the more common problems that may arise.

14.4.1. Unable to Connect to a Remote Host

There are many different manifestations of failing to connect to the target host. These break down into a number of categories, which you will then look at in order:

- No apparent communications between the two hosts in either direction; `ping` fails both ways.

- `ping` works one way, but not the other. No TCP connections can be established either way.

- `ping` works both ways, but TCP connections cannot be established—either both ways or just one way.

- Intermittent TCP connections can be established. They appear to fail in a random manner. Established TCP connections hang or reset in mid-flow.

Routing Problems

If there is no communication at all between hosts, log into both hosts locally and take a look at the routing tables. This can be done on most operating systems by typing `netstat -r`. Note that this still relies on DNS to be functioning correctly to do the hostname lookups. If you suspect that this is failing as well, use the `-n` option in conjunction with the `-r` option.

There are some differences in what information is reported and the format of the information provided by different operating systems. Here are two examples: The first is from Windows NT and the second is from UNIX.

The following is the output from `netstat -r -n` on Windows NT Workstation 4.0:

```
Route Table

Active Routes:
     Network Address          Netmask  Gateway Address        Interface  Metric
           0.0.0.0          0.0.0.0   158.84.55.111    158.84.55.223       1
         127.0.0.0        255.0.0.0       127.0.0.1        127.0.0.1       1
       158.84.55.0    255.255.255.0   158.84.55.223    158.84.55.223       1
     158.84.55.223  255.255.255.255       127.0.0.1        127.0.0.1       1
    158.84.255.255  255.255.255.255   158.84.55.223    158.84.55.223       1
         224.0.0.0        224.0.0.0   158.84.55.223    158.84.55.223       1
   255.255.255.255  255.255.255.255   158.84.55.223    158.84.55.223       1
```

This is output from `netstat -r -n` on DYNIX/PTX 2.1.6:

```
Routing tables (3 entries)
Destination      Gateway          Flags   ttl       Use  Interface
default          158.84.84.111    UGP     PERM  124825408  eg0
127.0.0.1        127.0.0.1        UHP     PERM      12480  loop
158.84.84        158.84.84.1      UP      PERM  305436773  eg0
```

We need to ensure that there is a route on the host at each end for packets that will be transmitted to the host at the other end (that is, the route exists in both directions). The first entry for both systems in this case is the default route. This is the route to which packets will be sent, should no other matching route be found.

If you don't have a default route and there is no other route that would match, you have a routing problem. This can be fixed in one of three ways: Add a default route to the host, or add a static route if the gateway to be used would not be the default one. The third way is if the host is running a routing daemon or equivalent, ensure that the correct route is advertised properly by your routers.

The other entries in the preceding table show the route to the loopback (`127.0.0.1`), multicast (`224.0.0.0`), and local interfaces (`158.84.55.223` and `158.84.84.1`), and should confirm that you have set your local IP addresses and netmask correctly.

If the routing tables on both hosts are correct, including subnet masks (check this carefully), there may be a problem with the routers in between the two hosts. Run a `traceroute` from both hosts to the other host. The following is an example:

```
Tracing route to dns1.rmplc.co.uk [194.238.48.3]over a maximum of 30 hops:
  1    <10 ms     10 ms   <10 ms   r55gbr3.noc.sequent.com [158.84.55.111]
  2    <10 ms   <10 ms   <10 ms   r3gbr1.noc.sequent.com [158.84.3.107]
  3    261 ms    270 ms    260 ms   r4rhe2.sequent.com [158.84.4.100]
  4    261 ms    260 ms    261 ms   r2rhe1.sequent.com [138.95.2.111]
  5    260 ms    311 ms    270 ms   r200rhe3.sequent.com [138.95.200.143]
  6    r200rhe3.sequent.com [138.95.200.143]   reports: Destination net unreachable.
Trace complete.
```

This shows us that we have a routing problem at hop 6: Either there is no onward route for the packet or it may be actively blocked by a firewall. Once this has been fixed, and the `traceroute` completes successfully, you can be sure that at least you have a path between the two hosts, so any failure to communicate is likely to be a problem at the local hosts, not on the network in-between.

If `traceroute` (or `ping`) completes one way, but cannot complete the other way, it is likely that there is a default route still missing on the host that cannot communicate. This happens because the ICMP layer responds to the MAC address of the incoming ICMP echo request. Hence it does not need a route to send the ICMP echo return, but the host cannot initiate a `ping` due to the missing route.

Incorrectly Configured Services

Now that you have established a route at the IP layer, it is important to ensure that the service that you are trying to connect to is working correctly, and that there are no other security measures blocking the path to the remote host.

First, check that there are no firewalls in the path between the two hosts for the protocol you are trying to use. For instance, you may find port 23 (telnet) blocked, but `ping` is not blocked and therefore still works.

Secondly, check that the remote service is running and configured correctly. On UNIX systems, you will need to check that the daemon for the appropriate service is running correctly, or that the right entry is in `inetd.conf`. Remember to send a HUP signal to the `inetd` daemon if you make changes to the configuration file.

For Windows NT, the TCP service you are attempting to connect to will probably have an associated system service. You can check on the service status by using the Services Control Panel. It may also be worth stopping and starting the service to reset it, and then check the system event log to see if any errors occurred during the reinitialization.

It is worth making a local call to the service, if you can, because this will go through the loopback interface and will confirm that all is well with the service. If this checks out, and you still cannot make a remote connection, check that the service has the correct permissions. For instance, you may find that the host is configured to block all incoming telnet sessions that are not from the local host.

Check that the daemon/service is running as the right user. This can be seen by using `ps` or checking the user and `Set UID` flag with `ls` on UNIX. For Windows NT, check the properties of the service. This will show whether it is using the system account or attempting to log on as a user. If it is attempting to log on as a user, check that the password in the Service Properties dialog box matches the relevant user's password.

Conflicting IP Addresses

Conflicting IP addresses are a common cause of intermittent connections. Sometimes the packet arrives at the right host, and the connection succeeds. Sometimes it will arrive at the duplicate host, where the service probably isn't configured, and therefore is refused. If the service is enabled on the duplicate, it will be fairly obvious that you are connecting to the wrong host.

The physical destination will be determined by the MAC destination MAC address and will therefore be dependent upon the ARP table in the routers or, if the target host is on the same subnet, the local host's ARP table. Depending on the algorithm for updating these entries, it will switch between the two conflicting hosts, therefore causing the intermittent behavior. If the MAC address is updated during an established connection, the session will hang and probably fail.

Operating systems, such as Windows 95 or Windows NT, attempt to detect duplicates and will report an error if they see somebody else using their IP address on the local network and inform you of the offending MAC address. To obtain the MAC address on a UNIX network, you will probably need to inspect the ARP tables in your routers. Unfortunately, this is only really useful where IP addresses are assigned to a host by MAC address (for example, BOOTP). Otherwise, the easiest way to isolate the duplicate is to turn off your host, and then, using a traffic analyzer elsewhere on the same subnet, you should be able to identify the duplicate host.

14.4.2. Slow Performance

Finding a performance problem can be difficult because there are so many possible causes. Start by looking for a pattern.

Physical Network Problems

Physical network problems are often indicated by all hosts on a particular subnet as being slow, although sometimes it's just the busy server that shows problems. There might be a cable fault (showing up as lots of illegally sized packets or corrupt packets), particularly on networks with a bus topology (such as Ethernet 10base2) or the network might be very busy (showing up as collisions on Ethernet; over 5% or 10% indicates a busy network).

Application Problems

Often the network isn't the problem at all! It may be that one particular application is slow, or perhaps the application is just using the network in an inefficient way. It's often necessary to take a network trace to prove that the network is not at fault. If the server is receiving a packet and not sending any response for a significant time, it may be a slow application or a slow server.

14.4.3. Printing to a Remote Host via LPD Doesn't Work

Printing to a remote host via LPD is a common bugbear, because there are quite a few things that can go wrong. When a print job is sent to the remote end, the following things happen (Note: The process used in debugging an LPD connection is typical of debugging other higher-level protocols such as telnet):

- IP packets are sent to the remote host. Check with `ping` that the remote host is up and running and that packets are reaching it.

- A TCP connection is established with the remote end. Try to telnet to the LPD port of the remote host (for example, `telnet printsrv 515`). If the connection is refused or no connection is made, the LPD server is not running properly on the remote end. A refusal to allow a connection will appear as a reset (`RST`) in a trace.

- A request is sent to the remote end, asking you to place a print job in the remote queue. Take a trace of the connection to the remote host, and check that the correct queue is being specified.

- The LPD server on the remote host has to allow you to send print jobs to the specified queue. If your machine is not in the list of permitted hosts, the connection will be terminated. The *authentication* is done by deriving the client's hostname from the incoming connection's IP address. The name is then matched to a list of permitted systems. The name is derived from the `hosts` file or by a reverse DNS lookup (see Chapter 12, "Naming Services"). Missing PTR records are often the culprit here.

14.4.4. Name Resolution Problems

Problems that seem to do with routing or connectivity often turn out to be caused by name resolution. Can't contact the server by typing `ping server`? Try using its IP address, such as `ping 1.2.3.4`. If the IP address works but the name doesn't, you've almost certainly have name resolution problems.

Check how the system is resolving names to IP addresses. Chapter 12, tells you all about this, but your first port of call is `/etc/resolv.conf` on a UNIX system, and in the Control Panel (networks section) under TCP/IP on a MS Windows box.

14.4.5. DNS Problems

Is your DNS name server down? Try `ping`. Are you set to access the correct name server? Is your local domain set correctly? Do you have the correct name for the remote host? Try its fully qualified domain name (for example, `foo.bar.com.`, not just `foo`). Can you manually retrieve the correct IP address for the machine you're trying to contact (you can use `nslookup` to do this).

Missing or incorrect reverse lookup records (PTR) can cause all sorts of problems. Most common is refusal of authentication. The remote host won't grant you access, although you're in the list of machines allowed access to that service. For example, a connection comes into a server from a host with IP address `1.2.3.4`; is this machine allowed access? The server tries to look up the name of the host to check through its access files, but, if the name is incorrect or unobtainable, you're unlikely to be allowed access.

Is mail not being sent, or is it being sent to the wrong mail server? Check your MX records. Remember that the preferred server is the one with the *lowest* numeric identifier.

If you have problems with the secondary name servers not replicating data properly, it's often caused by not incrementing the serial number of the primary's SOA record. It must be incremented after every change (see Chapter 12). Remember that records are cached, so changes may take some time to filter through.

If you have multiple zones in your domain, they *must* be delegated properly. That means having the appropriate NS records (and glue records if necessary) in the parent zone.

14.4.6. MAC Level Broadcast Storms

A broadcast storm will usually bring the network to a complete standstill, with high levels of collisions and little actual traffic due to the congestion. There are a number of different types, but one of the hardest to track is when a faulty piece of equipment starts transmitting rogue packets from MAC address FF:FF:FF:FF:FF:FF to FF:FF:FF:FF:FF:FF (that is, it is sending out a continuous stream of ones).

Due to the fact that most modern switches use cut-through switching, this type of packet will cross all ports and hence affect the whole network until a router is encountered. This makes it extremely difficult to trace because any network analyzer will show large numbers of duff packets, but will not give an indication of the source.

If you are using Ethernet over UTP, you may have hubs that will autopartition, which will help to block this sort of fault. However, if you are using thin Ethernet, or dumb hubs, this will not help. You are probably best starting at the center of your network and working outwards. Look for extremely busy incoming links during the storms and work from there.

Because these storms are likely to bring the whole network down anyway, temporarily disconnect the feed that you suspect is introducing the packets. If that was the correct segment, the rest of the network will stabilize almost immediately. You should then be able to repeat the process until you narrow it down to the device causing the problem.

There is a certain amount of guesswork involved in tracing this sort of fault, but if you know your network well enough, you should have some idea of what is normal traffic and what is abnormal.

14.5 Analyzing Packet Dumps and Examples of Common Sequences

If you've not looked at packet-level dumps before, it can be a little intimidating. To give you an idea of what some common packet structures look like, some sample packets from `tcpdump` are included in the following. Only the first section of each packet is done by `tcpdump`; I've done all the analysis for you.

We have used IPv4 headers, however, the analysis of IPv6 is not very different. The structure has already been described in Chapter 2, "A Close Look at IPv4 and IPv6." The two main fields used in the IP header are the source and destination addresses. Once you have established the ability to ping the remote host, any problem is likely to be in the TCP layer. Try to follow the analysis of the packets through, using the previous chapters as references.

14.5.1. An ICMP Echo Request

An ICMP echo request is more commonly known as `ping`, but in fact is only the outward bound part of a `ping`.

The following is the output from `tcpdump`:

```
11:44:04.29 158.84.50.2 > 158.84.31.99:
icmp: echo request (ttl 255, id 2215)

    45 00 00 54 08 A7 00 00 FF 01 24 F4 9E 54 32 02    E..T......$..T2.
    9E 54 1F 63 08 00 66 7D A4 26 00 00 00 00 00 00    .T.c..f}.&......
    DE E0 23 78 08 09 0A 0B 0C 0D 0E 0F 10 11 12 13    ..#x............
    14 15 16 17 18 19 1A 1B 1C 1D 1E 1F 20 21 22 23    ............ !"#
    24 25 26 27 28 29 2A 2B 2C 2D 2E 2F 30 31 32 33    $%&'()*+,-./0123
    34 35 36 37                                        4567
```

The IP header is

```
    45 00 00 54 08 A7 00 00 FF 01 24 F4 9E 54 32 02 9E 54 1F 63
```

IP Protocol Version:	4
Header Length:	20 bytes
Type of Service:	Routine
(Normal Reliability, Normal Throughput, Normal Delay)	
Total Length:	84 bytes
Datagram ID:	HEX: **08 A7** (Numeric: 2215)
Fragmentation:	May Fragment, Last Fragment
Fragment Offset:	0 bytes

Troubleshooting Common TCP/IP Problems

Time-To-Live (TTL):	255 seconds
Checksum:	HEX: 24 F4 (Numeric: 9460)
Checksum Integrity:	Correct
Protocol:	1
Protocol Name:	ICMP
Options:	None
Source IP Address:	158.84.50.2 (Class B)
Destination IP Address:	158.84.31.99 (Class B)

The ICMP header is

```
08 00 66 7D
```

Type:	8
Code:	0
Checksum:	HEX: 66 7D (Numeric: 26237)
Description:	Echo Request (ping)

Notes

Remember to check the IP version number before doing the packet breakdown by hand; the structure for IPv6 is different from IPv4. You won't normally find ping packets being fragmented because they are quite small. If you see this happening, with IPv4 it is likely you have a misbehaving router in the way, but with IPv6 it may mean that the MTU Path Discovery failed to work correctly as well.

14.5.2. An ICMP Echo Reply

This is what happens when a machine replies to a ping. You should only see one of these in response to an echo request.

The following is the output from tcpdump:

```
11:44:04.29 158.84.31.99 > 158.84.50.2:
icmp: echo reply (ttl 254, id 13411)

    45 00 00 54 34 63 00 00 FE 01 FA 37 9E 54 1F 63    E..T4c.....7.T.c
    9E 54 32 02 00 00 6E 7D A4 26 00 00 00 00 00 00    .T2...n}.&......
    DE E0 23 78 08 09 0A 0B 0C 0D 0E 0F 10 11 12 13    ..#x............
    14 15 16 17 18 19 1A 1B 1C 1D 1E 1F 20 21 22 23    ............ !"#
    24 25 26 27 28 29 2A 2B 2C 2D 2E 2F 30 31 32 33    $%&'()*+,-./0123
    34 35 36 37                                        4567
```

The IP header is

45 00 00 54 34 63 00 00 FE 01 FA 37 9E 54 1F 63 9E 54 32 02

IP Protocol Version:	4
Header Length:	20 bytes
Type of Service:	Routine
(Normal Reliability, Normal Throughput, Normal Delay)	
Total Length:	84 bytes
Datagram ID:	HEX: 34 63 (Numeric: 13411)
Fragmentation:	May Fragment, Last Fragment
Fragment Offset:	0 bytes
Time-To-Live (TTL):	254 seconds
Checksum:	HEX: FA 37 (Numeric: 64055)
Checksum Integrity:	Correct
Protocol:	1
Protocol Name:	ICMP
Options:	None
Source IP Address:	158.84.31.99 (Class B)
Destination IP Address:	158.84.50.2 (Class B)

The ICMP header is

00 00 6E 7D

Type:	0
Code:	0
Checksum	HEX: 6E 7D (Numeric: 28285)
Description:	Echo Reply (ping)

Notes

Don't expect to see an echo reply for every echo request packet sent. Over long links it is quite common for packets to be dropped, and routers will first discard ping packets before discarding real data when there is insufficient bandwidth. Check that the return packet size is the same—it should be!

14.5.3. Initiating a TCP Connection (Stage 1) TCP: SYN

Initiating a TCP connection requires both ends to send synchronization requests (SYN) to each other and for these to be acknowledged. This normally means a three-packet sequence. This is the first of these.

The following is the output from `tcpdump`:

```
11:44:16.56 158.84.50.2.1041 > 158.84.31.99.515:
S 425030450:425030450(0) win 16384 <mss 1460>
(ttl 64, id 2231)

   45 00 00 2C 08 B7 00 00 40 06 E4 07 9E 54 32 02    E..,....@....T2.
   9E 54 1F 63 04 11 02 03 19 55 73 32 00 00 00 00    .T.c.....Us2....
   60 02 40 00 37 7D 00 00 02 04 05 B4                '.@.7}......
```

The following is the IP header:

```
45 00 00 2C 08 B7 00 00 40 06 E4 07 9E 54 32 02 9E 54 1F 63
```

IP Protocol Version:	4
Header Length:	20 bytes
Type of Service:	Routine
(Normal Reliability, Normal Throughput, Normal Delay)	
Total Length:	44 bytes
Datagram ID:	HEX: 08 B7 (Numeric: 2231)
Fragmentation:	May Fragment, Last Fragment
Fragment Offset:	0 bytes
Time-To-Live (TTL):	64 seconds
Checksum:	HEX: E4 07 (Numeric: 58375)
Checksum Integrity:	Correct
Protocol:	6
Protocol Name:	TCP
Options:	None
Source IP Address:	158.84.50.2 (Class B)
Destination IP Address:	(Class B)

The following is the TCP header:

```
04 11 02 03 19 55 73 32 00 00 00 00 60 02 40 00 37 7D 00 00 02
➥04 05 B4
```

Source Port Number:	1041
Destination Port Number:	515 (Printer)
Sequence Number:	425030450
Acknowledgment Number:	0
Header Length:	24 bytes
TCP Flag:	SYN
Window Size:	16384 bytes
Option Kind (Length):	2 (4)
Option:	Max Segment Size: 1460
Data Analysis:	Line Printer Daemon Protocol

Notes

You should make sure that the port number corresponds to the service (for example, 515 is the LPD port). The source port is allocated by the host when the connection is opened, hence it will vary from one connection to another. However, the source port should not vary within the connection.

14.5.4. Initiating a TCP Connection (Stage 2) TCP: SYN, ACK

This is the second phase of the sequence. The remote host acknowledges the SYN request and sends its own SYN back.

The following is the output from `tcpdump`:

```
11:44:16.56 158.84.31.99.515 > 158.84.50.2.1041:
S 1149166080:1149166080(0) ack 425030451 win 24576 <mss 1460>
(ttl 63, id 13451)

    45 00 00 2C 34 8B 00 00 3F 06 B9 33 9E 54 1F 63    E..,4...?..3.T.c
    9E 54 32 02 02 03 04 11 44 7E E2 00 19 55 73 33    .T2.....D~...Us3
    60 12 60 00 F0 EC 00 00 02 04 05 B4                '.'.........
```

The following is the IP header:

```
    45 00 00 2C 34 8B 00 00 3F 06 B9 33 9E 54 1F 63 9E 54 32 02
```

IP Protocol Version:	4
Header Length:	20 bytes
Type of Service:	Routine
(Normal Reliability, Normal Throughput, Normal Delay)	
Total Length:	44 bytes
Datagram ID:	HEX: **34 8B** (Numeric: 13451)
Fragmentation:	May Fragment, Last Fragment
Fragment Offset:	0 bytes
Time-To-Live (TTL):	63 seconds
Checksum:	HEX: **B9 33** (Numeric: 47411)
Checksum Integrity:	Correct
Protocol:	6
Protocol Name:	TCP
Options:	None
Source IP Address:	**158.84.31.99** (Class B)
Destination IP Address:	**158.84.50.2** (Class B)

The following is the TCP header:

```
02 03 04 11 44 7E E2 00 19 55 73 33 60 12 60 00 F0 EC 00 00 02
➥04 05 B4
```

Source Port Number:	515 (Printer)
Destination Port Number:	1041
Sequence Number:	1149166080
Acknowledgment Number:	425030451
Header Length:	24 bytes
TCP Flag(s):	SYN, ACK
Window Size:	24576 bytes
Option Kind (Length):	2 (4)
Option:	Max Segment Size: 1460
Data Analysis:	Line Printer Daemon Protocol

Notes

The window size given here represents the maximum amount of data that remote host is able to accept. The local host will assume it can send up to this amount of data (24KB in this case) before it must receive an ACK from the remote host. Note the reversal of the source and destination ports.

14.5.5. Initiating a TCP Connection (Stage 3) TCP: ACK

This is the last stage of the sequence. We acknowledge the remote host's SYN packet. This is also typical of an ACK packet sent by the remote host for every packet of data we send.

The following is the output from `tcpdump`:

```
11:44:16.56 158.84.50.2.1041 > 158.84.31.99.515:
➥. ack 1 win 16384 (ttl 64, id 2232)

   45 00 00 28 08 B8 00 00 40 06 E4 0A 9E 54 32 02    E..(....@....T2.
   9E 54 1F 63 04 11 02 03 19 55 73 33 44 7E E2 01    .T.c.....Us3D~..
   50 10 40 00 28 AA 00 00                             P.@.(...
```

The following is the IP header:

```
45 00 00 28 08 B8 00 00 40 06 E4 0A 9E 54 32 02 9E 54 1F 63
```

IP Protocol Version:	4
Header Length:	20 bytes
Type of Service:	Routine

(Normal Reliability, Normal Throughput, Normal Delay)

Total Length:	40 bytes
Datagram ID:	HEX: **08 B8** (Numeric: 2232)
Fragmentation:	May Fragment, Last Fragment
Fragment Offset:	0 bytes
Time-To-Live (TTL):	64 seconds
Checksum:	HEX: **E4 0A** (Numeric: 58378)
Checksum Integrity:	Correct
Protocol:	6 (Shown in blue)
Protocol Name:	TCP
Options:	None
Source IP Address:	**158.84.50.2** (Class B)
Destination IP Address:	**158.84.31.99** (Class B)

The following is the TCP header:

```
04 11 02 03 19 55 73 33 44 7E E2 01 50 10 40 00 28 AA 00 00
```

Source Port Number:	1041
Destination Port Number:	515 (Printer)
Sequence Number:	425030451
Acknowledgment Number:	1149166081
Header Length:	20 bytes
TCP Flag(s):	ACK
Window Size:	16384 bytes
Data Analysis:	Line Printer Daemon Protocol

14.5.6. Sending Data via TCP (an EOF Character) TCP: PSH, ACK

If data is sent across a TCP connection, the push (PSH) flag is set. Here we are sending just one character ^D (EOF) to the remote end. The ACK flag is also set because we're acknowledging a previous packet (not shown).

The following is the output from `tcpdump`:

```
14:53:04.92 158.84.50.2.1045 > 158.84.31.99.23:
P 24:25(1) ack 267 win 16384 (ttl 64, id 2510)

  45 00 00 29 09 CE 00 00 40 06 E2 F3 9E 54 32 02    E..)....@....T2.
  9E 54 1F 63 04 15 00 17 46 55 2D BD 6D 3F 24 82    .T.c....FU-.m?$.
  50 18 40 00 D3 BD 00 00 04                         P.@......
```

The following is the IP header:

```
45 00 00 29 09 CE 00 00 40 06 E2 F3 9E 54 32 02 9E 54 1F 63
```

IP Protocol Version:	4
Header Length:	20 bytes
Type of Service:	Routine
(Normal Reliability, Normal Throughput, Normal Delay)	
Total Length:	41 bytes
Datagram ID:	HEX: 09 CE (Numeric: 2510)
Fragmentation:	May Fragment, Last Fragment
Fragment Offset:	0 bytes
Time-To-Live (TTL):	64 seconds
Checksum:	HEX: E2 F3 (Numeric: 58099)
Checksum Integrity:	Correct
Protocol:	6
Protocol Name:	TCP
Options:	None
Source IP Address:	158.84.50.2 (Class B)
Destination IP Address:	158.84.31.99 (Class B)

The following is the TCP header:

```
04 15 00 17 46 55 2D BD 6D 3F 24 82 50 18 40 00 D3 BD 00 00
```

Source Port Number:	1045
Destination Port Number:	23 (Telnet)
Sequence Number:	1179987389
Acknowledgment Number:	1832854658
Header Length:	20 bytes
TCP Flag(s):	PSH, ACK
Window Size:	16384 bytes
Data Analysis:	TELNET

The data is

```
04
```

Data Length:	1 bytes (Can show: 1 byte)
Data:	4 [EOF]

Notes

Although it is unlikely that a print job will consist of only one byte of data, when a telnet session is open, it is quite common to see every keystroke as an individual packet. This means that 41 bytes of data are sent for every key depressed, hence TCP is not a very efficient mechanism for ASCII data entry terminals.

14.5.7. Terminating a TCP Connection (Stage 1) TCP: FIN, ACK

Terminating a TCP connection requires each host to send a FIN to the remote end.

The following is the output from `tcpdump`:

```
11:44:16.69 158.84.31.99.515 > 158.84.50.2.1041:
F 1:1(0) ack 1 win 24576 (ttl 63, id 13468)

45 00 00 28 34 9C 00 00 3F 06 B9 26 9E 54 1F 63   E..(4...?..&.T.c
9E 54 32 02 02 03 04 11 44 7E E2 01 19 55 73 33   .T2.....D~...Us3
50 11 60 00 08 A9 00 00                            P.'.....
```

The following is the IP header:

```
45 00 00 28 34 9C 00 00 3F 06 B9 26 9E 54 1F 63 9E 54 32 02
```

IP Protocol Version:	4
Header Length:	20 bytes
Type of Service:	Routine
(Normal Reliability, Normal Throughput, Normal Delay)	
Total Length:	40 bytes
Datagram ID:	HEX: **34 9C** (Numeric: 13468)
Fragmentation:	May Fragment, Last Fragment
Fragment Offset:	0 bytes
Time-To-Live (TTL):	63 seconds
Checksum:	HEX: **B9 26** (Numeric: 47398)
Checksum Integrity:	Correct
Protocol:	6
Protocol Name:	TCP
Options:	None
Source IP Address:	**158.84.31.99** (Class B)
Destination IP Address:	**158.84.50.2** (Class B)

The following is the TCP header:

```
02 03 04 11 44 7E E2 01 19 55 73 33 50 11 60 00 08 A9 00 00
```

Source Port Number:	515 (Printer)
Destination Port Number:	1041
Sequence Number:	1149166081
Acknowledgment Number:	425030451
Header Length:	20 bytes
TCP Flag(s):	FIN, ACK
Window Size:	24576 bytes
Data Analysis:	Line Printer Daemon Protocol

Notes

Either end can send a FIN to close down the connection, and the other end will reply.

You should always see a pair of FINs. If you don't then you either have a very poor network connection or there is bug in the TCP code. The preceding FIN packet is the first of the pair. After a host has sent a FIN, it should discard any further data received for that connection—the remote host may be a long way away and hence there might be a high degree of latency in the connection, which delays the return FIN.

14.5.8. Terminating a TCP Connection (Stage 2) TCP: FIN, ACK

This is the second FIN, coming back the other way. The connection is now closed.

The following is the output from `tcpdump`:

```
11:44:16.69 158.84.50.2.1041 > 158.84.31.99.515: F 1:1(0) ack 2
win 16384 (ttl 64, id 2235)

45 00 00 28 08 BB 00 00 40 06 E4 07 9E 54 32 02    E..(....@....T2.
9E 54 1F 63 04 11 02 03 19 55 73 33 44 7E E2 02    .T.c.....Us3D~..
50 11 40 00 28 A8 00 00                             P.@.(...
```

The following is the IP header:

```
45 00 00 28 08 BB 00 00 40 06 E4 07 9E 54 32 02 9E 54 1F 63
```

IP Protocol Version:	4
Header Length:	20 bytes
Type of Service:	Routine
(Normal Reliability, Normal Throughput, Normal Delay)	
Total Length:	40 bytes
Datagram ID:	HEX: `08 BB` (Numeric: 2235)
Fragmentation:	May Fragment, Last Fragment
Fragment Offset:	0 bytes
Time-To-Live (TTL):	64 seconds
Checksum:	HEX: `E4 07` (Numeric: 58375)
Checksum Integrity:	Correct
Protocol:	6
Protocol Name:	TCP
Options:	None
Source IP Address:	`158.84.50.2` (Class B)
Destination IP Address:	`158.84.31.99` (Class B)

This is the TCP header:

```
04 11 02 03 19 55 73 33 44 7E E2 02 50 11 40 00 28 A8 00 00
```

Source Port Number:	1041
Destination Port Number:	515 (Printer)
Sequence Number:	425030451
Acknowledgment Number:	1149166082
Header Length:	20 bytes
TCP Flag(s):	FIN, ACK
Window Size:	16384 bytes
Data Analysis:	Line Printer Daemon Protocol

Notes

No further data should be sent by either side for this connection. If further packets are seen and if the connection is a long distance one, it could be a result of packets arriving out of order although it may indicate a bug in the TCP code. You will need to check the sequence and acknowledgment numbers carefully to determine the cause.

14.6. Summary

Debugging TCP and IP connections can be laborious, and it is unlikely that you will need to descend to this level of analysis very often. It is important, however, to have a feel for what should be happening because this will help you to spot diagnose a problem more quickly. Most errors in programming routers and DNS tables are caused by mistyping the IP address or hostname. When you are tired `129.65.29.3` rapidly becomes `129.65.129.3`, if you are not careful.

Should you need to inspect the datastream, most packet analyzers will help you find out that something is wrong, but they won't tell you what should be there instead. If you are working through a packet trace, remember to work from the start of the trace you're investigating. As with any form of debugging, the errors tend to snowball, and the first incorrect piece of data can cause a multitude of other errors to appear.

A. RFCs and Standards/
    Further References

B. Service Port Numbers

C. Technical Glossary

Part

VI

Appendixes

A.1. Internet Standards—
      An Overview

A.2. RFCs by Subject

A.3. Other References

Appendix

A

RFCs and Standards/ Further References

by Thomas Lee

This appendix presents some sources of additional information, above and beyond what is contained in the rest of this book. If you are a developer or you just wish to learn more about specific topics, this appendix will help. We set out details on where to get the RFCs, plus a comprehensive cross-reference index of these documents and references to other documents.

A.1. Internet Standards—An Overview

The formal definition of each of the protocols that encompass TCP/IP is formally contained in one or more documents. Each is known as a Request for Comments, or RFC. If you need to know how the protocol works, these documents are a great starting point. As a developer who develops TCP/IP–based products, I'd say having a good working knowledge of the RFCs is mandatory.

A.1.1. RFCs—What Are They?

The RFCs are the formal standards documents not only for TCP/IP but for much of the Internet as well. The first RFC, RFC 1, was published in April 1969. Another 26 RFCs were issued during 1969. At the time of this writing, the latest published RFC is RFC 2092.

The early RFC documents were written by a variety of people involved with the development of the ARPANET, the forerunner of today's Internet. These early RFCs were somewhat informal and described the early ARPANET. The more recent documents are being written by and for an increasingly diverse set of people.

Today, there over 2,000 published RFCs. A large number of those published are now obsolete. A key principle of RFCs is that they are never reissued. If they need to change, for example to correct errors or to reflect better approaches, they are reissued under a later RFC number. Thus, for example, the Documentation Conventions, first described in RFC 3, were updated by RFC 10, then by RFC 16, RFC 24, RFC 27, and so on.

> **NOTE** Why are they called Requests for Comments?
>
> After all, they are the standards documents, so why were they not called "ARPA Standards Documents" or something similar?
>
> One explanation relates to the people who developed the ARPANET. Largely academics, they were convinced that, at any minute, someone from industry would pop out of the woodwork and loudly proclaim, "You don't want to do it like THAT!" while pointing out the errors. To avoid any embarrassment when it happened, they call the documents Requests for Comments so that any comments from industry would be seen as being helpful! In hindsight, there were no gurus in industry who could do better, but the name stuck.
>
> The author does not know whether there is any actual truth in this theory. This explanation could just be yet another urban legend. But knowing academics, it does sound very plausible!

More recently, this approach has been improved by the issuing of Internet drafts. Once the comments have been collected and assimilated, they are formally issued as RFCs. This approach cuts down on the number of RFC updates and makes the RFCs a little more formal than was the case in the late 1960s and early 1970s.

Sadly, a number of the early RFCs are hard, if not impossible, to actually find. RFC 1, for example, could not be found in machine-readable form while this section of the book was being developed, although many might not regard this as necessarily a bad thing. The earliest RFC that could be found was RFC 3. Fortunately, these "lost" RFCs are largely irrelevant, having long since been overtaken by both later events and later RFCs. More recent RFCs are easy to find.

A.1.2. Do I Need an RFC?

RFCs contain a large amount of detail describing the way in which a protocol or Internet component (for example, MIME) will, or should, work. Some RFCs are published for information and have no direct relevance upon the developer or user community. Other RFCs are formal standards that implementations of the protocol are expected to follow.

If you are a developer and are implementing any of the protocols described in this book, a good understanding of the RFCs is essential. If you are an interested end user, you'll find that RFCs do contain a number of details.

A.1.3. Getting RFCs

So where do you get RFCs? There are a number of RFC repositories. Most Internet service providers have an FTP server with these documents available for download. A number of commercial publishers sell these documents on CD-ROM. As part of this book, we have obtained many of the RFCs available and have included them on the CD-ROM.

If you want to get an RFC, either to obtain one published after this book was sent for printing or if you don't have the CD readily available, there are a number of ways to get RFCs, using a variety of Internet tools, including FTP, WWW, and e-mail.

For the most up-to-date list of approaches, you should send an e-mail message to `RFC-INFO@ISI.EDU`, which is an autoresponder. The body of the e-mail message should have the following line:

```
HELP: ways_to_get_rfcs
```

When the autoresponder receives your e-mail message, it will send back an e-mail message giving you the current ways to get RFCs. The advice here was current as of January 1997, although things might have changed by the time you read this. Also, remember that a number of organizations, not described in the e-mail sent back, also hold copies of RFCs and are in addition to the suggestions made here.

There are several primary repositories for RFCs. These are as follows:

- `DS.INTERNIC.NET`—Provides FTP, e-mail, and WAIS access

- `NIS.NSF.NET`—Provides FTP and e-mail access

- `NISC.JVNC.NET`—Provides FTP and e-mail access

- `FTP.ISI.EDU`—Provides FTP and e-mail access

- `WUARCHIVE.WUSTL.EDU`—Provides FTP and NFS access

- `SRC.DOC.IC.AC.UK`—Located in the UK; provides FTP, e-mail, NTFTP, and ISO-FTAM access

- `FTP.NCREN.NET`—Via FTP, WAIS, and Gopher access

- `FTP.SESQUI.NET`—Provides FTP and FC access

- `NIS.GARR.IT`—Located in Italy; provides FTP, WWW, and e-mail access

In addition to these primary sites, which are generally good places to start, there are a number of secondary FTP repositories, as shown in Table A.1.

Table A.1. RFC repositories and their access methods.

Country	Site	Method
Australia/Pacific Rim	`munnari.oz.au` `ftp.progsoc.uts.edu.au`	FTP
Denmark	`ftp.denet.dk`	FTP
Finland	`nic.funet.fi`	FTP, e-mail
France	`info-server@inria.fr` `ftp.univ-lyon1.fr`	E-mail FTP
Germany	`ftp.Germany.EU.net`	FTP
Netherlands	`mcsun.eu.net`	FTP
Norway	`ugle.unit.no`	FTP
South Africa	`ftp.is.co.za`	FTP

Country	Site	Method
Sweden	`unic.sunet.se`	FTP
	`chalmers.se`	FTP
United States	`nic.cerf.net`	FTP
	`ftp.uu.net`	FTP
(DOD users only)	`NIC.DDN.MIL`	FTP

Full details of how to get RFCs from each of these sites, including directories to use, can be obtained from the `how_to_get_RFCs` e-mail previously noted.

Finally, if you want an RFC and you have an Internet connection, try using WWW search tools. Or better yet, ask someone at your Internet supplier—they're bound to know the closest place to find these documents.

A.1.4. Internet Drafts

Before an RFC is formally published, it is not normal for a draft to be issued to the wider Internet community. These are mainly issued by a member of one of the IETF working groups, but can, in theory, be created by anyone.

These documents can be obtained from the same sources as for RFCs.

A.1.5. FYIs

FYIs are a series of documents, also published as RFCs, that are of more general interest. Many of these FYI documents are dated, but possibly worth reading if only for the background.

FYI documents can be found at the same sites as RFC documents. An index of these documents can be found at `http://www.internic.net/fyi/`.

A.2. RFCs by Subject

This section notes the RFCs that relate to a particular subject. In some cases, some RFCs will be listed more than once because they relate to more than one subject area.

RFCs and Standards/Further References

A.2.1. Address Resolution Protocol/Reverse ARP (ARP/RARP)

Address Resolution Protocol (and Reverse Address Resolution Protocol) enables a host to convert an IP address into a hardware address (and vice versa).

RFC	Description
866	D. Plummer, "Ethernet Address Resolution Protocol: Or converting network protocol addresses to 48.bit Ethernet address for transmission on Ethernet hardware," 11/01/1982
903	R. Finlayson, T. Mann, J. Mogul, M. Theimer, "Reverse Address Resolution Protocol," 06/01/1984
1027	S. Carl-Mitchell, J. Quarterman, "Using ARP to implement transparent subnet gateways," 10/01/1987
1293	T. Bradley, C. Brown, "Inverse Address Resolution Protocol," 01/17/1992
1433	S. Alexander, R. Droms, "DHCP Options and BOOTP Vendor Extensions," 10/08/1993
1968	K. Sklower, G. Meyer, "The PPP DES Encryption Protocol (DESE)," 06/19/1996

A.2.2. April Fools Spoof RFCs

These RFCs show that even network nerds have a sense of humor! Not to be taken seriously, these RFCs can be a source of some amusement.

RFC	Description
748	M. Crispin, "Telnet randomly-lose option," 04/01/1978
1097	B. Miller, "Telnet subliminal-message option," 04/01/1989
1149	D. Waitzman, "A Standard for the Transmission of IP Datagrams on Avian Carriers," 04/01/1990
1217	V. Cerf, "Memo from the Consortium for Slow Commotion Research (CSCR)," 04/01/1991
1313	C. Partridge, "Today's Programming for KRFC AM 1313 Internet Talk Radio," 04/01/1992
1437	N. Borenstein, M. Linimon, "The Extension of MIME Content-Types to a New Medium," 04/01/1993
1605	W. Shakespeare, "SONET to Sonnet Translation," 04/01/1994
1606	J. Onions, "A Historical Perspective On The Usage Of IP Version 9," 04/01/1994
1607	V. Cerf, "A VIEW FROM THE 21ST CENTURY," 04/01/1994
1776	S. Crocker, "The Address is the Message," 04/01/1995
1925	R. Callon, "The Twelve Networking Truths," 04/01/1996

A.2.3. Assigned Numbers

This RFC sets out formally assigned values for all of the Internet standards.

RFC	Description
1700	J. Reynolds, J. Postel, "ASSIGNED NUMBERS," 10/20/1994

A.2.4. Asynchronous Transfer Method

These RFCs define Asynchronous Transfer Method (ATM) and how IP can be implemented over top of ATM.

RFC	Description
1483	J. Heinanen, "Multiprotocol Encapsulation over ATM Adaptation Layer 5," 07/20/1993
1626	R. Atkinson, "Default IP MTU for use over ATM AAL5," 05/19/1994
1755	S. Senum, "The PPP DECnet Phase IV Control Protocol (DNCP)," 03/01/1995
1932	R. Cole, D. Shur, C. Villamizar, "IP over ATM: A Framework Document," 04/08/1996

A.2.5. Bootstrap Protocol (BOOTP)

These documents define the BOOTP protocol for enabling a host to automatically get its TCP/IP host configuration.

RFC	Description
951	W. Croft, J. Gilmore, "Bootstrap Protocol," 09/01/1985
1497	J. Reynolds, "BOOTP Vendor Information Extensions," 08/04/1993
1532	W. Wimer, "Clarifications and Extensions for the Protocol," 10/08/1993
1533	S. Alexander, R. Droms, "DHCP Options and BOOTP Vendor Extensions," 10/08/1993

A.2.6. Border Gateway Protocol

These documents define the Border Gateway Protocol (BGP), an exterior routing protocol heavily used on the Internet backbones today.

RFC	Description
1163	K. Lougheed, Y. Rekhter, "A Border Gateway Protocol (BGP)," 06/20/1990
1164	J. Honig, D. Katz, M. Mathis, Y. Rekhter, J. Yu, "Application of the Border Gateway Protocol in the Internet," 06/20/1990
1267	K. Lougheed, Y. Rekhter, "A Border Gateway Protocol 3 (BGP-3)," 10/25/1991
1268	Y. Rekhter, "Experience with the BGP Protocol," 10/28/1991
1403	K. Varadhan, "BGP OSPF Interaction," 01/14/1993
1656	P. Traina, "BGP-4 Protocol Document Roadmap and Implementation Experience," 07/21/1994
1745	Y. Rekhter, "Experience with the BGP Protocol," 10/28/1991
1771	Y. Rekhter, T. Li, "A Border Gateway Protocol 4 (BGP-4)," 03/21/1995
1772	Y. Rekhter, P. Gross, "Application of the Border Gateway Protocol in the Internet," 03/21/1995

A.2.7. Classless Inter-Domain Routing

These documents define Classless Inter-Domain Routing (CIDR) and how it works.

RFC	Description
1517	R. Hinden, "Applicability Statement for the Implementation of Classless Inter-Domain Routing (CIDR)," 09/24/1993
1518	Y. Rekhter, T. Li, "An Architecture for IP Address Allocation with CIDR," 09/24/1993
1519	V. Fuller, T. Li, J. Yu, K. Varadhan, "Classless Inter-Domain Routing (CIDR): an Address Assignment and Aggregation Strategy," 09/24/1993

A.2.8. Dynamic Host Control Protocol

These documents describe Dynamic Host Control Protocol (DHCP), which is based largely on BOOTP. DHCP is a more advanced method of host configuration.

RFC	Description
1533	S. Alexander, R. Droms, "DHCP Options and BOOTP Vendor Extensions," 10/08/1993
1534	R. Droms, "Interoperation Between DHCP and BOOTP," 10/08/1993
1541	R. Droms, "Dynamic Host Configuration Protocol," 10/27/1993
1542	W. Wimer, "Clarifications and Extensions for the Bootstrap Protocol," 10/27/1993

A.2.9. Domain Name Service

These documents define how the Domain Name Service (DNS) works, for both IPv4 and IPv6.

RFC	Description
974	C. Partridge, "Mail routing and the domain system," 01/01/1986
1034	P. Mockapetris, "Domain names—concepts and facilities," 11/01/1987
1035	P. Mockapetris, "Domain names—implementation and specification," 11/01/1987
1183	R. Ullman, P. Mockapetris, L. Mamakos, C. Everhart, "New DNS RR Definitions," 10/08/1990
1383	C. Huitema, "An Experiment in DNS Based IP Routing," 12/28/1992
1706	B. Manning, R. Colella, "DNS NSAP Resource Records," 10/26/1994
1712	C. Farrell, M. Schulze, S. Pleitner, D. Baldoni, "DNS Encoding of Geographical Location," 11/01/1994
1713	A. Romao, "Tools for DNS debugging," 11/03/1994
1876	C. Davis, P. Vixie, T. Goodwin, I. Dickinson, "A Means of Expressing Location Information in the Domain Name System," 01/15/1996
1886	S. Thomson, C. Huitema, "DNS Extensions to support IP version 6," 01/04/1996

A.2.10. Exterior Gateway Protocol

Exterior Gateway Protcol (EGP) is another widely used routing protocol.

RFC	Description
904	International Telegraph and Telephone Co., D. Mills, "Gateway Protocol formal specification," 04/01/1984

A.2.11. File Transfer Protocol

These documents define File Transfer Protocol (FTP), a method of file transfer among heterogeneous systems. FTP is based on TCP.

RFC	Description
959	J. Postel, J. Reynolds, "File Transfer Protocol," 10/01/1985
1415	J. Mindel, R. Slaski, "FTP-FTAM Gateway Specification," 01/27/1993
1639	D. Piscitello, "FTP Operation Over Big Address Records (FOOBAR)," 06/09/1994

A.2.12. Finger

The finger protocol is used to provide information to an end user, typically about logged-in users.

RFC	Description
1288	D. Zimmerman, "The Finger User Information Protocol," 12/19/1991

A.2.13. Gopher

Gopher, a forerunner to the WWW, is defined by these documents. Gopher is not used much these days.

RFC	Description
1436	F. Anklesaria, M. McCahill, P. Lindner, D. Johnson, D. John, D. Torrey, B. Alberti, "The Internet Gopher Protocol (a distributed document search and retrieval protocol)," 3/18/1993

A.2.14. Hypertext Markup Language

Hypertext Markup Language (HTML) is the language for defining the content of WWW pages. HTML is carried by HTTP.

RFC	Description
1866	T. Berners-Lee, D. Connolly, "Hypertext Markup Language—2.0," 11/03/1995
2070	F. Yergeau, G. Nicol, G. Adams, M. Duerst, "Internationalization of the Hypertext Markup Language," 01/06/1997

A.2.15. Hypertext Transfer Protocol

These RFCs describe Hypertext Transfer Protocol (HTTP).

RFC	Description
1945	T. Berners-Lee, R. Fielding, H. Nielsen, "Hypertext Transfer Protocol—HTTP/1.0," 05/17/1996
2068	R. Fielding, J. Gettys, J. Mogul, H. Frystyk, T. Berners-Lee, "Hypertext Transfer Protocol—HTTP/1.1," 01/03/1997

A.2.16. Internet Control Message Protocol

The following RFCs describe Internet Control Message Protocol (ICMP).

RFC	Description
792	J. Postel, "Internet Control Message Protocol," 09/01/1981
1256	S. Deering, "ICMP Router Discovery Messages," 09/05/1991
1788	W. Simpson, "ICMP Domain Name Messages," 04/14/1995
1885	A. Conta, S. Deering, "Internet Control Message Protocol (ICMPv6) for the Internet Protocol Version 6 (IPv6)," 01/04/1996

A.2.17. Internet Group Multicasting Protocol

The following RFC describes Internet Group Multicasting Protocol (IGMP).

RFC	Description
1112	S. Deering, "Host extensions for IP multicasting," 08/01/1989

A.2.18. IPv4—Internet Protocol

The Internet Protocol is the heart of the TCP/IP suite and defines a datagram delivery service.

RFC	Description
791	J. Postel, "Internet Protocol," 09/01/1981
894	C. Hornig, "Standard for the transmission of IP datagrams over Ethernet networks," 04/01/1984
895	J. Postel, "Standard for the transmission of IP datagrams experimental Ethernet networks," 04/01/1984
1042	J. Postel, J. Reynolds, "Standard for the transmission of IP datagrams over IEEE 802 networks," 02/01/1988
1055	J. Romkey, "Nonstandard for transmission of IP datagrams over serial lines: SLIP," 06/01/1988
1108	S. Kent, "U.S. Department of Defense Security Options for the Internet Protocol," 11/27/1991
1149	D. Waitzman, "A Standard for the Transmission of IP Datagrams on Avian Carriers," 04/01/1990
1188	D. Katz, "A Proposed Standard for the Transmission of IP Datagrams over FDDI Networks," 10/30/1990
1191	J. Mogul, S. Deering, "Path MTU Discovery," 11/16/1990
1201	D. Provan, "Transmitting IP Traffic over ARCnet Networks," 02/01/1991
1226	B. Kantor, "Internet Protocol Encapsulation of AX.25 Frames," 05/13/1991

RFC	Description
1349	P. Almquist, "Type of Service in the Internet Protocol Suite," 07/06/1992
1390	D. Katz, "Transmission of IP and ARP over FDDI Networks," 01/05/1993
1469	T. Pusateri, "IP Multicast over Token-Ring Local Area Networks," 06/17/1993
1490	T. Bradley, C. Brown, A. Malis, "Multiprotocol Interconnect over Frame Relay," 07/26/1993
1501	E. Brunsen, "OS/2 User Group," 08/06/1993
1577	M. Laubach, "Classical IP and ARP over ATM," 01/20/1994

A.2.19. IPv6—Internet Protocol

IPv6 is an updated version of the Internet Protocol.

RFC	Description
1715	C. Huitema, "The H Ratio for Address Assignment Efficiency," 11/03/1994
1752	S. Bradner, A. Mankin, "The Recommendation for the IP Next Generation Protocol," 01/18/1995
1883	S. Deering, R. Hinden, "Internet Protocol, Version 6 (IPv6) Specification," 01/04/1996
1884	R. Hinden, S. Deering, "IP Version 6 Addressing Architecture," 01/04/1996
1897	R. Hinden, J. Postel, "IPv6 Testing Address Allocation," 01/25/1996
1972	M. Crawford, "A Method for the Transmission of IPv6 Packets over Ethernet Networks," 08/16/1996
2019	M. Crawford, "Transmission of IPv6 Packets Over FDDI," 10/17/1996

A.2.20. IPv6—Security

These RFCs define the security architecture for IPv6.

RFC	Description
1825	R. Atkinson, "Security Architecture for the Internet Protocol," 08/09/1995
1826	R. Atkinson, "IP Authentication Header," 08/09/1995
1827	R. Atkinson, "IP Encapsulating Security Payload (ESP)," 08/09/1995
1828	P. Metzger, W. Simpson, "IP Authentication using Keyed MD5," 08/09/1995
1829	P. Metzger, P. Karn, W. Simpson, "The ESP DES-CBC Transform," 08/09/1995

A.2.21. Internet Relay Chat

Internet Relay Chat (IRC) is a protocol that provides the capability to do real-time conferencing over IP.

RFC	Description
1459	J. Oikarinen, D. Reed, "Internet Relay Chat Protocol," 05/26/1993

A.2.22. Multipurpose Internet Mail Extension

Multipurpose Internet Mail Extension (MIME) provides a mechanism to support non-ASCII character sets when using SMPT and HTTP.

RFC	Description
1521	N. Borenstein, N. Freed, "MIME (Multipurpose Internet Mail Extensions) Part One: Mechanisms for Specifying and Describing the Format of Internet Message Bodies," 09/23/1993
1641	D. Goldsmith, M. Davis, "Using Unicode with MIME," 07/13/1994
1741	P. Faltstrom, D. Crocker, E. Fair, "MIME Content Type for Encoded Files," 12/22/1994
1767	D. Crocker, "MIME Encapsulation of EDI Objects," 03/02/1995
1847	J. Galvin, S. Murphy, S. Crocker, N. Freed, "Security Multiparts for MIME: Multipart/Signed and Multipart/Encrypted," 10/03/1995
1848	S. Crocker, N. Freed, J. Galvin, S. Murphy, "MIME Object Security Services," 10/03/1995
1892	G. Vaudreuil, "The Multipart/Report Content Type for the Reporting of Mail System Administrative Messages," 01/15/1996

A.2.23. NetBIOS

NetBIOS is an early LAN protocol and lives on in Microsoft and IBM networking.

RFC	Description
1001	Defense Advanced Research Projects Agency, End-to-End Services Task Force, Internet Activities Board, NetBIOS Working Group, "Protocol standard for a NetBIOS service on a TCP/UDP transport: Concepts and methods," 03/01/1987
1002	Defense Advanced Research Projects Agency, End-to-End Services Task Force, Internet Activities Board, NetBIOS Working Group, "Protocol standard for a NetBIOS service on a TCP/UDP transport: Detailed specifications," 03/01/1987

A.2.24. Network File System

Network File System (NFS) provides a way for UNIX systems to share files and entire file systems.

RFC	Description
1094	Sun Microsystems, Inc, "NFS: Network File System Protocol specification," 03/01/1989
1813	B. Callaghan, B. Pawlowski, P. Staubach, "NFS Version 3 Protocol Specification," 06/21/1995

A.2.25. Network News Transfer Protocol

This RFC describes the Network News Transfer Protocol (NNTP), the basis of Usenet newsgroups.

RFC	Description
977	B. Kantor, P. Lapsley, "Network News Transfer Protocol: A Proposed Standard for the Stream-Based Transmission of News," 02/01/1986

A.2.26. Open Shortest Path First

Open Shortest Path First (OSPF) is another popular interior-routing protocol.

RFC	Description
1583	J. Moy, "OSPF Version 2," 03/23/1994
1584	J. Moy, "Multicast Extensions to OSPF," 03/24/1994
1586	O. deSouza, M. Rodrigues, "Guidelines for Running OSPF Over Frame Relay Networks," 03/24/1994
1587	R. Coltun, V. Fuller, "The OSPF NSSA Option," 03/24/1994
1765	J. Moy, "OSPF Database Overflow," 03/02/1995

A.2.27. POP3—Post Office Protocol

POP3 enables an e-mail client to retrieve mail from a mail server. Many popular e-mail clients implement POP3 as a standard.

RFC	Description
1725	J. Myers, M. Rose, "Post Office Protocol—Version 3", 11/23/1994
1734	J. Myers, "POP3 AUTHentication command," 12/20/1994

A.2.28. Point-to-Point Protocol

Point-to-Point Protocol (PPP) is a protocol used via a point-to-point link (for example, a dial-up line). IP can run over PPP making PPP important for dial-up Internet users.

RFC	Description
1331	W. Simpson, "The Point-to-Point Protocol (PPP) for the Transmission of Multi-protocol Datagrams over Point-to-Point Links," 05/26/1992
1332	G. McGregor, "The PPP Internet Protocol Control Protocol (IPCP)," 05/26/1992
1333	W. Simpson, "PPP Link Quality Monitoring," 05/26/1992
1334	B. Lloyd, W. Simpson, "PPP Authentication Protocols," 10/20/1992
1377	D. Katz, "The PPP OSI Network Layer Control Protocol (OSINLCP)," 11/05/1992
1471	F. Kastenholz, "The Definitions of Managed Objects for the Link Control Protocol of the Point-to-Point Protocol," 06/08/1993
1472	F. Kastenholz, "The Definitions of Managed Objects for the Security Protocols of the Point-to-Point Protocol," 06/08/1993
1473	F. Kastenholz, "The Definitions of Managed Objects for the IP Network Control Protocol of the Point-to-Point Protocol," 06/08/1993
1474	F. Kastenholz, "The Definitions of Managed Objects for the Bridge Network Control Protocol of the Point-to-Point Protocol," 06/08/1993
1570	W. Simpson, "PPP LCP Extensions," 01/11/1994
1618	W. Simpson, "PPP over ISDN," 05/13/1994
1619	W. Simpson, "PPP over SONET/SDH," 05/13/1994
1638	F. Baker, R. Bowen, "PPP Bridging Control Protocol (BCP)," 06/09/1994
1661	W. Simpson, "The Point-to-Point Protocol (PPP)," 07/21/1994
1662	W. Simpson, "PPP in HDLC-like Framing," 07/21/1994
1663	D. Rand, "PPP Reliable Transmission," 07/21/1994
1717	K. Sklower, B. Lloyd, G. McGregor, D. Carr, "The PPP Multilink Protocol (MP)," 11/21/1994
1762	S. Senum, "The PPP DECnet Phase IV Control Protocol (DNCP)," 03/01/1995
2023	D. Haskin, E. Allen, "IP Version 6 over PPP," 10/22/1996

RFCs and Standards/Further References

A.2.29. Routing Information Protocol

Routing Information Protocol (RIP) is an early interior-routing protocol, somewhat overtaken by OSPF.

RFC	Description
1058	C. Hedrick, "Routing Information Protocol," 06/01/1988
1582	G. Meyer, "Extensions to RIP to Support Demand Circuits," 02/18/1994
1722	G. Malkin, "RIP Version 2 Protocol Applicability Statement," 11/15/1994
1723	G. Malkin, "RIP Version 2 Carrying Additional Information," 11/15/1994

A.2.30. Simple Mail Transfer Protocol

Simple Mail Transfer Protocol (SMTP), as the name suggests, is a simple protocol for the transmission of mail messages. SMTP is the backbone of Internet mail.

RFC	Description
821	J. Postel, "Simple Mail Transfer Protocol," 08/01/1982
822	D. Crocker, "Standard for the format of ARPA Internet text messages," 08/13/1982
1652	J. Klensin, N. Freed, M. Rose, E. Stefferud, D. Crocker, "SMTP Service Extension for 8-bit MIME transport," 07/18/1994
1854	N. Freed, A. Cargille, "SMTP Service Extension for Command Pipelining," 10/04/1995
1869	J. Klensin, N. Freed, M. Rose, E. Stefferud, D. Crocker, "SMTP Service Extensions," 11/06/1995
1870	J. Klensin, N. Freed, K. Moore, "SMTP Service Extension for Message Size Declaration," 11/06/1995
1891	K. Moore, "SMTP Service Extension for Delivery Status Notifications," 01/15/1996

A.2.31. Simple Network Management Protocol

Simple Network Management Protocol (SNMP) is a simple protocol for communication between network agents and a network management application.

RFC	Description
1157	M. Schoffstall, M. Fedor, J. Davin, J. Case, "A Simple Network Management Protocol (SNMP)," 05/10/1990
1187	J. Davin, K. McCloghrie, M. Rose, "Bulk Table Retrieval with the SNMP," 10/18/1990
1215	M. Rose, "A Convention for Defining Traps for use with the SNMP," 03/27/1991

RFC	Description
1228	G. Carpenter, B. Wijnen, "SNMP-DPI—Simple Network Management Protocol Distributed Program Interface," 05/23/1991
1352	J. Davin, J. Galvin, K. McCloghrie, "SNMP Security Protocols," 07/06/1992
1441	J. Case, K. McCloghrie, M. Rose, S. Waldbusser, "Introduction to version 2 of the Internet-standard Network Management Framework," 05/03/1993
1442	J. Case, K. McCloghrie, M. Rose, S. Waldbusser, "Structure of Management Information for version 2 of the Simple Network Management Protocol (SNMPv2)," 05/03/1993
1443	J. Case, K. McCloghrie, M. Rose, S. Waldbusser, "Textual Conventions for version 2 of the Simple Network Management Protocol (SNMPv2)," 05/03/1993
1444	J. Case, K. McCloghrie, M. Rose, S. Waldbusser, "Conformance Statements for version 2 of the Simple Network Management Protocol SNMPv2)," 05/03/1993
1445	J. Davin, K. McCloghie, "Administrative Model for version 2 of the Simple Network Management Protocol (SNMPv2)," 05/03/1993
1446	J. Galvin, K. McCloghrie, "Security Protocols for version 2 of the Simple Network Management Protocol (SNMPv2)," 05/03/1993
1448	J. Case, K. McCloghrie, M. Rose, S. Waldbusser, "Protocol Operations for version 2 of the Simple Network Management Protocol (SNMPv2)," 05/03/1993
1449	J. Case, K. McCloghrie, M. Rose, S. Waldbusser, "Transport Mappings for version 2 of the Simple Network Management Protocol (SNMPv2)," 05/03/1993
1451	J. Case, K. McCloghrie, M. Rose, S. Waldbusser, "Manager to Manager Management Information Base," 05/03/1993
1452	J. Case, K. McCloghrie, M. Rose, S. Waldbusser, "Coexistence between version 1 and version 2 of the Internet-standard Network Management Framework," 05/03/1993
1592	B. Wijnen, G. Carpenter, K. Curran, A. Sehgal, G. Waters, "Simple Network Management Protocol Distributed Protocol Interface Version 2.0," 03/03/1994
1901	J. Case, K. McCloghrie, M. Rose, S. Waldbusser, "Introduction to Community-based SNMPv2," 01/22/1996
1903	J. Case, K. McCloghrie, M. Rose, S. Waldbusser, "Textual Conventions for Version 2 of the Simple Network Management Protocol (SNMPv2)," 01/22/1996

RFCs and Standards/Further References

continues

RFC	Description
1904	J. Case, K. McCloghrie, M. Rose, S. Waldbusser, "Conformance Statements for Version 2 of the Simple Network Management Protocol (SNMPv2)," 01/22/1996
1908	J. Case, K. McCloghrie, M. Rose, S. Waldbusser, "Coexistence between Version 1 and Version 2 of the Internet-standard Network Management Framework," 01/22/1996
1909	K. McCloghrie, "An Administrative Infrastructure for SNMPv2," 02/28/1996
1910	G. Waters, "User-based Security Model for SNMPv2," 02/28/1996

A.2.32. SNMP—Management Information Bases

These RFCs define the information, the Management Information Base (MIB), which is the basis for SNMP.

RFC	Description
1212	K. McCloghrie, M. Rose, "Concise MIB Definitions," 03/26/1991
1213	K. McCloghrie, M. Rose, "Management Information Base for Network Management of TCP/IP-based Internets: MIB-II," 03/26/1991
1214	L. Labarre, "OSI Internet Management: Management Information Base," 04/05/1991
1229	K. McCloghrie, "Extensions to the Generic-Interface MIB," 08/03/1992
1230	R. Fox, K. McCloghrie, "IEEE 802.4 Token Bus MIB," 05/23/1991
1269	J. Burruss, S. Willis, "Definitions of Managed Objects for the Border Gateway Protocol (Version 3)," 10/26/1991
1285	J. Case, "FDDI Management Information Base," 01/24/1992
1354	F. Baker, "IP Forwarding Table MIB," 07/06/1992
1382	D. Throop, "SNMP MIB Extension for the X.25 Packet Layer," 11/10/1992
1406	F. Baker, J. Watt, "Definitions of Managed Objects for the DS1 and E1 Interface Types," 01/26/1993
1407	T. Cox, K. Tesink, "Definitions of Managed Objects for the DS3/ Interface Type," 01/26/1993
1414	M. St. Johns, M. Rose, "Ident MIB," 02/04/1993
1447	K. McCloghrie, J. Galvin, "Party MIB for version 2 of the Simple Network Management Protocol (SNMPv2)," 05/03/1993

RFC	Description
1450	J. Case, K. McCloghrie, M. Rose, S. Waldbusser, "Management Information Base for version 2 of the Simple Network Management Protocol (SNMPv2)," 05/03/1993
1493	E. Decker, P. Langille, A. Rijsinghani, K. McCloghrie, "Definitions of Managed Objects for Bridges," 07/28/1993
1512	J. Case, A. Rijsinghani, "FDDI Management Information Base," 09/10/1993
1514	P. Grillo, S. Waldbusser, "Host Resources MIB," 09/23/1993
1516	D. McMaster, K. McCloghrie, "Definitions of Managed Objects for IEEE 802.3 Repeater Devices," 09/10/1993
1525	E. Decker, K. McCloghrie, P. Langille, A. Rijsinghani, "Definitions of Managed Objects for Source Routing Bridges," 09/30/1993
1559	J. Saperia, "DECnet Phase IV MIB Extensions," 12/27/1993
1566	N. Freed, S. Kille, "Mail Monitoring MIB," 01/11/1994
1604	T. Brown, "Definitions of Managed Objects for Frame Relay Service," 03/25/1994
1611	R. Austein, J. Saperia, "DNS Server MIB Extensions," 05/17/1994
1612	R. Austein, J. Saperia, "DNS Resolver MIB Extensions," 05/17/1994
1628	J. Case, "UPS Management Information Base," 05/19/1994
1643	F. Kastenholz, "Definitions of Managed Objects for the Ethernet-like Interface Types," 07/13/1994
1657	S. Willis, J. Burruss, J. Chu, "Definitions of Managed Objects for the Fourth Version of the Border Gateway Protocol (BGP-4) using SMIv2," 07/21/1994
1665	Z. Kielczewski, D. Kostick, K. Shih, "Definitions of Managed Objects for SNA NAUs using SMIv2," 07/22/1994
1694	T. Brown, K. Tesink, "Definitions of Managed Objects for SMDS Interfaces using SMIv2," 08/23/1994
1695	M. Ahmed, K. Tesink, "Definitions of Managed Objects for ATM Management Version 8.0 using SMIv2," 08/25/1994
1696	F. Kastenholz, "Definitions of Managed Objects for the Ethernet-like Interface Types," 07/13/1994
1724	G. Malkin, F. Baker, "RIP Version 2 MIB Extension," 11/15/1994
1742	S. Waldbusser, K. Frisa, "AppleTalk Management Information Base II," 01/05/1995
1748	K. McCloghrie, E. Decker, "IEEE 802.5 MIB using SMIv2," 12/29/1994
1749	K. McCloghrie, F. Baker, E. Decker, "IEEE 802.5 Station Source Routing MIB using SMIv2," 12/29/1994

RFCs and Standards/Further References

continues

RFC	Description
1757	S. Waldbusser, "Remote Network Monitoring Management Information Base," 02/10/1995
1759	R. Smith, F. Wright, T. Hastings, S. Zilles, J. Gyllenskog, "Printer MIB," 03/28/1995
1850	F. Baker, R. Coltun, "OSPF Version 2 Management Information Base," 11/03/1995
1905	J. Case, K. McCloghrie, M. Rose, S. Waldbusser, "Protocol Operations for Version 2 of the Simple Network Management Protocol (SNMPv2)," 01/22/1996
1907	J. Case, K. McCloghrie, M. Rose, S. Waldbusser, "Management Information Base for Version 2 of the Simple Network Management Protocol (SNMPv2)," 01/22/1996

A.2.33. Systems Network Architecture

Systems Network Architecture (SNA) is an early IBM network architecture.

RFC	Description
1538	W. Behl, B. Sterling, W. Teskey, "Advanced SNA/IP: A Simple SNA Transport Protocol," 10/06/1993

A.2.34. Telnet

Telnet is a protocol designed to support terminal emulation.

RFC	Description
652	D. Crocker, "Telnet output carriage-return disposition option," 10/25/1974
653	D. Crocker, "Telnet output horizontal tabstops option," 10/25/1974
654	D. Crocker, "Telnet output horizontal tab disposition option," 10/25/1974
655	D. Crocker, "Telnet output formfeed disposition option," 10/25/1974
656	D. Crocker, "Telnet output vertical tabstops option," 10/25/1974
657	D. Crocker, "Telnet output vertical tab disposition option," 10/25/1974
698	T. Mock, "Telnet extended ASCII option," 07/23/1975
726	J. Day, "Minor pitfall in the Telnet Protocol," 04/27/1977
727	D. Crocker, "Telnet byte macro option," 05/13/1977
732	J. Day, "Telnet Data Entry Terminal option," 09/12/1977

RFC	*Description*
734	M. Crispin, "SUPDUP Protocol," 10/07/1977
735	D. Crocker, R. Gumpertz, "Revised Telnet byte macro option," 11/03/1977
736	M. Crispin, "Telnet SUPDUP option," 10/31/1977
749	B. Greenberg, "Telnet SUPDUP-Output option," 09/18/1978
779	E. Killian, "Telnet send-location option," 04/01/1981
854	J. Postel, J. Reynolds, "Telnet Protocol specification," 05/01/1983
855	J. Postel, J. Reynolds, "Telnet option specifications," 05/01/1983
856	J. Postel, J. Reynolds, "Telnet binary transmission," 05/01/1983
857	J. Postel, J. Reynolds, "Telnet echo option," 05/01/1983
858	J. Postel, J. Reynolds, "Telnet Suppress Go Ahead option," 05/01/1983
859	J. Postel, J. Reynolds, "Telnet status option," 05/01/1983
860	J. Postel, J. Reynolds, "Telnet timing mark option," 05/01/1983
861	J. Postel, J. Reynolds, "Telnet extended options: List option," 05/01/1983
885	J. Postel, "Telnet end of record option," 12/01/1983
927	B. Anderson, "TACACS user identification Telnet option," 12/01/1984
933	S. Silverman, "Output marking Telnet option," 01/01/1985
946	R. Nedved, "Telnet terminal location number option," 05/01/1985
1041	Y. Rekhter, "Telnet 3270 regime option," 01/01/1988
1043	A. Yasuda, T. Thompson, "Telnet Data Entry Terminal option: DODIIS implementation," 02/01/1988
1053	S. Levy, T. Jacobson, "Telnet X.3 PAD option," 04/01/1988
1073	D. Waitzman, "Telnet window size option," 10/01/1988
1079	C. Hedrick, "Telnet terminal speed option," 12/01/1988
1091	J. VanBokkelen, "Telnet terminal-type option," 02/01/1989
1096	G. Marcy, "Telnet X display location option," 03/01/1989
1184	D. Borman, "Telnet Linemode Option," 10/15/1990
1372	D. Borman, C. Hedrick, "Telnet Remote Flow Control Option," 10/23/1992
1408	D. Borman, "Telnet Environment Option," 01/26/1993
1411	D. Borman, "Telnet Authentication: Kerberos Version 4," 01/26/1993
1412	K. Alagappan, "Telnet Authentication: SPX," 01/27/1993
1416	D. Borman, "Telnet Authentication Option," 02/01/1993
1572	S. Alexander, "Telnet Environment Option," 01/14/1994
1647	B. Kelly, "TN3270 Enhancements," 07/15/1994
2066	R. Gellens, "TELNET CHARSET Option," 01/03/1997

A.2.35. Transmission Control Protocol

Transmission Control Protocol (TCP) is a reliable stream-oriented transmission protocol, implemented on top of IP.

RFC	Description
793	J. Postel, "Transmission Control Protocol," 09/01/1981
1144	V. Jacobson, "Compressing TCP/IP headers for low-speed serial links," 02/01/1990
1146	V. Jacobson, "Compressing TCP/IP headers for low-speed serial links," 02/01/1990
1323	D. Borman, R. Braden, V. Jacobson, "TCP Extensions for High Performance," 05/13/1992

A.2.36. Trivial File Transfer Protocol

Trivial File Transfer Protocol (TFTP) is a file transfer protocol based on UDP.

RFC	Description
1350	K. Sollins, "THE TFTP PROTOCOL (REVISION 2)," 07/10/1992
1782	G. Malkin, A. Harkin, "TFTP Option Extension," 03/28/1995
1783	G. Malkin, A. Harkin, "TFTP Blocksize Option," 03/28/1995
1784	G. Malkin, A. Harkin, "TFTP Timeout Interval and Transfer Size Options," 03/28/1995

A.2.37. User Datagram Protocol

User Datagram Protocol (UDP) is an unreliable end-to-end datagram delivery protocol, based on IP.

RFC	Description
768	J. Postel, "User Datagram Protocol," 08/28/1980

A.3. Other References

The following are a few more references that may be useful. Some of these may be hard to find.

A.3.1. Ethernet

This is a formal definition of the Ethernet protocol, which can be obtained directly from DEC.

This is a formal specification for Ethernet.

"The Ethernet, a Local Area Network: Data Link Layer and Physical Layer Specification," AA-K7959B-TK, Digital Equipment Corporation, Maynard, MA, USA, 1980.

A.3.2. Frequently Asked Questions

Frequently Asked Questions (FAQ) documents are usually produced by readers of a Usenet newsgroup. These volunteer efforts are often better than the vendor-supplied documentatation:

- Bernard D. Aboba, "`comp.protocols.tcp-ip.ibmpc` Frequently Asked Questions (FAQ)," Usenet news.answers, available via `ftp://ftp.netcom.com/pub/ma/mailcom/IBMTCP/ibmtcp.zip`

- John Hawkinson, "`cisco-networking-faq`," Usenet news.answers available via `http://www.lib.ox.ac.uk/internet/news/faq/archive/cisco-networking-faq.html`

- Chris Peckham, "`comp.protocols.tcp-ip.domains` FAQ," Usenet news.answers avaiable via `http://www.lib.ox.ac.uk/internet/news/faq/archive/internet.tcp-ip.domains-faq.part1.html` and `http://www.lib.ox.ac.uk/internet/news/faq/archive/internet.tcp-ip.domains-faq.part2.html`. An HTTP version of this FAQ can also be found at `http://www.users.pfmc.net/~cdp/cptd-faq/`.

A.3.3. Microsoft Whitepapers

Microsoft published a series of whitepapers that describe various aspects of its software. These documents provide a good overview to the subject and often augment formal documentation.

All these whitepapers are available as separate files from `ftp://ftp.microsoft.com/bussys/winnt/winnt-docs/papers`:

- Dave MacDonald, "Microsoft Windows NT 3.5/3.51/4.0: TCP/IP Implementation Details, TCP/IP Protocol Stack and Services, Version 2.0," (`TCPIPIMP2.DOC`), Part no. 098-66794, 1996

- Microsoft Corporation, "DNS and Microsoft® Windows NT® 4.0," (`DNSWP.EXE`), Part no. 098-67320, 1996

- Microsoft Corporation, "NT203 Administration Tools of Windows NT Advanced Server Dynamic Host Configuration Protocol, Windows Internet Naming Service," (`DHCPWINS.EXE`), Part no. 098-56544, 1995

- Microsoft Corporation, "Microsoft Windows NT™ from a UNIX® Point of View," (`NT4UNIX.EXE`), Part no. 098-61913, 1995

Appendix

B

Service Port Numbers

By Martin Bligh

This appendix lists which services run over which port numbers. It is particularly useful when trying to identify an unknown packet. The diversity of services running over TCP/IP is quite staggering.

Port numbers for UDP and TCP are independent, although they are normally kept the same for each service for simplicity.

Ports from 0 to 1023 are the *well known ports*, intended so that well known services can be contacted easily. Their allocation is controlled by the Internet Assigned Numbers Authority (IANA) and on most systems can only be used by privileged processes.

Ports from 1024 to 65535 are known as *registered ports* and can be used by user processes. Their allocation is not controlled by the IANA, so there are some conflicts in the table.

The information in Table B.1 is according to RFC 1700.

Table B.1. Assigned port numbers.

Service	Port	Protocol	Description
	0	tcp	Reserved
	0	udp	Reserved
tcpmux	1	tcp	TCP Port Service Multiplexer
tcpmux	1	udp	TCP Port Service Multiplexer
compressnet	2	tcp	Management Utility
compressnet	2	udp	Management Utility
compressnet	3	tcp	Compression Process
compressnet	3	udp	Compression Process
rje	5	tcp	Remote Job Entry
rje	5	udp	Remote Job Entry
echo	7	tcp	Echo
echo	7	udp	Echo
discard	9	tcp	Discard
discard	9	udp	Discard
systat	11	tcp	Active Users
systat	11	udp	Active Users

Service	Port	Protocol	Description
daytime	13	tcp	Daytime
daytime	13	udp	Daytime
qotd	17	tcp	Quote of the Day
qotd	17	udp	Quote of the Day
msp	18	tcp	Message Send Protocol
msp	18	udp	Message Send Protocol
chargen	19	tcp	Character Generator
chargen	19	udp	Character Generator
ftp-data	20	tcp	File Transfer [Default Data]
ftp-data	20	udp	File Transfer [Default Data]
ftp	21	tcp	File Transfer [Control]
ftp	21	udp	File Transfer [Control]
telnet	23	tcp	Telnet
telnet	23	udp	Telnet
	24	tcp	Any private mail system
	24	udp	Any private mail system
smtp	25	tcp	Simple Mail Transfer Protocol
smtp	25	udp	Simple Mail Transfer Protocol
nsw-fe	27	tcp	NSW User System FE
nsw-fe	27	udp	NSW User System FE
msg-icp	29	tcp	MSG ICP
msg-icp	29	udp	MSG ICP
msg-auth	31	tcp	MSG Authentication
msg-auth	31	udp	MSG Authentication
dsp	33	tcp	Display Support Protocol
dsp	33	udp	Display Support Protocol
	35	tcp	Any private printer server
	35	udp	Any private printer server

Service Port Numbers

continues

Table B.1. Continued.

Service	Port	Protocol	Description
time	37	tcp	Time
time	37	udp	Time
rap	38	tcp	Route Access Protocol
rap	38	udp	Route Access Protocol
rlp	39	tcp	Resource Location Protocol
rlp	39	udp	Resource Location Protocol
graphics	41	tcp	Graphics
graphics	41	udp	Graphics
nameserver	42	tcp	Host Name Server
nameserver	42	udp	Host Name Server
nicname	43	tcp	Who Is
nicname	43	udp	Who Is
mpm-flags	44	tcp	MPM FLAGS Protocol
mpm-flags	44	udp	MPM FLAGS Protocol
mpm	45	tcp	Message Processing Module [recv]
mpm	45	udp	Message Processing Module [recv]
mpm-snd	46	tcp	MPM [default send]
mpm-snd	46	udp	MPM [default send]
ni-ftp	47	tcp	NI FTP
ni-ftp	47	udp	NI FTP
auditd	48	tcp	Digital Audit Daemon
auditd	48	udp	Digital Audit Daemon
login	49	tcp	Login Host Protocol
login	49	udp	Login Host Protocol
re-mail-ck	50	tcp	Remote Mail Checking Protocol
re-mail-ck	50	udp	Remote Mail Checking Protocol
la-maint	51	tcp	IMP Logical Address Maintenance
la-maint	51	udp	IMP Logical Address Maintenance

Service	Port	Protocol	Description
xns-time	52	tcp	XNS Time Protocol
xns-time	52	udp	XNS Time Protocol
domain	53	tcp	Domain Name Server
domain	53	udp	Domain Name Server
xns-ch	54	tcp	XNS Clearinghouse
xns-ch	54	udp	XNS Clearinghouse
isi-gl	55	tcp	ISI Graphics Language
isi-gl	55	udp	ISI Graphics Language
xns-auth	56	tcp	XNS Authentication
xns-auth	56	udp	XNS Authentication
	57	tcp	Any private terminal access
	57	udp	Any private terminal access
xns-mail	58	tcp	XNS Mail
xns-mail	58	udp	XNS Mail
	59	tcp	Any private file service
	59	udp	Any private file service
	60	tcp	Unassigned
	60	udp	Unassigned
ni-mail	61	tcp	NI MAIL
ni-mail	61	udp	NI MAIL
acas	62	tcp	ACA Services
acas	62	udp	ACA Services
covia	64	tcp	Communications Integrator (CI)
covia	64	udp	Communications Integrator (CI)
tacacs-ds	65	tcp	TACACS–Database Service
tacacs-ds	65	udp	TACACS–Database Service
sql*net	66	tcp	Oracle SQL*NET
sql*net	66	udp	Oracle SQL*NET

Service Port Numbers

continues

Table B.1. Continued.

Service	Port	Protocol	Description
bootps	67	tcp	Bootstrap Protocol Server
bootps	67	udp	Bootstrap Protocol Server
bootpc	68	tcp	Bootstrap Protocol Client
bootpc	68	udp	Bootstrap Protocol Client
tftp	69	tcp	Trivial File Transfer
tftp	69	udp	Trivial File Transfer
gopher	70	tcp	Gopher
gopher	70	udp	Gopher
netrjs-1	71	tcp	Remote Job Service
netrjs-1	71	udp	Remote Job Service
netrjs-2	72	tcp	Remote Job Service
netrjs-2	72	udp	Remote Job Service
netrjs-3	73	tcp	Remote Job Service
netrjs-3	73	udp	Remote Job Service
netrjs-4	74	tcp	Remote Job Service
netrjs-4	74	udp	Remote Job Service
	75	tcp	Any private dial-out service
	75	udp	Any private dial-out service
deos	76	tcp	Distributed External Object Store
deos	76	udp	Distributed External Object Store
	77	tcp	Any private RJE service
	77	udp	Any private RJE service
vettcp	78	tcp	vettcp
vettcp	78	udp	vettcp
finger	79	tcp	Finger
finger	79	udp	Finger
www-http	80	tcp	World Wide Web HTTP
www-http	80	udp	World Wide Web HTTP

Service	Port	Protocol	Description
hosts2-ns	81	tcp	HOSTS2 Name Server
hosts2-ns	81	udp	HOSTS2 Name Server
xfer	82	tcp	XFER Utility
xfer	82	udp	XFER Utility
mit-ml-dev	83	tcp	MIT ML Device
mit-ml-dev	83	udp	MIT ML Device
ctf	84	tcp	Common Trace Facility
ctf	84	udp	Common Trace Facility
mit-ml-dev	85	tcp	MIT ML Device
mit-ml-dev	85	udp	MIT ML Device
mfcobol	86	tcp	Micro Focus COBOL
mfcobol	86	udp	Micro Focus COBOL
	87	tcp	Any private terminal link
	87	udp	Any private terminal link
kerberos	88	tcp	Kerberos
kerberos	88	udp	Kerberos
su-mit-tg	89	tcp	SU/MIT Telnet Gateway
su-mit-tg	89	udp	SU/MIT Telnet Gateway
dnsix	90	tcp	DNSIX Security Attribute Token Map
dnsix	90	udp	DNSIX Security Attribute Token Map
mit-dov	91	tcp	MIT Dover Spooler
mit-dov	91	udp	MIT Dover Spooler
npp	92	tcp	Network Printing Protocol
npp	92	udp	Network Printing Protocol
dcp	93	tcp	Device Control Protocol
dcp	93	udp	Device Control Protocol
objcall	94	tcp	Tivoli Object Dispatcher
objcall	94	udp	Tivoli Object Dispatcher

Service Port Numbers

continues

Table B.1. Continued.

Service	Port	Protocol	Description
supdup	95	tcp	SUPDUP
supdup	95	udp	SUPDUP
dixie	96	tcp	DIXIE Protocol Specification
dixie	96	udp	DIXIE Protocol Specification
swift-rvf	97	tcp	Swift Remote Virtual File Protocol
swift-rvf	97	udp	Swift Remote Virtual File Protocol
tacnews	98	tcp	TAC News
tacnews	98	udp	TAC News
metagram	99	tcp	Metagram Relay
metagram	99	udp	Metagram Relay
newacct	100	tcp	[Unauthorized use]
hostname	101	tcp	NIC Host Name Server
hostname	101	udp	NIC Host Name Server
iso-tsap	102	tcp	ISO-TSAP
iso-tsap	102	udp	ISO-TSAP
gppitnp	103	tcp	Genesis Point-to-Point Trans Net
gppitnp	103	udp	Genesis Point-to-Point Trans Net
acr-nema	104	tcp	ACR-NEMA Digital Imag. & Comm. 300
acr-nema	104	udp	ACR-NEMA Digital Imag. & Comm. 300
csnet-ns	105	tcp	Mailbox Name Nameserver
csnet-ns	105	udp	Mailbox Name Nameserver
3com-tsmux	106	tcp	3COM-TSMUX
3com-tsmux	106	udp	3COM-TSMUX
rtelnet	107	tcp	Remote Telnet Service
rtelnet	107	udp	Remote Telnet Service
snagas	108	tcp	SNA Gateway Access Server
snagas	108	udp	SNA Gateway Access Server

Service	Port	Protocol	Description
pop2	109	tcp	Post Office Protocol version 2
pop2	109	udp	Post Office Protocol version 2
pop3	110	tcp	Post Office Protocol version 3
pop3	110	udp	Post Office Protocol version 3
sunrpc	111	tcp	SUN Remote Procedure Call
sunrpc	111	udp	SUN Remote Procedure Call
mcidas	112	tcp	McIDAS Data Transmission Protocol
mcidas	112	udp	McIDAS Data Transmission Protocol
auth	113	tcp	Authentication Service
auth	113	udp	Authentication Service
audionews	114	tcp	Audio News Multicast
audionews	114	udp	Audio News Multicast
sftp	115	tcp	Simple File Transfer Protocol
sftp	115	udp	Simple File Transfer Protocol
ansanotify	116	tcp	ANSA REX Notify
ansanotify	116	udp	ANSA REX Notify
uucp-path	117	tcp	UUCP Path Service
uucp-path	117	udp	UUCP Path Service
sqlserv	118	tcp	SQL Services
sqlserv	118	udp	SQL Services
nntp	119	tcp	Network News Transfer Protocol
nntp	119	udp	Network News Transfer Protocol
cfdptkt	120	tcp	CFDPTKT
cfdptkt	120	udp	CFDPTKT
erpc	121	tcp	Encore Expedited Remote Procedure Call
erpc	121	udp	Encore Expedited Remote Procedure Call
smakynet	122	tcp	SMAKYNET
smakynet	122	udp	SMAKYNET

Service Port Numbers

continues

Table B.1. Continued.

Service	Port	Protocol	Description
ntp	123	tcp	Network Time Protocol
ntp	123	udp	Network Time Protocol
ansatrader	124	tcp	ANSA REX Trader
ansatrader	124	udp	ANSA REX Trader
locus-map	125	tcp	Locus PC-Interface Net Map Server
locus-map	125	udp	Locus PC-Interface Net Map Server
unitary	126	tcp	Unisys Unitary Login
unitary	126	udp	Unisys Unitary Login
locus-con	127	tcp	Locus PC-Interface Conn Server
locus-con	127	udp	Locus PC-Interface Conn Server
gss-xlicen	128	tcp	GSS X License Verification
gss-xlicen	128	udp	GSS X License Verification
pwdgen	129	tcp	Password Generator Protocol
pwdgen	129	udp	Password Generator Protocol
cisco-fna	130	tcp	Cisco FNATIVE
cisco-fna	130	udp	Cisco FNATIVE
cisco-tna	131	tcp	Cisco TNATIVE
cisco-tna	131	udp	Cisco TNATIVE
cisco-sys	132	tcp	Cisco SYSMAINT
cisco-sys	132	udp	Cisco SYSMAINT
statsrv	133	tcp	Statistics Service
statsrv	133	udp	Statistics Service
ingres-net	134	tcp	INGRES-NET Service
ingres-net	134	udp	INGRES-NET Service
loc-srv	135	tcp	Location Service
loc-srv	135	udp	Location Service
profile	136	tcp	PROFILE Naming System
profile	136	udp	PROFILE Naming System

Service	Port	Protocol	Description
netbios-ns	137	tcp	NetBIOS Name Service
netbios-ns	137	udp	NetBIOS Name Service
netbios-dgm	138	tcp	NetBIOS Datagram Service
netbios-dgm	138	udp	NetBIOS Datagram Service
netbios-ssn	139	tcp	NetBIOS Session Service
netbios-ssn	139	udp	NetBIOS Session Service
emfis-data	140	tcp	EMFIS Data Service
emfis-data	140	udp	EMFIS Data Service
emfis-cntl	141	tcp	EMFIS Control Service
emfis-cntl	141	udp	EMFIS Control Service
bl-idm	142	tcp	Britton–Lee IDM
bl-idm	142	udp	Britton–Lee IDM
imap2	143	tcp	Interim Mail Access Protocol v2
imap2	143	udp	Interim Mail Access Protocol v2
news	144	tcp	NewS
news	144	udp	NewS
uaac	145	tcp	UAAC Protocol
uaac	145	udp	UAAC Protocol
iso-tp0	146	tcp	ISO-IP0
iso-tp0	146	udp	ISO-IP0
iso-ip	147	tcp	ISO-IP
iso-ip	147	udp	ISO-IP
cronus	148	tcp	CRONUS-SUPPORT
cronus	148	udp	CRONUS-SUPPORT
aed-512	149	tcp	AED 512 Emulation Service
aed-512	149	udp	AED 512 Emulation Service
sql-net	150	tcp	SQL-NET
sql-net	150	udp	SQL-NET

Service Port Numbers

continues

Table B.1. Continued.

Service	Port	Protocol	Description
hems	151	tcp	HEMS
hems	151	udp	HEMS
bftp	152	tcp	Background File Transfer Program
bftp	152	udp	Background File Transfer Program
sgmp	153	tcp	SGMP
sgmp	153	udp	SGMP
netsc-prod	154	tcp	NETSC
netsc-prod	154	udp	NETSC
netsc-dev	155	tcp	NETSC
netsc-dev	155	udp	NETSC
sqlsrv	156	tcp	SQL Service
sqlsrv	156	udp	SQL Service
knet-cmp	157	tcp	KNET/VM Command/Message Protocol
knet-cmp	157	udp	KNET/VM Command/Message Protocol
pcmail-srv	158	tcp	PCMail Server
pcmail-srv	158	udp	PCMail Server
nss-routing	159	tcp	NSS-Routing
nss-routing	159	udp	NSS-Routing
sgmp-traps	160	tcp	SGMP-TRAPS
sgmp-traps	160	udp	SGMP-TRAPS
snmp	161	tcp	SNMP
snmp	161	udp	SNMP
snmptrap	162	tcp	SNMPTRAP
snmptrap	162	udp	SNMPTRAP
cmip-man	163	tcp	CMIP/TCP Manager
cmip-man	163	udp	CMIP/TCP Manager
cmip-agent	164	tcp	CMIP/TCP Agent
cmip-agent	164	udp	CMIP/TCP Agent

Service	Port	Protocol	Description
xns-courier	165	tcp	Xerox
xns-courier	165	udp	Xerox
s-net	166	tcp	Sirius Systems
s-net	166	udp	Sirius Systems
namp	167	tcp	NAMP
namp	167	udp	NAMP
rsvd	168	tcp	RSVD
rsvd	168	udp	RSVD
send	169	tcp	SEND
send	169	udp	SEND
print-srv	170	tcp	Network PostScript
print-srv	170	udp	Network PostScript
multiplex	171	tcp	Network Innovations Multiplex
multiplex	171	udp	Network Innovations Multiplex
cl/1	172	tcp	Network Innovations CL/1
cl/1	172	udp	Network Innovations CL/1
xyplex-mux	173	tcp	Xyplex
xyplex-mux	173	udp	Xyplex
mailq	174	tcp	MAILQ
mailq	174	udp	MAILQ
vmnet	175	tcp	VMNET
vmnet	175	udp	VMNET
genrad-mux	176	tcp	GENRAD-MUX
genrad-mux	176	udp	GENRAD-MUX
xdmcp	177	tcp	X Display Manager Control Protocol
xdmcp	177	udp	X Display Manager Control Protocol
nextstep	178	tcp	NextStep Window Server
nextstep	178	udp	NextStep Window Server

Service Port Numbers

continues

Table B.1. Continued.

Service	Port	Protocol	Description
bgp	179	tcp	Border Gateway Protocol
bgp	179	udp	Border Gateway Protocol
ris	180	tcp	Intergraph
ris	180	udp	Intergraph
unify	181	tcp	Unify
unify	181	udp	Unify
audit	182	tcp	Unisys Audit SITP
audit	182	udp	Unisys Audit SITP
ocbinder	183	tcp	OCBinder
ocbinder	183	udp	OCBinder
ocserver	184	tcp	OCServer
ocserver	184	udp	OCServer
remote-kis	185	tcp	Remote-KIS
remote-kis	185	udp	Remote-KIS
kis	186	tcp	KIS Protocol
kis	186	udp	KIS Protocol
aci	187	tcp	Application Communication Interface
aci	187	udp	Application Communication Interface
mumps	188	tcp	Plus Five's MUMPS
mumps	188	udp	Plus Five's MUMPS
qft	189	tcp	Queued File Transport
qft	189	udp	Queued File Transport
gacp	190	tcp	Gateway Access Control Protocol
gacp	190	udp	Gateway Access Control Protocol
prospero	191	tcp	Prospero Directory Service
prospero	191	udp	Prospero Directory Service
osu-nms	192	tcp	OSU Network Monitoring System
osu-nms	192	udp	OSU Network Monitoring System

Service	Port	Protocol	Description
srmp	193	tcp	Spider Remote Monitoring Protocol
srmp	193	udp	Spider Remote Monitoring Protocol
irc	194	tcp	Internet Relay Chat Protocol
irc	194	udp	Internet Relay Chat Protocol
dn6-nlm-aud	195	tcp	DNSIX Network Level Module Audit
dn6-nlm-aud	195	udp	DNSIX Network Level Module Audit
dn6-smm-red	196	tcp	DNSIX Session Mgt Module Audit Redir
dn6-smm-red	196	udp	DNSIX Session Mgt Module Audit Redir
dls	197	tcp	Directory Location Service
dls	197	udp	Directory Location Service
dls-mon	198	tcp	Directory Location Service Monitor
dls-mon	198	udp	Directory Location Service Monitor
smux	199	tcp	SMUX
smux	199	udp	SMUX
src	200	tcp	IBM System Resource Controller
src	200	udp	IBM System Resource Controller
at-rtmp	201	tcp	AppleTalk Routing Maintenance
at-rtmp	201	udp	AppleTalk Routing Maintenance
at-nbp	202	tcp	AppleTalk Name Binding
at-nbp	202	udp	AppleTalk Name Binding
at-3	203	tcp	AppleTalk Unused
at-3	203	udp	AppleTalk Unused
at-echo	204	tcp	AppleTalk Echo
at-echo	204	udp	AppleTalk Echo
at-5	205	tcp	AppleTalk Unused
at-5	205	udp	AppleTalk Unused
at-zis	206	tcp	AppleTalk Zone Information
at-zis	206	udp	AppleTalk Zone Information

Service Port Numbers

continues

Table B.1. Continued.

Service	Port	Protocol	Description
at-7	207	tcp	AppleTalk Unused
at-7	207	udp	AppleTalk Unused
at-8	208	tcp	AppleTalk Unused
at-8	208	udp	AppleTalk Unused
tam	209	tcp	Trivial Authenticated Mail Protocol
tam	209	udp	Trivial Authenticated Mail Protocol
z39.50	210	tcp	ANSI Z39.50
z39.50	210	udp	ANSI Z39.50
914c/g	211	tcp	Texas Instruments 914C/G Terminal
914c/g	211	udp	Texas Instruments 914C/G Terminal
anet	212	tcp	ATEXSSTR
anet	212	udp	ATEXSSTR
ipx	213	tcp	IPX
ipx	213	udp	IPX
vmpwscs	214	tcp	VM PWSCS
vmpwscs	214	udp	VM PWSCS
softpc	215	tcp	Insignia Solutions
softpc	215	udp	Insignia Solutions
atls	216	tcp	Access Technology License Server
atls	216	udp	Access Technology License Server
dbase	217	tcp	dBASE UNIX
dbase	217	udp	dBASE UNIX
mpp	218	tcp	Netix Message Posting Protocol
mpp	218	udp	Netix Message Posting Protocol
uarps	219	tcp	Unisys ARPs
uarps	219	udp	Unisys ARPs
imap3	220	tcp	Interactive Mail Access Protocol v3
imap3	220	udp	Interactive Mail Access Protocol v3

Service	Port	Protocol	Description
fln-spx	221	tcp	Berkeley rlogind with SPX authority
fln-spx	221	udp	Berkeley rlogind with SPX authority
rsh-spx	222	tcp	Berkeley rshd with SPX authority
rsh-spx	222	udp	Berkeley rshd with SPX authority
cdc	223	tcp	Certificate Distribution Center
cdc	223	udp	Certificate Distribution Center
sur-meas	243	tcp	Survey Measurement
sur-meas	243	udp	Survey Measurement
link	245	tcp	LINK
link	245	udp	LINK
dsp3270	246	tcp	Display Systems Protocol
dsp3270	246	udp	Display Systems Protocol
pdap	344	tcp	Prospero Data Access Protocol
pdap	344	udp	Prospero Data Access Protocol
pawserv	345	tcp	Perf Analysis Workbench
pawserv	345	udp	Perf Analysis Workbench
zserv	346	tcp	Zebra server
zserv	346	udp	Zebra server
fatserv	347	tcp	Fatmen Server
fatserv	347	udp	Fatmen Server
csi-sgwp	348	tcp	Cabletron Management Protocol
csi-sgwp	348	udp	Cabletron Management Protocol
clearcase	371	tcp	Clearcase
clearcase	371	udp	Clearcase
ulistserv	372	tcp	UNIX Listserv
ulistserv	372	udp	UNIX Listserv
legent-1	373	tcp	Legent Corporation
legent-1	373	udp	Legent Corporation

Service Port Numbers

continues

Table B.1. Continued.

Service	Port	Protocol	Description
legent-2	374	tcp	Legent Corporation
legent-2	374	udp	Legent Corporation
hassle	375	tcp	Hassle
hassle	375	udp	Hassle
nip	376	tcp	Amiga Envoy Network Inquiry Protocol
nip	376	udp	Amiga Envoy Network Inquiry Protocol
tnETOS	377	tcp	NEC Corporation
tnETOS	377	udp	NEC Corporation
dsETOS	378	tcp	NEC Corporation
dsETOS	378	udp	NEC Corporation
is99c	379	tcp	TIA/EIA/IS-99 modem client
is99c	379	udp	TIA/EIA/IS-99 modem client
is99s	380	tcp	TIA/EIA/IS-99 modem server
is99s	380	udp	TIA/EIA/IS-99 modem server
hp-collector	381	tcp	HP performance data collector
hp-collector	381	udp	HP performance data collector
hp-managed-node	382	tcp	HP performance data managed node
hp-managed-node	382	udp	HP performance data managed node
hp-alarm-mgr	383	tcp	HP performance data alarm manager
hp-alarm-mgr	383	udp	HP performance data alarm manager
arns	384	tcp	A Remote Network Server system
arns	384	udp	A Remote Network Server system
ibm-app	385	tcp	IBM application
ibm-app	385	tcp	IBM application
asa	386	tcp	ASA Message Router Object Default
asa	386	udp	ASA Message Router Object Default
aurp	387	tcp	AppleTalk Update-Based Routing Protocol
aurp	387	udp	AppleTalk Update-Based Routing Protocol

Service	Port	Protocol	Description
unidata-ldm	388	tcp	Unidata LDM Version 4
unidata-ldm	388	udp	Unidata LDM Version 4
ldap	389	tcp	Lightweight Directory Access Protocol
ldap	389	udp	Lightweight Directory Access Protocol
uis	390	tcp	UIS
uis	390	udp	UIS
synotics-relay	391	tcp	SynOptics SNMP Relay Port
synotics-relay	391	udp	SynOptics SNMP Relay Port
synotics-broker	392	tcp	SynOptics Port Broker Port
synotics-broker	392	udp	SynOptics Port Broker Port
dis	393	tcp	Data Interpretation System
dis	393	udp	Data Interpretation System
embl-ndt	394	tcp	EMBL Nucleic Data Transfer
embl-ndt	394	udp	EMBL Nucleic Data Transfer
netcp	395	tcp	NETscout Control Protocol
netcp	395	udp	NETscout Control Protocol
netware-ip	396	tcp	Novell NetWare over IP
netware-ip	396	udp	Novell NetWare over IP
mptn	397	tcp	Multi Protocol Transport Network
mptn	397	udp	Multi Protocol Transport Network
kryptolan	398	tcp	Kryptolan
kryptolan	398	udp	Kryptolan
work-sol	400	tcp	Workstation Solutions
work-sol	400	udp	Workstation Solutions
ups	401	tcp	Uninterruptible Power Supply
ups	401	udp	Uninterruptible Power Supply
genie	402	tcp	Genie Protocol
genie	402	udp	Genie Protocol

Service Port Numbers

continues

Table B.1. Continued.

Service	Port	Protocol	Description
decap	403	tcp	decap
decap	403	udp	decap
nced	404	tcp	nced
nced	404	udp	nced
ncld	405	tcp	ncld
ncld	405	udp	ncld
imsp	406	tcp	Interactive Mail Support Protocol
imsp	406	udp	Interactive Mail Support Protocol
timbuktu	407	tcp	Timbuktu
timbuktu	407	udp	Timbuktu
prm-sm	408	tcp	Prospero Resource Manager System Manager
prm-sm	408	udp	Prospero Resource Manager System Manager
prm-nm	409	tcp	Prospero Resource Manager Node Manager
prm-nm	409	udp	Prospero Resource Manager Node Manager
decladebug	410	tcp	DECLadebug Remote Debug Protocol
decladebug	410	udp	DECLadebug Remote Debug Protocol
rmt	411	tcp	Remote MT Protocol
rmt	411	udp	Remote MT Protocol
synoptics-trap	412	tcp	Trap Convention Port
synoptics-trap	412	udp	Trap Convention Port
smsp	413	tcp	SMSP
smsp	413	udp	SMSP
infoseek	414	tcp	InfoSeek
infoseek	414	udp	InfoSeek
bnet	415	tcp	BNet
bnet	415	udp	BNet
silverplatter	416	tcp	Silverplatter
silverplatter	416	udp	Silverplatter

Service	Port	Protocol	Description
onmux	417	tcp	Onmux
onmux	417	udp	Onmux
hyper-g	418	tcp	Hyper-G
hyper-g	418	udp	Hyper-G
ariel1	419	tcp	Ariel
ariel1	419	udp	Ariel
smpte	420	tcp	SMPTE
smpte	420	udp	SMPTE
ariel2	421	tcp	Ariel
ariel2	421	udp	Ariel
ariel3	422	tcp	Ariel
ariel3	422	udp	Ariel
opc-job-start	423	tcp	IBM Operations Planning and Control Start
opc-job-start	423	udp	IBM Operations Planning and Control Start
opc-job-track	424	tcp	IBM Operations Planning and Control Track
opc-job-track	424	udp	IBM Operations Planning and Control Track
icad-el	425	tcp	ICAD
icad-el	425	udp	ICAD
smartsdp	426	tcp	smartsdp
smartsdp	426	udp	smartsdp
svrloc	427	tcp	Server Location
svrloc	427	udp	Server Location
ocs_cmu	428	tcp	OCS_CMU
ocs_cmu	428	udp	OCS_CMU
ocs_amu	429	tcp	OCS_AMU
ocs_amu	429	udp	OCS_AMU
utmpsd	430	tcp	UTMPSD
utmpsd	430	udp	UTMPSD

Service Port Numbers

continues

Table B.1. Continued.

Service	Port	Protocol	Description
utmpcd	431	tcp	UTMPCD
utmpcd	431	udp	UTMPCD
iasd	432	tcp	IASD
iasd	432	udp	IASD
nnsp	433	tcp	NNSP
nnsp	433	udp	NNSP
mobileip-agent	434	tcp	MobileIP-Agent
mobileip-agent	434	udp	MobileIP-Agent
mobilip-mn	435	tcp	MobilIP-MN
mobilip-mn	435	udp	MobilIP-MN
dna-cml	436	tcp	DNA-CML
dna-cml	436	udp	DNA-CML
comscm	437	tcp	comscm
comscm	437	udp	comscm
dsfgw	438	tcp	dsfgw
dsfgw	438	udp	dsfgw
dasp	439	tcp	dasp
dasp	439	udp	dasp
sgcp	440	tcp	sgcp
sgcp	440	udp	sgcp
decvms-sysmgt	441	tcp	decvms-sysmgt
decvms-sysmgt	441	udp	decvms-sysmgt
cvc_hostd	442	tcp	cvc_hostd
cvc_hostd	442	udp	cvc_hostd
https	443	tcp	https MCom
https	443	udp	https MCom
snpp	444	tcp	Simple Network Paging Protocol
snpp	444	udp	Simple Network Paging Protocol

Service	Port	Protocol	Description
microsoft-ds	445	tcp	Microsoft–DS
microsoft-ds	445	udp	Microsoft–DS
ddm-rdb	446	tcp	DDM–RDB
ddm-rdb	446	udp	DDM–RDB
ddm-dfm	447	tcp	DDM–RFM
ddm-dfm	447	udp	DDM–RFM
ddm-byte	448	tcp	DDM–BYTE
ddm-byte	448	udp	DDM–BYTE
as-servermap	449	tcp	AS Server Mapper
as-servermap	449	udp	AS Server Mapper
tserver	450	tcp	TServer
tserver	450	udp	TServer
exec	512	tcp	Remote process execution
biff	512	udp	Used to notify users of new mail
login	513	tcp	Remote login a la Telnet
who	513	udp	Who's logged on to a machine
cmd	514	tcp	Like exec, with automatic authentication
syslog	514	udp	
printer	515	tcp	spooler
printer	515	udp	spooler
talk	517	tcp	Like tenex link, but across machine
talk	517	udp	Like tenex link, but across machine
ntalk	518	tcp	
ntalk	518	udp	
utime	519	tcp	UNIX time
utime	519	udp	UNIX time
efs	520	tcp	Extended filename server
router	520	udp	Variant of Xerox NS

Service Port Numbers

continues

Table B.1. Continued.

Service	Port	Protocol	Description
timed	525	tcp	timeserver
timed	525	udp	timeserver
tempo	526	tcp	newdate
tempo	526	udp	newdate
courier	530	tcp	rpc
courier	530	udp	rpc
conference	531	tcp	chat
conference	531	udp	chat
netnews	532	tcp	readnews
netnews	532	udp	readnews
netwall	533	tcp	For emergency broadcasts
netwall	533	udp	For emergency broadcasts
apertus-ldp	539	tcp	Apertus Technologies Load Determination
apertus-ldp	539	udp	Apertus Technologies Load Determination
uucp	540	tcp	uucpd
uucp	540	udp	uucpd
uucp-rlogin	541	tcp	uucp-rlogin
uucp-rlogin	541	udp	uucp-rlogin
klogin	543	tcp	
klogin	543	udp	
kshell	544	tcp	krcmd
kshell	544	udp	krcmd
new-rwho	550	tcp	new-who
new-rwho	550	udp	new-who
dsf	555	tcp	
dsf	555	udp	
remotefs	556	tcp	rfs server
remotefs	556	udp	rfs server

Service	Port	Protocol	Description
rmonitor	560	tcp	rmonitord
rmonitor	560	udp	rmonitord
monitor	561	tcp	
monitor	561	udp	
chshell	562	tcp	chcmd
chshell	562	udp	chcmd
9pfs	564	tcp	plan 9 file service
9pfs	564	udp	plan 9 file service
whoami	565	tcp	whoami
whoami	565	udp	whoami
meter	570	tcp	demon
meter	570	udp	demon
meter	571	tcp	udemon
meter	571	udp	udemon
ipcserver	600	tcp	Sun IPC server
ipcserver	600	udp	Sun IPC server
nqs	607	tcp	nqs
nqs	607	udp	nqs
urm	606	tcp	Cray Unified Resource Manager
urm	606	udp	Cray Unified Resource Manager
sift-uft	608	tcp	Sender-Initiated/Unsolicited File Transfer
sift-uft	608	udp	Sender-Initiated/Unsolicited File Transfer
npmp-trap	609	tcp	npmp-trap
npmp-trap	609	udp	npmp-trap
npmp-local	610	tcp	npmp-local
npmp-local	610	udp	npmp-local
npmp-gui	611	tcp	npmp-gui
npmp-gui	611	udp	npmp-gui

Service Port Numbers

continues

Table B.1. Continued.

Service	Port	Protocol	Description
ginad	634	tcp	ginad
ginad	634	udp	ginad
mdqs	666	tcp	
mdqs	666	udp	
doom	666	tcp	DOOM ID software
doom	666	tcp	DOOM ID software
elcsd	704	tcp	errlog copy/server daemon
elcsd	704	udp	errlog copy/server daemon
entrustmanager	709	tcp	EntrustManager
entrustmanager	709	udp	EntrustManager
netviewdm1	729	tcp	IBM NetView DM/6000 server/client
netviewdm1	729	udp	IBM NetView DM/6000 server/client
netviewdm2	730	tcp	IBM NetView DM/6000 send/tcp
netviewdm2	730	udp	IBM NetView DM/6000 send/tcp
netviewdm3	731	tcp	IBM NetView DM/6000 receive/tcp
netviewdm3	731	udp	IBM NetView DM/6000 receive/tcp
netgw	741	tcp	netGW
netgw	741	udp	netGW
netrcs	742	tcp	Network-based Revision Control System
netrcs	742	udp	Network-based Revision Control System
flexlm	744	tcp	Flexible License Manager
flexlm	744	udp	Flexible License Manager
fujitsu-dev	747	tcp	Fujitsu Device Control
fujitsu-dev	747	udp	Fujitsu Device Control
ris-cm	748	tcp	Russell Info Sci Calendar Manager
ris-cm	748	udp	Russell Info Sci Calendar Manager
kerberos-adm	749	tcp	kerberos administration
kerberos-adm	749	udp	kerberos administration

Service	Port	Protocol	Description
rfile	750	tcp	
loadav	750	udp	
pump	751	tcp	
pump	751	udp	
qrh	752	tcp	
qrh	752	udp	
rrh	753	tcp	
rrh	753	udp	
tell	754	tcp	send
tell	754	udp	send
nlogin	758	tcp	
nlogin	758	udp	
con	759	tcp	
con	759	udp	
ns	760	tcp	
ns	760	udp	
rxe	761	tcp	
rxe	761	udp	
quotad	762	tcp	
quotad	762	udp	
cycleserv	763	tcp	
cycleserv	763	udp	
omserv	764	tcp	
omserv	764	udp	
webster	765	tcp	
webster	765	udp	
phonebook	767	tcp	phone
phonebook	767	udp	phone

continues

Table B.1. Continued.

Service	Port	Protocol	Description
vid	769	tcp	
vid	769	udp	
cadlock	770	tcp	
cadlock	770	udp	
rtip	771	tcp	
rtip	771	udp	
cycleserv2	772	tcp	
cycleserv2	772	udp	
submit	773	tcp	
notify	773	udp	
rpasswd	774	tcp	
acmaint_dbd	774	udp	
entomb	775	tcp	
acmaint_transd	775	udp	
wpages	776	tcp	
wpages	776	udp	
wpgs	780	tcp	
wpgs	780	udp	
concert	786	tcp	Concert
concert	786	udp	Concert
mdbs_daemon	800	tcp	
mdbs_daemon	800	udp	
device	801	tcp	
device	801	udp	
xtreelic	996	tcp	Central Point Software
xtreelic	996	udp	Central Point Software
maitrd	997	tcp	
maitrd	997	udp	

Service	Port	Protocol	Description
busboy	998	tcp	
puparp	998	udp	
garcon	999	tcp	
applix	999	udp	Applix ac
puprouter	999	tcp	
puprouter	999	udp	
cadlock	1000	tcp	
ock	1000	udp	
	1023	tcp	Reserved
	1023	udp	Reserved
	1024	tcp	Reserved
	1024	udp	Reserved
blackjack	1025	tcp	network blackjack
blackjack	1025	udp	network blackjack
iad1	1030	tcp	BBN IAD
iad1	1030	udp	BBN IAD
iad2	1031	tcp	BBN IAD
iad2	1031	udp	BBN IAD
iad3	1032	tcp	BBN IAD
iad3	1032	udp	BBN IAD
instl_boots	1067	tcp	Installation Bootstrap Protocol Server
instl_boots	1067	udp	Installation Bootstrap Protocol Server
instl_bootc	1068	tcp	Installation Bootstrap Protocol Client
instl_bootc	1068	udp	Installation Bootstrap Protocol Client
socks	1080	tcp	Socks
socks	1080	udp	Socks
ansoft-lm-1	1083	tcp	Anasoft License Manager
ansoft-lm-1	1083	udp	Anasoft License Manager

Service Port Numbers

continues

Table B.1. Continued.

Service	Port	Protocol	Description
ansoft-lm-2	1084	tcp	Anasoft License Manager
ansoft-lm-2	1084	udp	Anasoft License Manager
nfa	1155	tcp	Network File Access
nfa	1155	udp	Network File Access
nerv	1222	tcp	SNI R&D network
nerv	1222	udp	SNI R&D network
hermes	1248	tcp	
hermes	1248	udp	
alta-ana-lm	1346	tcp	Alta Analytics License Manager
alta-ana-lm	1346	udp	Alta Analytics License Manager
bbn-mmc	1347	tcp	Multimedia conferencing
bbn-mmc	1347	udp	Multimedia conferencing
bbn-mmx	1348	tcp	Multimedia conferencing
bbn-mmx	1348	udp	Multimedia conferencing
sbook	1349	tcp	Registration Network Protocol
sbook	1349	udp	Registration Network Protocol
editbench	1350	tcp	Registration Network Protocol
editbench	1350	udp	Registration Network Protocol
equationbuilder	1351	tcp	Digital Tool Works (MIT)
equationbuilder	1351	udp	Digital Tool Works (MIT)
lotusnote	1352	tcp	Lotus Note
lotusnote	1352	udp	Lotus Note
relief	1353	tcp	Relief Consulting
relief	1353	udp	Relief Consulting
rightbrain	1354	tcp	RightBrain Software
rightbrain	1354	udp	RightBrain Software
intuitive edge	1355	tcp	Intuitive Edge
intuitive edge	1355	udp	Intuitive Edge

Service	Port	Protocol	Description
cuillamartin	1356	tcp	CuillaMartin Company
cuillamartin	1356	udp	CuillaMartin Company
pegboard	1357	tcp	Electronic PegBoard
pegboard	1357	udp	Electronic PegBoard
connlcli	1358	tcp	CONNLCLI
connlcli	1358	udp	CONNLCLI
ftsrv	1359	tcp	FTSRV
ftsrv	1359	udp	FTSRV
mimer	1360	tcp	MIMER
mimer	1360	udp	MIMER
linx	1361	tcp	LinX
linx	1361	udp	LinX
timeflies	1362	tcp	TimeFlies
timeflies	1362	udp	TimeFlies
ndm-requester	1363	tcp	Network DataMover Requester
ndm-requester	1363	udp	Network DataMover Requester
ndm-server	1364	tcp	Network DataMover Server
ndm-server	1364	udp	Network DataMover Server
adapt-sna	1365	tcp	Network Software Associates
adapt-sna	1365	udp	Network Software Associates
netware-csp	1366	tcp	Novell NetWare Comm Service Platform
netware-csp	1366	udp	Novell NetWare Comm Service Platform
dcs	1367	tcp	DCS
dcs	1367	udp	DCS
screencast	1368	tcp	ScreenCast
screencast	1368	udp	ScreenCast
gv-us	1369	tcp	GlobalView to UNIX Shell
gv-us	1369	udp	GlobalView to UNIX Shell

Service Port Numbers

continues

Table B.1. Continued.

Service	Port	Protocol	Description
us-gv	1370	tcp	UNIX Shell to GlobalView
us-gv	1370	udp	UNIX Shell to GlobalView
fc-cli	1371	tcp	Fujitsu Config Protocol
fc-cli	1371	udp	Fujitsu Config Protocol
fc-ser	1372	tcp	Fujitsu Config Protocol
fc-ser	1372	udp	Fujitsu Config Protocol
chromagrafx	1373	tcp	Chromagrafx
chromagrafx	1373	udp	Chromagrafx
molly	1374	tcp	EPI Software Systems
molly	1374	udp	EPI Software Systems
bytex	1375	tcp	Bytex
bytex	1375	udp	Bytex
ibm-pps	1376	tcp	IBM Person-to-Person Software
ibm-pps	1376	udp	IBM Person-to-Person Software
cichlid	1377	tcp	Cichlid License Manager
cichlid	1377	udp	Cichlid License Manager
elan	1378	tcp	Elan License Manager
elan	1378	udp	Elan License Manager
dbreporter	1379	tcp	Integrity Solutions
dbreporter	1379	udp	Integrity Solutions
telesis-licman	1380	tcp	Telesis Network License Manager
telesis-licman	1380	udp	Telesis Network License Manager
apple-licman	1381	tcp	Apple Network License Manager
apple-licman	1381	udp	Apple Network License Manager
udt_os	1382	tcp	
udt_os	1382	udp	
gwha	1383	tcp	GW Hannaway Network License Manager
gwha	1383	udp	GW Hannaway Network License Manager

Service	Port	Protocol	Description
os-licman	1384	tcp	Objective Solutions License Manager
os-licman	1384	udp	Objective Solutions License Manager
atex_elmd	1385	tcp	Atex Publishing License Manager
atex_elmd	1385	udp	Atex Publishing License Manager
checksum	1386	tcp	CheckSum License Manager
checksum	1386	udp	CheckSum License Manager
cadsi-lm	1387	tcp	Computer Aided Design Software Inc License Manager
cadsi-lm	1387	udp	Computer Aided Design Software Inc License Manager
objective-dbc	1388	tcp	Objective Solutions Database Cache
objective-dbc	1388	udp	Objective Solutions Database Cache
iclpv-dm	1389	tcp	Document Manager
iclpv-dm	1389	udp	Document Manager
iclpv-sc	1390	tcp	Storage Controller
iclpv-sc	1390	udp	Storage Controller
iclpv-sas	1391	tcp	Storage Access Server
iclpv-sas	1391	udp	Storage Access Server
iclpv-pm	1392	tcp	Print Manager
iclpv-pm	1392	udp	Print Manager
iclpv-nls	1393	tcp	Network Log Server
iclpv-nls	1393	udp	Network Log Server
iclpv-nlc	1394	tcp	Network Log Client
iclpv-nlc	1394	udp	Network Log Client
iclpv-wsm	1395	tcp	PC Workstation Manager software
iclpv-wsm	1395	udp	PC Workstation Manager software
dvl-activemail	1396	tcp	DVL Active Mail
dvl-activemail	1396	udp	DVL Active Mail
audio-activmail	1397	tcp	Audio Active Mail

continues

Service Port Numbers

Table B.1. Continued.

Service	Port	Protocol	Description
audio-activmail	1397	udp	Audio Active Mail
video-activmail	1398	tcp	Video Active Mail
video-activmail	1398	udp	Video Active Mail
cadkey-licman	1399	tcp	Cadkey License Manager
cadkey-licman	1399	udp	Cadkey License Manager
cadkey-tablet	1400	tcp	Cadkey Tablet Daemon
cadkey-tablet	1400	udp	Cadkey Tablet Daemon
goldleaf-licman	1401	tcp	Goldleaf License Manager
goldleaf-licman	1401	udp	Goldleaf License Manager
prm-sm-np	1402	tcp	Prospero Resource Manager
prm-sm-np	1402	udp	Prospero Resource Manager
prm-nm-np	1403	tcp	Prospero Resource Manager
prm-nm-np	1403	udp	Prospero Resource Manager
igi-lm	1404	tcp	Infinite Graphics License Manager
igi-lm	1404	udp	Infinite Graphics License Manager
ibm-res	1405	tcp	IBM Remote Execution Starter
ibm-res	1405	udp	IBM Remote Execution Starter
netlabs-lm	1406	tcp	NetLabs License Manager
netlabs-lm	1406	udp	NetLabs License Manager
dbsa-lm	1407	tcp	DBSA License Manager
dbsa-lm	1407	udp	DBSA License Manager
sophia-lm	1408	tcp	Sophia License Manager
sophia-lm	1408	udp	Sophia License Manager
here-lm	1409	tcp	Here License Manager
here-lm	1409	udp	Here License Manager
hiq	1410	tcp	HiQ License Manager
hiq	1410	udp	HiQ License Manager
af	1411	tcp	AudioFile

Service	Port	Protocol	Description
af	1411	udp	AudioFile
innosys	1412	tcp	InnoSys
innosys	1412	udp	InnoSys
innosys-acl	1413	tcp	InnoSys-ACL
innosys-acl	1413	udp	InnoSys-ACL
ibm-mqseries	1414	tcp	IBM MQSeries
ibm-mqseries	1414	udp	IBM MQSeries
dbstar	1415	tcp	DBStar
dbstar	1415	udp	DBStar
novell-lu6.2	1416	tcp	Novell LU6.2
novell-lu6.2	1416	udp	Novell LU6.2
timbuktu-srv1	1417	tcp	Timbuktu Service 1 Port
timbuktu-srv1	1417	tcp	Timbuktu Service 1 Port
timbuktu-srv2	1418	tcp	Timbuktu Service 2 Port
timbuktu-srv2	1418	udp	Timbuktu Service 2 Port
timbuktu-srv3	1419	tcp	Timbuktu Service 3 Port
timbuktu-srv3	1419	udp	Timbuktu Service 3 Port
timbuktu-srv4	1420	tcp	Timbuktu Service 4 Port
timbuktu-srv4	1420	udp	Timbuktu Service 4 Port
gandalf-lm	1421	tcp	Gandalf License Manager
gandalf-lm	1421	udp	Gandalf License Manager
autodesk-lm	1422	tcp	Autodesk License Manager
autodesk-lm	1422	udp	Autodesk License Manager
essbase	1423	tcp	Essbase Arbor Software
essbase	1423	udp	Essbase Arbor Software
hybrid	1424	tcp	Hybrid Encryption Protocol
hybrid	1424	udp	Hybrid Encryption Protocol
zion-lm	1425	tcp	Zion Software License Manager

Service Port Numbers

continues

Table B.1. Continued.

Service	Port	Protocol	Description
zion-lm	1425	udp	Zion Software License Manager
sas-1	1426	tcp	Satellite-data Acquisition System 1
sas-1	1426	udp	Satellite-data Acquisition System 1
mloadd	1427	tcp	mloadd monitoring tool
mloadd	1427	udp	mloadd monitoring tool
informatik-lm	1428	tcp	Informatik License Manager
informatik-lm	1428	udp	Informatik License Manager
nms	1429	tcp	Hypercom NMS
nms	1429	udp	Hypercom NMS
tpdu	1430	tcp	Hypercom TPDU
tpdu	1430	udp	Hypercom TPDU
rgtp	1431	tcp	Reverse Gosip Transport
rgtp	1431	udp	Reverse Gosip Transport
blueberry-lm	1432	tcp	Blueberry Software License Manager
blueberry-lm	1432	udp	Blueberry Software License Manager
ms-sql-s	1433	tcp	Microsoft SQL Server
ms-sql-s	1433	udp	Microsoft SQL Server
ms-sql-m	1434	tcp	Microsoft SQL Monitor
ms-sql-m	1434	udp	Microsoft SQL Monitor
ibm-cics	1435	tcp	IBM CISC
ibm-cics	1435	udp	IBM CISC
sas-2	1436	tcp	Satellite-data Acquisition System 2
sas-2	1436	udp	Satellite-data Acquisition System 2
tabula	1437	tcp	Tabula
tabula	1437	udp	Tabula
eicon-server	1438	tcp	Eicon Security Agent/Server
eicon-server	1438	udp	Eicon Security Agent/Server
eicon-x25	1439	tcp	Eicon X25/SNA Gateway

Service	Port	Protocol	Description
eicon-x25	1439	udp	Eicon X25/SNA Gateway
eicon-slp	1440	tcp	Eicon Service Location Protocol
eicon-slp	1440	udp	Eicon Service Location Protocol
cadis-1	1441	tcp	Cadis License Management
cadis-1	1441	udp	Cadis License Management
cadis-2	1442	tcp	Cadis License Management
cadis-2	1442	udp	Cadis License Management
ies-lm	1443	tcp	Integrated Engineering Software
ies-lm	1443	udp	Integrated Engineering Software
marcam-lm	1444	tcp	Marcam License Management
marcam-lm	1444	udp	Marcam License Management
proxima-lm	1445	tcp	Proxima License Manager
proxima-lm	1445	udp	Proxima License Manager
ora-lm	1446	tcp	Optical Research Associates License Manager
ora-lm	1446	udp	Optical Research Associates License Manager
apri-lm	1447	tcp	Applied Parallel Research LM
apri-lm	1447	udp	Applied Parallel Research LM
oc-lm	1448	tcp	OpenConnect License Manager
oc-lm	1448	udp	OpenConnect License Manager
peport	1449	tcp	PEport
peport	1449	udp	PEport
dwf	1450	tcp	Tandem Distributed Workbench Facility
dwf	1450	udp	Tandem Distributed Workbench Facility
infoman	1451	tcp	IBM Information Management
infoman	1451	udp	IBM Information Management
gtegsc-lm	1452	tcp	GTE Government Systems License Manager
gtegsc-lm	1452	udp	GTE Government Systems License Manager
genie-lm	1453	tcp	Genie License Manager

Service Port Numbers

continues

Table B.1. Continued.

Service	Port	Protocol	Description
genie-lm	1453	udp	Genie License Manager
interhdl_elmd	1454	tcp	interHDL License Manager
interhdl_elmd	1454	tcp	interHDL License Manager
esl-lm	1455	tcp	ESL License Manager
esl-lm	1455	udp	ESL License Manager
dca	1456	tcp	DCA
dca	1456	udp	DCA
valisys-lm	1457	tcp	Valisys License Manager
valisys-lm	1457	udp	Valisys License Manager
nrcabq-lm	1458	tcp	Nichols Research Corporation
nrcabq-lm	1458	udp	Nichols Research Corporation
proshare1	1459	tcp	Proshare Notebook Application
proshare1	1459	udp	Proshare Notebook Application
proshare2	1460	tcp	Proshare Notebook Application
proshare2	1460	udp	Proshare Notebook Application
ibm_wrless_lan	1461	tcp	IBM Wireless LAN
ibm_wrless_lan	1461	udp	IBM Wireless LAN
world-lm	1462	tcp	World License Manager
world-lm	1462	udp	World License Manager
nucleus	1463	tcp	Nucleus
nucleus	1463	udp	Nucleus
msl_lmd	1464	tcp	MSL License Manager
msl_lmd	1464	udp	MSL License Manager
pipes	1465	tcp	Pipes Platform
pipes	1465	udp	Pipes Platform mfarlin@peerlogic.com
oceansoft-lm	1466	tcp	Ocean Software License Manager
oceansoft-lm	1466	udp	Ocean Software License Manager
csdmbase	1467	tcp	CSDMBASE

Service	Port	Protocol	Description
csdmbase	1467	udp	CSDMBASE
csdm	1468	tcp	CSDM
csdm	1468	udp	CSDM
aal-lm	1469	tcp	Active Analysis Limited License Manager
aal-lm	1469	udp	Active Analysis Limited License Manager
uaiact	1470	tcp	Universal Analytics
uaiact	1470	udp	Universal Analytics
csdmbase	1471	tcp	csdmbase
csdmbase	1471	udp	csdmbase
csdm	1472	tcp	csdm
csdm	1472	udp	csdm
openmath	1473	tcp	OpenMath
openmath	1473	udp	OpenMath
telefinder	1474	tcp	Telefinder
telefinder	1474	udp	Telefinder
taligent-lm	1475	tcp	Taligent License Manager
taligent-lm	1475	udp	Taligent License Manager
clvm-cfg	1476	tcp	clvm-cfg
clvm-cfg	1476	udp	clvm-cfg
ms-sna-server	1477	tcp	ms-sna-server
ms-sna-server	1477	udp	ms-sna-server
ms-sna-base	1478	tcp	ms-sna-base
ms-sna-base	1478	udp	ms-sna-base
dberegister	1479	tcp	dberegister
dberegister	1479	udp	dberegister
pacerforum	1480	tcp	PacerForum
pacerforum	1480	udp	PacerForum
airs	1481	tcp	AIRS

Service Port Numbers

continues

Table B.1. Continued.

Service	Port	Protocol	Description
airs	1481	udp	AIRS
miteksys-lm	1482	tcp	Miteksys License Manager
miteksys-lm	1482	udp	Miteksys License Manager
afs	1483	tcp	AFS License Manager
afs	1483	udp	AFS License Manager
confluent	1484	tcp	Confluent License Manager
confluent	1484	udp	Confluent License Manager
lansource	1485	tcp	LANSource
lansource	1485	udp	LANSource
nms_topo_serv	1486	tcp	nms_topo_serv
nms_topo_serv	1486	udp	nms_topo_serv
localinfosrvr	1487	tcp	LocalInfoSrvr
localinfosrvr	1487	udp	LocalInfoSrvr
docstor	1488	tcp	DocStor
docstor	1488	udp	DocStor
dmdocbroker	1489	tcp	dmdocbroker
dmdocbroker	1489	udp	dmdocbroker
insitu-conf	1490	tcp	insitu–conf
insitu-conf	1490	udp	insitu–conf
anynetgateway	1491	tcp	anynetgateway
anynetgateway	1491	udp	anynetgateway
stone-design-1	1492	tcp	stone–design–1
stone-design-1	1492	udp	stone–design–1
netmap_lm	1493	tcp	netmap_lm
netmap_lm	1493	udp	netmap_lm
ica	1494	tcp	ica
ica	1494	udp	ica
cvc	1495	tcp	cvc

Service	Port	Protocol	Description
cvc	1495	udp	cvc
liberty-lm	1496	tcp	liberty-lm
liberty-lm	1496	udp	liberty-lm
rfx-lm	1497	tcp	rfx-lm
rfx-lm	1497	udp	rfx-lm
watcom-sql	1498	tcp	Watcom-SQL
watcom-sql	1498	udp	Watcom-SQL
fhc	1499	tcp	Federico Heinz Consultora
fhc	1499	udp	Federico Heinz Consultora
vlsi-lm	1500	tcp	VLSI License Manager
vlsi-lm	1500	udp	VLSI License Manager
sas-3	1501	tcp	Satellite-data Acquisition System 3
sas-3	1501	udp	Satellite-data Acquisition System 3
shivadiscovery	1502	tcp	Shiva
shivadiscovery	1502	udp	Shiva
imtc-mcs	1503	tcp	Databeam
imtc-mcs	1503	udp	Databeam
evb-elm	1504	tcp	EVB Software Engineering License Manager
evb-elm	1504	udp	EVB Software Engineering License Manager
funkproxy	1505	tcp	Funk Software, Inc.
funkproxy	1505	udp	Funk Software, Inc.
ingreslock	1524	tcp	ingres
ingreslock	1524	udp	ingres
orasrv	1525	tcp	Oracle
orasrv	1525	udp	Oracle
prospero-np	1525	tcp	Prospero Directory Service non-priv
prospero-np	1525	udp	Prospero Directory Service non-priv
pdap-np	1526	tcp	Prospero Data Access Protocol non-priv

Service Port Numbers

continues

Table B.1. Continued.

Service	Port	Protocol	Description
pdap-np	1526	udp	Prospero Data Access Protocol non-priv
tlisrv	1527	tcp	Oracle
tlisrv	1527	udp	Oracle
coauthor	1529	tcp	Oracle
coauthor	1529	udp	Oracle
issd	1600	tcp	
issd	1600	udp	
nkd	1650	tcp	
nkd	1650	udp	
proshareaudio	1651	tcp	Proshare conf audio
proshareaudio	1651	udp	Proshare conf audio
prosharevideo	1652	tcp	Proshare conf video
prosharevideo	1652	udp	Proshare conf video
prosharedata	1653	tcp	Proshare conf data
prosharedata	1653	udp	Proshare conf data
prosharerequest	1654	tcp	Proshare conf request
prosharerequest	1654	udp	Proshare conf request
prosharenotify	1655	tcp	Proshare conf notify
prosharenotify	1655	udp	Proshare conf notify
netview-aix-1	1661	tcp	netview-aix-1
netview-aix-1	1661	udp	netview-aix-1
netview-aix-2	1662	tcp	netview-aix-2
netview-aix-2	1662	udp	netview-aix-2
netview-aix-3	1663	tcp	netview-aix-3
netview-aix-3	1663	udp	netview-aix-3
netview-aix-4	1664	tcp	netview-aix-4
netview-aix-4	1664	udp	netview-aix-4
netview-aix-5	1665	tcp	netview-aix-5

Service	Port	Protocol	Description
netview-aix-5	1665	udp	netview–aix–5
netview-aix-6	1666	tcp	netview–aix–6
netview-aix-6	1666	udp	netview–aix–6
licensedaemon	1986	tcp	Cisco license management
licensedaemon	1986	udp	Cisco license management
tr-rsrb-p1	1987	tcp	Cisco RSRB Priority 1 port
tr-rsrb-p1	1987	udp	Cisco RSRB Priority 1 port
tr-rsrb-p2	1988	tcp	Cisco RSRB Priority 2 port
tr-rsrb-p2	1988	udp	Cisco RSRB Priority 2 port
tr-rsrb-p3	1989	tcp	Cisco RSRB Priority 3 port
tr-rsrb-p3	1989	udp	Cisco RSRB Priority 3 port
mshnet	1989	tcp	MSHnet system
mshnet	1989	udp	MSHnet system
stun-p1	1990	tcp	Cisco STUN Priority 1 port
stun-p1	1990	udp	Cisco STUN Priority 1 port
stun-p2	1991	tcp	Cisco STUN Priority 2 port
stun-p2	1991	udp	Cisco STUN Priority 2 port
stun-p3	1992	tcp	Cisco STUN Priority 3 port
stun-p3	1992	udp	Cisco STUN Priority 3 port
ipsendmsg	1992	tcp	IPsendmsg
ipsendmsg	1992	udp	IPsendmsg
snmp-tcp-port	1993	tcp	Cisco SNMP TCP port
snmp-tcp-port	1993	udp	Cisco SNMP TCP port
stun-port	1994	tcp	Cisco serial tunnel port
stun-port	1994	udp	Cisco serial tunnel port
perf-port	1995	tcp	Cisco perf port
perf-port	1995	udp	Cisco perf port
tr-rsrb-port	1996	tcp	Cisco remote SRB port

Service Port Numbers

continues

Table B.1. Continued.

Service	Port	Protocol	Description
tr-rsrb-port	1996	udp	Cisco remote SRB port
gdp-port	1997	tcp	Cisco Gateway Discovery Protocol
gdp-port	1997	udp	Cisco Gateway Discovery Protocol
x25-svc-port	1998	tcp	Cisco X.25 service (XOT)
x25-svc-port	1998	udp	Cisco X.25 service (XOT)
tcp-id-port	1999	tcp	Cisco identification port
tcp-id-port	1999	udp	Cisco identification port
callbook	2000	tcp	
callbook	2000	udp	
dc	2001	tcp	
wizard	2001	udp	curry
globe	2002	tcp	
globe	2002	udp	
mailbox	2004	tcp	
emce	2004	udp	CCWS mm conf
berknet	2005	tcp	
oracle	2005	udp	
invokator	2006	tcp	
raid-cc	2006	udp	raid
dectalk	2007	tcp	
raid-am	2007	udp	
conf	2008	tcp	
terminaldb	2008	udp	
news	2009	tcp	
whosockami	2009	udp	
search	2010	tcp	
pipe_server	2010	udp	
raid-cc	2011	tcp	raid

Service	Port	Protocol	Description
servserv	2011	udp	
ttyinfo	2012	tcp	
raid-ac	2012	udp	
raid-am	2013	tcp	
raid-cd	2013	udp	
troff	2014	tcp	
raid-sf	2014	udp	
cypress	2015	tcp	
raid-cs	2015	udp	
bootserver	2016	tcp	
bootserver	2016	udp	
cypress-stat	2017	tcp	
bootclient	2017	udp	
terminaldb	2018	tcp	
rellpack	2018	udp	
whosockami	2019	tcp	
about	2019	udp	
xinupageserver	2020	tcp	
xinupageserver	2020	udp	
servexec	2021	tcp	
xinuexpansion1	2021	udp	
down	2022	tcp	
xinuexpansion2	2022	udp	
xinuexpansion3	2023	tcp	
xinuexpansion3	2023	udp	
xinuexpansion4	2024	tcp	
xinuexpansion4	2024	udp	
ellpack	2025	tcp	

Service Port Numbers

continues

Table B.1. Continued.

Service	Port	Protocol	Description
xribs	2025	udp	
scrabble	2026	tcp	
scrabble	2026	udp	
shadowserver	2027	tcp	
shadowserver	2027	udp	
submitserver	2028	tcp	
submitserver	2028	udp	
device2	2030	tcp	
device2	2030	udp	
blackboard	2032	tcp	
blackboard	2032	udp	
glogger	2033	tcp	
glogger	2033	udp	
scoremgr	2034	tcp	
scoremgr	2034	udp	
imsldoc	2035	tcp	
imsldoc	2035	udp	
objectmanager	2038	tcp	
objectmanager	2038	udp	
lam	2040	tcp	
lam	2040	udp	
interbase	2041	tcp	
interbase	2041	udp	
isis	2042	tcp	
isis	2042	udp	
isis-bcast	2043	tcp	
isis-bcast	2043	udp	
rimsl	2044	tcp	

Service	Port	Protocol	Description
rimsl	2044	udp	
cdfunc	2045	tcp	
cdfunc	2045	udp	
sdfunc	2046	tcp	
sdfunc	2046	udp	
dls	2047	tcp	
dls	2047	udp	
dls-monitor	2048	tcp	
dls-monitor	2048	udp	
shilp	2049	tcp	
shilp	2049	udp	
dlsrpn	2065	tcp	Data Link Switch Read Port Number
dlsrpn	2065	udp	Data Link Switch Read Port Number
dlswpn	2067	tcp	Data Link Switch Write Port Number
dlswpn	2067	udp	Data Link Switch Write Port Number
ats	2201	tcp	Advanced Training System Program
ats	2201	udp	Advanced Training System Program
rtsserv	2500	tcp	Resource Tracking system server
rtsserv	2500	udp	Resource Tracking system server
rtsclient	2501	tcp	Resource Tracking system client
rtsclient	2501	udp	Resource Tracking system client
hp-3000-telnet	2564	tcp	HP 3000 NS/VT block mode Telnet
www-dev	2784	tcp	World Wide Web—development
www-dev	2784	udp	World Wide Web—development
NSWS	3049	tcp	
NSWS	3049	udp	
ccmail	3264	tcp	cc:Mail/Lotus
ccmail	3264	udp	cc:Mail/Lotus

continues

Table B.1. Continued.

Service	Port	Protocol	Description
dec-notes	3333	tcp	DEC Notes
dec-notes	3333	udp	DEC Notes
mapper-nodemgr	3984	tcp	MAPPER network node manager
mapper-nodemgr	3984	udp	MAPPER network node manager
mapper-mapethd	3985	tcp	MAPPER TCP/IP server
mapper-mapethd	3985	udp	MAPPER TCP/IP server
mapper-ws_ethd	3986	tcp	MAPPER workstation server
mapper-ws_ethd	3986	udp	MAPPER workstation server
bmap	3421	tcp	Bull Apprise portmapper
bmap	3421	udp	Bull Apprise portmapper
udt_os	3900	tcp	Unidata UDT OS
udt_os	3900	udp	Unidata UDT OS
nuts_dem	4132	tcp	NUTS Daemon
nuts_dem	4132	udp	NUTS Daemon
nuts_bootp	4133	tcp	NUTS Bootp Server
nuts_bootp	4133	udp	NUTS Bootp Server
unicall	4343	tcp	UNICALL
unicall	4343	udp	UNICALL
krb524	4444	tcp	KRB524
krb524	4444	udp	KRB524
rfa	4672	tcp	Remote file access server
rfa	4672	udp	Remote file access server
commplex-main	5000	tcp	
commplex-main	5000	udp	
commplex-link	5001	tcp	
commplex-link	5001	udp	
rfe	5002	tcp	Radio free Ethernet
rfe	5002	udp	Radio free Ethernet

Service	Port	Protocol	Description
telelpathstart	5010	tcp	TelepathStart
telelpathstart	5010	udp	TelepathStart
telelpathattack	5011	tcp	TelepathAttack
telelpathattack	5011	udp	TelepathAttack
mmcc	5050	tcp	Multimedia conference control tool
mmcc	5050	udp	Multimedia conference control tool
rmonitor_secure	5145	tcp	
rmonitor_secure	5145	udp	
aol	5190	tcp	America Online
aol	5190	udp	America Online
padl2sim	5236	tcp	
padl2sim	5236	udp	
hacl-hb	5300	tcp	# HA cluster heartbeat
hacl-hb	5300	udp	# HA cluster heartbeat
hacl-gs	5301	tcp	# HA cluster general services
hacl-gs	5301	udp	# HA cluster general services
hacl-cfg	5302	tcp	# HA cluster configuration
hacl-cfg	5302	udp	# HA cluster configuration
hacl-probe	5303	tcp	# HA cluster probing
hacl-probe	5303	udp	# HA cluster probing
hacl-local	5304	tcp	
hacl-local	5304	udp	
hacl-test	5305	tcp	
hacl-test	5305	udp	
x11	6000-6063	tcp	X Window System
x11	6000-6063	udp	X Window System
sub-process	6111	tcp	HP SoftBench Sub-Process Control
sub-process	6111	udp	HP SoftBench Sub-Process Control

continues

Service Port Numbers

Table B.1. Continued.

Service	Port	Protocol	Description
meta-corp	6141	tcp	Meta Corporation License Manager
meta-corp	6141	udp	Meta Corporation License Manager
aspentec-lm	6142	tcp	Aspen Technology License Manager
aspentec-lm	6142	udp	Aspen Technology License Manager
watershed-lm	6143	tcp	Watershed License Manager
watershed-lm	6143	udp	Watershed License Manager
statsci1-lm	6144	tcp	StatSci License Manager—1
statsci1-lm	6144	udp	StatSci License Manager—1
statsci2-lm	6145	tcp	StatSci License Manager—2
statsci2-lm	6145	udp	StatSci License Manager—2
lonewolf-lm	6146	tcp	Lone Wolf Systems License Manager
lonewolf-lm	6146	udp	Lone Wolf Systems License Manager
montage-lm	6147	tcp	Montage License Manager
montage-lm	6147	udp	Montage License Manager
xdsxdm	6558	udp	
xdsxdm	6558	tcp	
afs3-fileserver	7000	tcp	File server itself
afs3-fileserver	7000	udp	File server itself
afs3-callback	7001	tcp	Callbacks to cache managers
afs3-callback	7001	udp	Callbacks to cache managers
afs3-prserver	7002	tcp	Users & groups database
afs3-prserver	7002	udp	Users & groups database
afs3-vlserver	7003	tcp	Volume location database
afs3-vlserver	7003	udp	Volume location database
afs3-kaserver	7004	tcp	AFS/Kerberos authentication service
afs3-kaserver	7004	udp	AFS/Kerberos authentication service
afs3-volser	7005	tcp	Volume management server
afs3-volser	7005	udp	Volume management server

Service	Port	Protocol	Description
afs3-errors	7006	tcp	Error interpretation service
afs3-errors	7006	udp	Error interpretation service
afs3-bos	7007	tcp	Basic overseer process
afs3-bos	7007	udp	Basic overseer process
afs3-update	7008	tcp	Server-to-server updater
afs3-update	7008	udp	Server-to-server updater
afs3-rmtsys	7009	tcp	Remote cache manager service
afs3-rmtsys	7009	udp	Remote cache manager service
ups-onlinet	7010	tcp	Onlinet uninterruptable power supplies
ups-onlinet	7010	udp	Onlinet uninterruptable power supplies
font-service	7100	tcp	X Font Service
font-service	7100	udp	X Font Service
fodms	7200	tcp	FODMS FLIP
fodms	7200	udp	FODMS FLIP
man	9535	tcp	
man	9535	udp	
isode-dua	17007	tcp	
isode-dua	17007	udp	

Appendix

C

Technical Glossary

by Christopher Fisher

!

10Base-2   Ethernet network standard that uses coaxial RG-58 A/U wiring (such as television cable). Also known as Thinnet or Cheapernet; it uses the bus topology. Cable is commonly attached to computers and equipment using metal twist on devices called BNC connectors. The *10* stands for 10Mbps, the *Base* means baseband, and the *2* denotes that the maximum length of a single cable run is 200 meters.

10Base-5   Ethernet network standard specified by the original Ethernet standards. This standard uses a thick 50-ohm coaxial cable and is sometimes referred to as Thickwire Ethernet. The *10* stands for 10Mbps, the *Base* means baseband, and the *5* denotes that the maximum length of a single cable run is 500 meters.

10Base-T   Ethernet local area network that uses twisted-pair wiring; this is currently the most common Ethernet implementation. 10Base-T networks are physically laid out in a star topology, where each piece of equipment on the network is connected to a central hub. The wiring is connected to devices using a plug that resembles a phone jack, called an RJ-45. The *10* stands for 10Mbps, the *Base* means baseband, and the *T* denotes that this standard uses twisted-pair cable.

100Base-T   The *100* stands for 100Mbps, the *Base* means baseband, and the *T* denotes that this standard uses twisted-pair cable. *See 10Base-T.*

100VG-AnyLan Ethernet   This is an AT&T– and Hewlett-Packard–designed approach to higher-speed networking. Like Fast Ethernet, it allows for a 100Mbps transfer rate; however, it can operate on lower grades of media from category 3 up, allowing it to interconnect with existing Ethernet networks.

802   This is IEEE's set of standards for local area network communications.

A

address mask   *See subnet mask.*

ADSL (Asymmetric Digital Subscriber Line)   A variation of Digital Subscriber Line, that is optimized for one-way data flow. Ideal for Internet connections where data volumes are much greater from server to client (for example, Web browsing).

ANSI (American National Standards Institute)   A private nonprofit membership organization that sets and develops U.S. standards in areas including computers and communications.

API (Application Program Interface)   The programming interface that is used to access operating system functions and other services.

AppleTalk   This is a proprietary local area network protocol for linking Macintosh computers and peripherals. There are two implementations: LocalTalk (230.4Kbps) and EtherTalk (10Mbps).

application layer   The seventh layer of the OSI data communication model that dictates how applications talk to the network.

ARCnet (Attached Resource Computer Network)   This is an early and, for quite some time, popular type of local area network. ARCnet had a large market share in the late 1980s as it was almost as fast and cheaper than Ethernet. Over the past several years it has lost all of its market share to Ethernet and Token Ring networks.

ARP (Address Resolution Protocol)   A protocol within the TCP/IP suite residing at the Internet layer. It enables a host Ethernet address to be found from its IP address. See RFC 826.

ARPANET (Advanced Research Projects Agency Network)   A Department of Defense wide area network that was operational in the late 1960s. Tying together systems in universities, governments, and businesses, it was used for networking research and was a central backbone for the development of the Internet.

asynchronous communication   The opposite of synchronous or, literally, not synchronous. This is a common method of communication for computers in which information is sent at irregular intervals. Communication is indicated by a start bit followed by a data element and ended with a stop bit. Due to the overhead of start and stop bits, asynchronous communication is slower than other more expensive methods of communication.

ATM (Asynchronous Transfer Mode)   A high-speed transmission technology that can dynamically allocate bandwidth. ATM is a connection-oriented switching and asynchronous multiplexing technique that transports fixed-size packets (called cells). ATM has been selected by the International Telecommunications Union (ITU) as the basis for the future of broadband networking.

B

B channel   Bearer channel, a component of ISDN; it has a transmission rate of 64Kbps and can carry both voice and data.

backbone   A high-speed line between two or more networks.

bandwidth   The amount of data that can be sent through a given communications medium in a given time interval.

baseband   A transmission medium through which digital signals are sent without frequency division. Only one signal is transmitted at a time. Baseband is the most common type of transmission used in local area networks. Ethernet is an example of a baseband network.

BIND   *See Domain Name System.*

BNC (Bayonet Neil Concelman, also known as Bayonet Navy Connector, British Naval Connector, and Bayonet Nut Connection)   A connector for coaxial cable which has a bayonet-type shell with two small knobs on the T-shaped female connector, which lock into spiral slots in the male connector when it is twisted on.

Bonding (Bandwidth ON Demand INteroperability Group)   A group that develops common control and synchronization standards to manage high-speed data over the public network.

BOOTP (Boot Protocol or Bootstrap Protocol)   A TCP/IP protocol that allows an Internet node to discover startup information such as an IP address. See RFCs 951 and 1084.

BRI (Basic Rate Interface)   BRI is a type of Integrated Services Digital Network (ISDN) service commonly found as a residential service. It consists of two 64KB bearer channels and a single delta channel (2B+D). The B channels are used for voice or data, and the D channel is used for signaling.

bridge   A communication device that operates at the data link layer of the OSI model, connects two or more networks, and exchanges packets between them.

broadband   A transmission medium that is capable of carrying multiple signals. Broadband achieves this by supporting a wide range of frequencies and dividing the total capacity of the medium into multiple, independent channels, with each channel operating on a specific range of frequencies.

bus network   A network topology in which all devices share a common path. A single cable runs around the network, attaching to individual computers and equipment via drop cables. Bus networks are common because they are easy to install and use little cable. A major drawback of this type of network, however, is the fact that a single break in the cable can bring down the entire network.

C

Category 3, 4, 5   These are labels of the quality of wire for data rates and reliability. Category 3 will cleanly transmit 16MHz communications and is used to handle voice and LAN traffic up to 10Mbps; Category 4 transmits cleanly 20MHz communications and handles data up to 20Mbps; and Category 5 transmits cleanly 100MHz communications and will handle network traffic up to 155Mbps networks.

CCITT (Consultative Committee for International Telephone and Telegraph)   Commite' Consultatif International de Telegraphique et Telephonique. CCITT changed its name to ITU-T in 1993. *See ITU-T.*

CGI (Common Gateway Interface)   A scripting facility that allows HTML pages to link to other data sources and programs.

client/server   A common form of distributed system in which the workload is split between desktop computers and larger servers.

connectionless protocol   A data communication method in which communication occurs between hosts with no previous setup.

CRC (Cyclic Redundancy Check)   A common error-checking algorithm employed in data communication.

CSLIP   A version of SLIP that compresses the TCP header. *See SLIP.*

CSMA/CD (Collision Sense Multiple Access with Collision Detection) A low-level, network arbitration protocol used on Ethernet.

D

D channel (delta channel)   Delta channel is a component of ISDN. It has a transmission rate of 16Kbps and is used for carrying control and signaling information.

daemon   A background process that handles low-level operating system tasks continuously operating on a UNIX server. Daemons provide resources to client systems on the network.

DAP (Directory Access Protocol)   A protocol used in an X.500 directory system.

DARPA (Defense Advanced Research Project Agency)   The original developers of ARPANET and TCP/IP for internetworking.

data link layer   The second layer of the OSI model responsible for putting messages together and coordinating their flow.

datagram   A self-contained packet of data carrying sufficient information to be independently routed from its source to its destination, without reliance on earlier exchanges between this source and destination computer and the transporting network. Datagrams are the basic units of information passed across the Internet.

demultiplexing   The act of splitting up signals that have been combined for transmission over a shared medium.

DHCP (Dynamic Host Configuration Protocol)   A protocol used for automatic TCP/IP configuration for notes across a network. DHCP dynamically assigns addresses to nodes and allows for the central administration of addresses.

DMA (Direct Memory Access)   A method of directly transferring information to and from a computer's memory, bypassing the CPU.

DNS (Domain Name System)   A commonly accepted way of giving computers names in UNIX-based networks. Sometimes called the BIND service from its roots in BSD UNIX. A DNS server maintains a list of hostnames and IP addresses, allowing computers that query them to find remote computers by specifying hostnames rather than IP addresses. DNS is a distributed database and therefore DNS servers can be configured to use a sequence of name servers, based on the domains in the name being looked for.

domain   Microsoft uses the term domain to denote computers that share a common domain database and security policy. On the Internet, domain refers to computers that share a common suffix, such as commercial (`.COM`).

domain name   Refers to the domain address of a computer or network of computers on the Internet (for example, `MCP.COM`).

E

EGP (External Gateway Protocol)   An Internet protocol for exchanging routing information between systems.

EIGRP (Enhanced Interior Gateway Routing Protocol)   A proprietary routing algorithm from Cisco.

Ethernet   A local area network that connects computers and devices. Operates over twisted-pair or coaxial cable at speeds up to 10Mbps. Like so many other things that the computer industry takes for granted, the Ethernet specification came from Xerox's Palo Alto Research Center. Currently Ethernet is the most widely used network access method.

F

Fast Ethernet   A 100Mbps implementation of Ethernet.

finger   A standard protocol that allows a user who invokes it to see information about a user or all users logged on the system or a remote system.

firewall   A dedicated hardware and/or software system that protects against intrusion from systems external to the network. A firewall sits between networks, monitoring and blocking unauthorized access. Firewalls protect networks by tracking and filtering packets based on their IP address and/or port. As traffic passes between a network and the Internet, it's examined by the firewall that denies access to any traffic that has not been previously expressly permitted.

FQDN (fully qualified domain name)   Refers to the full domain address of a computer on the Internet (for example, `MACMIN.MCP.COM`).

frame   Generally, a packet of data that contains the header and trailer information required by the physical medium. Usually a frame will also contain control information for addressing and error checking. A frame is a basic logical unit of data transmission.

Frame Relay   A form of packet switching that uses smaller packets and requires less error checking. Frame Relay handles high-speed bursty traffic over wide area networks well.

FTP (File Transfer Protocol)   A client/server protocol that allows a user on one computer to transfer files to and from another computer over a TCP/IP network. FTP also allows users to do basic file management, such as listing directories and renaming and deleting files. See RFC 959.

G

gateway   A device that provides a link between systems using different data formats. The term is used to denote a connection between two incompatible networks, and is also used to describe a connection between two differing software packages, such as a mail gateway.

Gopher   Gopher was designed as a menu system to allow easy retrieval of distributed documents on the Internet. It has been largely displaced with the World Wide Web. See RFC 1436.

H

H channel   Similar to a B channel, but is 384Kbps instead of 64Kbps. Found on PRIs.

header   Generally the portion of a message or packet that contains the source and destination addresses as well as routing instructions and error checking and other fields. The header is used to guide the data entity to its destination.

HTML (Hypertext Markup Language)   The standard language used to create documents for the World Wide Web.

HTTP (Hypertext Transfer Protocol)   A client/server TCP/IP protocol used on the World Wide Web for moving of HTML documents on the Internet.

hub   The center of the star in a network based on a star topology or the point where multiple circuits on a network are connected. A hub allows for centralized wiring management and easy troubleshooting of failed network segments.

hybrid   A network that is made up of different topologies.

I

IAB (Internet Architecture Board)   The technical body that oversees the development of the Internet suite of protocols. It has two arms: the Internet Engineering Task Force and the Internet Research Task Force.

ICMP (Internet Control Message Protocol)   An integrated part of IP that allows for the generation of error messages and diagnostic functions that are sent to hosts. See RFC 792.

IEEE (Institute of Electrical and Electronic Engineers)   A standards body responsible for many computing and other standards. The IEEE is the world's largest technical professional society, covering aerospace, biomedical technology, computers and communications, and electric power and consumer electronics.

IETF (Internet Engineering Task Force)   A technical body of the Internet Activities Board, the IETF coordinates the operation, management, and evolution of the Internet. The primary working body developing TCP/IP standards for the Internet.

IGRP (Interior Gateway Routing Protocol)   A protocol used to distribute routing information between routers belonging to a single Autonomous System (a single administrative domain). See RFC 1371.

IMAP   An Internet UNIX protocol that allows clients to access and manipulate electronic mail messages on a server. The protocol is currently at version 4. See RFC 1730.

Internet   The Internet is the largest network in the world; its roots can be traced back to ARPANET. The TCP/IP protocol suite is central to its operation.

internetworking   The interconnection of two or more networks, usually local area networks, so that data can pass between hosts on different networks as though they were one network. This requires some kind of router or gateway.

InterNIC (Internet Network Information Center)   A collaborative project between AT&T, General Atomics, and Network Solutions, Inc. Established in 1993, InterNIC serves as the Internet central naming registry.

intranet   A customized network operating within an organization that is based on Internet technology.

IP (Internet Protocol)   A connectionless protocol that allows a packet to travel across multiple networks on its way to its destination. IP is the network layer of the TCP/IP suite. See RFC 791.

IP address   A unique address that identifies a TCP/IP host on a network. In IPv4 this is a 32-bit address; in IPv6 it is a 128-bit address.

IPv4   The current version of Internet Protocol that supports 32-bit addressing.

IPv6   The IP standard that will probably replace the current version of Internet Protocol. It offers 16-byte addressing rather than 4-byte addressing and is designed to resolve the problem of the shortage of IP addresses. See RFC 1550.

IPX/SPX (Internet Packet Exchange and Sequenced Packet Exchange)   These are network protocols. IPX is Novell NetWare's LAN communication protocol. SPX works on top of IPX and is responsible for flow control.

IRC (Internet Relay Chat)   An Internet application that allows real-time conversation among many users.

IRQ (Interrupt Request Line)   A circuit used by I/O devices to send an interrupt request to the CPU.

IRTF (Internet Research Task Force)   The IRTF is chartered by the Internet Architecture Board and is comprised of a community of network researchers. They look at Internet issues from a theoretical point of view.

ISDN (Integrated Service Digital Network)   A set of communication standards that allow a single wire or optical fiber to carry voice, digital network services, and video. ISDN is a wide area communications service and is intended to eventually replace the plain old telephone system.

ISO (International Standards Organization)   An organization devoted to defining international and national data communications. ISO is a voluntary, non-treaty organization that is chartered by the United Nations.

ISP (Internet service provider)   An organization that provides access to Internet services such as e-mail, World Wide Web browsing, and Internet Relay Chat groups.

ITU-T (International Telecommunications Union)   The telecommunication standardization sector of ITU. It is responsible for technical recommendations about telephone and data communications systems. The group works with all standards organizations to achieve uniform communication standards.

L

LAN (local area network)   A network designed to allow systems in a small geographical location, such as a campus or a building, to communicate with each other.

LDAP (Lightweight Directory Access Protocol)   A protocol for accessing online directory services, which allows a user to look up people from directories over the Internet.

leased line   A phone line that is rented for exclusive 24-hour, 7 days a week, use from one location to another.

link-state   A routing protocol that exchanges routing tables when modifications are made. Updates are provided only when needed and only the changed information is sent.

M

MAN (metropolitan area network)   A network designed to allow systems in a geographical location the size of a large city to communicate.

MIB (Management Information Base)   The store of information gathered by Simple Network Management Protocol. See RFC 1213.

MIME (Multipurpose Internet Mail Extensions)   The standard for attaching binary files to Internet mail messages. See RFC 1521.

MPPP (Multilink PPP)   Commonly used protocol to link both B channels in a BRI simultaneously to create a 128bps connection. Can also be used to connect multiple POTS lines.

multiplexer   A device that allows two or more signals to be sent over one analog or digital communication circuit. Also known as a mux.

multiplexing   The act of combining two or more signals for transmission on a shared medium. The signals are combined at the transmitter by a multiplexer and split up at the receiver by a demultiplexer.

mux   *See multiplexer.*

N

NetBEUI (NetBIOS Extended User Interface.)   An extension to NetBIOS used by all of Microsoft's network systems.

NetBIOS   A standard interface for networking PCs, NetBIOS is a set of drivers for simple hardware support.

network layer   The third layer of the OSI communications model. It determines routing of packets of data from sender to receiver via the data link layer and is used by the transport layer. A sample protocol is IP.

NFS (Network File System)   A method developed by Sun Microsystems that allows a computer to access files over a heterogeneous network as if they were on its local disks. This protocol is now a de facto standard implemented in many vendors' hardware and software systems. See RFC 1094.

NIC (Network Interface Card)   The physical device that is installed in a computer to provide a physical connection to a network.

NIS/YP (Network Information Service/Yellow Pages)   Formerly known as Yellow Pages, NIS/YP is a client/server protocol for distributing system configuration data such as usernames and hostnames between computers on a network.

NOS (Network Operating System)   An operating system that includes software that controls the communication with other computers over a network. Examples include LANtastic, Novell NetWare, LAN Manager, and Windows NT.

NT-1 (Network Termination)   A device that connects the customer's data or telephone equipment to the local ISDN exchange carrier's line. The NT device provides a connection for terminal equipment and terminal adapter (TA) equipment to the local loop.

O

ODI (Open Data Link Interface)   A Novell-developed network card device driver standard that provides media and protocol independence. ODI allows the sharing of a single card by multiple protocols.

OSI model (Open Systems Interconnect Reference model)   The only internationally accepted set of standards for communication between different systems from different vendors. The model organizes the communications process into seven categories dependent on their relationship to the user. These are 1) physical layer, 2) data link layer, 3) network layer, 4) transport layer, 5) session layer, 6) presentation layer, 7) application layer. Each layer builds on the layer below it and provides a service to the layer above.

OSPF (Open Shortest Path First)   A link state protocol that is one of the Internet standard Interior Gateway Protocols. See RFC 1247.

P

packet   The unit of data and additional information required for transmitting to the correct network note. Packets are broken into frames for transmission across a medium.

peer-to-peer   A network typically found in small companies in which all computers are equal. A file server is not required. Peer-to-peer networks are extremely popular and many new operating systems allow peer-to-peer networking right out of the box.

PGP (Pretty Good Privacy)   A cryptographic program that uses RSA public-key encryption for encoding computer data and mail. PGP allows for the secure and private exchange of information.

physical layer   The lowest level in the OSI model of data communications. The physical layer is comprised of the hardware, cables, and wires that link equipment to the network.

Ping (Packet Internet Groper)   A program used to determine the presence of a computer on a network and to measure the time it takes to communicate with it.

POP (Post Office Protocol)   A protocol designed to allow single-user hosts to retrieve electronic mail from a server. Gradually being replaced by IMAP. See RFC 1081.

port   A logical access point in a communication system. Internet transfer protocols use ports to distinguish between multiple simultaneous connections to a host.

POTS (Plain Old Telephone System)   The standard telephone service provided to homes. Also known as the public-switched telephone network; it is the most common type of telephone system used around the world.

PPP (Point-to-Point Protocol)   The Internet standard method for transmitting IP packets over serial point-to-point links. PPP is used to connect systems using standard telephone lines and modems to the Internet and allow them to use the TCP/IP protocol suite. PPP replaces SLIP in this regard. See RFC 1171.

PPTP (Point-to-Point Tunneling Protocol)   A protocol that allows point-to-point connections across the Internet by creating a tunnel between the host and the server.

presentation layer   The sixth layer in the OSI model of data communication. This layer controls functions such as text compression and the format of data screens and files.

PRI (Primary Rate Interface)   A type of Integrated Services Digital Network (ISDN) service commonly used to connect a customer's PBX to the telephone company. In North America and Japan, it consists of 23 64K bearer channels and a single delta channel (23B+D). In Europe, a PRI is (30B+D). The B channels are used for voice or data, and the D channel is used for signaling.

proxy gateway   A system that passes on requests for URLs from a World Wide Web browser to an outside server and returns the results. This provides clients using the gateway with a level of protection by sealing them off from the Internet. *See also proxy server.*

proxy server   This server provides extra security between an insecure system and a local network such as a firewall. A Web proxy server provides a cache of items available on other servers.

Q

QOS (Quality of Service)   The quality of telephone service provided to a subscriber. Also used to describe the assurance of bandwidth on a network.

R

RARP (Reverse Address Resolution Protocol)   A TCP/IP protocol that provides the reverse function of ARP. RARP maps a hardware address to an Internet address, allowing an Internet address to be found from an Ethernet address. See RFC 903.

RFC (Request For Comments)   Numbered Internet informational documents and standards started in 1969. The document process where proposed standards and generally accepted ideas are published. IETF and the IESG publish their specification documents on the Internet Protocol suite via RFCs.

ring topology   This topology uses a closed loop with devices connected to it and is associated with token-passing protocols. In this type of system, the data travels from computer to computer until it returns to its source. Advantages of this type of system are the capability to self-heal if the cable is broken and little attenuation due to signal regeneration at each station. Disadvantages include large cable requirements and short wiring distances between each node.

RIP (Routing Information Protocol)   An Internet standard Interior Gateway Protocol used by routers to determine the shortest distance between two paths. The connectivity status is determined in terms of the number of hops between two points. See RFC 1388.

router   This is a device that interconnects different access methods and protocols. Routers act like bridges forwarding traffic between networks but have greater functionality. They are used to build wide area networks.

RPC (remote procedure call)   A protocol that governs how a program running on one host can cause events to happen on another host. RPCs are used to implement client/server computing in a distributed network environment.

RSVP (Resource reSerVation Protocol)   A protocol that is used for installing and maintaining resource reservations on a network. The RSVP protocol is part of an effort to enhance the current Internet architecture with support for Quality of Service flows.

RTP (Real Time Transport Protocol)   A protocol that provides end-to-end network transport functions suitable for applications transmitting real-time data, such as audio, video, or simulation data.

S

segment   A part of a network that is electrically continuous, usually consisting of the same wire communication between segments as performed by a router.

server   A system that provides services to workstations over a network. There are different types of servers, such as print servers, mail servers, and database servers. Several servers can exist on the same computer.

session layer   The fifth layer in the OSI model of data communication. The session handles security and creation of sessions, allowing clients on a network to send data to each other.

SLIP (Serial Line Interface Protocol)   A method for transmitting IP packets over serial point-to-point links. SLIP is used to connect systems using standard telephone lines and modems to the Internet, and to allow them to use the TCP/IP protocol suite. SLIP has largely been replaced by PPP. See RFC 1055.

SMTP (Simple Mail Transfer Protocol)   A TCP/IP protocol that governs transfers and receipt of electronic mail between computers. See RFC 821.

SNA (Systems Network Architecture)   A proprietary, high-level networking protocol standard used by IBM and IBM-compatible mainframes.

sniffer   A network monitoring program that can capture and decode packets from a network.

SNMP (Simple Network Management Protocol)   Developed as an Internet standard protocol to manage nodes on an IP network. It has also been widely implemented on Ethernet. See RFC 1157.

socket   A virtual connection between processes by pairing of IP addresses and port numbers.

spoofing   The act of intercepting, altering, and retransmitting information to mislead the receiving host system as to who the sender is. Also used to reduce network traffic in wide area networks.

star topology   This topology uses a hub or concentrator to connect to workstations. Each computer uses a single cable to attach to the central hub. This topology gets its name because logically all connections radiate out from the hub in a star fashion. Unlike networks that use the bus topology, a break in such a connection will not bring down an entire network; however, the initial cost of a star network is higher because it uses a lot more cable and large portions of a network will stop functioning if a hub fails.

subnet   A portion of a network that may be a physically independent network segment, which shares a network address with other portions of the network and is distinguished by a subnet number.

subnet mask   Also known as an address mask. A bit-mask used to identify which bits in an IP address correspond to the network address and subnet portions of the address.

synchronous communication   The communication of data that is controlled by a master clock. Information arrives at a specified time in a predetermined order. Rather than start and stop bits as used in asynchronous communication, packets are spaced by time. Synchronous communication is used widely by mainframe computers.

T

T-1   A point-to-point digital communications link that has a capacity of 1.544Mbps made up of 24 64,000bps channels.

T-3   A point-to-point digital communications link that has capacity of 44.736Mbps and is made up of 28 T-1 lines.

TA (terminal adapter)   A device that allows non-ISDN equipment, such as standard telephones, to operate over an ISDN line.

TCP (Transmission Control Protocol)   A connection- and stream-oriented, end-to-end protocol developed for use on ARPANET. TCP is the most common transport layer protocol used on Ethernet and the Internet. See RFC 793.

TCP/IP (Transmission Control Protocol/Internet Protocol)   A protocol suite developed by the U.S. Department of Defense to link dissimilar computers across different kinds of networks. TCP/IP is the transport protocol employed by the Internet and is commonly used on Ethernet networks.

Telnet   A program that runs on top of TCP/IP, it is the Internet standard protocol for remote login. Originally developed for ARPANET. See RFC 854.

token   A packet of data passed around on a network that ensures synchronized access to resources. When a system on a network has the token, it then has permission to transmit data.

token ring   A scheme in local area networking in which devices are logically connected in a ring. Collision is avoided by the passing of tokens, which give permission to transmit data. The note on the network keeps the token while transmitting its data. If it has no data to transmit, the token is passed on to the next station.

topology   The physical or logical configuration that describes a local area network showing the links between hosts. Common types are bus, ring, and star.

transport layer   The fourth layer in OSI model of data communication responsible for how connections are made and unmade, message structure, and error checking.

twisted pair   Two insulated copper wires twisted around each other. Several sets of twisted-pair wires can be enclosed in one cable. The twists in the wire reduce induction and thus interference from one wire to another.

U

UDP (User Datagram Protocol)   A TCP/IP protocol that provides simple datagram services. UDP is a connectionless mode protocol that is layered on top of IP. UDP does not guarantee delivery and is potentially unreliable. See RFC 768.

URL (Uniform Resource Locator)   A standardized method of specifying an address on the World Wide Web. It's used in HTML documents to specify the target of a hyperlink.

Usenet   A worldwide system of discussion groups with well over 10,000 discussion areas, called newsgroups.

UTP (unshielded twisted pair)   A cable in which one or more twisted pairs of copper wire are bound together in a covered sheath. Telephone wire is an example.

V

VPN (virtual private network)   A network that takes advantage of the public network to provide a simulated private network.

W

WAN (wide area network)   A network designed to operate over a large area. It uses links from telephone companies to connect networks in different cities or countries.

WINS (Windows Internet Name Service)   A Microsoft name resolution service that resolves computer names to IP addresses.

Winsock   A networking programming interface that provides a single API for application developers. Used to establish connection and to send and receive data.

X

X.25 A standard protocol suite used worldwide for communication over a packet–switched network, which allows devices from mainframes to microcomputers to communicate.

X.400 A standard for electronic mail services that allows different mail systems to exchange messages with each other.

X.500 The set of ITU–T standards covering electronic directory services such as whitepages, Knowbot, and whois.

Technical Glossary

Index

Symbols

10Base-2, 440
10Base-5, 440
10Base-T, 440
16-bit Windows sockets, 206
32-bit Windows sockets, 207
100Base-T, 440
100VG-AnyLan Ethernet, 440
802 standards, 440

A

AALs (ATM Adaption Layers), 188
ABORT command
  FTP sessions, 254
  TCP processes, 201
abortive releases, 173
accept function, BSD socket model, 204
access restrictions for routers, 320
ACK flag
  TCP headers, 163
  TCP processes, 169
ACK requests
  packet dump analysis, 353-355
  terminating TCP connections, 358
Acknowledgment field, TCP datagrams, 163
active routers, 104
active routes, routing tables, 101
active/passive flag, TCP processes, 199
Add Group Name service, NetBIOS, 231

Add Name service, NetBIOS, 231
additional section, DNS queries, 295
address allocation database, static entries for servers, 120
addresses
  ARP, static, 89-90
  IP addresses, network design issues, 311
  IPv4 types, 38-39
  IPv6, 49-50, 55
  MAC, router access restrictions, 320
  multicasting, 61
  private addressing ranges, network design issues, 311
  see also IP addresses
addressing
  Ethernet nodes, 95
  IP
    reasons for protocol, 94-96
    routing, 96
    scheme, 58-65
  IPv4
    host address, 59
    network identifier, 59
    reserved addresses, 65
    subnetting, 62
    variable length subnetting, 67
  IPv6, 68-78
    anycast addresses, 75
    global provider-based unicast addresses, 73
    Link-Local unicast addresses, 74
    loopback address, 74

    minimum required address support, 77-78
    multicast addresses, 75-77
    reserved multicast addresses, 76
    Site-Local unicast addresses, 74
    transient multicast addresses, 76
    unicast, 71-74
    unspecified address, 74
    well-known multicast addresses, 76
  MAC (Media Access Control), 95
admission control module, RSVP, 182
ADSL (Asymmetric Digital Subscriber Line), 440
advantages
  dynamic address allocation, 120
  switches and routers, 316
agents, NFS operations, 227
algorithms, distance vector and link state, 103
allocation policies for IP addresses, 119
Allow header field, HTTP requests, 274
analyzers, troubleshooting problems, 337-338
ANSI (American National Standards Institute), 440
answers to DNS queries, 295
anycast addresses, IPv6, 49, 75
AO function, Telnet sessions, 247
APIs (Application Program Interfaces), 440

APP packet, RTCP, 180
AppleTalk, 441
application entities, SNMP, 219
application layer, 194, 441
OSI model, 22
TCP/IP model, 24, 212
application messages, TCP processes, 201
application performance problems, 346
application protocols, 7
application requests, TCP processes, 198–201
application services, 238
ARCnet, 441
arguments option, TCP/IP UNIX services, 204
ARP (Address Resolution Protocol), 80, 96–97, 368, 441
addresses, static, 89–90
cache, 97
cache table, 88
IP addresses, conflicts, 82–88
packet format, 88–89
packet reception, 81
queries, 96
ARPANET, 4, 441
ASCII
conversions from binary via UUENCODE/UUDECODE, 268
FTP transfers, 258
values, Telnet session negotiation commands, 243
association modes, NTP servers, 215
asynchronous communication, 441
asynchronous file writes, NFS, 228
Asynchronous Transfer Mode, *See* ATM
AT&T System V UNIX version, TCP/IP services, 205
ATM (Asynchronous Transfer Mode), 9, 188–189, 369, 441
authentication, HTTP, 272

Authenticaton, NTP datagrams, 217
Authentication Header, IPv6, 46
authentication parameters, NFS service requests, 228
authentication process commands, FTP sessions, 253
authentication types, Telnet, 246
authority section, DNS queries, 295
Authorization header field, HTTP requests, 274
automatic address allocation, 119
AYT function, Telnet sessions, 247

B

B channel, 441
backbones, considerations in network design, 313–315, 441
backup strategies and network design issues, 331–334
bandwidth, 441
data links, 339
network design issues, 310
baseband, 441
bastion hosts, firewalls, 324–325
BEL code, Telnet NVT, 240
BGP (Border Gateway Protocol), 113, 369
BGP4 (Border Gateway Protocol 4), 53
binary FTP transfers, 258
binary to ASCII conversions via UUENCODE/UUDECODE, 268
BIND (Berkley Internet Naming Daemon), 282
BIND resolver, 289
BNC, 442

Bonding (Bandwidth ON Demand INteroperability Group), 442
boot file size option, BOOTP/DHCP extensions, 129
BOOTP (boot protocol), 121–122, 442
bootreply messages, 122
bootrequest messages, 121
packets, 122
relay agents, 126
RFCs, 369
static address allocation, 121
vendor extensions, 127–135
bootreply messages, BOOTP, 122
bootrequest messages, BOOTP, 121
BRI (Basic Rate Interface), 442
bridges, 98–99, 442
local, 109–111
remote, 109
translational bridging, 110
transparent, 99
broadband transmission concepts, 186–187, 442
broadcast address option, BOOTP/DHCP extensions, 130
broadcast addresses, IPv4, 38
broadcast NTP association mode, 216
BROADCAST option, TCP/IP UNIX services, 203
broadcast registration, NetBIOS names, 301
broadcast storms, 348
broadcast/collision model, 9
BS code, Telnet NVT, 240
BSD UNIX
sockets, 204
TCP/IP service configuration, 202–204
building firewalls, 322
bus network, 442
BYE packet, RTCP, 180

C

C socket class, 207

cabling issues and network design, 314

cache, ARP, 97

cache table, IP/ARP address pairs, 88

caching proxy servers, network design issues, 317

Call session service, NetBIOS, 231

capacity planning, 329-330

CAsyncSocket class, 207

Categories 3, 4, 5, 442

CCITT (Consultative Committee for International Telephone and Telegraph), 442

CDUP command, FTP sessions, 254

central location of IP address data on host, 118

CGI (Common Gateway Interface), 443

Checksum field
TCP datagrams, 163
UDP headers, 175

CIDR (Classless Inter-Domain Routing), 50, 65-68, 370

class-based IPv4 subnetting, 63-64

classes of IPv4 network addresses, 59

client/server, 443
NTP association mode, 215
protocols, 238
relationship in TCP/IP networks, 10-12

clients
BOOTP, 126
DNS, resolvers, 282, 288-289
FTP, 248-250
HTTP, server response messages, 271
MTA, 261
RARP, 121
Telnet, 239

CLOSE command, TCP processes, 200

close function, BSD socket model, 204

CLOSE-WAIT state, TCP processes, 198

command options for Telnet, 244-245

commands
FTP sessions, authentication process, 253
SMTP mail transfers, 261-264

COMMIT procedure, NFS, 228

common problem troubleshooting, 343-348

communities, SNMP application entities, 219

comparisons
IPv4 and IPv6, 49-55
switches and routers, 316

Compression-Protocol option, IPv6CP, 151

computer naming schemes, 282-283

configuration
DNS resolvers, 288-289
IPv4 hosts, 52
IPv6CP options, 150
NTP server subnets, 215-218
service troubleshooting, 345

Configure-Ack packets, PPP protocol, 145

Configure-Nak packets, PPP protocol, 146

Configure-Reject packets, PPP protocol, 146

Configure-Request packets, PPP protocol, 145

conflicts
domain names, 284
IP address problems, 345
ARP-generated, 82

congestion and TCP processes, 170-171

connect function, BSD socket model, 204

connections

failure troubleshooting, 343-346
TCP process
initiatiation, 165
negotiation, 168-169
states, 195-198
termination, 173

Connection: header field, HTTP requests, 275

connectionless protocol, 443

Content-Encoding field, HTTP requests, 274

Content-Length field, HTTP requests, 274

Content-Type field, HTTP requests, 274

control flags, TCP headers, 163

control functions, Telnet, 247-248

convergence, routing tables, 103

conversion to IPv6 issues, 115-116

cookie server option, BOOTP/DHCP extensions, 129

count to infinity problems, router hop problems, 105

CR code, Telnet NVT, 240

CRC (Cyclical Redundancy Check), 28, 443

criteria filtering, troubleshooting problems, 337

CSLIP, 443

CSMA/CD (Collision Sense Multiple Access with Collision Detection), 443

CSRC list field, RTP headers, 179

CWD command, FTP sessions, 253

D

D channel, 443
daemons, 202, 443
DAP (Directory Access
  Protocol), 443
DARPA (Defense Advanced
  Research Project Agency),
  443
DATA command, SMTP mail
  transfers, 262
Data field
  TCP datagrams, 163
  UDP headers, 175
data link layer
  OSI model, 7, 21, 443
  protocols, 7
data transfer commands, FTP
  sessions, 254
data transfer file types for
  FTP, 258-259
data-link protocols, 138
datagram services, NetBIOS,
  232
datagrams, 443
  IP, encapsulation in NetBIOS,
    233
  IPv4
    basic format, 29-30
    fragmentation, 36-38
    version numbers, 31
  NetBIOS formats, 233
  NTP, 216-218
  PPP encapsulation, 141-144
  RST (reset), 173
  SLIP encapsulation, 139
  TCP
    encapsulation, 161
    FIN flag, 173
    format, 162-164
    headers, 162
Date header field, HTTP
  requests, 275
demultiplexing, 443
debugging DNS setups
  nslookup tool, 296-297
  networks, 336
  see also troubleshooting
    problems

default gateways, routers, 97
definitions of domain names,
  283-284
DELE command, FTP
  sessions, 254
DELETE method, HTTP 1.1,
  278
Delete Name service,
  NetBIOS, 231
deleting DHCP leases, 125-126
demultiplexing network
  stacks, 28-29
designing networks, 310-311
  backbones, 313
  backup strategies, 331-334
  cabling options, 314
  capacity planning, 329-330
  fault tolerance issues, 315-316
  firewalls, 321
  ISP issues, 317-318
  netmasks, 315
  remote sites, 331
  routers, 311, 316-317
  satellite sites, 331
  security issues, 319-329
  service access restrictions for
    security, 323-324
  subnets, 315
  switches, 312, 316-317
  TCP wrappers, 326-327
  workstations, 312
Destination Address, IPv6, 42
Destination field
  TCP datagrams, 162
  UDP headers, 175
Destination IP Address field,
  IPv4, 35
Destination Options header,
  IPv6, 48
device {device type} options,
  TCP/IP UNIX services, 202
DHCP (Dynamic Host
  Configuration Protocol),
  123-126, 443
  leases, 123
    deleting leases, 125-126
    initial allocation, 123-124
  option field formats, 127
  packets, 125
  RFCs, 370

DHCP message type option,
  BOOTP/DHCP extensions,
  134
DHCPACK message, 124
DHCPDECLINE message, 124
DHCPDISCOVER message,
  123
DHCPNAK message, 124
DHCPOFFER message, 123
DHCPRELEASE message, 125
DHCPREQUEST message,
  124
dial-up access protocols, 138
Digital Equipment Corporation VAX minicomputers, 5
directory-level services, NFS,
  228
disadvantages
  dynamic address allocation, 120
  manual address allocation, 119
  switches and routers, 316
Discard-Request packets, LCP
  packets, 148
distance vector algorithms,
  router protocols, 103
DM command, Telnet sessions,
  247
DMA (Direct Memory
  Access), 444
DNS (Domain Name System),
  12, 282-283, 444
  debugging setups, 296-297
  glue records, 292-293
  queries, 282, 293-295
    additional section, 295
    answers, 295
    authority section, 295
    headers, 293-294
    questions, 294-295
  resource records, 289-292
  RFCs, 371
  terminology, 283-289
  troubleshooting problems,
    347-348
  underlying concepts, 283-289
  zones, 286-287
DNS clients, resolvers, 282,
  288-289
DNS servers, 282

DO request, Telnet sessions, 242

#DOM:<domain> keyword, LMHOSTS file, 300

domain name option, BOOTP/DHCP extensions, 130

domain name server option, BOOTP/DHCP extensions, 128

domain names, 444
definitions, 283-284
FQDNs (fully qualified domain names), 284
namespace, 283-285
naming conflicts, 284
PQDNs (partially qualified domain names), 284
resolution, 296
reverse lookups, 285-286, 296
storage formats, 290
WINS resolution, 298

domains
DNS zones, 286-287, 444
name resolution, 287

DONT request, Telnet sessions, 243

DTP (User Data Transfer Process), 250-252

dual-homing and network design issues, 318

dynamic address allocation, 119

E

e-mail, 259-269

EC function, Telnet sessions, 247

Echo-Reply packets, PPP protocol, 148

Echo-Request packets, PPP protocol, 148

EGP (Exterior Gateway Protocol), 444
external LAN routing, 104, 111
RFCs, 371

EIGRP (Enhanced Interior Gateway Routing Protocol), 108-109, 444

EL function, Telnet sessions, 247

embedded IPv4 addresses, 73

encapsulation
network stacks, 27-29
PPP
datagrams, 141-144
Multilink packets, 185
packets, 143
SLIP datagrams, 139
TCP datagrams, 161

END character, SLIP protocol, 139

end nodes in NetBIOS services, 232

end option, BOOTP/DHCP extensions, 128

envelope component, SMTP mail transfers, 266

EOF characters, packet dump analysis, 355

ephemeral ports, FTP connections, 252

ESC character, SLIP protocol, 139

ESP (Encapsulating Security Payload) extension header, IPv6, 47

establish function, BSD socket model, 204

ESTABLISHED state, TCP process, 197

Ethernet, 444
frames, 28
networks, MAC addressing, 95
RFCs, 384

EtherTalk, 441

Expires field, HTTP requests, 275

EXPN command, SMTP mail transfers, 262

extension headers, IPv6
Authentication Header, 46
Destination Options, 48
Encapsulating Security Payload, 47
Fragmentation, 46
Hop-by-Hop, 43
Routing, 45

extensions for BOOTP, 127-135

external nodes, namespace trees, 283-284

extranets, 9

F

failed connection trouble-shooting, 343-346

FAQs (Frequently Asked Questions), 385

Fast Ethernet, 444

fault tolerance, network design issues, 315-316

FF code, Telnet NVT, 241

file-level services, NFS, 228

files
FTP data transfer types, 258-259
LMHOSTS, 299-300
locks, NFS resource access, 227
resource access under NFS, 227

filtering
by criteria, troubleshooting problems, 337
packets for security, 321
tcpdump IP packet tracing, 341

filterspec, RSVP, 183

FIN flag
TCP datagrams, 173
TCP headers, 164

FIN packet, TCP processes, 198

FIN requests, terminating TCP connections, 357-358

Finger, 444

Finger protocol RFCs, 372

firewalls, 321, 444
bastion hosts, 324-325
building guidelines, 322
proxy hosts, 325-326

Flags field, IPv4, 33

flow control, TCP processes, 169-172

flowspec, RSVP, 183
formal Internet standards
    RFCs, 369
Format Prefixes, IPv6, 70
formats
    ARP packets, 88–89
    BOOTP vendor extensions,
        127
    TCP datagrams, 162–164
forward paths, MAIL and
    RCPT parameters, 264
forwarders, nameservers, 288
FQDNs (fully qualified
    domain names), 284, 445
fragmentation
    IPv4, 36–38
    minimizing, 38
Fragmentation header, IPv6,
    46
Fragmentation Offset field,
    IPv4, 33
Frame Relay, 187–188, 445
frames, 7, 445
    Ethernet, 28
    PPP protocol, 142
From header field, HTTP
    requests, 275
FTP (File Transfer Protocol),
    12, 248–259, 445
    clients, 248–250
    data transfer file types, 258–259
    DTP port connections, 252
    ephemeral port connections,
        252
    response messages, 256–258
    RFCs, 371
    servers, 249–250, 365
    sessions, 251–258
future developments in HTTP,
    277
FYIs, 367

G

gateways, 8, 97, 445
general principles for problem
    troubleshooting, 336
GET method, HTTP requests,
    272

GetBulkRequest-PDU,
    SNMPv2, 226
GGP (Gateway to Gateway
    protocol), 112
global provider-based, unicast
    IPv6 addresses, 73
glue records, 292–293
Gopher, 372, 445
GPS system (Global Position-
    ing Satellite), 214
graphics workstations,
    network design issues, 312
groups, MIB, 221
guidelines
    firewall construction, 322
    network design, 311

H

H channel, 445
Hang Up session service,
    NetBIOS, 231
HEAD method, HTTP
    requests, 272
Header Checksum field, IPv4,
    34
header fields, HTTP requests
    and responses, 273–275
header processing comparison
    between IPv4 and IPv6, 52
header_information field
    RTP headers, 178
    TCP datagrams, 163
headers, 445
    DNS queries, 293–294
    IP, ICMP echo request analysis,
        349
    IPv4 structural layout, 30–35
    IPv6 structural layout, 39–42
    Multilink PPP, 185
    RTP, 178–179
    SMTP mail transfers, 266
    TCP
        control flags, 163
        datagram fields, 162
        maximum segment sizes,
            164–165
        MTU, 165
    UDP, 175

Hello protocol, routing, 106
HELO command, SMTP mail
    transfers, 261
HELP command, FTP
    sessions, 256
hold down RIP routing, 105
hop count metric, active
    routers, 104
Hop Limit field, IPv6, 42
Hop-by-Hop extension
    header, IPv6, 43
host address
    IPv4 addressing, 59
    IPv6, 77
host name option, BOOTP/
    DHCP extensions, 129
host routing troubleshooting,
    344
hosts
    IPv4, configuring, 52
    multihomed, IP address
        queries, 289
    namespace tree nodes, 284
hosts file, 282
HT code, Telnet NVT, 240
HTML RFCs, 372
HTTP (Hypertext Transfer
    Protocol), 12, 269–278, 445
    authentication, 272
    clients, server response
        messages, 271
    future developments, 277
    methods, 272–273
    requests, 270
        header fields, 273–275
        URI format and syntax,
            275–276
    responses
        codes, 276–277
        header fields, 273–275
    RFCs, 372
    servers, request format, 270
HTTP 1.1, 277–278
hub, 445
hysterical overview of TCP/IP,
    4–6

I-J

IAB (Internet Architecture Board), 13, 446

IAC (Interpret-as command) escape character, Telnet sessions, 243

IANA (Internet Assigned Numbers Authority), 13

ICMP (Internet Control Message Protocol), 26, 446
  packet dump analysis
    echo replies, 350-351
    echo requests, 349-350
  RFCs, 373

Identification field, IPv4, 33

IDRP (Inter-domain Routing Protocol), 53, 113

IEEE (Institute of Electrical and Electronic Engineers), 446

IESG (Internet Engineering Steering Group), 13

IETF (Internet Engineering Task Force), 13, 446

If-Modified-Since header field, HTTP requests, 275

IGMP (Internet Group Multicasting Protocol), RFCs, 373

IGPs (Interior Gateway Protocols), LAN routing, 104

IGRP (Interior Gateway Routing Protocol), 446

IMAP, 446

implied foreign sockets, TCP processes, 200

#INCLUDE statements, LMHOSTS file, 300

INET options, TCP/IP UNIX services, 202

inetd (Internet Daemon), 202

Information field, PPP protocol, 143

InformRequest-PDU, SNMPv2, 226

initiating connections, TCP process, 165

integrated layer processing, 177

interactive audio/video conferencing with RTP, 179

interactive mode, nslookup, 296

interface token option, IPv6CP, 150-151

internal nodes, namespace trees, 283-284

Internet, 5, 446
  drafts, 365-367
  Internet Daemon (inetd), 202
  standards and RFCs, 364-365

Internet Header Length, IPv4, 32

Internet Information Server, TCP/IP server facilities, 208

Internet layer, TCP/IP model, 24

internetworking, 446

InterNIC, 13-14, 446

intranets, 9, 327-328, 446

IP (Internet Protocol), 4, 8-9, 20, 58-65, 446
  datagram encapsulation in NetBIOS, 233
  headers
    ICMP echo reply analysis, 351
    ICMP echo request analysis, 349
    TCP connection initiation analysis, 352-353
  multicasting, 176
  packet tracing, tcpdump utility, 340-341
  pathways, 9

IP addresses, 446
  allocation policies, 119-120
  ARP conflicts, 82
  central location of data for host, 118
  compared to LAN addressing, 94
  lease time option, BOOTP/DHCP extensions, 134
  mapping machine names to, 282
  network design issues, 311
    new allocations, 330

  reasons for protocol, 94-96
  reverse lookups, 285
  troubleshooting conflicts, 345-346

IP function, Telnet sessions, 247

IP Header Option field, IPv4, 35

IP routing, 96-97

IPFORWARDING option, TCP/IP UNIX services, 202

IPSENDREDIRECTS option, TCP/IP UNIX services, 203

IPv4, 447
  addresses, 38-39
  addressing, 58-65
  CIDR, 65-68
  comparison to IPv6, 49-55
  datagrams
    fragmentation, 36-38
    version numbers, 31
  Destination IP Address field, 35
  Flags field, 33
  Fragmentation Offset field, 33
  Header Checksum field, 34
  headers
    comparison to IPv6, 52
    structural layout, 30-35
  hosts, configuring, 52
  Identification field, 33
  Internet Header Length, 32
  IP Header Option field, 35
  multicasting, 61-62
  network classes, 59-60
  packets, structural overview, 29-39
  Path MTU, 36
  Protocol field, 34
  reverse lookups, 285-286
  RFCs, 373
  Source IP address field, 35
  subnet masks, 64-65
  subnetting, 62-64
    class-based, 63-64
    variable length subnetting, 67
  supernetting, 67
  TOS field, 32
  Total Length field, 33
  TTL (Time-To-Live) field, 33

IPv6, 68-78, 447
addresses, 68-69
anycast, 49, 75
Link-Local unicast
addresses, 74
loopback address, 74
minimum required address
support, 77-78
multicast, 49, 55, 75-77
reserved multicast addresses,
76
Site-Local unicast addresses,
74
space allocations, 50
transient multicast addresses,
76
types, 69-71
unicast, 49, 71-74
unspecified address, 74
well-known multicast
addresses, 76
comparison to IPv4, 49-55
Destination address, 42
embedded IPv4 addresses, 73
extension headers, 42-48
Format Prefixes, 70
headers
comparison to IPv4, 52
structural layout, 39-42
Hop Limit field, 42
migration considerations,
113-116
multicasting, 54
Network Control Protocol,
149
Next Header field, 41
packets, structural overview,
39-49
Payload Length field, 41
PPP encapsulation, 149
PPP protocol, 149-151
Priority field, 40
priority values, 40
reverse lookups, 286
RFCs, 374
Source Address, 42
stateless autoconfiguration, 52
Version field, 40

IPv6CP
Compression-Protocol option,
151
configuration options, 150
interface token option,
150-151
packets, code options, 150
**IPX/SPX (Internet Packet
Exchange/Sequenced Packet
Exchange), 447**
**IRC (Internet Relay Chat)
RFCs, 375, 447**
**IRQ (Interrupt Request Line),
447**
**IRTF (Internet Research Task
Force), 447**
**IS-IS protocol (Intermediate
Host to Intermediate Host),
108**
**ISDN (Integrated Service
Digital Network), 187, 447**
**ISO (International Standards
Organization), 20, 447**
ISOC (Internet Society), 13
**ISPs (Internet service
providers), network design
issues, 317-318, 447**
**iterative queries, local
nameservers, 288**
**ITU-T (International Tele-
communications Union), 447**

K

keepalive timers, 173
keyboard, NVT, 240

L

L2F (Layer 2 Forwarding), 153
**L2TP (Layer Two Tunneling
Protocol), 153-154, 158**
**LANs (local area networks),
447**
addressing schemes compared
to IP addressing, 94
gateways, 8

NFS protocol operations, 227
outside router protocols,
109-113
routing protocols, 103-109
**LAST-ACK state, TCP
processes, 198**
**Last-Modified field, HTTP
requests, 275**
latency, data links, 339
layered protocols, 5
**LCP (Link Control Protocol),
PPP protocol, 144-149**
Code-Reject packets, 147
configuration negotiation, 145
Discard-Request packets, 148
loopback checking, 148
protocol rejects, 148
termination, 147
**LDAP (Lightweight Directory
Access Protocol), 447**
**Leap Indicator, NTP
datagrams, 216**
leases
DHCP, 123
deleting leases, 125-126
initial allocation, 123-124
leased lines, 448
**Length field, UDP headers,
175**
LF code, Telnet NVT, 240
**licensing issues for networks,
331**
limitations of SLIP, 140
**link control options for
Multilink PPP, 186**
**link operations, PPP protocol,
143-148**
**link state algorithms, router
protocols, 103, 448**
**Link-Local unicast addresses,
IPv6, 74**
**Listen session service,
NetBIOS, 231**
**LISTEN state, TCP process,
197**
LMHOSTS file, 299-300
local bridges, 109-111
local nameservers, 282, 288
LocalTalk, 441

Lock Manager, NFS, 227
log server option, BOOTP/
DHCP extensions, 129
logins, Telnet remote options,
238
loopback address, IPv6, 74
loopback checking, LCP
packets, 148
LPD printing problems, 346

M

MAC (Media Access Control)
addresses, 95
ARP resolution, 80
broadcast storms, 348
router access restrictions, 320
troubleshooting IP conflicts,
345
vendor address list, IP address
conflict resolution, 83
MAIL command, SMTP mail
transfers, 261
mail servers, security, 328-329
mail transfer SMTP com-
mands, 261-264
managing networks, 329-334
mandatory objects, SNMP
MIB, 222
MANs (metropolitan area
networks), 448
manual address allocation, 119
mapping machine names to
IP addresses, 282
maximum segment sizes for
TCP headers, 164-165
MBONE virtual network, 176
MD command, FTP sessions,
255
media access protocols, 7
message transmission via
SNMP, 220
methods, HTTP, 272-273
MIB (Management
Information Base), 448
RFCs, 380
SNMP, 219-225
group definitions, 221
mandatory objects, 222

Microsoft
FTP server response messages,
257
Internet Information Server,
TCP/IP server facilities, 208
whitepapers, 385
Windows TCP/IP services,
206-208
migration to IPv6 considerations, 113-116
MIME (Multipurpose Internet
Mail Extensions), 448
data conversions for mail
transfers, 268
RFCs, 375
minimizing fragmentation, 38
minimum required address
support, IPv6, 77-78
mixers for RTP multicast
streams, 177
Mode Indicator, NTP
datagrams, 217
monitoring networks for
capacity planning, 330
MOUNT operation, NFS,
227-228
MPPP (Multilink PPP), 9, 448
MTAs (Mail Transfer Agents),
259, 348
MTU (Maximum Transmis-
sion Unit), TCP headers, 165
multicast addresses
IPv4, 38
IPv6, 49, 55, 75-77
multicast IP, 176
multicast NTP association
mode, 216
multicasting, 54, 61-62
multihomed hosts, IP address
queries, 289
Multilink PPP, 183-186
headers, 185
link control options, 186
packet encapsulation, 185
multimedia, RSVP protocol,
182
multiplexing, 160-161, 448
packet-based, 187
TCP, 165-169

N

Nagle's algorithm, TCP data
flow control, 171
name encoding, NetBIOS, 305
name option, TCP/IP UNIX
services, 203
name registration for
NetBIOS, 301-304
name release requests,
NetBIOS, 304
name resolution
NetBIOS names to addresses,
303
primary servers, 287
problem troubleshooting, 347
secondary servers, 287
name services, NetBIOS, 231
name types for NetBIOS,
298-299
nameservers, 282
forwarders, 288
local, 282
iterative and recursive
queries, 288
NetBIOS, 297-305
root, resource records, 287
slaves, 288
namespace, domains, 283-285
namespace trees, external or
internal nodes, 283-284
naming computers, 282-283
naming conflicts in domain
names, 284
NBDD (NetBIOS Datagram
Distribution) server, 232
NBNS (NetBIOS Name
Server), 232
negotiation
TCP connection process,
168-169
Telnet session options, 242
NetBEUI (NetBIOS Extended
User Interface), 448
NetBIOS, 230-233, 448
datagrams
formats, 233
services, 232

names
encoding, 305
registration, 301-304
release requests, 304
resolution, 303
types, 298-299
nameservers, 297-305
obtaining name data, 300
RFCs, 375
services, 230-232
datagrams, 232
names, 231
scope of end nodes, 232
sessions, 231-233
**NetBIOS node type option,
BOOTP/DHCP extensions,
133**
**NetBIOS over TCP/IP,
230-233**
**NetBIOS over TCP/IP name
server option, BOOTP/
DHCP extensions, 133**
**netmasks, network design
issues, 315**
netstat -r command, 343
**Network Access layer, TCP/IP
model, 24**
network classes, IPv4, 59-60
**Network Control Protocol,
IPv6, 149**
**network identifier, IPv4
addressing, 59**
**network information servers
option, BOOTP/DHCP
extensions, 131**
**network information service
domain option, BOOTP/
DHCP extensions, 131**
**network layer, OSI model, 7,
22, 448**
network management, 329-334
**Network Monitor, network
and packet analysis, 341-342**
networks
ARPANET, 4
bridges, 98-99
demultiplexing, 28-29
designing, 310-311
backbones, 313
backup strategies, 331-334
cabling options, 314

capacity planning, 329-330
fault tolerance issues,
315-316
firewalls, 321
ISP issues, 317-318
netmasks, 315
remote sites, 331
routers, 311, 316-317
satellite sites, 331
security issues, 319-329
service access restrictions
for security, 323-324
subnets, 315
switches, 312, 316-317
TCP wrappers, 326-327
workstations, 312
encapsulation, 27-29
Ethernet, MAC addressing, 95
failed connection troubleshooting, 343-346
IPv6 migration considerations,
114
MBONE, 176
packet-switched, 4
physical problems, 346
protocols, 7
repeaters, 98
routers, 99-102
routing tables
active routes, 101
simple example, 100
static route entries, 101-102
segment connection options,
98-102
TCP/IP
client/server relationship,
10-12
server roles, 11-12
service functions, 11-12
troubleshooting problems,
337-338
Next Header field, IPv6, 41
**NFS (Network File System),
14, 226-230, 448**
asynchronous file writes, 228
COMMIT procedure, 228
directory-level services, 228
file resource access, 227
file-level services, 228
Lock Manager, 227

MOUNT operations, 227-228
operation agents, 227
RFCs, 376
RPCs (Remote Procedure
Calls), 226-228
Sun Microcomputers, 12
WRITE procedure, 228
XDR (eXternal Data
Representation), 227
**NICs (network interface
cards), 7, 449**
**NIS/YP (Network Informa-
tion Service/Yellow Pages),
449**
**NNTP (Network News
Transfer Protocol), RFCs,
376**
nodes
addresses, 95
namespace trees, 283-284
types for NetBIOS name data,
300
**non-interactive mode,
nslookup, 296**
**NOOP command, SMTP mail
transfers, 262**
**NOS (Network Operating
System), 449**
nslookup tool
debugging DNS setups,
296-297
zone transfers, 296
**NT-1 (Network Termination),
449**
**NTP (Network Time Proto-
col), 12, 213-218**
datagrams
Authenticator, 217
format, 216-218
Leap Indicator, 216
Mode Indicator, 217
Originate Timestamp, 217
Poll Interval, 217
Precision integer, 217
Receive Timestamp, 217
Reference Clock Identifier,
217
Reference Timestamp, 217

Root Delay, 217
Root Dispersion, 217
servers, 214–215
  association modes, 215
  subnet configuration,
    215–218
  Stratum, 217
  Transmit Timestamp, 217
  Version Number Indicator,
    216
NUL code, Telnet NVT, 240
**NVT (Network Virtual
  Terminal), Telnet protocol,
  239–241**

stack architecture model, 6
TCP/IP relationship, 20–29
transport layer, 22
**OSPF (Open Shortest Path
  First), 107–108, 376, 449**
**outside LAN router protocols,
  109–113**
**over capacity planning for
  networks, 314**
overviews
  historical development of
    TCP/IP, 4–6
  Multilink PPP, 184
  PPP process, 140

Multilink PPP, encapsulation,
  185
NetBIOS
  formats, 233
  session services, 233
PPP protocol
  Configure-Ack, 145
  Configure-Nak, 146
  Configure-Reject, 146
  Configure-Request, 145
  Echo-Reply, 148
  Echo-Request, 148
  encapsulation, 143
  Terminate-Request, 147
RARP, 97, 120–121
RST, TCP processes, 198
RTCP, 180
RTP, 179
SYN, TCP connections, 197
timestamps, 213
**pad option, BOOTP/DHCP
  extensions, 128**
Padding field
  PPP protocol, 143
  TCP datagrams, 163
**PASS command, FTP sessions,
  252–253**
passive routers, 104
**passwords, network security
  issues, 319–320**
Path MTU, IPv4, 36
pathways (IP), 9
Payload Length field, IPv6, 41
**PDUs (protocol data units),
  SNMP, 220, 226**
peer-to-peer, 449
**perform mask discovery
  option, BOOTP/DHCP
  extensions, 130**
**performance problem
  troubleshooting, 346**
**permanent host group
  addresses, 61**
**persist timer, TCP processes,
  172**
**persistent routes, routing
  tables, 101**
**PGP (Pretty Good Privacy),
  449**

O

**objects, mandatory for SNMP
  MIB, 222**
**ODI (Open Data Link
  Interface), 449**
**OPEN command, TCP
  processes, 199**
**Open Systems Interconnect
  Reference Model,** *see* **OSI
  model**
**open systems nature of
  TCP/IP, 11**
operations, NFS, 227–228
**option field formats for
  DHCP, 127**
**option negotiation, Telnet
  sessions, 241–246**
**Options field, TCP datagrams,
  163**
**Originate Timestamp, NTP
  datagrams, 217**
**OSI Open Systems Intercon-
  nect) model, 449**
  application layer, 22
  comparison to TCP/IP model,
    26–27
  data link layer, 21
  network layer, 22
  physical layer, 21
  presentation layer, 22
  session layer, 22

P

packet, 449
packet classifiers, RSVP, 182
packet dump analysis, 349–359
**packet filtering for security,
  321–322**
packet format for ARP, 88–89
**packet-based multiplexing,
  187**
packet-switched networks, 4
packets
  ARP, 81
  BOOTP, 122
  DHCP, 125
  FIN, TCP processes, 198
  IP transmission, 96
  IPv4, structural overview,
    29–39
  IPv6, structural overview,
    39–49
  IPv6CP, code options, 150
  LCP
    Code-Reject packets, 147
    configuration negotiation,
      145
    Discard-Request packets,
      148
    loopback checking, 148
    PPP protocol, 144
    protocol rejects, 148
    termination, 147

physical layer, OSI model, 21, 450

physical network problems, 346

PI (User Protocol Interface), FTP clients, 250

ping (Packet Internet Groper, 450

ICMP echo reply analysis, 350-351

packet dump analysis, 349-350

troubleshooting system connections, 338-339

poison reverse RIP routing, 106

policies for security, 319

policy control module, RSVP, 182

Poll Interval, NTP datagrams, 217

POP (Post Office Protocol), 260, 450

POP3 RFCs, 376

PORT command, FTP sessions, 254

ports, 450

ephemeral, FTP connections, 252

port 20, FTP server well-known TCP port, 253

port 21, FTP server well-known port, 250

port number references for TCP/IP services, 388

router access restrictions, 320

TCP process connections, 166

POST method, HTTP requests, 272

POTS (Plain Old Telephone System), 450

PPP (Point-To-Point Protocol), 138-148, 377, 450

Configure-Ack packets, 145

Configure-Nak packets, 146

Configure-Reject packets, 146

Configure-Request packets, 145

datagram encapsulation, 141-144

Echo-Reply packets, 148

Echo-Request packets, 148

frames, 142

Information field, 143

IPv6 encapsulation, 149

IPv6 revisions, 149-151

LCP (Link Control Protocol), 144-149

link operations, 143-148

packet encapsulation, 143

Padding field, 143

Protocol field, 142

Terminate-Request packets, 147

PPTP (Point-to-Point Tunneling Protocol), 152, 158, 450

PQDNs (partially qualified domain names), 284

#PRE keyword, LMHOSTS file, 300

Precision integer, NTP datagrams, 217

presentation layer, OSI model, 22, 450

PRI (Primary Rate Interface), 450

primary digit values for SMTP reply codes, 265

primary servers

domain name resolution, 287

zone transfers, 295

printer, NVT, 240

printing, LPD problems, 346

Priority field, IPv6, 40

private addressing ranges, network design issues, 311

problem troubleshooting

analyzers and sniffers, 337-338

common problems and solutions, 343-348

DNS, 347-348

IP addressing conflicts, 345-346

LPD printing, 346

MAC broadcast storms, 348

MTAs, 348

name resolution, 347

Network Monitor, network and packet analysis, 341-342

ping options, 338-339

poor performance, 346

service configurations, 345

tcpdump options, 340-341

traceroute options, 339-340

processes, TCP

congestion management, 170-171

flow control, 169-172

terminating connections, 173

processing comparison for headers between IPv4 and IPv6, 52

programs, problem troubleshooting tools, 338-341

protocol entities, SNMP, 219

Protocol field

IPv4, 34

PPP protocol, 142

protocol fields for PPP, 142

protocol option, TCP/IP UNIX services, 203

protocol stacks, 21

demultiplexing, 28-29

encapsulation, 27-29

protocols

application, 7, 212

ARP, 96

BGP, 113

BOOTP, 121-122

client/server, 238

data link, 7, 138

DHCP, 123-126

dial-up access, 138

EGP, 112

EIGRP, 108-109

FTP, 248-259

GGP, 112

Hello, 106

HTTP, 269-278

IDRP, 113

IP, 8-9

IS-IS, 108

L2F, 153

L2TP, 9, 153-154

media access, 7

Multilink PPP, 183-186

NetBIOS, 230-233

network, 7

NTP, 12, 213-218
OSPF, 107-108
POP, 260
PPP, 138-148
    datagram encapsulation, 141-144
    Echo-Reply packets, 148
    Echo-Request packets, 148
    frames, 142
    Information field, 143
    link operations, 143-148
    packet encapsulation, 143
    Padding field, 143
    Protocol field, 142
PPTP, 152
RARP, 97
RIP, 104-106
router, 103
RSVP, 181-183
RTP, 176-180
SLIP, 138-140
    datagram encapsulation, 139
    END character, 139
    ESC character, 139
    limitations, 140
SMTP, 259-269
SNMP, 12, 218-226
SNMPv2, 225-226
SNTP, 218
stacked, 5
T/TCP, 173
TCP, 159-174
    datagram encapsulation, 161
    multiplexing, 160-161
TCP/IP, stack model architecture, 6-8, 23-24
Telnet, 238-248
transport, 7
X.25, 5
provider-based unicast IPv6 addresses, 73
proxy agents, WINS, 304
Proxy ARP, 90
proxy gateways, 450
proxy hosts, firewalls, 325-326
proxy servers, 450

caching and network design issues, 317
network design issues, 311
pseudo-device loop options, TCP/IP UNIX services, 202
pseudo-device pty options, TCP/IP UNIX services, 202
pseudoheaders, UDP, 175-176
PSH flag
    TCP headers, 164
    packet dump analysis, 355
PUSH flag, TCP processes, 200
PUT method, HTTP 1.1, 278
PWD command, FTP sessions, 256

Q

QOS (Quality of Service), 158-159, 451
queries
    ARP, 96
    DNS, 282, 293-295
        additional section, 295
        answers, 295
        authority section, 295
        headers, 293-294
        questions, 294-295
    iterative and recursive, local nameservers, 288
questions, DNS queries, 294-295
QUIT command
    FTP sessions, 254
    SMTP mail transfers, 262

R

RARP (Reverse Address Resolution Protocol), 451
    packets, 97, 120-121
    RFCs, 368
RCPT command, SMTP mail transfers, 261
read function, BSD socket model, 204

Rebinding (T2) time value option, BOOTP/DHCP extensions, 135
Receive Broadcast Datagram service, NetBIOS, 232
RECEIVE command, TCP processes, 200
Receive Datagram service, NetBIOS, 232
Receive Session service, NetBIOS, 231
Receive Timestamp, NTP datagrams, 217
Receiver Report packet, RTCP, 180
receiver requests, Telnet sessions, 242
reception of ARP packets, 81
recursive queries, local nameservers, 288
Reference Clock Identifier, NTP datagrams, 217
Reference Timestamp, NTP datagrams, 217
Referer header field, HTTP requests, 275
registered ports, TCP/IP services, 388
registering names for NetBIOS, 301-304
relationship of client/server in TCP/IP networks, 10-12
relay agents for BOOTP, 126
remote bridges, 109
remote hosts, printing problems, 346
remote logins with Telnet, 238
remote sites, network design planning, 331
Renewal (T1) time value option, BOOTP/DHCP extensions, 135
repeaters, 98
replication, WINS, 304
reply codes for SMTP mail transfers, 264-266
Report-PDU, SNMPv2, 226
repositories for RFCs, 365

Requested IP address option, BOOTP/DHCP extensions, 134

requests, HTTP, 270
    header fields, 273-275
    URI format and syntax, 275-276

reservations, DHCP addresses, 123

reserved addresses, IPv4, 65

reserved multicast addresses, IPv6, 76

reset datagrams, 173

resolvers
    BIND, 289
    DNS clients, 282, 288-289
    stub, 289

resolving names, *see* name resolution

Resource Class, DNS resource records, 289

Resource Data, DNS resource records, 290

Resource Name, DNS resource records, 289

resource records
    DNS structure, 289-292
    root nameservers, 287

Resource Type, DNS resource records, 289

Response-PDU, SNMPv2, 226

responses
    FTP sessions, 256-258
    HTTP header fields, 273-277

restricting service access for security, 323

RETR command, FTP sessions, 254

reverse lookups, domain names, 285-286, 296

reverse paths, MAIL and RCPT parameters, 264

RFC (Request for Comments), 13, 451
    Internet standards, 364-365
    IP network transmission methods, 26
    listed by subject, 367-384
    repositories, 365

ring topology, 451

RIP (Routing Information Protocol), 104-106, 378, 451

RMD command, FTP sessions, 255

RNFR command, FTP sessions, 254

RNTO command, FTP sessions, 254

Root Delay, NTP datagrams, 217

Root Dispersion, NTP datagrams, 217

root nameservers, resource records, 287

root path option, BOOTP/DHCP extensions, 130

route aggregation, 53

router address support, IPv6, 77

router fragmentation, IPv4, 36

router option, BOOTP/DHCP extensions, 128, 131

router ports, network design issues, 311

router protocols
    LAN options, 103-109
    outside LAN options, 109-113

routers, 9, 12, 64, 96, 99-102, 451
    active and passive, 104
    default gateways, 97
    network design issues, 311-312, 316-317
        access restrictions, 320
        security, 320-321

routing
    addresses with IP, 96
    Hello protocol, 106
    troubleshooting host communication, 343

Routing extension header, IPv6, 45

routing tables
    active routes, 101
    convergence, 103
    simple example, 100
    static route entries, 101-102
    troubleshooting host communication, 343

RPCs (remote procedure calls), 226-228, 451

RST (reset) datagrams, 173

RST control flag, TCP headers, 164

RST packet, TCP processes, 198

RSVP (Resource reSerVation Protocol), 181-183, 451
    admission control module, 182
    flow descriptors, 183
    packet classifiers, 182
    policy control module, 182

RTCP (Real Time Control Protocol), 177, 180

RTP (Real Time Protocol), 180, 451
    headers, 178-179
    interactive audio/video conferencing, 179

S

satellite sites, network design planning, 331

SB command, Telnet sessions, 243

scope of end nodes in NetBIOS services, 232

SE command, Telnet sessions, 243

SEAL (Simple and Efficient Adaption Layer), 189

search lists, nslookup, 296

second digit values for SMTP reply codes, 265

secondary RFC repositories, 366

secondary servers
    domain name resolution, 287
    zone transfers, 295

security
    network design issues, 310
        bastion hosts, 324-325
        firewalls, 321
        intranets, 327-328
        mail servers, 328-329

passwords, 319–320
proxy hosts, 325–326
routers, 320–321
TCP wrappers, 326–327
policies, 319
TCP/IP UNIX services, 205
**Security Parameters Index,
IPv6 AH header, 47**
segments, 452
**Send Broadcast Datagram
service, NetBIOS, 232**
**SEND command, TCP
processes, 199**
**Send Datagram service,
NetBIOS, 232**
Send service, NetBIOS, 231
**Sender Report packet, RTCP,
180**
**sender requests, Telnet
sessions, 242**
**Sequence field, TCP
datagrams, 163**
**Sequence number field, RTP
headers, 178**
**Server header field, HTTP
requests, 275**
**Server identification option,
BOOTP/DHCP extensions,
135**
**server option, TCP/IP UNIX
services, 204**
**server usage commands, FTP
clients, 255**
servers, 452
ARP proxy, 90
DNS, 282
FTP, 249–250
HTTP, request format, 270
mail servers, security, 328–329
MTA, 261
NTP, 214
association modes, 215
subnet configuration,
215–218
primary
domain name resolution,
287
zone transfers, 295
proxy, network design issues,
311

RARP, 97, 121
secondary, domain name
resolution, 287
SMTP proxy, mail server
security, 328
static entries, address allocation
database, 120
Stratum Three, 214
Stratum Two, 214
TCP/IP network roles, 11–12
services
access restrictions for security,
323–324
NetBIOS, 230–232
datagram service, 232
name service, 231
session service, 231
TCP/IP
network roles, 11–12
port number references,
388
timekeeping and tracking,
213–218
troubleshooting configuration
problems, 345
**session layer, OSI model, 22,
452**
sessions
FTP, 251–258
NetBIOS session services,
231–233
Telnet, 239
**silly window syndrome, TCP
links, 171–172**
**SITE command, FTP sessions,
256**
**Site-Local unicast addresses,
IPv6, 74**
**size considerations for
network design, 314**
slaves, nameservers, 288
**SLIP (Serial Line Interface
Protocol), 138–140, 452**
datagram encapsulation, 139
END character, 139
ESC character, 139
limitations, 140

**slow convergence, router hop
problems, 105**
**SMTP (Simple Mail Transfer
Protocol), 259–269, 452**
Internet transfer example, 269
mail format, 266–268
mail message example, 267
mail transfers
commands, 261–264
envelope component, 266
header component, 266
reply codes, 264–266
RFCs, 378
**SMTP proxy servers, mail
server security, 328**
**SNA (Systems Network
Architecture), 382, 452**
**sniffers, troubleshooting
problems, 337–338, 452**
**SNMP (Simple Network
Management Protocol), 12,
218–226, 452**
application entities, 219
message transmission, 220
MIB (Management Informa-
tion Base), 219–225
group definitions, 221
mandatory objects, 222
PDUs (protocol data units),
220
protocol entities, 219
RFCs, 378
SNMPv2, 225–226
**SNTP (Simple Network Time
Protocol), 213, 218**
sockets, BSD UNIX, 204, 452
**soft state management, RSVP,
183**
**software problem trouble-
shooting tools, 338–341**
Source address, IPv6, 42
**Source Description packet,
RTCP, 180**
Source field
TCP datagrams, 162
UDP headers, 175
**source host fragmentation,
IPv4, 36**

Source IP address field, IPv4, 35

source routing bridges, 99

space allocations for IPv6 addresses, 50

spanning tree bridges, 99

split horizon update, RIP routing, 105

spoof RFCs, 368

spoofing, 452

SSRC field, RTP headers, 179

stacks, protocols, 5, 21

star topology, 452

STAT command, FTP sessions, 256

state transitions in TCP connections, 196

stateless autoconfiguration, IPv6, 52

static address allocation, BOOTP, 121

static ARP addresses, 89–90

static entries for servers, address allocation database, 120

static route entries, routing tables, 101–102

static route option, BOOTP/ DHCP extensions, 131

STATUS command, TCP processes, 201

STOR command, FTP sessions, 254

storage formats for domain names, 290

strategies for network backups, 331–334

Stratum
NTP datagrams, 217
Stratum One sources, 214
Stratum servers, 214

structural
layouts
IPv4 headers, 30–35
IPv6 headers, 39–42
overviews
IPv4 packets, 29–39
IPv6 packets, 39–49

stub resolver, 289

sub-option negotiation, Telnet sessions, 243

subdomains, namespace tree nodes, 284

subnet mask option, BOOTP/ DHCP extensions, 128

subnet masks, IPv4, 64–65, 453

subnets, 62–64, 67, 452
network design issues, 315
NTP server configuration, 215–218

SUBNETSARELOCAL option, TCP/IP UNIX services, 203

Sun Microcomputers Network File System, 12

supernetting, IPv4, 67

swap server option, BOOTP/ DHCP extensions, 130

switches
network design issues, 312, 316–317
network sizing issues, 314

symmetric-active NTP, association mode, 215

SYN flag
TCP headers, 164
TCP processes, 168

SYN header, TCP processes, 168

SYN packets, TCP connections, 197

SYN requests, packet dump analysis, 351

SYN-RECEIVED state, TCP process, 197

SYN-SENT state, TCP process, 197

SYNCH command, Telnet sessions, 247

synchronous communication, 453

system security, TCP/IP UNIX services, 205

T

T-1 lines, 187, 453

T-3 lines, 453

T/TCP (Transaction TCP), 173–174

TA (terminal adapter), 453

TCP (Transmission Control Protocol), 4, 159–174, 453
application
messages, 201
requests, 198–201
application interface model, 194–201
connections
initiation analysis, 351
initiation process, 165
negotiation process, 168–169
termination process, 173
data flow control with Nagle's algorithm, 171
datagrams
encapsulation, 161
FIN flag, 173
format, 162–164
header fields, 162
FIN packets, 198
headers
control flags, 163
maximum segment sizes, 164–165
MTU (Maximum Transmission Unit), 165
TCP connection initiation analysis, 352–354
multiplexing, 160–161, 165–169
processes
congestion management, 170–171
flow control, 169–172
RFCs, 384
RST packets, 198
silly window syndrome, 171–172
states
CLOSE-WAIT, 198

connection options,
195-198
ESTABLISHED, 197
LAST-ACK, 198
LISTEN, 197
SYN-RECEIVED, 197
SYN-SENT, 197
TIME_WAIT, 198
timers, 172-173
Well-Known Port Numbers,
166-167
wrappers, 326-327
**TCP/IP (Transmission
Control Protocol/Internet
Protocol), 453**
networks
client/server relationship,
10-12
designing, 310-311
server roles, 11-12
service functions, 11-12
protocol model, 23-24
relationship to OSI model,
20-29
server facilities, Internet
Information Server, 208
stack model architecture, 6-8
TCP/IP model
application layer, 24
comparison to OSI model,
26-27
Internet layer, 24
Network Access layer, 24
Transport layer, 24
TCP/IP services
MS Windows versions,
206-208
port number references, 388
UNIX
arguments option, 204
AT&T System V version
options, 205
BROADCAST option, 203
BSD UNIX configuration,
202-204
device {device type}
options, 202
INET options, 202
IPFORWARDING option,
202

IPSENDREDIRECTS
option, 203
name option, 203
protocol option, 203
pseudo-device ether
options, 202
pseudo-device loop options,
202
pseudo-device pty options,
202
server option, 204
SUBNETSARELOCAL
option, 203
system security, 205
uid option, 203
wait_status option, 203
**tcpdump utility, IP packet
tracing, 340-341**
Telnet, 238-248, 453
AO function, 247
authentication types, 246
AYT function, 247
command options, 244-245
control functions, 247-248
DM command, 247
EC function, 247
EL function, 247
IAC escape character, 243
IP function, 247
mail sessions
log example, 263
SMTP reply code example,
265
NVT (Network Virtual
Terminal), 240
receiver requests, 242
RFCs, 382
SB command, 243
SE command, 243
sender requests, 242
session option negotiation,
241-246
sub-option negotiation, 243
SYNCH command, 247
**TelnetD Server, Windows NT,
239**
**Terminate-Request packet,
PPP protocol, 147**
**terminating TCP connections,
173**

ACK requests, 358
FIN requests, 357-358
terminology of DNS, 283-289
**TFTP (Trivial File Transfer
Protocol), 384**
**third digit values for SMTP
reply codes, 265**
**three-way handshake, TCP
connections, 168**
time services, 213-218
**TIME_WAIT state, TCP
processes, 198**
**timers for TCP processes,
172-173**
timestamps
packet tracking, 213
RTP headers, 178
tokens, 453
Token Ring, 453
topology, 453
TOS field, IPv4, 32
Total Length field, IPv4, 33
**traceroute utility, trouble-
shooting routing and
connectivity, 339-340**
**tracking packets with
timestamps, 213**
**transient multicast addresses,
IPv6, 76**
translational bridges, 99, 110
**translators for RTP multicast
streams, 177**
**Transmit Timestamp, NTP
datagrams, 217**
transparent bridges, 99
transport layer, 453
OSI model, 22
TCP/IP model, 24
transport protocols, 7
troubleshooting problems
analyzers and sniffers, 337-338
common problems and
solutions, 343-348
DNS, 347-348
IP addressing conflicts,
345-346
LPD printing, 346
MAC broadcast storms, 348
MTAs, 348

name resolution, 347
Network Monitor, network and packet analysis, 341–342
ping options, 338–339
poor performance, 346
service configurations, 345
tcpdump options, 340–341
traceroute options, 339–340
trusted timing information, 214
TTL (Time-To-Live)
DNS resource records, 289
IPv4, 33
tunneling via PPTP, VPNs, 151–154
TURN command, SMTP mail transfers, 262
twisted pair, 454

U

UCT (Universal Coordinated Time), 213
UDP (User Datagram Protocol), 8, 174–176, 454
headers, 175
pseudoheaders, 175–176
RFCs, 384
UI (user interface), FTP client, 250
uid option, TCP/IP UNIX services, 203
unicast
addresses
IPv4, 38
IPv6, 49, 71–74
registration, NetBIOS names, 301
UNIX operating system, 5
BSD UNIX sockets, 204
TCP/IP services
arguments option, 204
AT&T System V version options, 205
BROADCAST option, 203
BSD UNIX configuration, 202–204

device {device type} options, 202
INET options, 202
IPFORWARDING option, 202
IPSENDREDIRECTS option, 203
name option, 203
protocol option, 203
pseudo-device ether options, 202
pseudo-device loop options, 202
pseudo-device pty options, 202
server option, 204
SUBNETSARELOCAL option, 203
system security, 205
uid option, 203
wait_status option, 203
unspecified address, IPv6, 74
URG control flag, TCP headers, 163
Urgent field, TCP datagrams, 163
Urgent flag
TCP processes, 200
Telnet DM command, 247
URIs (Universal Resource Identifiers), HTTP requests, 270, 275–276
URLs (Uniform Resource Locators), 454
USASCII codes, NVT supported, 240
USENET, 454
User Agents, e-mail, 259
USER command, FTP sessions, 252–253
user commands, TCP supported, 199
User-Agent header field, HTTP requests, 275
utilities
ping, troubleshooting system connections, 338–339
tcpdump, IP packet tracing, 340–341

traceroute, troubleshooting routing and connectivity, 339–340
UTP (unshielded twisted pair), 454
UUENCODE/UUDECODE, binary to ASCII conversions, 268

V

variable length subnetting, 67
VAX minicomputers, 5
VCs (virtual circuits), Frame Relay, 188
vendor address list of MAC addresses, IP address conflict resolution, 83
vendor extensions for BOOTP, 127–135
vendor-specific information option, BOOTP/DHCP extensions, 132
Version field, IPv6, 40
Version Number Indicator, NTP datagrams, 216
version numbers, IPv4 datagrams, 31
VLANs (virtual local area networks), 313–314
VPNs (virtual private networks), tunneling via PPTP, 151–154, 454
VRFY command, SMTP mail transfers, 262
VT code, Telnet NVT, 240

W

wait_status option, TCP/IP UNIX services, 203
WANs (wide area networks), gateways, 8, 454
Web sites, InterNIC RFCs, drafts and proposals, 14
WebNFS, 229–230

Well-Known Port Numbers,
TCP processes and services,
166–167, 388
well-known multicast
addresses, IPv6, 76
WILL request, Telnet sessions,
242
window, TCP process flow
control, 169
Window field, TCP datagrams,
163
Windows (Microsoft)
Mail Transfer Agents, 260
TCP/IP service versions,
206–208
Windows NT, TelnetD Server,
239
WinInet API, 207–208
WINS (Windows Internet
Name Service), 297–298, 454
LMHOSTS files, 299–300
proxy agents, 304
replication, 304
WinSock, 206–207, 454
WONT request, Telnet
sessions, 243
word processing workstations,
network design issues, 312
workstations
dynamic address allocation, 120
network design issues, 312
wrappers, *see* TCP wrappers
write function, BSD socket
model, 204
WRITE procedure, NFS, 228

Z

zone transfers
nslookup, 296
primary servers, 295
zones, DNS domains, 286–287

X-Y

X.25 protocol, 5, 455
X.400, 455
X.500, 455
XDR (eXternal Data Repre-
sentation), NFS, 227

MACMILLAN COMPUTER PUBLISHING USA

A VIACOM COMPANY

 **Support:**

If you need assistance with the information in this book or with a CD/Disk
accompanying the book, please access the Knowledge Base on our Web
site at **http://www.superlibrary.com/general/support**. Our most
Frequently Asked Questions are answered there. If you do not find the
answer to your questions on our Web site, you may contact Macmillan
Technical Support **(317) 581-3833** or e-mail us at **support@mcp.com**.

TCP/IP Unleashed

— Timothy Parker, Ph.D.

This book starts with the installation of the most popular TCP/IP products on each platform, then proceeds through the configuration and troubleshooting of each product. Subsequent chapters increase the reader's understanding of the theory and practice of TCP/IP, both from an administrative and a user point of view.

Book covers TCP/IP for DOS, Windows, Macintosh, and UNIX systems. Includes configuration and troubleshooting information. CD-ROM includes source code from the book.

Price: $55.00 USA/$74.95 CDN   User Level: New-Casual
ISBN: 0-672-30603-4   880 pages

The Internet 1997 Unleashed

— Jill Ellsworth, et al.

Internet 1997 Unleashed is the definitive bible for Internet users everywhere. This comprehensive guide stakes out new ground as it details the hottest Internet tools and upcoming technologies. Written by the world's top experts in Internet fields, this book provides improved coverage of common tools and takes a futuristic look at the Internet of tomorrow.

Book includes over 200 pages of an easy-to-use, well-organized listing of the top 1,000 resources on the Internet. Covers the WWW browsers, Internet commerce, and Internet virtual reality. CD-ROM contains all the software needed to get connected to the Internet, regardless of computing platform—Windows 3.1, Windows 95, Macintosh, or UNIX.

Price: $49.99 USA/$70.95 CDN   User Level: Casual-Advanced
ISBN: 1-57521-185-8   1,328 pages

The World Wide Web 1997 Unleashed

— John December

This book has unleashed the latest Web topics, previously known only to the field experts. It is designed to be the only book readers will need from the initial logon to the Web to creating their own Web pages.

The book takes readers on an updated tour of the Web, highlights sites, and outlines browsing techniques. Includes Sams.net Web 1,000 Directory—the "yellow pages" of the Internet. CD-ROM contains everything from starter software to advanced Web site development tools.

Price: $49.99 USA/$70.95 CDN   User Level: All User Levels
ISBN: 1-57521-184-X   1,300 pages

Peter Norton's Complete Guide to Windows 95, Second Edition

— Peter Norton & John Mueller

Following the success of the best-selling *Peter Norton Premier* series, this complete reference provides users with in-depth, detailed insights into this powerful operating system. Users will master all the tricks of the trade, as well as learn how to create a Web page.

Covers the new Internet Explorer interface, DSD, OEM Service Pack 2.1 enhancements, and more. Provides advanced tips, optimization techniques, and detailed architectural information. Extensive coverage of the Microsoft Plus! Pack. Peter's Principles, quick reference, and tear-out survival guide make learning easy.

Price: $35.00 USA/$49.95 CDN   User Level: New–Expert
ISBN: 0-672-31040-6   1,224 pages

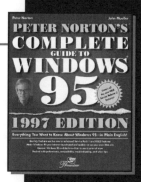

Robert Cowart's Windows NT 4 Unleashed, Professional Reference Edition

— Robert Cowart

The only reference Windows NT administrators need to learn how to configure their NT systems for maximum performance, security, and reliability. This comprehensive reference explains how to install, maintain, and configure an individual workstation as well as connect computers to peer-to-peer networking. Includes comprehensive advice for setting up and administering an NT server network, and focuses on the new and improved administration and connectivity features of version 4.0. CD-ROM includes source code, utilities, and sample applications from the book.

Price: $59.99 USA/$84.95 CDN *User Level: Intermediate–Expert*
ISBN: 0-672-31001-5 *1,400 pages*

Windows NT 4 and Web Site Resource Library

— Sams Development Group

This comprehensive library is the most complete reference available for Windows NT and Web administrators and developers. Six volumes and more than 3,200 pages of key information about the Windows NT Registry, Web site administration and development, networking, BackOffice integration, and much more.
Three bonus CD-ROMs include networking utilities, third-party tools, support utilities, Web site development tools, HTML templates, CGI scripts, and more!

Price: $149.99 USA/$210.95 CDN *User Level: Accomplished-Expert*
ISBN: 0-672-30995-5 *3,200 pages*

Red Hat Linux Unleashed

— Kamran Husain, Tim Parker, et al.

Programmers, users, and system administrators will find this a must-have book for operating the Linux environment. Everything from installation and configuration to advanced programming and administration techniques are covered in this valuable reference.
Book includes coverage of PPP, TCP/IP, networking, and setting up an Internet site. CD-ROM includes source code from the book and powerful utilities.

Price: $49.99 USA/$67.99 CDN *User Level: Accomplished-Expert*
ISBN: 0-672-30962-9 *1,176 pages*

Slackware Linux Unleashed, Third Edition

— Kamran Husain, Tim Parker, et al.

Slackware Linux is a 32-bit version of the popular UNIX operating system. In many ways, it enhances the performance of UNIX and UNIX-based applications. Slackware is a free operating system that can be downloaded from the Internet. Because it is free, there is very little existing documentation for the product. This book fills that void and provides Slackware Linux users with the information they need to effectively run the software on their computers or networks.
Teaches editing, typesetting, and graphical user interfaces. Discusses Linux for programmers and system administrators. CD-ROM includes powerful source code and two best-selling books in HTML format.

Price: $49.99 USA/$70.95 CDN *User Level: Advanced–Expert*
ISBN: 0-672-31012-0 *1,392 pages*

Add to Your Sams Library Today with the Best Books for Programming, Operating Systems, and New Technologies

The easiest way to order is to pick up the phone and call

1-800-428-5331

between 9:00 a.m. and 5:00 p.m. EST.

For faster service please have your credit card available.

ISBN	Quantity	Description of Item	Unit Cost	Total Cost
0-672-30603-4		TCP/IP Unleashed (Book/CD-ROM)	$55.00	
1-57521-185-8		The Internet 1997 Unleashed (Book/CD-ROM)	$49.99	
1-57521-184-x		The World Wide Web 1997 Unleashed (Book/CD-ROM)	$49.99	
0-672-31040-6		Peter Norton's Complete Guide to Windows 95, Second Edition	$35.00	
0-672-31001-5		Robert Cowart's Windows NT 4 Unleashed, Professional Reference Edition (Book/CD-ROM)	$59.99	
0-672-30995-5		Windows NT 4 and Web Site Resource Library (6 Books/3 CD-ROMs)	$149.99	
0-672-30962-9		Red Hat Linux Unleashed (Book/CD-ROM)	$49.99	
0-672-31012-0		Slackware Linux Unleashed (Book/CD-ROM)	$49.99	
		Shipping and Handling: See information below.		
		TOTAL		

Shipping and Handling: $4.00 for the first book, and $1.75 for each additional book. Floppy disk: add $1.75 for shipping and handling. If you need to have it NOW, we can ship product to you in 24 hours for an additional charge of approximately $18.00, and you will receive your item overnight or in two days. Overseas shipping and handling adds $2.00 per book and $8.00 for up to three disks. Prices subject to change. Call for availability and pricing information on latest editions.

201 W. 103rd Street, Indianapolis, Indiana 46290

1-800-428-5331 — Orders   1-800-835-3202 — FAX   1-800-858-7674 — Customer Service

Book ISBN 0-672-31055-4

What's on the Disc

The companion CD-ROM contains an assortment of third-party tools and product demos. The disc creates a new program group for this book and utilizes Windows Explorer. Using the icons in the program group and Windows Explorer, you can view information concerning products and companies and install programs with just a few clicks of the mouse.

To create the program group for this book, follow these steps.

Windows NT Installation Instructions

NOTE For best results, set your monitor to display between 256 and 64,000 colors. A screen resolution of 640×480 pixels is also recommended. If necessary, adjust your monitor settings before using the CD-ROM.

1. Insert the CD-ROM disc into your CD-ROM drive.

2. With Windows NT installed on your computer and the AutoPlay feature enabled, a Program Group for this book is automatically created whenever you insert the disc into your CD-ROM drive. Follow the directions provided in the installation program.

   If Autoplay is not enabled, using Windows Explorer, choose `Setup.exe` from the root level of the CD-ROM to create the Program Group for this book.

3. Double-click on the "Browse the CD-ROM" icon in the newly created Program Group to access the installation programs of the software or reference material included on this CD-ROM.

   To review the latest information about this CD-ROM, double-click on the icon "About this CD-ROM."

Technical Support

If you need assistance with the information in this book or with the CD-ROM accompanying this book, please access the Knowledge Base on our Web site at

`http://www.superlibrary.com/general/support`

Our most frequently asked questions are answered there. If you do not find the answer to your questions on our Web site, you may contact Macmillan Technical Support at (317) 581-3833 or e-mail us at `support@mcp.com`.